D1576392

SOAS, University of London

18 0847158 9

# OUTCAST LABOUR
## IN ASIA

# OUTCAST LABOUR
# IN ASIA

Circulation and Informalization
of the Workforce at the Bottom of the Economy

### JAN BREMAN

OXFORD
UNIVERSITY PRESS

# OXFORD
## UNIVERSITY PRESS

YMCA Library Building, Jai Singh Road, New Delhi 110 001

Oxford University Press is a department of the University of Oxford. It furthers the
University's objective of excellence in research, scholarship, and education
by publishing worldwide in

Oxford   New York

Auckland   Cape Town   Dar es Salaam   Hong Kong   Karachi   Kuala Lumpur
Madrid   Melbourne   Mexico City   Nairobi   New Delhi   Shanghai   Taipei   Toronto

With offices in

Argentina   Austria   Brazil   Chile   Czech Republic   France   Greece   Guatemala
Hungary   Italy   Japan   Poland   Portugal   Singapore   South Korea   Switzerland
Thailand   Turkey   Ukraine   Vietnam

Oxford is a registered trademark of Oxford University Press
in the UK and in certain other countries

Published in India
by Oxford University Press, New Delhi

ISBN-13: 978-019-806632-3
ISBN-10: 019-806632-5

Typeset in 10.5/12.5 Adobe Garamond Pro
by Excellent Laser Typesetters, Pitampura, Delhi 110 034
Printed in India at De Unique, New Delhi 110 018
Published by Oxford University Press
YMCA Library Building, Jai Singh Road, New Delhi 110 001

# Contents

## V  THE DYNAMICS OF EXCLUSION

# Preface

This volume includes a set of essays, written during the last ten years either as conference papers, as invited contributions to edited volumes, or as book reviews published in various journals. These writings may earlier have appeared in a slightly different format to meet with editorial instructions and I have also cut passages in order to avoid repetition in my narratives and analyses. The themes dealt with revolve around labour migration and informalization of employment, issues on which I have focused my micro-studies carried out in different parts of Asia. While they seem economic in nature, I have elaborated on the social, political, and cultural dynamics of work and life at the bottom of the rural and urban economy. To comprehend what is happening in the world of today, a historical and comparative perspective is required. Besides linking the present to the past, I have tried to contextualize the great transformation, the emergence of post-peasant societies and economies, in the wider setting of Asia. I am indebted to publishers and editors of journals for their permission to reprint my essays in this volume.

# Publisher's Acknowledgements

The publisher acknowledges the following for permission to include articles/extracts in this volume.

Intermediate Technology Publications for 'Of Labour and Landlessness in South and Southeast Asia', in D. Bryceson, C. Kay, and J. Mooij (eds), *Disappearing Peasantries*, London, 2000, pp. 231–46.

Routledge for 'The Political Economy of Agrarian Change', in Paul R. Brass (ed.), *Handbook of South Asian Politics*, London and New York, (forthcoming), pp. 468–90.

*Economic and Political Weekly* for 'Coming to Kolkata: Pathways to a Better Life or Lost in Dead-end Alleys?', vol. 38, no. 39, 2003, pp. 4151–8; 'How to Find Space, Shop Around, and Move Up in the Informal Sector', vol. 40, no. 25, 2005, pp. 2500–6; and 'The Eventual Return of Social Darwinism', vol. 39, no. 35, 2004, pp. 3869–72.

*New Left Review* for 'Slumlands', vol. 40, July–August 2007, pp. 141–8; and 'Myths of the Global Safety Net', no. 59, September–October 2009, pp. 1–8.

Sage Publications for 'The Study of Industrial Labour in Post-colonial India: The Formal Sector' and 'The Study of Industrial Labour in Post-colonial India: The Informal Sector, a Concluding Review', in J. Parry, J. Breman, and K. Kapadia (eds), *The World View of Industrial Labour in India*, New Delhi, 1999, pp. 1–41 and pp. 407–31 respectively.

International Labour Organization for 'Social Exclusion in the context of Globalization', Working Paper No. 18, Policy Integration Department, Geneva, 2004.

*Indian Journal of Labour Economics* for 'The Political Economy of Unfree Labour in South Asia: Determining the Nature and Scale of Debt Bondage', vol. 52, no. 1, January–March 2010.

# Abbreviations

| | |
|---|---|
| BPS | *Badan Pusat Statistik* |
| BPL | below poverty line |
| BJP | Bharatiya Janata Party |
| CPI(M) | Communist Party of India (Marxist) |
| DA | Dearness Allowance |
| ESIS | Employees State Insurance Scheme |
| GDP | gross domestic product |
| GoI | Government of India |
| HSS | Halpati Seva Sangh |
| ICFTU | International Congress of Free Trade Union |
| *IHT* | *International Herald Tribune* |
| ILO | International Labour Organization |
| IMF | International Monetary Fund |
| KHAM | kshatriyas, harijans, adivasis, and Muslims |
| MNC | multinational corporation |
| NPA | National Progressive Alliance |
| NCEUS | National Commission for Enterprises in the Unorganized Sector |
| NCL | National Commission on Labour |
| NCRL | National Commission on Rural Labour |
| NPC | National Planning Committee |
| NREGA | National Rural Employment Guarantee Act |
| NSS | National Sample Survey |
| NSSO | National Sample Survey Organization |
| NGO | non-governmental organization |
| NRI | non-resident Indian |
| SAP | Structural Adjustment Programme |
| SC | Scheduled Caste |

| ST | Scheduled Tribe |
| SEWA | Self-Employed Women's Association |
| SEZ | Special Economic Zone |
| SOE | state-owned enterprise |
| SOAS | School for Oriental and African Studies |
| TISCO | Tata Iron and Steel Company |
| TLA | Textile Labour Association |
| TVE | Town and Village Enterprise |
| UK | United Kingdom |
| UN | United Nations |
| UNESCO | United Nations Educational, Scientific and Cultural Organization |
| USA | United States of America |
| *WSJ* | *Wall Street Journal* |
| WTO | World Trade Organization |

# Introduction
## The Great Transformation in the Setting of Asia[*]

## A CIVILIZATIONAL SWITCH

We are in the midst of a major civilizational switch from a rural–agrarian to an urban–industrial mode of life and work. The long era, spanning over two thousand years, during which the march of mankind was dominated by peasant economies and peasant societies has ended. Propelled by the economic forces of capitalist production, large masses of people are driven out of agriculture and away from their habitat in the countryside. The great transformation was how Karl Polanyi analysed the onslaught of capitalism that disentangled the economy from the political, social, and cultural framework in which it had been embedded.

Industrialization, in tandem with urbanization, was the organizing principle of the market-driven transformation that took place, in the first instance, in the Atlantic community. Polanyi insisted that the new order that emerged was already global in nature, an observation that led him to label the fringe zones as the colonial and semi-colonial jungle. Europe, and Great Britain in particular, was the heartland on which his seminal work focused, and he described the landscape that arose as a veritable abyss of human degradation:

Before the process had advanced very far, the laboring people had been crowded together in new places of desolation, the so-called industrial towns of England;

* This paper was presented as Acceptance Speech on Receipt of Honorary Doctorate from the Institute of Social Studies on the 57th Dies Natalis, held in The Hague on 29 October 2009.

the country folk had been dehumanized into slum dwellers; the family was on
the road to perdition; and large parts of the country were rapidly disappearing
under the slack and scrap heaps vomited forth from the 'satanic mills'.[1]

The exodus of rural labour began, in Europe, in the early decades of the
nineteenth century. In the wake of decolonization in the second half
of the twentieth century, a similar expansion spread to what came to
be called the Third World. The exodus from agriculture and the countryside has now become a global phenomenon resulting from a process
in which people with little or no land to cultivate become redundant
in primary production and are converted into a huge reserve army of
labour. The opening up of the countryside and reduction in the cost
of transport has accelerated labour mobility on a larger scale than ever
before. During the initial stage of this worldwide upheaval, migration
was truly intercontinental, leading to an influx into the underpopu-
lated countries of North America, South America, Southern Africa, and
Australia. Passage to already developed zones of the world has since
become increasingly difficult, and people who were in the past lauded
as enterprising colonists are now denigrated and stigmatized as
economic refugees. Consequently, migration, by and large, tends to
remain restricted to movement within the same country or local region.

Intra-rural mobility is quite significant, no doubt, but the main
emphasis is now on the trek from rural to urban destinations. It needs
to be stated at the outset that, although the pace of urbanization has
accelerated, it is generally not accompanied by a rapid expansion in
industrial employment. Migrants who settle down in the urban fringes
fail, to a large extent, to become absorbed in steady jobs in factories,
mills, or even small-scale sweatshops. Instead, they find a niche in the
service sector as waged workers or remain self-employed. They get stuck
in the informal sector economy, the defining features of which are low
wages, payment by piece rate or job work, un- or low-skilled work,
casual and intermittent employment, erratic working hours, no written
labour contracts, and an absence of institutional representation. These
features dominate in the slum habitats where most of the newcomers
from the hinterland congregate.

From the early 1960s onwards, the main focus of my investigations
has been on monitoring the rural–urban transition and the social identity and dynamics of poverty, first in South Asia and then in Southeast

[1] K. Polanyi, *The Great Transformation: The Political and Economic Origins of
Our Times*, Boston: Beacon Press, 1944, p. 39.

Asia. The attempts made by a huge rural reserve army of labour to get urbanized are being frustrated by the growing saturation of employment niches, however defined, in the informal sector of the economy, as well as a marked reluctance by the well-settled urban inhabitants to tolerate the presence of poor people in their midst. Thus, migrant labour has remained footloose, a phenomenon which has led to the continual circulation rather than to the permanent outmigration of workers from the countryside. I have documented the conditions of massive labour nomadism in my field-based research in India and Indonesia and, more recently, also in China. In a collection of essays, I have brought together my writings on these issues over the last ten years.

Going out and coming back again was also a major trend in the West, when the exodus from the countryside began to accelerate in the second half of the nineteenth century. However, fairly soon, such recurrent mobility decreased and migrants settled down in their new habitat, usually towns or cities. They left their rural habitat behind and became urban citizens, often as industrial workers. As Polanyi observed, what started as a catastrophe turned out to be the beginning of a vast movement of economic improvement that signified the growing control of human society (again) over runaway markets. The great transformation which changed the character of the Atlantic world eventually succeeded in harnessing the forces of predatory capitalism. Is this also the outcome of the upheaval caused by dislocation, essentially a trajectory of social progress, in the setting of contemporary Asia?

## LABOUR CIRCULATION RATHER THAN MIGRATION

In various parts of Asia, a large number of people who leave the villages nowadays do not 'arrive' in the cities. To the extent their mobility is intra-rural in nature, it is usually only for the duration of a season: they return to their place of origin when their presence is no longer required. Thus, labour migration is actually labour circulation. My fieldwork for the last half century has focused on the coming and going of these people in south Gujarat, a region of high economic growth on the western coast of India. Those who belong to this nomadic workforce remain outsiders in the area to which they have been recruited on a temporary and casual basis, and are treated as transients by those who make use of their labour power. Informality and circulation together allow us to define these people as a reserve army of labour.[2]

[2] J. Breman, *Footloose Labour: Working in India's Informal Economy*, Cambridge: Cambridge University Press, 1996.

In considering the main features of their identity, the first thing that comes to mind is that as socially deprived contingents, that is, as members of low or backward communities and sections of tribal or religious minorities, they belong to the land-poor or landless underclasses of rural society. In their search for work and income outside agriculture, they lack not only physical but also social capital (low education achievements and lacking the network which would make them eligible for steady and better work). In the absence of social, economic, and political qualifications, they remain stuck at the bottom of the economy, both in their places of origin as well as in their new place of work. Pushed out because of their redundancy in the rural–agrarian labour process, they are driven back again because of their temporary and time-bound incorporation elsewhere. At both ends of their axis of mobility, they are hired only for as long as they are willing and are fit enough to work, and are fired when there is a downturn in the demand for their labour power or when they have lost their capacity to work.

Circulation is work related. As dependent members of the household, women and children can come along or are even required to come along on the basis of their ability to take part in the labour process. Those who are not fit to work, because they are too young or too old to earn at least their own keep, are discouraged from accompanying members of the household who move off. It means that labour power, not the social unit of which it is part, is made mobile. Recruitment once started is both local and group based. The pattern of segmentation in the labour market that has emerged, rather haphazardly, tends to become repetitive over time in the sense that other factors than a particular aptitude seem to be the main trigger and driving force. Labour circulation has a chain effect and cannot be explained in terms of the supply/demand mechanism operating in the formal labour market. Labour brokers, acting on behalf of employers, form another link in the chain of circulation for the foot-loose workforce and explains why they seldom have access to other jobs wherever they go, even in the informal sector. Opting out of the circuit with the aim of staying on and settling down at the new worksite is next to impossible. On the other hand, work-specific segmentation such as I found in brick kilns, stone quarries, salt pans, and on construction sites perpetuates circulation.

Drifting in and out is not necessarily caused by local shortage, a lack of hands available, or a willingness to work. The preference for outsiders is often part of a strategy resorted to by employers to command a pliable and vulnerable labour force which, by their status as aliens and transients, have, on both sides, forfeited their bargaining power. Consequently, because of migrants moving in, local labour becomes superfluous to demand and has to go out in search of alternative employment. They fall victim to the same process of failing to get access to steady work and, in turn, are made to join the reserve army of labour. Thus, influx and exodus are closely related to each other in a perpetual pattern of circulation.

What is the magnitude of people in India who work for the whole year or a substantial part of it away from home? Numbers are difficult to come by because the phenomenon of labour remaining footloose is hugely understated in census statistics and macro-level surveys such as reported by National Sample Survey (NSS). Moreover, there is a lack of consensus on the definition of migration, operationalized in terms of distance (demarcated by the boundaries of district or state) as well as length of absence (week, season, year, or more). Are workers commuting from the village to the nearby town migrants, or do they only become so if they stay on at the worksite for more than a day, a week, or longer? On the other hand, there are long-distance migrants such as the powerloom operators who go off at a young age to Surat and go home only for brief visits but who settle back down again in their place of origin in Orissa and Andhra Pradesh when they are worn out. As semi-permanent migrants, they spend a large part of their working life in loneliness until economic compulsion, due to job loss or old age, ultimately drives them back to 'where they belong'. At both ends, the migratory scale is fluid rather than fixed, difficult to comprehend in a research jargon that is heavily biased by formal sector concepts.

Based on the 1991 *Report of the National Commission on Rural Labour* in India, a migrant is a person who migrates temporarily from his place of residence to another area, either rural or urban, with a view to getting waged employment. A separate study group specified this further by stating that a migrant labourer is one who works as part of a temporary workforce in different sectors and returns to her/his place of origin. Rather arbitrarily, that is, on the basis of incomplete estimates, more in the nature of guesswork than backed up by verifiable accounts, the National Commission on Rural Labour (NCRL) calculated in its 1991 report that about 10 million rural workers went out in search of work. With the caveat that seasonal migration had been the commission's primary concern, this tally included 4.5 million interstate rural migrants and around 6 million intra- or inter-district rural migrant workers temporarily employed inside or outside agriculture. The change in composition of the national economy, both sector-wise and as far as the shift in the rural–urban balance of labour is concerned, accelerated dramatically after the report came out. But it is quite clear that the magnitude of circulation in the preceding decades had not been covered adequately. In addition to heavily underestimating the participation rate of females and children in the annual trek, both the rural–urban and the intra-rural migration rate must have been at least double the reported size. While it is a matter of dispute whether in south Gujarat either the short-distance sojourners (example, the village commuters going off to work in the Vapi industrial estate) or the long-stay migrants (such as the powerloom workers in Surat city) should be included in the figure on labour circulation, even when narrowing down the score to seasonal migrants, the stated figures are much too low. This was duly noted by the special study group on migrant labour. In a reference to my own published fieldwork findings, this panel of experts wrote:

It appears that circular migration is much higher than what can be discerned from the NSS and Census data. Moreover both the NSS and Census data is dated; the developments since the mid-seventies, such as the Green Revolution, are not reflected. For instance, the presence of migrant workers from Maharashtra who speak Khandeshi seems to have been ignored by the 1981 Census in three taluks of Surat district—Kamrej, Bardoli and Palsana—where according to micro in-depth studies, around 60,000–70,000 migrant workers during that period worked in sugarcane farms. But the Census reports only 11,373 Marathi and only 6 Khandeshi speaking persons. And the Marathi speaking persons reported by the Census seem to be non-farm employees.[3]

Do recent statistics show a higher degree of accuracy and reliability? I am afraid not, and, once again, even that observation has no foundation in factual and reliable data. According to the latest estimate with which I am familiar, the total number of migrant workers is supposed to hover around 30 million for the whole of India.[4] The source from which I derive this figure refers, as a typical example, to at least half a million seasonal migrants belonging to Muslim communities in the rice belt

[3] National Commission on Rural Labour (NCRL), *Report of the National Commission on Rural Labour, Vol. II: Report of Study Groups,* New Delhi: Ministry of Labour, Government of India (GoI), 1991, p. K-17.

[4] R. Srivastava and S.K. Sasikumar, 'An Overview of Migration in India, its Impact and Key Issues', paper presented at the 'Regional Conference on Migration, Development and Pro-Poor Policy Choices in Asia', Dhaka, Bangladesh, 22–4 June 2003.

of West Bengal during the harvesting period. In view of incomplete coverage—caused by the same mixture of absence of investigative zeal, lack of definitional rigour, a politically inspired reluctance, or outright unwillingness to take stock of what is going on in the lower echelons of the economy and society—I am inclined to suggest that, presently, at least 50 million people are and remain on the move in order to make up for the income and employment deficit the households they belong to face at home for a major part of the year. Migration findings presented by the Census and National Sample Survey Organization (NSSO) for 1991–2001 suggest that long-term work related mobility (more than ten years) is the largest category of migrant workers, representing a little more than half of the total, while the category in the range from one to nine years went up in the same interval to 41 per cent, with a residual category of 7 per cent migrants staying away for less than one year. Indeed, the NSSO reported a decline in short-term migration in the course of the 1990s, coming down to 11 million workers in 1999–2000 who went off for two to six months, of which 8.5 million were employed in rural areas.

What is shown as a residual category in the census and NSSO reports has remained a highly understated segment of the total labour force in the research carried out by those agencies specialized in the collection of statistical data but which fall short in the qualitative and contextual analysis of their database. Although circulation is not restricted to mobile men and women who work away from home for less than one year, I would argue that this residual category going off but coming back within a short interval represents a much bigger proportion of all migrants in search of employment than a mere 7 per cent. The report brought out by the National Commission for Enterprises in the Unorganized Sector (NCEUS) unequivocally states that the numbers of such migrants (that is, circulating for up to one year) is much larger than that estimated in official sources.[5]

Many features relating to labour circulation or migration are poorly documented, for instance, information on the part of the household

[5] National Commission for Enterprises in the Unorganized Sector (NCEUS), *Report on Conditions of Work and Promotion of Livelihoods in the Unorganised Sector*, New Delhi: Academic Foundation, 2008, p. 96. A recent study puts the figure of temporary migrants at 10 crores, an estimate which is not backed up by firm data. See Priya Deshingkar and John Farrington (eds), *Circular Migration and Multilocational Livelihood Strategies in Rural India*, New Delhi: Oxford University Press, 2009, p. 16.

budget earned while working outside the place of residence. There is a
dearth of data on both the amount of cash brought back home or sent as
remittances that is spent on daily requirements, as well as on the expenses
that are incurred during life-cycle events. From another perspective, we
should not talk about savings but understand these transactions as 'loans'
advanced by the employer or a broker/contractor as payment for labour
to be performed later on. Practices of neo-bondage are often the modus
operandi of such work contracts.[6] While it is quite clear that the money
needed for survival is met from what migrants manage to save, details of
how family members back home contribute to the cost of reproduction
in terms of child care, care for the old, and the cost of medication in
the case of failing health are often not taken into account. The kind of
jobs for which footloose labour qualify makes them prone to diseases,
injuries, and accidents which impair the physical and mental condition
of workers who, undernourished and overworked, are already suffering
from all kinds of health deficiencies.

## IN SEARCH OF WORK AND SHELTER

The people pushed out of agriculture do not give up the habitat which
keeps them embedded in the village of their origin; first and foremost,
because they may have been accepted in the urban space as temporary
workers but not as residents. It means, of course, that they simply
cannot afford to vacate the shelter left behind in the hinterland. This is
in addition to the fact that dependent members of their household do
not join them on departure. Here we notice a major contrast with the
transformation that went on in the western world when the rural exodus
escalated one and half centuries ago. When the working classes in Europe
started to move out of the countryside, they brought their families along
to the cities where they settled down. Public housing was sponsored by
the state/municipality or by corporations set up by the newly arrived
citizens themselves. In India, housing societies for factory labour did
not become a prominent part of the urban expansion in most parts of
the country. Unlike in Europe, where housing cooperatives are part of
working-class neighbourhoods, in India, this term invariably signals
the presence of middle-class owners who have bought their bungalows
and apartments from private contractors. Working-class colonies used
to be built by employers either as coolie lines on the plantations and

---

[6] J. Breman, *Labour Bondage in West India: From Past to Present*, New Delhi:
Oxford University Press, 2007.

in the mine belt or as *chawls*, consisting of dead-end alleys filled with cheap tenements which came up around the textile mills in, for example, Bombay (henceforth Mumbai) and Ahmedabad. Due to the relentless informalization of the economy, of which casualized employment is a major feature, the need to keep a stable workforce and to provide even a modicum of housing to them has gone.

Informal sector workers who have reached the city where they try to find a more permanent niche in the urban economy have to make their own arrangements. This they manage to do by squatting on unoccupied land or by finding a foothold in one of the settlements, usually on the outskirts, as portrayed by Mike Davis in his book, *Planet of Slums*.[7] Their self-built shelters, grouped in colonies and built from recycled material, lack basic facilities such as tap water, sanitation, electricity, a school, and proper access roads and are difficult to reach by public transport. But colonies inhabited by the low castes or classes in the villages are not of a better quality. For no good reason at all, the word slum has an urban connotation, while the shanties spread out in the countryside are similarly populated by residents living in utter degradation. Still, on both sides of the rural–urban axis, the labouring poor have at least a fixed abode, ramshackle though it may be. It is a space in which they can retreat from the harshness of their daily work, from the bullying of the employer or his agent, and from the nagging of neighbours.

Circulating migrants, however, are often made to live without a proper shelter and do not enjoy the comfort of privacy. This goes for the powerloom workers in Surat who sleep in a packed room in the company of workmates, construction workers who arrange a sort of bivouac at the building site, brick makers who erect a makeshift hut of broken and rejected bricks, gangs of paddy harvesters allowed to cook their food and pass the night in the farmer's courtyard, and the mobile army of sugarcane cutters who camp along the roadside or in the open field in a tent of plastic canvas sheets; for the duration of the working season, they have to make do without drinking water and toilet facilities. One worker had the courage to tell a group of officials that had come to find out about the way they were treated by the mill management that 'even dogs are better off'. This was more than twenty years ago, and since then nothing has changed. But the anger with which these labour nomads react to their plight of exploitation and subordination shows that they are not only in search of regular jobs but also in search of

---

[7] M. Davis, *Planet of Slums*, London and New York: Verso, 2006.

decency and dignity. One wonders what the prospects are for realizing these ambitions which are fuelled by the rightful demand for a better quality of life. The degradation and dehumanization which Polanyi highlighted as features characteristic for the initial stage of the great transformation, made way for a decisive improvement in the further transition to an urban–industrial livelihood in the Atlantic world. The advance made in that direction so far does not seem to give ground for optimism about a better future for the much larger working classes of contemporary Asia.

What needs to be emphasized is the strong interdependence that exists between the ongoing practice of labour circulation and employment in the informal economies of the globalized South. Recruitment of labour for a limited time period, lasting no longer than one season, is in line with the time-bound nature of many informal sector operations: the harvesting of various crops (such as paddy, sugarcane, tobacco, cotton, and mangoes), the quarrying of stones, the moulding of bricks, or the manufacture of sea salt, are all operations that can only take place during the dry months of the year. The same goes for other industries, rural and urban, carried out under fair weather conditions in the open air and for construction work: production comes to a halt before the onset of the monsoon. As a matter of fact, labour circulation facilitates informal sector activity and, also the other way round, the progressive informalization of the economy puts a premium on movement by a highly casualized workforce.

Conducive to the ongoing nature of migration/circulation is an improved mobility infrastructure: transport by mechanized vehicles and communication on where to go and what to do made available at both the beginning and the end of the route. The result is that distance can be bridged in a relatively short time by train, bus, or truck, while, at the same time, travel costs have gone down. Having said this, I would also like to point out that it is usually not the employer or his agent who bears the cost of the journey made, but the migrants themselves. Ferrying them from the village to the worksite when they are hired, and back again when they are fired, involves expenses charged to their account, adding to the debt which is the start of the contract. The poor resource base of the massive army forced to participate in the annual trek to other destinations to work long hours at low pay rates is a direct consequence of their inability to qualify for better type of jobs yielding higher incomes at home. For the large majority of these people, poorly educated or totally illiterate, labour circulation is not a free choice, but a strenuous and tiresome expedition that has to be repeated again and again, rarely rewarded by getting skilled or bringing back savings that can be used for productive investment leading to a more secure economic condition. Circulation is at best a survival strategy, a route taken to cope with the threat of unemployment and the lack of means needed to keep the household going.

When, in the wake of India's independence, land reforms were carried out—as was promised by the nationalist leadership in its efforts to mobilize the peasantry for the struggle against colonial rule—those segments of the rural workforce which had no or very little land did not benefit from the redistribution of agrarian capital. Their exclusion at that critical moment of restructuring ownership of resources explains why they remained bypassed in the processes of socio-economic development that came about during the second half of the twentieth century. The NCRL backed up its verdict in 1991 on the political and policy failure to strengthen the asset base of the rural underclasses with the following statement:

Even a small piece of land can serve not only as a supplementary source of income for the rural labour household, but also as a source of security. Land-base, however slender, can weaken the dependency syndrome in the rural setting. Despite two rounds of land reform legislation, the surplus land acquired and distributed among the rural poor was below 2 per cent of total cultivated area. Thus, due to most unsatisfactory implementation of ceiling laws in several of the States, the objective of acquiring surplus land and distribution among the landless has not been achieved. Moreover, there was hardly any attempt to influence the land market in favour of the rural poor by advancing long-term loans to them for purchase of land.[8]

After independence, the stalwarts of the Congress party announced that there was simply not enough land to provide all peasant classes with a viable holding. Pressure on agrarian resources had already surpassed critical levels in most regions of the country. Instead of handing out tiny plots which would not yield adequate employment and income, the land poor and landless were told that a better future would await them outside agriculture, as mill hands in the city. Factories were going to open up to provide skilled and decent jobs for all those whose labour power had become redundant in the rural economy. The breakthrough to an urban-industrial mode of production appeared to take longer than anticipated

[8] NCRL, *Report of the National Commission on Rural Labour, Vol. I: Main Report*, New Delhi: Ministry of Labour, GoI, 1991, pp. v–vi.

by the political designers and policy planners, but then the notion of an informal sector was ingenuously construed as a stop-gap solution to the problem of underprivileged contingents who were encouraged to leave the villages in search of alternative employment. The state, however, did nothing to take care of people who were made footloose or to support and protect them in their search for work and shelter.

## Informalization as a Strategy to Reduce Labour Cost

The initial understanding was that the informal sector acted as a waiting room for migrants who had found their way to the urban economy. Growing accustomed to the pace of urban life and work, they were supposed to move up in the labour hierarchy. However, that scenario turned out to have been too optimistic. While a rapidly increasing flow of steady job seekers kept coming, they were only offered casual work, rotated around as temporary rather than regular hands. Instead of finalizing their migratory status as new arrivals and finding a first niche from which to upgrade themselves in the urban economy, many of those who enter the city have to leave again. If not when the season or year runs out, then when they have lost the labour power needed to hang on. Even if they succeed in extending the duration of their urban stay, in the end, they fail to escape from their membership of a footloose army.

Another unduly optimistic notion was the suggestion that the informal sector is able to accommodate any number of newcomers. Even if the city is already flooded with shoeshine boys, *rickshawvalas*, construction workers, head loaders, street vendors, beggars, and so on, the prevalent notion is 'no problem', more can enter these trades and find a ready supply of customers willing to buy their services. It is the myth of the infinite absorption capacity of the informal sector and it is just that: a myth. Unemployment and underemployment of the footloose workforce are highly neglected issues which require focused and detailed investigation to shed light on this side of life at the urban and rural bottom which so far has remained in the shadow. In my last round of fieldwork in south Gujarat, carried out between 2004 and 2006, I found that both intra-rural and rural–urban labour circulation had gone down in the localities of my recurrent research. Not because more and better employment opportunities had locally become available in or at short distance away from the village but, as I was told, because migrants found themselves crowded out of the job markets with which they were familiar. I am inclined to read this as a signal that the informal sector is getting saturated with an oversupply of labour that is already in a state of reserve.

Polanyi suggested that the free labour market which emerged in Great Britain with the abolition of the poor law arrangements in 1830s— provisions that had discouraged outmigration to urban localities—was ultimately beneficial to the displaced segment of the workforce: 'No relief any longer for the able-bodied unemployed, no minimum wages either, nor a safeguarding of the right to live. Labor should be dealt with as that which it was, a commodity which must find its price in the market.'[9] The new regime was harsh but received praise, in retrospect, as a blessing in disguise, because the unleashed market organization became counterproductive and led inevitably to the building up of pressure for protection. And this protectionist countermovement, Polanyi argues, was a reaction against a dislocation which attacked the fabric of society, and which, in the end, would have destroyed the very organization of production that the market had called into being. Is this then the change for better times to come that can be discerned in the booming economies of Asia today? One wonders if it is really possible for the vast masses redundant in their rural habitat to opt out and find regular employment elsewhere. What I tend to see is a supply of labour far in excess to the structural demand for this factor of production. It helps to explain why a bottom segment of land-poor and landless peasants do not drift around freely in the labour market but remain as a casualized workforce bonded in debt.[10] They are made mobile in a state of immobility. This leads me to challenge the assumption that the kind of restless circulation in which a substantial part of mankind is presently involved will be replaced by a decent and dignified work regime that offers security and protection for the labouring poor as it did one century ago in the Atlantic world.

Earlier estimates that less than half of the working population came to depend for their livelihood on the proceeds of the informal sector have since been revised to include at least three-quarters, or even more than four-fifths, of all those who are gainfully employed. In addition to demographic growth, a complex of economic and social mecha-nisms—mainly fragmentation of land holdings and mechanization of

---

[9] Polanyi, *The Great Transformation*, p. 117.

[10] J. Breman, *The Poverty Regime in Village India: Half a Century of Work and Life at the Bottom of the Rural Economy in South Gujarat*, New Delhi: Oxford University Press, 2007.

farm work—has led to a rapid fall in the volume of labour in agriculture. The recognition of this trend has led to a reconsideration of the view that the process of transformation in the Third World is essentially a delayed repetition of the industrialization and urbanization scenario that laid the foundations for the western welfare state in the early twentieth century.

This critical review of the initial notion of an evolutionary trajectory based on the western model has major policy implications. The new political correctness is to state that efforts should no longer focus on formalizing the labour system. In a major deviation from the previous route to development, the suggestion now is that the privileges enjoyed by an exceedingly small proportion of the working population must end. The protection enjoyed by a vanguard of the workforce—which in Third World countries represents no more than a tenth of the total population living on the sale of their labour power—is detrimental, according to this argument, to the efforts of the vast majority to improve the conditions in which they live. This 'unfair' competition could be avoided by abolishing the security of employment, minimum wages, maximum working hours, and secondary labour rights which usually apply in the formal sector.

But, should we not then worry that things will get even worse? No. Those who call for flexibility to give employers a free hand to hire and fire as they please suggest that this approach would actually lead to more and better work, and a rise in real wages. The idea that efforts should no longer be focused on increasing formalization of the labour system seems to have become the received wisdom in the milieu of neo-liberal policymakers. Analyses focusing on the positive side of the regime of economic informality are designed to refute the idea that leaving the formal sector and joining the informal sector will automatically imply a deterioration in living standards. Such a view often tends to culminate in an ode to the virtues of micro-enterprise and self-employment. The World Bank has been a leading proponent of the policy of informalization, which goes together with the erosion of the rights of formal sector workers. This was the basic message of the *World Development Report 1995*, which discusses the position of labour in the globalized economy.[11]

[11] World Bank, *World Development Report 1995: Workers in an Integrating World*, New York: Oxford University Press, 1995.

## INSISTING ON MIGRATION AS THE ROADMAP TO PROGRESS

The World Bank is in the forefront of all those who argue that because of the pressure on agrarian resources—the man–land ratio is becoming even more unfavourable than it has been for a long time already—migration to wherever non-agrarian work and income can be found is a must. Actually, the verdict is more positive than that and is summed up in the latest *World Development Report 2009*.[12] The case of China, in particular, is supposed to have demonstrated that the exodus of huge contingents of labour (at a figure of more than 150–200 million by 2008) from the rural hinterland to the urban growth poles is a win-win situation for all stakeholders: for migrants, who get more employment and higher wages; for the places of destination in need of more manpower than locally available; and for the places of origin, which stand to benefit from remittances sent back home.

In offering its recipe of large-scale labour mobility as a pro-growth strategy, the World Bank has carefully refrained from referring to evidence that shows what migrants often lose rather than win. In the first place, because departure of many landless and land-poor peasants is a form of distress migration, away from misery or even destitution without necessarily resulting in better work and higher wages, it is an escape for the duration of a season, a short-term remedy in response to the structural lack of wherewithal to survive by staying put. For many of them, migration is bound to remain circular in nature because of the dearth of physical and social capital to settle down elsewhere. The decision to leave is also not based on the exercise of free but of forced choice imposed by the need to sell one's labour power in advance and thus, become entrapped in a relationship of debt bondage.[13]

Heralding departure from home as the way out of poverty, the *World Development Report 2009*[14] strongly condemns what it calls the setting up of barriers against labour mobility. Efforts to increase rural employment opportunities such as the newly introduced scheme in India to generate public works, are rejected as a waste of time and money, ill-advised because such interventions tend to undercut the free flow of labour praised as being in the best interests of all parties concerned.

---

[12] World Bank, *World Development Report 2009: Reshaping Economic Geography*, New York: Oxford University Press, 2009.

[13] J. Breman, Isabelle Guérin, and Aseem Prakash (eds), *India's Unfree Workforce: Of Bondage Old and New*, New Delhi: Oxford University Press, 2009.

[14] World Bank, *World Development Report 2009*, p. 163.

In a sharp critique of the World Bank's judgment, the beneficial side of the National Rural Employment Guarantee Act (NREGA) is brought to the fore:

Media reports since the introduction to the programme indicate that in many areas of the country, the NREGA, described by the Report as retarding labour mobility, has enhanced the confidence of rural workers who have intensified their demands for higher wages. In failing to reference the politics behind the NREGA, the Report effectively disavows such struggles and their (however limited) success in winning a modicum of rights and thereby a 'spatial' advantage for migrant workers. Representations in the Report of this policy and practice as ill-conceived effectively erase not only the (emotional and physical) injuries that becoming mobile entails for large numbers of people, but also the responsiveness of governments to democratic pressure.[15]

Of course, together with other policymakers, the World Bank is fully aware that migrants require at least a foothold to enable them to settle down more permanently in the urban milieu. By not attending to their basic needs, the newly arrived may find the terrain to which they have come not congenial for staying on. Without access to minimal welfare services such as cheap shelter and food subsidies made available to other inhabitants, the cost of long-term city life becomes prohibitively high. The same logic suggests that granting property rights and tenure security to the plots on which the slum dwellers have built their shelter—leaves clearly taken from de Soto's notebook[16]—helps migrants to ease their journey along the winding road, leading to their acceptance as regularized urban residents endowed with a legal status. The question, of course, is to what extent is this minimum packet presented in the World Bank's document as 'selective interventions' put into practice? Hardly or not at all, it seems.

While the pressure on resources in the rural hinterland is building up, the growth rate of the urban population in India is, contrary to what we would expect, not rising but declining. Why is that? According to Kundu,[17] it is not because labour mobility is going down. The

[15] A. Mariganti *et al.*, 'Where is the Geography? World Bank's WDR 2009', *Economic and Political Weekly,* vol. XLIV, no. 19, 2009, pp. 45–51.

[16] J. Breman, *The Labouring Poor in India: Patterns of Exploitation, Subordination and Exclusion*, New Delhi: Oxford University Press, 2003.

[17] A. Kundu, 'Urbanisation and Urban Governance: Search for a Perspective beyond Neoliberlism', *Economic and Political Weekly,* vol. 38, no. 29, 2003, pp. 3079–87.

restructuring of the balance between countryside and town appears to taper off, he suggests, because the urban arena has turned markedly hostile to outsiders who have come not only to work but also to occupy space for their livelihood. Finding access to agencies charged with issuing permits required for urban citizenship is next to impossible for slum dwellers, blamed from day one as squatters with no right to the waste land, either in public or private hands, on which they have built their makeshift shelter. The space they encroach is required for building roads, bridges, canals, and power stations as part of an expanding urban infrastructure, or is taken up by housing colonies for people with higher and regular incomes. The squatters are forced to leave again before the construction works begin. Drifting around the outskirts of the city, they have to keep a low profile because they cannot afford to buy the plot on which they erect a bivouac of sorts since land prices are far beyond their budget. Without assets and contacts with the municipal authorities, these settlers do not, of course, qualify for property rights and tenure security. They are what I have called 'nowhere people', drifting around in a nowhere landscape. Reporting on the outcome of my fieldwork findings in rural south Gujarat, I observed that:

These working men, women and children are sometimes needed in the towns and sometimes in the countryside. Sometimes they are put to work in the obscure and degraded landscape in between these two extremes: alongside the highways and railway lines, in agro-industrial enclaves, brick kilns, quarries and saltpans, gathered together in temporary camps that arise where rivers are dammed, where earth has to be moved to dig canals or lay pipelines, where roads have to be laid or bridges and viaducts built, and so on. They live and work at these sites as long as the job lasts. The rest of the time they are confined in slum-like sprawling settlements of the fringes of villages, squatting with no legal title, waiting until the call comes for them to leave again. If the work is relatively close to home they commute back and forth each day, if it is farther afield they stay away longer, sometimes for whole seasons. But sooner or later the work is completed again and they return to their waiting room that lies beyond the purview of politicians and policymakers.[18]

Those who manage to gain a foothold in one of the more regularized slums belong to the somewhat better-off category of migrants. It does not mean, however, that they have found a more permanent niche in which they are safe from forced removal. Even when they are put on record in the municipal books, their houses get demolished because

[18] Breman, *The Poverty Regime in Village India*, p. 409.

the cheap land they occupy becomes a target for real estate dealers or building contractors who terrorize the slum dwellers to vacate and move off. The hostile reception awaiting resourceless migrants in the urban arena is inspired also by new civic movements launched by bourgeois and politically well-connected sections of the population to disenfranchise slum dwellers arguing that their illegal status poses a threat to the maintenance of law and order.[19] The labour power of these outsiders is required, on and off, but not their cumbersome and defiling presence as regular inhabitants.

The growing prosperity of the more well-to-do, living far above the poverty line, has encouraged local governments to design projects for the beautification of city space. A clear example is the corporation in Ahmedabad, set up as a public–private partnership to develop the banks of the Sabarmati river, bifurcating the city into a rest and recreation zone for its middle-class citizens. Shopping malls, cinemas, playgrounds for children, fountains, and statues are going to decorate the boulevard on both sides of the river along which middle-class citizens will stroll and spend their leisure time. The price paid for the good life is at the cost of the poor who had settled on the riverbanks. Hundreds of households have been evicted, to be resettled in a swamp far outside Ahmedabad. Here, I found them at the end of September 2009, deprived of the basic amenities that make life somewhat decent and trying desperately to hold on to their niche in the urban job market as hawkers, security guards, housemaids, rickshaw drivers, garbage collectors, waste pickers, and such like.

## BLOCKING ACCESS TO MAINSTREAM SOCIETY

The NCRL report of 1991 held the slow increase in per capita income, as well as the labour-unfriendly policy framework, responsible for the deprivation in which the lower classes in the countryside remained stuck and concluded that the trickle-down effects of growth had been negligible for India's rural poor. This assessment came after more than four decades of development praxis as specified in the five year planning documents that formed the directory for the policies to be followed. A major shift came when, under the spell of the neo-liberal doctrine from the 1980s onwards, the state retreated from interference in the business of economic growth—at least, as far as the interests of labour,

---

[19] D. Mahadevia (ed.), *Inside the Transforming Urban Asia: Processes, Policies and Public Action*, New Delhi: Concept Publishing Company, 2008, chapters 12 and 18.

not those of capital, were concerned—to leave the field open for the free interplay of market forces. It essentially meant relying on a totally different approach to poverty alleviation, suggesting that rather than the problem, informality is the solution in the attempt to raise production and generate more and better employment opportunities. The restructuring which went on explains why the NCEUS found that by 2008, 93 per cent of the total workforce in India had become dependent for its livelihood, either as waged labour or as self-employed earners, on the informal sector of the economy. It should immediately be pointed out that not all of them are living in dire circumstances. Actually, a sizable category enjoys higher incomes than the lower grades of formal sector workers. But these better-paid workers, generally, do not belong to the deprived castes and communities which is the social identity of the lower segments of the labour force in the informal economy.

Flexibilization of employment and deregulation of the economy is said to have resulted in bringing down the number of people in India who survive below the poverty line, and statistics are produced to back up this welcome message. It is a mystifying operation meant to disguise the fact that life has not become better for the huge underclasses rotating around a variety of worksites in the informal sector. The NCEUS reported that at the end of 2004–5 about 836 million or 77 per cent of the population had to make do with less than 20 rupees per day, that is, less than half a dollar per capita. These people are the backbone of India's informal economy and their life in abject poverty was conditioned by the lack of any legal protection of their jobs and the absence of decent standards of employment and social security. The members of this National Commission do not hesitate to identify migrants as one of the most vulnerable segments within the workforce:

Migrant workers, particularly at the lower end, including casual labourers and wage workers in industries and construction sites, face adverse work as well as living conditions. This group is highly disadvantaged because they are largely engaged in the unorganised sector with weakly implemented labour laws. Migration often involves longer working hours, poor living conditions, social isolation and inadequate access to basic amenities ... These groups of migrants are characterized by meagre physical and human capital and belong to socially deprived groups such as Scheduled Castes (SCs) and Scheduled Tribes (STs) and weaker groups such as the women.[20]

[20] NCEUS, *Report on Conditions of Work and Promotion of Livelihoods in the Unorganised Sector*, p. 97.

Although floating around in large numbers, their presence is often not acknowledged and their muted voices remain unheard. They are redundant in a labour market that is already flooded with men, women, and children who constitute the reserve footloose army. But the denigration shown to them is related also to their inferior status in the social hierarchy. Of relevance here is the interrelationship that Kannan, a member of the NCEUS, has traced between the regime of poverty and the social structure based on inequality.[21] Ongoing labour circulation and lack of representation reinforce each other in a vicious circle. The constant coming in and going off again pre-empts the building up of cohesion and mutual trust that workers need to engage in collective action. Keeping the workforce in a state of flux by instant hire and fire procedures is a strategy to which employers or their agents resort in order to avoid being confronted by the politics of solidarity from below. While the workforce thus remains unorganized, those who make use of their casual labour power find ways and means to coordinate their action. To call the informal sector unorganized is to overlook how employers operating in this vast terrain manage to lay down the terms of the contract by engaging in collective action.

Fragmentation is the outcome of a strategy of recruitment that brings together a heterogeneous workforce, internally separated by having no other option than to articulate their primordial loyalties. In their effort to realize a better deal for themselves, the diverse sections do not close ranks but fall prey to competing with each other in the narrow bargaining space left to them. And if they rise to the occasion, stand up to fight for steady jobs, higher pay, a basic dignity, they are dealt with as a law and order problem and have to face the ire of the employers as well as the heavy hand of the state intolerant of demonstrations of 'indiscipline'.

Since informality is mainly, if not exclusively, discussed as a phenomenon of the economy, I want to argue that it is a dimension of governance as well. While public space and public institutions have shrunk with the retreat of the state, many politicians and bureaucrats cash in on their role as civil servants to line their own pockets. Turning public power into private gain is the sort of fraud that is criticized when indulged in

[21] K.P. Kannan, 'Dualism, Informality and Social Inequality: An Informal Economy Perspective of the Challenge of Inclusive Development in India', Presidential Address, 50th Annual Conference of the Indian Society of Labour Economics, Lucknow, 13–15 December 2008.

by high-ranking officials and power brokers, but it is at the lower echelons of the government machinery, at the district and sub-district levels,
that we have to focus our attention on the wheeling and dealing of petty
bureaucrats and political cadre. In collusion with vested interests, this
set of local influentials operates at the interface between the informal
and formal sector institutions and manipulates their legal standing to
take illegal cuts from the capital which is accumulated in their domain
beyond the purview of the state. Of course, these transactions remain
hidden to the public eye and fail to turn up in the database produced by
formal sector agencies. It is one of the reasons why such tailored findings
are a poor reflection of what goes on in the real economy, which is for a
very large part informal.

It should come as no surprise that, as reported by the NCEUS, poverty lingers on much more massively than is acknowledged by those who
have put their faith in the kind of wishful thinking which suggests that
the percentage of people unable to satisfy their basic needs has decreased.
As before, new schemes have been announced promising that life will
also become better for all those who have not benefited much, or even at
all, from the growth of the steadily informalized economy. The National
Rural Employment Guarantee Act is meant to provide work and income
for households belonging to the land-poor and landless underclasses in
the countryside. It is still too early to tell whether it will be able to stem
the tide of circular migration. Of similar importance is the introduction
of social security provisions for the workforce in the informal sector.
Already, the NCRL commented in its 1991 report that such a scheme
was long overdue:

The expenditure on social security in India hardly accounts for 2.5 per cent of
GDP. This is among the lowest in the world. Most of the social security benefits
from this meagre allocation accrue to the well organised urban work force, who
account for only one-tenth of the total work force. However, there is now a
growing realisation among the States and the Centre about the need to provide
adequate social security to the rural labour. A wide variety of social security
schemes for rural labour are currently in operation in different States, although
the coverage and the scale of assistance are far from being adequate.[22]

It has taken more time than suggested in this passage. Nearly two decades
later, in order to cope with adversities that are a regular feature of the
working poor, the NCEUS took the lead in framing a social security

---

[22] NCRL, *Report of the National Commission on Rural Labour, Vol. I*, p. viii.

bill to reduce the vulnerability which keeps these households in a state of dependency that often takes the shape of neo-bondage. Without stipulating the basic provisions that will soon be introduced—related to health care insurance and some minimal support at old age—it needs to be clarified that the bill that was finally passed was a heavily diluted version of the original proposal. The main policymakers decided that the financial outlay required was too high to be paid out of the public budget and scaled down both the cost of the operation and the coverage of the scheme. In the face of these setbacks, it is difficult to remain confident that the political will exists to honour the rightful claims of a labour force for which the relentless thrust towards informalization has meant that they continue to be dealt with as no more than reserve workers and marginalized citizens. The latest school of thought pushed by economists aligning themselves with the World Bank policies suggests that in the current global crisis, the informal sector economy figures as a cushion for people who have lost their formal sector employment.[23] The message conveyed in this kind of statement is clear: informal sector workers are able to cope with adversities that are part of their day-to-day life and do not need public support or social security. The policymakers have now decided that the large masses of wage hunters and 'own-account workers' have somehow managed to find their own safety net: the informal sector.

## A TRANSFORMATION ABORTED?

Polanyi spelled out what the triumph of the market from the mid-nineteenth century onward meant for the 'native' economies outside Europe: a catastrophe.

The three or four large famines that decimated India under the British rule since the Rebellion were thus neither a consequence of the elements, nor of exploitation, but simply of the new market organization of labor and land which broke up the old village without actually solving its problems. While under the regime of feudalism and the village community, *noblesse oblige,* clan solidarity, and regulation of the corn market checked famines,under the rule of the market the people could not be prevented from starving according to the rules of the game.[24]

The author then goes on to argue that 'economically, India may have been—and in the long run, certainly was—benefited, but socially she

    [23] J. Breman, 'Myths of the Global Safety Net', *New Left Review*, vol. 59, September–October 2009, pp. 1–8.
    [24] Polanyi, *The Great Transformation*, p. 160.

was disorganized and thus thrown a prey to misery and degradation'.[25] In these words he essentially concludes that the path of India to development did not differ from the one followed in Great Britain: things had to get worse before they could become better.[26] Polanyi did not mince words in his description of what the self-regulating market meant for the people pushed out of their rural habitat in Great Britain. However, he also clarified that the pauperization which went on in the nineteenth century was the start of a trajectory that led, from the early twentieth century onwards, to economic improvement for the urban–industrial workforce. Besides, the depeasantized labourer on the European continent did not pass through the kind of horrendous misery and degradation that was the fate of the British workforce:

From the status of a villein he changed—or rather rose—to that of a factory worker. Thus he escaped the cultural catastrophe which followed in the wake of the Industrial Revolution in England. Moreover, the Continent was industrialized at a time when adjustment to the new productive techniques had already become possible, thanks, almost exclusively, to the imitations of English methods of social protection.[27]

Can a similar turning point be expected in Asia now that the land poor and landless, redundant in agriculture and in the countryside, are driven out in such massive numbers? I happen to be quite sceptical about such an optimistic forecast. Polanyi ended his treatise on a hopeful note when he concluded that the economic system has ceased to lay down the law to society and that the primacy of society over that system is secured once and for all. He illustrated the triumph of society over the market with the statement that 'not only conditions in the factory, hours of work, and modalities of contract, but the basic wage itself are determined outside the market'.[28] Of course, in the light of the labour regimes prevalent in contemporary Asia, this is an untenable proposition. At least in the setting of Asia, we seem to be back again in the first and ugly phase of the great transformation.

[25] Ibid.
[26] In *Late Victorian Holocausts: El Niño Famines and the Making of the Third World*, London: Verso, 2001, Davis rightly criticizes Polanyi's view of the way in which markets operate, but in doing so he may have overstated the traditional village community as an institution characterized by reciprocity and redistribution between the haves and the have-nots.
[27] Polanyi, *The Great Transformation*, p. 175.
[28] Ibid., p. 251.

A major feature of my analysis has focused on circulation in combination with informalization, which I have interpreted as ways to organize economic activity with a high return to capital and an excessively low return to labour. A more even distribution of the rewards gained by both factors of production would be a hopeful sign, but is difficult to discern. The huge but also highly differentiated and fragmented workforce in the informal sector of Asia's economy has not been able to withstand the onslaught of the free market, let alone come together on a common platform. The countervailing power of collective action to which Polanyi, quite correctly, attributed so much weight in reversing the trajectory of pauperization is still to make itself manifest. In a critical essay, Parry argues that Polanyi has understated the formidable obstacles that 'active society' must confront in its quest to rein in the market and nor did he adequately explain how a downtrodden and demoralized working class was able to assert itself.[29]

The erosion of the welfare state in the West, as well as its halting development where it had only just begun to come into sight in other parts of the world, can be seen as confirmation of a trend in which the steadily advancing emancipation of labour during the twentieth century appears to be reversing into its opposite, that is, dependency and growing insecurity, in the Asian region emphatically so. The progressive polarization of social classes accompanying these dynamics has given rise to a debate that concentrates on the inclusion–exclusion contrast. It seems to mark the return of the old dualism concept in yet another form. The growing inequality between the well-to-do and the underprivileged classes has contributed to the separation of the latter from mainstream society. The most vulnerable sections of the rural poor try to cope with their social exclusion by remaining footloose. As circular migrants, they have to face many hardships that go together with a life that begins and ends in poverty. They are the victims more than the beneficiaries of the transnationalized politics of development and are even blamed for their failure to work themselves out of their state of deficiency. In the morality dominating the dynamics of growth, based on a doctrine of inequity, these people at the tail end stand accused of defects in their behaviour which keep them stagnating in poverty. It is an ideology that comes close to the main tenets of social Darwinism. The hopeful notion remains, of

---

[29] J. Parry, '"Sociological Marxism" in Central India: Polanyi, Gramsci and the Case of the Unions', in C. Hann and K. Hart (eds), *Market and Society: The Great Transformation Today*, Cambridge: Cambridge University Press, 2009, p. 177.

course, that the neglect of social interests must eventually generate a political breakdown and a retreat of market fundamentalism.[30] Indeed, cracks have appeared in the façade of neo-liberal hegemony. Is this the beginning of the final episode of transformation in a globalized world that Polanyi had in mind?

[30] Hann and Hart (eds), *Market and Society*, p. 8.

# I

# THE AGRARIAN BACKGROUND

# 1

# Labour and Landlessness in South and Southeast Asia*

A central theme of Kautsky's classic analysis of agrarian dynamics in Europe at the end of the nineteenth century is the impact of the capitalist mode of production on rural class formation.[1] According to Kautsky, capitalist penetration differentiated what had been a more or less homogeneous peasantry in the *ancien régime* and gave rise to a class of landless labourers. In colonial Asia, the emergence of a landless class of agricultural labour has likewise, conventionally, been explained with reference to the penetration of capitalism into the rural economy. This essay critically evaluates these interpretations of European and Asian rural development and argues that landlessness existed in Asia long before agriculture became organized along capitalist lines.

* This paper was presented at an international conference on agrarian question, held in Wageningen in May 1995. It was subsequently published as 'Of Labour and Landlessness in South and Southeast Asia', in D. Bryceson, C. Kay, and J. Mooij (eds), *Disappearing Peasantries*, London: Intermediate Technology Publications, 2000, pp. 231–46.

[1] K. Kautsky, *Die Agrarfrage*, Stuttgart: Dietz, 1899. A French edition of the first volume was published in 1900 and subsequently reprinted by Maspero, Paris, in 1970. Jairus Banaji published an English summary of the French translation, 'Summary of Selected Parts of Kautsky's "The Agrarian Question"', *Economy and Society*, vol. 5, no. 1, 1976, pp. 2–49, and it is from this that my quotations are taken. An overview of Kautsky's work for English language readers can be found in A. Hussain, 'Theoretical Writings on the Agrarian Question', in A. Hussain and K. Tribe (eds), *Marxism and the Agrarian Question*, 2nd edition, vol. I, London: Macmillan, 1981, pp. 102–32. Kautsky's work has subsequently been translated into English by Pete Burgess and published in two volumes (K. Kautsky, *The Agrarian Question*, London: Zwan Publications, 1988).

A second argument developed in this essay relates to the different trajectories of capitalism in Europe and Asia. In Europe, a large part of the rural proletariat became both industrialized and urbanized in the course of the eighteenth to twentieth centuries, whilst in Asia's colonial regimes, the rural underclass remained dependent on agricultural work and income. It is only during the second half of the twentieth century, following political independence, that the rural economies of Asia became more diversified.

This essay begins by discussing Kautsky's views on the development of rural capitalism in Europe in more detail. The focus then shifts to Asia, and a discussion of the extent to which landlessness already existed in pre-colonial and colonial South and Southeast Asia. I argue that a distinct underclass existed in much of rural Asia even before the advent of colonialism, just as in Europe before capitalism started to penetrate rural life. This underclass is, however, difficult to define precisely because it varied according to time and place and because the boundary between land-poor and landless was often blurred. I then go on to describe the development of the rural underclass in the decades following political independence. In particular, the diversification of the rural economy, increased labour mobility, and the casualization of employment are examined. The essay concludes by highlighting the different impacts of capitalist development in Asia and Europe, particularly on the most marginal segments of the peasantry.

The problem addressed in this essay arises out of two considerations. The first refers to the interest shown by Marx and his followers in the agrarian situation of Asia in particular. As Banaji[2] notes, European Marxists of Engels' and Kautsky's generation showed little awareness of colonial questions and their reflections on the 'Asiatic mode of production' were speculative and based on weak empirical evidence. My purpose here is to draw renewed attention to this weakness. Furthermore, having engaged in historical and anthropological research in rural Asia, notably India and Indonesia, for the past thirty years, I am struck by the need to take into account the highly variable nature of the agrarian question, an issue which also formed the focus of Kautsky's analysis.

---

[2] Banaji, 'Summary of Selected Parts of Kautsky's "The Agrarian Question"', footnote 8.

## THE AGRARIAN QUESTION IN EUROPE

According to Kautsky, a protracted process of economic differentiation ended the once homogeneous composition of the European peasantry. In medieval Europe, the peasant family

composed an economic society that was entirely, or almost entirely, self-sufficient, a society that produced not only its own food, but built its own home, furniture and utensils, forged its own implements of production, etc. Naturally the peasant went to market, but he sold only his surplus produce, and bought only trivialities, except for iron, which he used only sparsely.[3]

Uniformity at the base of rural society was accompanied by the subordination of the agricultural workforce to feudal landowners. This implies that, in Kautsky's scheme of development, pre-capitalist society was stratified into two groups—the elite and the masses. The landlord–peasant relationship was the organizing principle of the feudal mode of production and a separate class of landless labourers did not exist.

Kautsky argued that the penetration of capitalism transformed this self-reproducing rural economy, which combined agricultural and artisanal production, in two ways. First, the growth of urban industry and trade deprived the peasantry of its composite resource base. Loss of all-round self-sufficiency forced peasants to become agrarian producers exclusively and to sell their crops for cash to meet their non-agrarian needs. The division of labour between town and countryside gradually subjected the peasant masses to market mechanisms over which they had no control. Second, exploitation by mercantile capital meant indebtedness and later, alienation from the means of production, leading to progressive economic differentiation.

The emerging process of commoditization in agriculture resulted in a large part of the rural population becoming almost or totally landless. Kautsky relates this slipping down the agrarian ladder to imbalances in the annual cycle of peasant labour. The decline of home industry made it necessary to reduce the household size. Peasant families began to push out some household members, either temporarily or indefinitely. These people had to find alternative sources of employment. The introduction of a new, machine-based technology had a similar impact. At the same time, the remaining workforce was insufficient to meet agricultural needs at peak times of the agricultural calendar. This shortfall was met

[3] Ibid., p. 3.

by hiring seasonal workers, mostly from peasant families seeking supplementary incomes for the surplus labour of adult members or children.

The same development which on the one hand creates a demand for wage
labourers, creates, on the other hand, these wage labourers themselves. It pro-
letarianises masses of peasants, cuts down the size of the peasant family and
throws the redundant members on the labour market. Finally, this process
enhances the peasants' dependence on secondary resources of income: as they
find it impossible to earn an income from the sale of agricultural produce, they
sell their labour power. Up until the 17th century we only rarely encounter
day workers or farm hands. Their employment becomes widespread around
this time. As wage labourers come to replace the family members who have left,
the conditions of the others, who stay behind, deteriorates to the level of wage
labour, subordinated to the head of the family. The old society centred on the
self-sufficient peasant family is thus replaced by troops of hired labour engaged
on the big peasant holdings.[4]

In his subsequent analysis, however, Kautsky rejected the orthodox
Marxist thesis of concentration and accumulation and emphasized the
preservation of petty commodity production in agriculture. That preservation took the form of the subordination of the peasant (pseudo-)
proletariat to the urban–industrial economy. Only through the sale
of labour power, both within and outside agriculture, could the final
eclipse of the agrarian family enterprise be prevented.

According to Kautsky, the resulting social formation illustrated the
coexistence of agrarian capitalism with pre-capitalist production relations. Petty cultivators, who were unable to consolidate their position
as marginal peasants, notwithstanding the recurrent sale of their labour
power, abandoned the countryside and became fully proletarianized
industrial workers. This explains why the landless underclass, which
was assumed to be almost non-existent under Europe's ancien régime,
showed only a moderate increase as capitalism advanced in agriculture.

As pointed out by Banaji,[5] Kautsky's view of the historical evolution
of capitalism has no conception of an internal development of
agriculture prior to the growth of modern industry in the nineteenth
century. By ignoring the history of agriculture (in contrast to Weber),
Kautsky greatly underestimated the extent of market relationships in the
pre-industrial world. Banaji rejects the notion of a sudden development

---

[4] Ibid., p. 5.

[5] J. Banaji, 'Illusions about the Peasantry: Karl Kautsky and the Agrarian Question', *Journal of Peasant Studies*, vol. 17, no. 2, 1990, p. 289.

of commodity production in the countryside and draws attention to widespread practices of waged labour in Europe much earlier than Kautsky acknowledges.

Almost 100 years after Kautsky wrote *Die Agrarfrage*, similar interpretations can still be found. For example, Hobsbawm and Rudé[6] imply that rural landlessness was alien to the peasant landscape in earlier times.[7] De Vries and van der Woude[8] argue in similar fashion with respect to the lack of dynamism in Dutch agriculture. As long as new land could be opened up for cultivation, agricultural work remained embedded in the peasant household. Proletarianization only took place when the peasant resource base was exhausted and the emergence of larger holdings stimulated demand for hired labour. The transition to a situation of closed resources only came about at the beginning of the nineteenth century.[9]

The fact that Kautsky's views on the late origin of a landless class of agrarian labour continue to find strong support among agrarian historians of Europe may have something to do with the perspective adopted. In an authoritative work on Europe's agrarian history, Slicher van Bath[10] argues that studies which take landownership as their point of departure tend to focus on the propertied classes and neglect the lower classes that are just as significant for understanding rural society. Drawing on research in the eastern Netherlands, Slicher van Bath concludes that wage labourers and marginalized peasants increased in number during the 1800s, but that signs of a pauperized residual class could already be found at the beginning of the century.[11] More attention to labour migration, as the studies of Jan Lucassen illustrate, could form a significant starting point for a reappraisal of the debate on the agrarian question in Europe.[12]

---

[6] See E.J. Hobsbawm and G. Rudé, *Captain Swing*, Harmondsworth: Penguin, 1973.

[7] In their seminal study on agrarian riots around 1830 in south England, however, Hobsbawm and Rudé are puzzled by the general lack of interest in the agricultural labourer in the agrarian history literature (ibid., p. 6).

[8] J. De Vries and A. van der Woude, *Nederland 1500–1815: De eerste ronde van moderne economische groei*, Amsterdam: Uitgeverij Balans, 1995.

[9] Ibid., pp. 642–3.

[10] B.H. Slicher van Bath, *De Agrarische Geschiedenis van West-Europa*, Utrecht and Antwerpen: Aula, 1960.

[11] Ibid., pp. 340–56.

[12] New historical research on the Netherlands, such as that by J. Lucassen, *Migrant Labour in Europe 1600–1900: The Drift to the North Sea*, London: Croom

## LANDLESSNESS IN COLONIAL ASIA

Conventional interpretations of landlessness in colonial Asia tend to emphasize the closed character of the pre-colonial economic and political system. Alongside the increasing exposure of the Asian population to colonial rule during the nineteenth century, came a growing need for the colonial state to gather intelligence on the nature, shape, and management of the Asian agricultural economy. In the vast terrain, mapped principally by government officials, the village community was considered to be the cornerstone of the social order.[13] In descriptions of that institution as a micro-cosmos, emphasis was placed on the closed character of the local economy, its considerable degree of political autonomy, organization as a collectivity, and on the elementary division of labour between agriculture and artisanal manufacture. Insofar as such an autarky did not remain more or less contained within the sphere of the peasant household, a pattern of localized exchange met the diverse, albeit modest, needs of the villager, as mediated through the caste system in parts of the South Asian subcontinent. Cooperation, reciprocity, and redistribution are a few of the keywords used to underline the quid pro quo character of interaction between rural producers.

Not only were these characteristics seen to be the cause of economic and social stagnation, they were also regarded as distinguishing Asian pre-colonial society from European pre-capitalist society. While Kautsky and his contemporaries perceived the landlord–peasant configuration in Europe as a linkage transcending the locality, in Asia, no such configuration seemed to exist. Indeed, the concept of the Asiatic mode of production was developed by Marxist and non-Marxist theories to emphasize the differences between Asian and European pre-capitalist rural life.

According to the received wisdom, there was no evidence of a distinct landless class of subaltern peasants, although individual sources sporadically refer to landlessness or vagrancy. Van Vollenhoven, architect of

---

Helm, 1987, shows that landless and land-poor peasants migrated over long distances and frequently for long periods to hire out their labour power. De Vries and van der Woude, *Nederland 1500–1815*, pp. 95–6, likewise draw attention to large-scale seasonal migration during an even earlier period than that studied by Lucassen. Extra-economic coercion played an important role in this labour mobility. See G. Jaritz and A. Müller (eds), *Migration in der Feudalgesellschaft*, Ludwig-Boltzmann-Institut für Historische Sozialwissenschaft, Frankfurt and New York: Campus, 1988.

[13] J. Breman, 'The Shattered Image: Construction and Deconstruction of the Village in Colonial Asia', *Comparative Asian Studies 2*, Dordrecht: Foris Publications, 1988, pp. 1–9.

customary law in the Netherlands Indies, divided the rural population into three categories: descendants of the village founders who shared fully in communal landownership; cultivators who were given rights of usage but had no hereditary claim on the land; and the landless who were attached as farm servants to the households of more substantial peasants. Van Vollenhoven added that the boundary between these three groups was fluid, movement between them being dependent on age and status in the local community.[14]

The creation of a class of landless labourers in British India was held to be the outcome of commercialization and monetization, which, in the late colonial period, led to a radical shift in the social relations of agrarian production. As expressed by Patel in the early 1950s: 'In pre-nineteenth century India there were domestic and menial servants; but their numbers were small, and they did not form a definite group … The large class of agricultural labourers represents a new form of social relationship that emerged during the late nineteenth and early twentieth centuries in India.'[15]

More recent research, however, has led to a fundamental reappraisal of the course of rural transformation in Asia during colonial rule. In a pioneering study of early colonial society in south India, Kumar[16] refers to a sizeable landless segment, which she estimated to constitute 10–15 per cent of the total population. Her findings are supported by my own historical research in west India, which found that former generations of the agrarian underclass used to be employed as attached labourers by landowning households at the beginning of the nineteenth century.[17] This earlier underclass consisted of tribals, who had, until the arrival of caste Hindus, made their living as hunters and gatherers or, more often, as shifting cultivators. Their gradual insertion into the larger Hindu society was accompanied by a loss of control over the territory where they lived and over their means of subsistence. The confinement of what were originally outsiders to the bottom rung of a more complex agrarian hierarchy was due to political domination—the exercise of coercive

---

[14] Ibid., p. 5.

[15] S.J. Patel, *Agricultural Labourers in Modern India and Pakistan,* Bombay: Current Book House, 1952, p. 32.

[16] D. Kumar, *Land and Caste in South India: Agricultural Labour in the Madras Presidency during the Nineteenth Century,* Cambridge: Cambridge University Press, 1965 (reprinted with a new Introduction, New Delhi: Manohar, 1992).

[17] J. Breman, *Patronage and Exploitation: Changing Agrarian Relations in South Gujarat,* Berkeley: University of California Press, 1974.

force—rather than economic regression. In a more recent publication, I have elaborated on the slow process of tribal incorporation in Hindu economy and society.[18]

Elsewhere in India, tribals were likewise incorporated—and subordinated—into the expanding caste society.[19] A determining structural feature of Hindu civilization forbade members of high castes to cultivate the land. By assigning this unclean activity to a clientele especially maintained for the purpose, the rural elite reinforced their claim to a high position in the ritual order. I regard this culture-specific interpretation as a variation of the explanation of the bonding of labour in terms of political economy.

In an ethnological study published in 1910, Nieboer argued that slavery occurs in situations of open resources.[20] This thesis was later extended by Kloosterboer[21] to refer to bonded labour in general. Whenever land is, in principle, freely accessible to all, people will make their labour power available to others only if extra-economic force is brought to bear. However, when land is a scarce commodity—in other words, when resources become closed—force becomes unnecessary. In such circumstances, landlessness is due not to the imposition of power but to the effect of economic differentiation combined with rising population pressure on agrarian resources, ultimately resulting in the creation of a voluntary labour supply. This perspective explains both the practice of bonded labour in the countryside of early colonial British India and its subsequent erosion.[22]

Colonial literature in British India did not give proper consideration to the existence of a subaltern landless class held captive in a state of unfreedom. Only very occasionally did its magnitude come to light, as,

---

[18] J. Breman, *Labour Bondage in West India: From Past to Present*, New Delhi: Oxford University Press, 2007.

[19] G. Prakash, 'Bonded Histories: Genealogies of Labour Servitude in Colonial India', *Cambridge South Asian Studies No. 44*, Cambridge: Cambridge University Press, 1990.

[20] H.J. Nieboer, *Slavery as an Industrial System: Ethnological Researches*, 2nd edition, The Hague: Martinus Nijhoff, 1910.

[21] W. Kloosterboer, *Onvrije arbeid na de afschaffing van slavernij* (Unfree Labour after the Abolition of Slavery), The Hague: Willemina/Excelsior, 1954.

[22] Breman, *Patronage and Exploitation*; J. Breman, *Of Peasants, Migrants and Paupers: Rural Labour Circulation and Capitalist Production in West India*, Oxford: Clarendon Press and New Delhi: Oxford University Press, 1985; Breman, *Labour Bondage in West India*.

for example, during the debate on the abolition of slavery, when the British Parliament demanded an official report from its colonies on the phenomenon of agrarian bondage. Such stocktaking did not lead to their shackles being removed, however. The priority given to the levying of taxes prevented any more radical government interference in the social organization of peasant production. Consequently, the rural landless remained largely invisible to colonial authorities and commentators.

Accounts of the Javanese countryside, dating from the beginning of the nineteenth century or earlier, also reported a sizeable and internally differentiated underclass that was denied access to land. These subordinate workers were employed as sharecroppers or as farm servants by an upper segment of the peasantry. I have emphasized elsewhere the bonded status of these landless clients who, individually or together with their families, belonged to the household of their landowning patron. Rather than adhering to the conventional wisdom of a homogeneous village community, I consider these corporate and internally differentiated peasant households as having been the primary social formation in Asia's pre-capitalist regime.[23]

Others have also argued that there was social differentiation in colonial Java. Boomgaard[24] concludes from an analysis of available sources that the landless section of Java's rural population was considerable in the early nineteenth century, though with substantial local variations. On the basis of detailed archival research, Elson[25] also reports that landlessness was very common. He connects this phenomenon with the arrival of outsiders who had fled an uncertain existence elsewhere.

[23] J. Breman, *The Village on Java and the Early Colonial State* (translated from Dutch), Rotterdam: Comparative Asian Studies Programme, 1980; J. Breman, 'Control of Land and Labour in Colonial Java: A Case Study of Agrarian Crisis and Reform in the Region of Cirebon during the First Decades of the Twentieth Century', Verhandelingen Koninklijk Instituut voor Taal-, Land- en Volkenkunde 101, Dordrecht: Foris Publications, 1983; J. Breman, *Koloniaal profijt van onvrije arbeid: het Preanger stelsel van gedwongen koffieteelt op Java, 1720–1870* (Colonial Profit from Unfree Labour: The Preanger System of Forced Coffee Cultivation on Java, 1720–1870), Amsterdam: Amsterdam University Press, (forthcoming).

[24] P. Boomgaard, 'Children of the Colonial State: Population Growth and Economic Development in Java, 1795–1880', *CASA Monographs*, Amsterdam: Free University Press, 1989, p. 60.

[25] R.E. Elson, 'Village Java under the Cultivation System, 1830–1870', *Southeast Publications Series No. 25*, Asian Studies Association of Australia, Sydney: Allen and Unwin, 1994.

Those newly arrived might have no option but to enter dependency relationships with more established and prosperous peasants which precluded them from holding land; in the absence of alternative means of sustenance, they might find themselves in a permanently servile condition which allowed their patrons correspondingly to enhance their wealth and power through the shrewd deployment of their clients' labour power.[26]

The introduction of the forced cultivation of cash crops on Java already early in the eighteenth century, initiated an agrarian policy which aimed to accelerate Java's integration into the world economy.[27] Peasants were forced to set aside a considerable part of their arable land and their labour power for the cultivation of export crops such as coffee, indigo, and sugar. In order to broaden the taxable basis, the colonial government granted members of the landless underclass access to the expanding agricultural resource base. However, this attempt to communalize peasant ownership and production was only moderately successful as the established landowning class tenaciously resisted the redistribution of agrarian property. Only by holding fast to their exclusive rights could heads of the corporate peasant households meet the exorbitant levies imposed on the rural economy by the colonial government. In short, land remained concentrated in the hands of the rural elite.

## A Distinct yet Difficult-to-define Underclass

The image of a landless class tied in bondage to peasant households is difficult to reconcile with early colonial reports of a proletariat *avant-la-lettre* which led an extremely footloose existence in the countryside of Java. Early colonial writings frequently describe such people as wanderers and vagrants. Boomgaard[28] distinguishes between young bachelors who worked temporarily as farm labourers for a local landowning household and a class of free and unattached workers who roamed over a larger area in search of a wage. The first form of employment was temporary, being an apprenticeship of a few years which young men served before being admitted to the established local peasantry with all its rights and duties. It is the second group which Boomgaard considers as belonging to a subaltern class, permanently obliged to depend on casual work, both in and outside agriculture, for its living.[29] In a more cautious assessment

---

[26] Ibid., p. 20.
[27] Breman, *Koloniaal profijt van onvrije arbeid.*
[28] Boomgaard, 'Children of the Colonial State'.
[29] Ibid., pp. 65–6.

of the divergent and partly contradictory source material, Elson opines that the dividing lines between the various rural classes were quite fluid and that landlessness did not crystallize into a distinct lifestyle which was reproduced across the generations.[30]

Although Boomgaard and Elson agree that landlessness did exist in colonial Java, they do not regard those peasants who had no direct command over agrarian resources as forming a distinct, let alone pro-letarianized, social class. One thing that can surely be concluded is that in both South and Southeast Asia, '[t]he history of the bottom layers of the . . . countryside is obscure, with plenty of room, indeed a crying need, for further research'.[31]

My own view is that peasant work and life under the ancien régime cannot be understood within the framework of a static, homogeneous, and closed order—the reputed Asiatic mode of production—but needs to be interpreted in a more open and differentiated frontier context. In this shifting landscape, I do not assume that mobility and bondage at the bottom of the agrarian order were mutually exclusive. On the contrary, I argue that their coexistence determined the dynamics of the peasant economy.[32]

At the beginning of the nineteenth century, the size of the landless segment in the Asian countryside varied from a fifth to a third of the total rural population. It is unclear whether late colonial policy caused a greater congestion at the foot of the agrarian hierarchy or not. Certainly, increased population density during the late nineteenth and the first half of the twentieth century had a direct influence on the diminishing size of the peasant household enterprise. It is more difficult to establish whether a sharp fall down the agrarian ladder took place, in which land-owners were downgraded first to tenants and then to landless labourers.

During the last 150 years of colonial rule, non-agrarian sources of employment in the rural economy probably increased very little or perhaps even decreased. This is arguably the case in parts of South Asia where, according to the deindustrialization thesis, the loss of artisanal production was organized as home industry increased the pressure on

---

[30] Elson, 'Village Java under the Cultivation System, 1830–1870', p. 22.

[31] B. Moore Jr, *Social Origins of Dictatorship and Democracy: Lord and Peasant in the Making of the Modern World*, Boston: Beacon Press, 1966, p. 369.

[32] See Breman, 'The Shattered Image', pp. 28–37; Breman, *Koloniaal profijt van onvrije arbeid*, chapter 2. I would add that a landless underclass was also present in pre-capitalist Europe and that Kautsky's image of a fairly homogeneous peasantry firmly embedded in well-established villages should be modified.

employment in the agricultural economy. Whatever the case, there was little sign of any advance of industrial capitalism, such as had absorbed the surplus peasant proletariat in the countryside of Europe. Insofar as new industries were established in the colonial metropolises of Asia, rural labour was only admitted on a partial and conditional basis: non-working family members had to remain behind in the village and the labourers themselves were only tolerated in the urban milieu for the duration of their working lives.[33] This also applied to the army of landless people who were recruited as coolies for the mines and on plantations in the Asian hinterlands or were shipped overseas. When the contract period expired, most were sent back home or to a destination which passed as such.[34] The congestion at the bottom of the agrarian economy cannot have escaped the notice of the colonial authorities, although they tended to emphasize land fragmentation rather than land alienation as the main cause.

This short overview of conditions in late colonial Asia leads me to conclude that it was the combination of economic and demographic changes which led to progressive land impoverishment. Landownership at the village level continued to be highly concentrated and a growing portion of the agrarian population was denied access, with the result that the landless class expanded. However, adequate and reliable statistics to support this quantitative shift in the class structure of the peasantry are lacking. In addition, it is difficult, in practice, to distinguish between the class of small landowners and that of agricultural workers. As Thorner comments with reference to small producers in his well-known analysis of the agrarian structure in India in the mid-twentieth century:

Families in this class may indeed have tenancy rights in the soil, or even property rights, but the holdings are so small that the income from cultivating them or from renting them out comes to less than the earnings from field work.[35]

Thus, in order to understand the process of (pseudo-) proletarianization in rural Asia, it is imperative not to make a sharp divide between land-poor and landless. It then becomes evident that, in the densely populated

[33] J. Breman, 'The Study of Industrial Labour in Post-colonial India: The Formal Sector', in J.P. Parry, J. Breman, and K. Kapadia (eds), *The Worlds of Indian Industrial Labour*, New Delhi: Sage Publications, 1999, pp. 1–41.

[34] J. Breman, 'Labour Migration and Rural Transformation in Colonial Asia', *Comparative Asian Studies 5*, Amsterdam: Free University Press, 1990.

[35] D. Thorner, *The Agrarian Prospect in India*, 2nd edition (with a new Introduction written in 1973), Bombay: Allied Publishers, 1976, p. 11.

rural regions at the end of colonial rule, these two groups combined comprised from a half to about two-thirds of the peasantry.

## THE LANDLESS IN THE TRANSITION TO CAPITALISM

Quantitative changes notwithstanding, at the end of colonial rule, there was also a qualitative shift in the social relations of production. Life as an agricultural worker became moulded along new lines. This transformation continued in the post-colonial era as capitalism increasingly influenced the rural economy.[36]

## The Impact of the Green Revolution

The much-discussed Green Revolution of the 1960s, which introduced a modernization package consisting of high-yielding seed varieties, fertilizers and pesticides, credit, new technology, agricultural extension services, and better water management, illustrates the growing trend towards capitalism in agriculture. In contrast to East Asia, the transformation in South and Southeast Asia was not, as in China, preceded by a drastic redistribution of agrarian resources. Large landed estates, where they still existed, were abolished and tenancy relationships were reformed with a view to encouraging a capitalist orientation amongst a well-established class of owner–cultivators in India, usually drawn from locally dominant castes. This class in particular was charged with the task of increasing production and productivity.[37]

The shift in the rural balance of power which accompanied the Green Revolution development strategy caused the vulnerable position of sharecroppers and agricultural labourers to deteriorate further. Even a very moderate land reform which would have benefited the agrarian underclass lands was not on the agenda. Resources still held in common, the village waste in particular, were rapidly privatized and usually fell into the hands of the landowning elite. In Indonesia, the military coup

---

[36] T.J. Byres, 'The Agrarian Question and Differing Forms of Capitalist Agrarian Transition: An Essay with Reference to Asia', in J. Breman and S. Mundle (eds), *Rural Transformation in Asia*, New Delhi: Oxford University Press, 1991, pp. 3–76.

[37] T.J. Byres, 'The New Technology, Class Formation and Class Action in the Indian Countryside', *Journal of Peasant Studies*, vol. 8, no. 4, 1981, pp. 423–7; Byres, 'The Agrarian Question and Differing Forms of Capitalist Agrarian Transition', pp. 63–4; G. Myrdal, *Asian Drama: An Inquiry Into the Poverty of Nations, Vol. II*, New York: The Twentieth Century Fund, 1968, pp. 1366–84; W.F. Wertheim, *East-West Parallels: Sociological Approaches to Modern Asia*, The Hague: W. van Hoeve, 1964, pp. 259–77.

d'etat of 1965 put an end to efforts initiated from below to introduce
an agrarian law, which would improve the position of marginal and
landless peasants, who formed the majority of people living in Java's
countryside.[38]

My conclusion is that the capitalist-oriented agricultural development policy pursued in the post-colonial era has further exacerbated
the vulnerability of life at the bottom of the rural economy. Although
initial reports of a mass expulsion of labour following the introduction of rationalized and mechanized cultivation methods proved
unfounded, the expansion of agricultural employment as a net effect of
the Green Revolution has not kept pace with the growth of the Asian
rural population.

The *World Labour Report*, published annually by the International
Labour Organization (ILO), shows that self-employment in agriculture is
gradually but steadily giving way to waged labour. It would be premature
to explain this trend purely as a sign of progressive proletarianization.
The replacement of own or family labour by hired workers is also due
to the emergence of a different lifestyle, which leads even middle-sized
landowners to prefer hiring and supervising outside labour. This trend
has been a contributing factor to the creation of a rural labour market
in the capitalist sense.

The continuing abject poverty of the great majority of the landless is
due to the fact that the supply of labour far exceeds demand. This excess
labour supply helps to explain why earlier forms of labour bondage have
considerably weakened. After independence, national policymakers
anticipated that the surplus rural proletariat would be absorbed as mill
workers in the urban economy. In these Asian countries, however, the
expansion of large-scale industry has been far slower and above all, far
less labour intensive than envisaged. Opportunities to escape to the
cities are therefore limited, while emigration overseas is an equally
unrealistic option. For the Asian rural surplus, there is no New World
in which to settle, as there had been for the proletarianized mass from
Europe a century earlier.

In sum, Asia's rural proletariat, after the colonial era, was far greater
in size than Europe's rural proletariat had been after capitalism had
transformed the ancien régime. Furthermore, the sluggish pace of
the industrialization process in Asia since the mid-twentieth century,
together with a population growth rate which has only recently started

---

[38] Breman, 'Control of Land and Labour in Colonial Java', pp. 122–6.

to decline, drastically intensified the pressure on those at the bottom of the rural economy.

## Diversification, Mobility, and Casualization

It would be incorrect, however, to infer that the nature of the landless existence has hardly changed since the end of colonial rule. After political independence, capitalist dynamics came to dominate the countryside, causing drastic changes in the social relations of production.

We can distinguish three interconnected processes. The first refers to the diversification of the rural economy. With the growing demand for labour from agro-industry, infrastructural works, trade, transport, and the service sector, agriculture has lost significance in the overall rural employment pattern. Such diversification has not occurred everywhere to the same degree, but the trend is unmistakeable. In some cases, off-farm employment is an expression of the growing underutilization of labour in agriculture. In other instances, however, it reflects real growth in peasant production which has an impact on other branches of the economy. In the villages of west India where I did most of my fieldwork, and in the state of Gujarat more generally, working in the fields is no longer the predominant source of employment and income for the landless. Rural diversification means that work at the bottom of the rural economy is characterized by occupational multiplicity. From having been an agrarian proletariat, this class has remoulded itself into a more general rural proletariat.

A second and related process which has transformed the situation of the landless relates to the increased mobility of labour. Non-agricultural work usually involves work outside the village of residence and sometimes, seasonal migration to towns and cities. Although the drift towards urban centres has increased, the majority of migrants have little chance of settling there, being concentrated in the informal sector, which is the greatest reservoir of employment in the urban economy. The informal sector is not a stepping stone towards a better and settled urban life but a temporary abode for labour which can be pushed back to its place of origin when no longer needed.[39] This continual to-ing and fro-ing between urban and rural sectors indicates the linkage, rather than the rupture, of rural and urban labour markets.

This interconnectedness of urban and rural labour markets is not caused by the unwillingness of the workforce to commit itself to an

[39] J. Breman, *Wage Hunters and Gatherers: Search for Work in the Urban and Rural Economy of South Gujarat*, New Delhi: Oxford University Press, 1994.

industrial way of life, as Thompson seems to suggest was the case in Europe.[40] Rather, it is the lack of economic and physical space which prevents the army of newcomers from establishing themselves as permanent urban citizens.

Labour not only circulates between village and town but also does so within the rural milieu. In previous publications on intra-rural labour mobility, I stressed the connection between massive long-distance seasonal migration and the emergence of a more pronounced capitalist mode of production.[41] In relation to Java, the transport revolution enabled the rapid and cheap movement of labour so that members of households with little, if any, land can circulate in a greatly enlarged labour market.[42]

Diversification of the rural economy and increased labour mobility are, in turn, connected to a third process which has significantly changed the experience of the landless, namely, the casualization of employment. The peasant economy shows a tendency for permanent farmhands to be replaced by daily wage earners and for indefinite employment to be replaced by short-term labour contracts based on the hire-and-fire principle. This form of employment facilitates the hire of outsiders who are usually cheaper and more docile than local workers. Labour is now paid principally or exclusively in cash rather than in kind, and remunerated on a piecework or contracting out basis rather than on a time rate basis as before.

This casualization of labour does not mean that production relations have been cleansed of all pre-capitalist elements. Labour's prerogative to hire itself out at any moment, and for the highest possible price, is subject to many restrictions. Although labour has become abundant, the transition to a situation of closed resources, that is, land scarcity, has not stopped employers from resorting to new forms of labour bondage. For example, acceptance of a cash advance frequently entails a contract which immobilizes labour power. Employers also defer wage payment as a means of ensuring that the required quantity of labour continues to be supplied.

Nevertheless, the lack of freedom entailed in such bonding mechanisms differs essentially from the coercive regime to which agricultural labour was subjected in the past. I employ the term 'neo-bondage' to

---

[40] E.P. Thompson, *Customs in Common*, London: Penguin, 1991, p. 398.

[41] Breman, *Of Peasants, Migrants and Paupers*.

[42] J. Breman, 'Work and Life of the Rural Proletariat in Java's Coastal Plain', *Modern Asian Studies*, vol. 29, no. 1, 1995, pp. 21–2.

refer to the practices adopted by present-day employers to ensure a sufficient and cheap supply of labour. As argued by Miles,[43] among others, these bonding mechanisms which restrict the liberty of the worker do not necessarily diminish the capitalist character of the production process.[44]

* * *

Kautksy's view that '[c]apitalism concentrates the working masses in the towns … favouring their organisation, their intellectual development, their capacity to struggle as a class'[45] is not confirmed by the development route followed by various Asian societies. In both India and Indonesia, the rural proletariat is still undoubtedly the largest working class. Furthermore, those who have found a niche in the urban economy lead an extremely fragile existence in the informal sector. Their capacity to take action as a class is seriously hampered by their lack of organization and their low level of literacy. Finally, capitalism's penetration into the countryside has caused a qualitative change in social relations, both in and outside agriculture, in ways which show affinity with urban dynamics. The need to be available for employment in diverse branches of industry rather than to specialize, the pressure towards spatial mobility which often takes on the character of circulation, and the casual mode of employment with its corresponding modalities of wage payment, are all mechanisms which frustrate collective bargaining and the formation of a common front from this composite underclass. The articulation of class interests finds a weak basis in this milieu. That is why, with rare exceptions, trade unions are absent in the informal sector. Pressure at the bottom of the economy is so great that there is fierce rivalry for any work that becomes available. In a situation of surplus labour, recruitment on the basis of primordial loyalties preserves lines of demarcation other than that of class.

The capitalist development which large regions of Asia are currently experiencing differs drastically from that which took place in western societies. In Europe, capitalist development went together with an

[43] R. Miles, *Capitalism and Unfree Labour: Anomaly or Necessity?*, London and New York: Tavistock, 1987.

[44] The production process is defined as capitalist because production is for the capitalist market. Ultimately, the reproduction of the labour process depends on a generalized system of commodity production.

[45] Banaji, 'Summary of Selected Parts of Kautsky's "The Agrarian Question"', p. 47.

enormous expansion of the formal labour market, government intervention to protect labour, trade unionism, and a general increase in the standard of living. In much of urban and rural Asia, the pattern of rapid growth during the past few decades is still based on a strongly informalized labour system, and government protection is absent or ineffective. Furthermore, previous patterns of care provision within the family or by means of patron–client relations, which went some way to redressing the sharply unequal social distribution, have been eroded without being replaced by more formal and horizontally structured forms of social security. The lack of any organized countervailing power to the commoditization of labour illustrates the extreme vulnerability of the working masses. As yet, capitalist dynamics in Asia's economies appear to be unaffected by the emancipation of labour. The trend is towards a bifurcated order which excludes a very substantial segment of the world's population from enjoying a secure and decent life.

# 2

# The Political Economy of
# Agrarian Change*

## SETTLING THE AGRARIAN QUESTION

At the time of independence, in the middle of the twentieth century, India could firmly be classified as a peasant society. The rural based mode of existence had remained dominant from generation to generation, and the large majority of the population continued to live in the countryside and work in agriculture. A series of village monographs, most of which were published between the 1950s and 1970s as the outcome of anthropological research, showed that the habitat of peasants included a wide variety of non-agrarian households and that, moreover, the peasantry was highly differentiated. A major point of departure in the populist course steered by the nationalist leadership was the restoration of a social order that had been eroded under colonial rule. The owner–cultivator, reported to have steadily lost ground in the transition to a market economy, was to be shored up as the backbone of agricultural production. Solving the agrarian question stood high on the political agenda of the Congress movement that came to power at both the central and state level. In preparation for the takeover of government, a National Planning Committee (NPC) was set up under the chairmanship of Jawaharlal Nehru and given the task to frame the main outlines of economic policy after decolonization. Radhakamal Mukherjee drafted a paper on the land issue that was first discussed in his working group on agriculture and then endorsed by experts and politicians in a plenary meeting of the NPC at the end of June 1940. Landlordism was to be abolished and ownership rights transferred to

* Originally published as 'The Political Economy of Agrarian Change', in Paul R. Brass (ed.), *Handbook of South Asian Politics*, London and New York: Routledge (forthcoming), pp. 468–90.

the actual tillers of the soil. The family farm would remain the main unit of cultivation and its size should neither be larger nor smaller than an economic holding. It should provide adequate employment and income for the family without making use, at least not permanently, of outside labour.

The architects of the post-colonial era clearly envisaged an agricultural economy of self-cultivating owners. In their directives, the planners seemed to have ignored the existence, in most parts of the subcontinent, of a vast agrarian underclass completely bereft of landownership. Their disregard for this landless mass was operationalized in the decision not to include them in the redistribution of the surplus land that would become available with the fixation of a ceiling on landownership and the abolition of absentee ownership. By way of consolation, the planning document suggested that agricultural labourers be allowed access to land not yet under cultivation, village commons, and other waste land waiting to be taken into production; perhaps not by the straightforward handing out of individualized ownership rights, but indirectly, through the establishment of land-tilling cooperatives in which various agrarian classes would join and collaborate.

The cooperative model was one of the vaguely phrased socialist ideas which appealed to some sections of the Congress movement but which were never taken seriously in the execution of mainstream policies firmly heading in a capitalist direction. Of similar symbolic value was the promise that agricultural labourers would be released from bondage when they had been indebted to landowners for more than five years. A large-scale, nation-wide survey of agricultural labour conducted a few years after independence showed that a substantial segment worked in a state of attachment which took away their freedom of employment.[1] The land reform operation was closely monitored. Thorner was one of many observers who came to the conclusion that the redistribution of property rights, both in making the design for a new agrarian blueprint and in the subsequent stage of implementation, fell short of what had been promised in the decades leading up to independence by the Congress leadership.[2] Myrdal minced no words when he concluded halfway in his

---

[1] Government of India (GoI), *All India Agricultural Labour Enquiry Report on Intensive Survey of Agricultural Labour, 1950–51, Vol. 1*, Delhi: Manager of Publications, 1955.

[2] Daniel Thorner, *The Agrarian Prospect in India: Five Lectures on Land Reform Delivered in 1955 at the Delhi School of Economics*, 2nd edition, Bombay: Allied, 1976.

three-volume *Asian Drama*[3] that the opportune moment for a radical reshaping of the agrarian structure had passed. The land reforms, he wrote, have bolstered the political, social, and economic position of the rural better-off segments on which the post-colonial government depended for crucial support. The policy was not merely tilted in favour of the more well-to-do but had an anti-poor bias as well. 'Measures that would deprive the upper strata in the villages of land and power, and would genuinely confer dignity and status on the underprivileged and the landless, are among the last that those in power would find acceptable.'[4]

## PRACTISING THE LAND REFORMS IN GUJARAT

What was the shape and outcome of the agrarian question in the villages of south Gujarat where I started my fieldwork in the early 1960s? Under the provisions of the Bombay Tenancy and Agricultural Lands Act of 1948, the Maratha *inamdar* (land holder), who lived in Baroda, lost most of the agrarian property which his family had held in Gandevigam village for many generations. The Anavil Brahmans, who were already the dominant landowners, received the title deeds for the plots which they used to cultivate as his tenants. Bania moneylenders and urban traders forfeited whatever land they had taken over from farmers indebted to them. The same happened in Chikhligam, the second site of my fieldwork. For the Anavil Brahmans, Tillers' Day—April 1957—heralded their consolidation as the landed elite in the region. On the other hand, the subaltern castes—in Gandevigam, the Kolis, and in Chikhligam, the tribal Dhodhias—lost out in the land transfer deals. In the past, local Anavil farmers had leased out plots to them on a sharecropping basis and under the new legislation, the low-caste cultivators could lay a claim to these fields. To avoid losing property, the main landowners decided to discontinue most sharecropping arrangements even though their clients swore that they would never dare to register their names in the local record of rights. The land poor were only beneficiaries if the land they worked belonged to owners not residing in the village. A land ceiling, fixed in 1960 and scaled down in 1974, could have threatened the privileged position of the Anavil Brahmans, but because of the many exemptions and loopholes in the act, the members of this dominant caste—which to the present day average no more than 15 per cent of

---

[3] Gunnar Myrdal, *Asian Drama: An Enquiry into the Poverty of Nations, Vol. II*, New York: The Twentieth Century Fund, 1968.

[4] Ibid., p. 1375.

the village population—managed to appropriate two-thirds to three-quarters of the total arable land in the locality.

The landless were, of course, excluded from the reallocation of the meagre amount of surplus land that became available. One of the reasons given for their non-qualification was that they had never been, even in their own memory, owner–cultivators. Their huts used to be built on land owned by the Anavil landlords who had tied them as farm servants in a relationship of bondage, which was passed on from father to son. In the years between independence and the enactment of the land reform, they were thrown out of the plots they had inhabited in their masters' fields. When I came for the first round of my research nearly half a century ago, I found them living on the outskirts of the village, occupying homesteads for which they had not been issued title deeds. The withholding of a legal status, either as owners or tenants, meant that the landless could be blamed for having invaded as squatters the public domain kept as a reserve open to the local community at large for grazing cattle, cutting grass, collecting firewood, and, not least, for defecation. The promise made by the NPC that members of the agrarian underclass be given access to the still undivided waste land under the control of the village panchayat was more often broken than honoured.

On the contrary, in a subsequent round of land reform, the commons were privatized, surreptitiously and in collusion with the local bureaucracy, resulting in the registration of ownership rights for what had always been communal property in the names of the dominant caste. As one of my informants in Chikhligam caustically commented: 'Even when I go for shitting to the field where I always have been doing that in the morning I stand accused of trespassing.' And when the agricultural labourers went on strike in Gandevigam in their fight for higher wages, the landowners retaliated with the threat that they would stop the landless women and children gathering firewood on 'their' land. One last effort was made to hand out land to the landless for self-cultivation. Acharya Vinoba Bhave started the *Bhoodan* (land gift) campaign in the 1950s to deradicalize agrarian struggles such as the agitation that had been going on in Telengana. In his opinion, the Gandhian approach would persuade the well-endowed elite to part with their surplus land. The movement turned out to be a failure,[5] although it was quite popular for some time in south Gujarat where a network of Gandhian institutions had become firmly entrenched in the late colonial era. Social

---

[5] See Thorner, *The Agrarian Prospect in India*, pp. 70–1.

activists were told that agricultural labourers lacked the wherewithal and discipline to work the land on their own account. There was, however, a more genuine argument why the landless segment should not benefit from restructuring of the agrarian order. The widely held verdict was that it made no sense to burden households with a tiny piece of land which would in any case be inadequate for them to make a decent living. It would simply act as an obstacle to their mobility.

Swami Sahajanand, the national leader of the *kisan sabha*, the peasant union, had come to the same conclusion. He pointed out that the agricultural economy was unable to provide enough employment for the mass of agricultural labour.[6] At least half of them would have to get out and seek a better future in the urban industries that were going to emerge after independence. This was also the destiny that the NPC had in mind for the large number of households at the bottom of the village economy.[7] It was in line with what Sardar Patel had advised the Dublas of south Gujarat to do towards the end of the 1930s if they wanted to be free: to go elsewhere.[8] All those who said that they were guided by what would be best for the rural underclass suggested that a more dignified life was awaiting these hapless people outside agriculture. Migration to the cities and factory employment were thus highlighted as an end to the misery of the landless and the final solution for the agrarian question.

## SOCIAL PROFILE OF THE LANDLESS PROLETARIAT

The large majority of the agricultural labourers in south Gujarat are Dublas (or Halpatis, as they came to be called later). Their earlier name had been given a derogatory meaning and *sala Dubla*[9] is still a common curse. The denigration resonated in the suggestion that the word Dubla was to be understood as weakling, a reference to the inferior character ascribed to the members of this community. Classified as a scheduled

[6] Walter Hauser, *Sahajanand on Agricultural Labour and the Rural Poor*, New Delhi: Manohar, 1994. Also, Walter Hauser, *Culture, Vernacular Politics and the Peasants*, New Delhi: Manohar, 2006.

[7] See J. Breman, 'The Study of Indian Industrial Labour in Post-Colonial India', in Jonathan Parry, J. Breman, and Karin Kapadia (eds), *The Worlds of Indian Industrial Labour in India*, New Delhi: Sage Publications, 2002, pp. 2–4.

[8] J. Breman, *Labour Bondage in West India: From Past to Present*, New Delhi: Oxford University Press, 2007, p. 168.

[9] Sala, literally brother-in-law, is also very commonly used as a term of abuse, so the meaning here is, more or less, 'miserable weakling', but is really much stronger than that in Hindi and Marathi.

tribe in the colonial bookkeeping, the Dublas had been tied to high-caste landowners such as the Anavil Brahmans for many generations. Their work as farm servants included using the plough, which their employers had to avoid if they wanted to retain their purity. Although they were bonded, the Dublas were not ranked as unclean and both men and women performed household chores, releasing their masters from having to do such demeaning work themselves. In my initial fieldwork, I still found traces of the earlier bondage. My investigations focused on the changes which had come about in the relations between these landowning and landless castes-cum-classes at opposing ends of the social hierarchy. In my opinion, the fading away of bondage in the preceding decades was more the result of internal dynamics—on one side, landowners shedding clients whom they no longer wished to grant full employment and, on the other side, agricultural labourers refusing to consider themselves debt-bonded to masters who impinged on their freedom of movement—than outside intervention. The external forces at work were either the state, unwilling to condone any longer practices of unfree labour, or civil agencies, Gandhian activists in particular, attempting in the late colonial era to uplift the Dublas.[10] There is no doubt that Mahatma Gandhi himself had tried to elevate their social standing by renaming them Halpatis, lords of the plough, to wipe out their dismal history as Dublas. Summing up my findings, I reported in my fieldwork account that while features of patronage had disappeared over time, the dimension of exploitation had remained as strong as ever.[11]

The agricultural labourers continued to live in deep poverty because of the extremely low wages they received for their work: less than one rupee per day in the early 1960s. It was far less than what they needed to meet their basic needs. Outside agriculture, there was hardly any work available in the village. In the slack season, their already low food intake declined further and many families could not still their hunger for days on end. Undernourishment, a lack of clothes to cover the bodies of adults and children, and inadequate shelter in huts that gave no protection against cold and rain made them vulnerable to health risks, leading to high morbidity, particularly for the youngest and oldest age groups. Only a handful of children would attend school for a few standards,

[10] I have elaborated on these issues in Breman, *Labour Bondage in West India*, chapter 1.

[11] J. Breman, *Patronage and Exploitation: Changing Agrarian Relations in South Gujarat*, Berkeley: University of California Press, 1974.

but illiteracy was the general state of affairs. The Minimum Wage Act, announced in 1948, was not put into effect, and this did not change when the first and second Agricultural Labour Enquiries, held in 1950–1 and 1955–6 respectively, provided abundant evidence of the deprivation of the lowest class in the rural economy. In 1966, a panel of experts urged the Government of Gujarat to fix a floor price for agricultural labour to prevent tensions which had been building up in several parts of the state from boiling over into open clashes. A better deal could not wait for much longer, the committee's report warned, in order to pre-empt organized political radicalism from surfacing.[12] It took six more years of deliberation and consultation before a legal minimum rate was finally introduced, later and lower than the downright conservative advisors had deemed both wise and fair. Further delay would have risked losing a major vote bank of the Congress party: the landless electorate that made up more than half (55 per cent in 1982) of the agrarian workforce in south Gujarat.

Gandhian activists had begun to mobilize the Halpatis in the late-colonial era and remained active as political agents who delivered the votes of these downtrodden people to the Congress party in the early decades after independence. The well-established landowners who had rallied behind Congress in the struggle for independence did not appreciate the mainstream party voicing and articulating the interests of the rural poor. This was one of the major reasons why Mahatma Gandhi never became a popular figure in his own home state, in contrast to the strong-handed Sardar Patel who became idolized as the hero of the Bardoli *satyagraha*.[13] Already at this early stage, the elite formations in the countryside began to distance themselves from Congress stalwarts and backed candidates who canvassed for Jan Sangh and Swatantra. My informants among the dominant caste insisted that giving Halpatis the right to vote, as ordained by the principle of universal suffrage, had been a grave blunder. Such lowly people had fewer needs than full citizens—a major argument why their wages should not be fixed above reproduction level—and should have remained excluded from participating in the regular political process. While the new Congress high command did not go beyond paying mere lip service to the *garibi hatao* (ban poverty) slogan when it was coined after the split in the party, it was good enough reason for the landed interests to side with veterans such as Morarji

---

[12] Government of Gujarat, *Report of the Minimum Wages Advisory Committee for Employment in Agriculture*, Ahmedabad: Government of Gujarat, 1966.

[13] See Breman, *Labour Bondage in West India*, chapter 3.

Desai who established their leadership of the old Congress (Congress-O) in opposition to Indira Gandhi, whose new Congress came to be called Congress (I) ('I' for Indira). The rupture between the rural rich and poor further escalated when the main landowners transferred their allegiance first to Janata and, after the failure of that intermezzo at the central and state level, to the Bharatiya Janata Party (BJP), which appealed to the rapidly spreading mood of Hindu fundamentalism in the 1980s and 1990s. Extending their power base to the upwardly mobile castes helped the BJP and its front organizations to tackle and defeat the political strategy of new Congress that had formed the KHAM alignment, carrying for some time the vote banks of kshatriyas, harijans, adivasis, and Muslims.

## THE FAILURE OF THE GANDHIAN GOSPEL

In the shifting political constellation during the last quarter of the twentieth century, the Halpatis, by and large, remained faithful to the Congress party. Their voting behaviour was more inspired by confronting the successive choices made by their caste-cum-class opponents, who cast their votes for candidates belonging to opposition parties. The Halpatis never wavered from their loyalty to Congress, although not out of gratitude for concrete material gains. The minimum wage legislation came too late and offered too little to be hailed as clear proof of successful representation. In a violent incident that took place in 1976 in a village close to the sites of my research, two Halpatis were killed by *zim rakha*s, private guards contracted by the landlords to protect their fields against crop theft. A committee of inquiry reported that the agricultural labourers had become restive because they were paid much less than the prescribed legal wage. Heeding these signals, the Government of Gujarat set up a rural labour inspectorate in 1981, with the mandate to check whether farmers paid for the labour they utilized in accordance with the law. But, during their rounds, the government labour inspectors collected bribes rather than fines, so that employers could buy off prosecution for non-compliance.[14]

Nevertheless, Indira Gandhi has remained a cult figure in the Halpati milieu until the present day. If *Mataji* could not deliver what she promised, freedom from exploitation and oppression, it was because

---

[14] See J. Breman, 'I Am the Government Labour Officer…', *Economic and Political Weekly*, vol. 20, no. 24, 1985, pp. 1043–55. Reprinted in J. Breman, *Wage Hunters and Gatherers: Search for Work in the Urban and Rural Economy of South Gujarat*, New Delhi: Oxford University Press, 1994, chapter 4.

of the collusion between the vested interests at the local level and the officials in charge of the district and sub-district bureaucracies. This political–bureaucratic front of high-caste domination had prevented the rural landless from making their numerical weight felt. There was the famous statement made by a Congress minister who, when *gherao*ed (surrounded) by angry farmers protesting against a rise in the minimum wage rate for agricultural labour, went on public record saying: 'Some laws are not meant to be implemented'. However, when I came back in the late 1980s for a restudy of my initial fieldwork villages, I noticed some signs of progress in the landless quarters. The huts had become houses, and although they were not *pakka* (well made of brick), they were definitely better than the shacks in which I had found them before. The floor space had not increased much but the walls were higher and the thatched roofs were now tiled or covered with asbestos or corrugated iron sheets. Not having to bend down low in order to pass through the opening, but instead to enter through a door of sorts, and to be able to stand erect once inside testified to an increase in dignity.

Housing schemes were a major instrument with which Congress bought the support of the rural poor. The Halpatis required public subsidies to build their accommodation in the new colonies because they needed at least four-fifths of their daily income for food intake. What helped in this respect was the public distribution system that provided a monthly ration of low-price grain to households officially declared as living below the poverty line. As a consequence, the number of days without at least one meal decreased. More children had started going to school, to some extent motivated by the introduction of a noon meal scheme. Although the dropout rate remained high, a small minority managed to complete their basic education. Disease and debilitation were still rampant, but access to public health care helped to moderate the impact of chronic or recurrent illness. The primary health centres opened in sub-district towns played an important role in bringing down morbidity.

The Halpati Seva Sangh (HSS), founded in 1946 by Gandhian activists and led by them ever since, became a useful instrument for spreading the public welfare benefits among the landless of south Gujarat. The staff of social workers belonging to the *ujliparaj*, the higher castes, considered themselves to be engaged in a mission to civilize the tribal communities. Acting as a front organization for Congress, the HSS was rewarded for its mobilizing role in election campaigns with large grants spent on a network of boarding schools and social welfare schemes. Propagating

vegetarianism and abstinence from drinking country liquor, a favourite
pastime among the landless, the HSS leadership tried to convert its
clientele to a Hinduized way of life and, by strengthening communal
sentiments, to instil in the Halpatis a sense of caste identity. The leaders
of this social movement firmly refused to turn it into a trade union
fighting for freedom from bondage and higher wages for agricultural
labourers. Its ideological stance was based on preaching harmony.
Whenever conflicts broke out, caused by the antagonistic relationship
between landowners and landless, the Gandhian missionaries rushed
to the scene and appealed to those they considered part of their flock to
abstain from militant confrontation. The aim of their mediation was to
reach a compromise, which invariably meant systematically understating
and misrepresenting the interests of the dominated class.[15] This leads me
to conclude that the role played by civil society in raising the visibility
and the voice of the landless mass and in helping them to acquire better
political representation has been more negative than positive.

## OPENING UP THE COUNTRYSIDE AND MODERNIZING
## THE FORCES OF PRODUCTION

Equally important as the efforts made by various state agencies in the
1970s and 1980s to alleviate poverty somewhat was the accelerated
diversification of the rural economy arising on account of road building
and motorized transport. Distances could be bridged much easier than
before and new modes of communication resulted in more information
about what was going on beyond the local boundaries. I have never
endorsed the view that, in the past, there had ever been a closed labour
market at the village level, but it would be difficult to deny that agricultural
labourers became more mobile than they had been before. They started
to operate in a wider and more fluid labour market and moved around
both in spatial terms, going to sites of employment that had been
beyond their reach in the past, and in finding access to other economic
sectors than agriculture. Not only did seasonal migration increase but
also daily commuting to the industrial estates that had sprung up in
most district towns. Gaining access to these new employment niches
was only possible for those who owned a bicycle, which thus became a

---

[15] I have seen no reason to change my assessment on the role played by the Halpati
Seva Sangh (HSS) after my first critical report in J. Breman, 'Mobilisation of Landless
Labourers: Halpatis of South Gujarat', *Economic and Political Weekly*, vol. 9, no. 12, 1974,
pp. 489–96.

major asset, also for the younger generation of landless who continued to work as agricultural labourers.

What I found quite striking was that only a few Halpatis left the village to settle down in the urban localities alongside the railway line, which rapidly expanded from the 1980s onwards. Migration became circulatory, with labourers leaving home to work, but coming back at the end of the day, every few weeks, or at the onset of the monsoon. Urbanization, in the sense of staying on more indefinitely in the town or city, required, apart from access to low-cost housing, a modicum of educational qualifications and proper skills, a network of contacts to find shelter, and a regular job. That kind of social capital was rare in the bottom of the rural milieu. Consequently, the Halpatis had no other option but to remain footloose, hired and fired according to the needs of the moment at a wage level which was not much higher than that paid by the farmers. Leaving the village had become easier, but in and outside their home base, the landless mass turned into a reserve army of labour dependent for irregular work and low income on the steadily expanding informal sector of the economy.[16] Their hopes for a better future lay in the prospect that a process of formalization would eventually take place that would absorb the surplus labour redundant in agriculture into the better paid and more skilled jobs that were bound to become available, if not in the village then elsewhere.

In the second half of the twentieth century, agricultural production became less dependent on rainfall. The construction of, first, the Kakrapar dam and then, the Ukai dam in the Tapti river led to a significant extension of the irrigated area in the central plain of south Gujarat. Crops could now be cultivated throughout the year. The lengthening of the agrarian cycle resulted in a growing demand for labour, although this was somewhat lessened by the mechanization of farming operations and transport—the introduction of tractors and power tillers. More damaging for the local landless, however, was the influx of seasonal labour from the remote hinterland. Throughout the region, sugarcane became the major cash crop and the agro-industry managing its production and processing recruited harvesting gangs from far-off destinations for the duration of the season. Elaborating on

---

[16] This was the theme of my fieldwork in south Gujarat during the last decade of the twentieth century; see J. Breman, *Footloose Labour: Working in India's Informal Economy*, Cambridge: Cambridge University Press, 1996. On the same theme, see also, *The Jan Breman Omnibus*, Introduction by S. Patel, New Delhi: Oxford University Press, 2007.

the political economy of labour migration, I pointed out that the decision to bring in these outsiders was not caused by a local shortage of
labour but was conditioned by an employment strategy that reduced
the cost of the brutal work regime to the lowest possible level.[17] Labour
migrants are easy to discipline, are not allowed to bring non-working
dependents along, can be put to work day and night, and have to leave
the region again when their presence is no longer required. While the
local landless have to remain at home idle, an army of more than a
hundred thousand men, women, and children camp along the roadside
or in the open fields from October to June to cut the cane and take it to
the cooperative sugar mills which have been set up in nearly every *taluka*
(sub-division of a district).

As I was able to observe in Bardoligam, which became the third
village of my fieldwork at the end of the 1970s, growing sugarcane has
been a very profitable business for the landowners whose prosperity has
significantly increased in the last half century. The houses in which they
used to live have been replaced by *haveli*s, mansions two or even three
storeys high, with well-furnished interiors designed to demonstrate the
wealth of the inhabitants. They no longer use mopeds or scooters to
get around, but are the proud owners of motorcars, preferably expensive
foreign models. The members of the dominant castes had already given
up working in the fields one or two generations ago, and their growing
detachment from agriculture is expressed in an unwillingness to invest
time and money in farming. In recent decades, milk cattle have followed
draught animals in disappearing from the high-caste neighbourhoods.
When I asked why, I was told that keeping them was too much of a
nuisance, despite the fact that looking after the animals and cleaning the
stables were chores done by the farm servants and maids anyway.

Anavil Brahmans and Kanbi Patidars have dissociated themselves
from the agrarian lifestyle of their ancestors. Settling down in towns and
cities has become increasingly popular among the younger generations
and attending college in a nearby town helps them to prepare for a life
oriented more towards the world beyond the village. Sons and, more
particularly, daughters do not see a future for themselves living in the
village and working in agriculture. They really want to become embedded in an urban environment, but because of the soaring prices of real

---

[17] J. Breman, *Of Peasants, Migrants and Paupers: Rural Labour Circulation and
Capitalist Production in West India*, Oxford: Clarendon Press and New Delhi
Oxford University Press, 1985.

estate—the cost of even a small and rather basic apartment in a high-rise building in the municipalities of Valsad, Navsari, Bardoli, or Surat runs to more than four lakh (hundred thousand) rupees—not all can afford it. Fathers complain that they find it difficult to get suitable girls to marry their sons because coming to the village inevitably implies having to take up the role of the dutiful daughter-in-law. For the rich, their rural lifestyle has become sufficiently urbanized, with all the modern gadgets and conveniences until recently only available in the town. The infrastructure has been upgraded and distances can be easily bridged by scooter or motorcar. It is therefore nowadays acceptable to continue to live in the village, also for the younger generation, but it is important to have a proper urban job, that is, white collar and in the managerial ranks or, preferably, having your own business so as to be your own boss. It is interesting to note that the trend away from agriculture at the higher end of the village hierarchy rarely leads to land being sold off. A new class of 'absentee' landlords has emerged who own most of the land but desist from ploughing their earnings back to raise production. They manage their property by remote control and in a leisurely fashion—having fruit orchards and growing sugarcane—rather than as active, let alone innovative, agrarian entrepreneurs.

## THE WIDENING DIVIDE BETWEEN WINNERS AND LOSERS

The members of the village elite are, however, not content to just shed their rurality. Their real ambition is to settle abroad and join their caste mates as non-resident Indians (NRIs). Leaving for other shores is not a new phenomenon in south Gujarat, but the number of migrants going overseas has increased enormously in the last quarter century. An earlier generation went to East Africa and later on to the United Kingdom (UK), but nowadays, the United States of America (USA) is the favoured destination. Getting hold of a green card to send a son or daughter to America is a high priority in many well-established households. What they do there depends on the educational qualifications of the migrants. Running your own business is the dream of every Patidar youngster and the popular saying, 'hotel–motel–patel', in which the community at large takes pride, illustrates the strength of their presence in this branch of trade. Much less widely known is that at least part of the money spent on buying a motel somewhere in the US comes from the profits reaped from agriculture at home. Sugarcane in particular has been a real money spinner, and the Rs 500 shares that a farmer had to buy many years ago to register himself as member of the cooperative agro-industry processing the cane are now sold for not less than Rs 150,000– Rs 250,000 on the open market. The landowners not only indulge in conspicuous consumption but also help to provide the cash their sons need to buy the overseas property that has made them such successful emigrants. If it comes to the crunch, they are even willing to sell a piece of land because they see it as an investment in the future well-being of their children and grandchildren abroad.

To that extent, the NRIs regard themselves as frontrunners in building up a globalized identity, not afraid to move themselves and their capital around in the pursuit of happiness. They come home to relax, to charge their religious batteries, to find marriage partners, to check on the family property, to seek medical care (the cost of which is much lower than in the USA), or to spend their retirement, but not to engage in business. The dominant castes are strong, even vehement, supporters of the BJP. Narendra Modi, the *Hindutva* supremo and Chief Minister of Gujarat, is their hero. They affectionately call him *chhote* Sardar, the little lion, who has stepped into the shoes of his famous namesake, Sardar Patel. Although a close associate of Gandhi in the struggle for independence, Patel but was strongly opposed to the doctrine of piety preached by the father of the nation and his steadfast concern for upliftment of the poor.[18] So far, however, Modi has not been successful in his appeal to the NRIs to bring their overseas profits back to the state where they were born and bred. It has been made clear to him that a precondition to their willingness to build and run hotels and motels in Gandhi's homeland would be the repeal of prohibition. Given the huge illegal intake of alcohol in all quarters, that moment may actually not be far off.

In the ongoing discussion on the shape and magnitude of the current stagnation in agrarian investment and production, most, if not all, attention has usually been given to economic factors. I have just argued that an important feature of the crisis is that the main owners of agrarian property are distancing themselves from active farming, a way of life with which they no longer feel comfortable. For totally different reasons, the class of agricultural labourers is also turning away from what has been, until now, the primary economic sector. They are being pushed out from cultivating the land because they get neither enough work nor a wage that enables them to satisfy their basic needs. Lack of sufficient employment has reached the point at which the rural landless in south

---

[18] See Breman, *Labour Bondage in West India*, chapters 3 and 4.

Gujarat cannot be occupationally classified any longer as spending most of their working days in agriculture. What have conventionally been registered as subsidiary sources of income in other sectors of the economy have become the main ones. It boils down to a wide assortment of unskilled jobs, such as digging, hauling, and lifting work, which taxes their bodily strength and stamina and for which they get a wage not much higher than that paid by the farmers: in 2005–6, that was Rs 30–Rs 40 for eight hours, and less even than that if their presence was required for only half a day.

Have the poor become poorer since my investigations in Gandevigam and Chikhligam nearly half a century ago? That statement would be difficult to substantiate if only because their condition then could hardly have been worse than the intense misery in which I found them in the early 1960s: steeped in hunger, prone to illness, having only one set of clothes, and without adequate shelter. As I have already pointed out, in all these respects some progress has been made. But today, with a few exceptions, the Halpatis are still stuck firmly below the poverty line. It seems that more progress was made in the 1970s and 1980s than since. The annual income of most households does not exceed Rs 15,000–Rs 20,000. That means that an average household of four to five members can spend at best Rs 50–Rs 60 a day on their basic needs, which is less than 40 cents daily for each of them. My informants in the landless colonies are not impressed when I tell them that their parents and grandparents were even poorer than they are now. 'How does that help us today?,' they reply, 'We know it was very bad then but that does not mean that our condition is much better now.' They are right of course; they should not be compared with the indigence of an earlier generation, but with the highly visible comfort, if not luxury, in which their employers live. What they experience is relative deprivation, an acute awareness that those who were already much better off in the past have appropriated most of the fruits of economic growth. All stakeholders acknowledge that the cake has become bigger, but the way it is cut up shows even greater inequity than before. And why not, is the widely held opinion in the milieu of those who have become much better off. They have no problem arguing that the poor masses are non-deserving because of their defective way of life.

## POLICIES OF EXCLUSION

While in the past the landless used to live in the shadow of the landown-ers, who kept a close check on their bonded servants, the demise of the beck-and-call relationship meant that having a permanent and abundant supply of agricultural labour had become more of a nuisance than a comfort. In all the sites of my fieldwork, the Halpatis were thrown off their master's land and became squatters on the waste land at the outskirts of the village. As already noted, the houses in which they live—though an improvement on the earlier huts—are small, jerry built, and lack the basic amenities, such as drinking water and sewage, which have upgraded the accommodation of the non-poor. Electricity lines reach the landless colonies but many households cannot afford to have a meter installed and pay the price of the two-monthly subscription. The uneven terrain on which the colonies are built makes them difficult to access and the *kachha* (rough) roads leading to the outskirts are not properly maintained, making them difficult to walk or ride on, particularly in the monsoons. What I am describing are nothing less than slums. For no good reason at all, this term is reserved for labelling the settlements in which the urban poor congregate. Such quarters in the countryside may be smaller and somewhat less congested, but they are otherwise similar to the deficient habitat of those who live a down-and-out existence in the urban milieu. The inhabitants buy their daily provisions in small shops or *gallas*, roadside cabins in their own neighbourhood which sell a narrow range of commodities, since, in terms of both quantity and quality, the customers have to be modest in their daily purchases. Also, in this respect, the contrast with mainstream society stands out because the non-poor are not shy in demonstrating their ability to consume more and better. All this contributes to making the gap in material well-being more visible than ever.

Living in slums and being constantly exposed to the deprivations that are inherent to such a dire existence is only part of a more comprehensive policy of exclusion that has turned the landless into a new class of untouchables. The deterioration of public health care over the last two decades, in the wake of the drive towards privatization, has made the Halpatis more vulnerable to disease. Because of the prohibitive cost, they delay seeking medical help. Only if the problem becomes unbearable do they consult professionals (with lower qualifications than the doctors), clinics, and hospitals frequented by the non-poor. Finally, segregation is a prominent feature in seeking access to education. Although the percentage of Halpati children going to school has steadily increased, still, only half of them at best complete primary school. A small minority go on to secondary school, but they, too, tend to drop out after the first few standards. If they have become literate, their ability to read and write soon wanes again because of lack of practice. By and large, the children belonging to the higher castes continue their education for much longer. Moreover, the route they follow is different from the very beginning. The public school in the village is nowadays only attended by the local poor. The high-caste parents send their children to private schools in town that are considered to offer better quality education. Apart from better teachers, the return on the investment is also growing up in the company of age mates who share a similar elevated caste–class identity. The growing *apartheid* of the rural underclass is the inevitable outcome of a policy of exclusion in all walks of life.

## ABSENCE OF COLLECTIVE ACTION

To cope with deprivation is a full-time occupation and most people living precariously do not have much energy left for engaging in joint activities leading to redemption from their indigence. I am not suggesting that the Halpatis' way of life comes close to, or actually is, a culture of poverty. Their behaviour is indeed marked by improvidence but this is mainly because the demand for their labour power is intermittent and the employment for which they qualify as unskilled or self-skilled workers is casual rather than regular, and is invariably paid on piece rates at the lowest possible level. Due to a chronic shortage of income, many Halpatis have no other option than to ask for payment in advance. They refuse, however, to consider themselves subservient to one or more employers who have bought a prior claim on their labour power at some later stage. Nevertheless, using debt as an instrument for what I have called practices of neo-bondage, adds to the dependency, which is a major feature of poverty itself. Resistance against oppression and exploitation is difficult to organize when the supply of labour is structurally so much higher than the demand for it. The vested interests, on the other hand, face fewer problems in taking a united stand when their domination is challenged. This does not mean that the Halpatis accept with docility the harsh treatment meted out to them. Agrarian relations are fragile as well as tense, and what begins as a quarrel may escalate into a regular fight. I reported on one such incident that began when an agricultural worker was beaten to death to punish him for his impudence.[19]

Strikes do break out every now and then to articulate claims for a higher wage. But, they tend to be spontaneous rather then well planned,

[19] J. Breman, *The Labouring Poor in India*, New Delhi and Oxford: Oxford University Press, 2003, chapter 2.

usually remain localized instead of spreading to other villages, and are short in duration because the landless have no reserves to live on. Lack of food brings them back to work after only a couple of days, and if this does not happen, the landowners back up their refusal to bargain by bringing in outside labour. It is true that the opening up of the rural economy has made the landless more mobile, but going out of the village or trying to gain access to regular work outside agriculture is not so easy. A proper job is difficult to come by since the eagerly awaited formalization of informal sector employment has not taken place. On the contrary, labour has become firmly informalized in all sectors of the economy.[20] Instead of changing their occupational profile from agricultural to industrial workers, the landless masses remain footloose, but in a fluid and already saturated labour market. It is a workforce without skills, social capital, and political leverage, a reserve army stuck in their rural slums, pushed out for some time and then pushed back again. They are fragmented over a wide range of short-term work niches and continually rotate between them. The pretension that they are self-employed in whatever they do at any moment needs to be addressed critically. Their mode of employment is a contractualized and casualized waged labour relationship, but one that makes it difficult to unite them in solidarity for concerted action.

## PAUPERISM

Of the many problems I have with the Great Debate on Poverty, as it is complacently called by a closed shop of number-crunching economists,[21] the major one is the fixing of a highly debatable poverty line and then clustering together all those who live beneath it as if they constitute a more or less homogeneous segment.[22] This kind of incomprehension shows the lack of insight concerning the various layers of deprivation, ranging below and above a decent livelihood, and of the differences among them. The households inhabiting the rural slums are differentiated from each other in composition and size as well as in levels of consumption. Reducing these variations to average figures

[20] See ibid., chapter 6.

[21] See Angus Deaton and Valerie Kozel (eds), *The Great Indian Poverty Debate*, New Delhi: Macmillan, 2005.

[22] The only concession made in part of the literature is to separate the poor from the very poor or destitute, a distinction in which the latter category is identified as having less than three-quarters of the amount of the cut-off point for the poverty line.

would ignore a range of lifestyles, running from coping with adversities without being overwhelmed by them to having lost even minimal control over the circumstances conditioning one's life and giving up the fight for a better existence.

In contrast to the vast amount of literature on poverty, not much has been written on pauperism, but this is what strikes the eye when going around the landless colonies in the villages of my fieldwork: Gandevigam, Chikhligam, and Bardoligam. It is expressed in symptoms suggesting that planning for today or tomorrow, let alone investment in future well-being, is impossible. Income from work is haphazardly spent without giving priority to the most basic needs, in particular a sufficient and adequate intake of food. Addiction to drink means that up to a quarter or even half of the wages earned is set aside for the purchase of illegally distilled alcohol. Quarrels with neighbours or within the household are a frequent occurrence. Husband and wife fall out with each other, unable to handle the misery in which they find themselves, and because of desertion or neglect, children already have to fend for themselves at a very young age. Sometimes, the men are unable or unwilling to be the main providers for their households, but in other cases, it is the women who default on their role as caretakers. Outside intervention to avoid the situation getting worse is rare. Neighbours or relatives are often too much bothered by their own problems to spend time on mediation or giving support to the victims. 'We can't afford to live and act in solidarity,' one of my Halpati informants commented. Communal institutions, such as the *panch*, which used to play an important role in maintaining social mores, arranging the celebration of religious festivals, and settling internal disputes, have disappeared and have not been replaced by new conventions cementing togetherness in the landless milieu.

Certainly, there is a section aspiring to achieve more respectability, to gain in dignity by demonstrating behaviour expressive of the desire to belong to mainstream society. Women seem, more than men, to be at the forefront of that endeavour. Their ambition is to run a self-contained, well-ordered, and sober household; to avoid abuse or being abused; to live within one's means and not to indulge in consumerism; to encourage their children to get educated beyond primary school; to economize on the inevitable *rites de passage*; to consolidate what they have; and to reach out for more. Their presence is significant because it shows that not all the inhabitants of the landless colonies can be classed as lumpen. Having said that, I also want to emphasize that, among the Halpatis, the 'deserving poor' are a minority segment. They swim against the tide of deprivation and discrimination, and reaching where they want to be, out of indigence, is a long haul. Sliding back proves to be easier than moving up.

## A Dangerous Class?

Mass poverty tends to be seen as a political risk to the established order. In this line of thinking, the reserve army of labour does not remain sunk in apathy but can be mobilized for all kinds of subversive activities which put the security and comfort of well-established citizens at risk. It has been argued that the threat the restive and unwieldy lumpenproletariat posed to political stability was a major reason for giving this underclass access to mainstream society. To defuse their nuisance value, the poor had to be given a fair deal and be co-opted into the social security and other benefits which became available. This is why and how, according to de Swaan, the welfare state came into being during the restructuring of western economies from a rural–agrarian to an urban–industrial mode of production.[23] Is it possible to discern such a sobering reappraisal in the code of conduct of those who are better off and who see themselves not only as the driving force of 'Shining India' but also as its natural beneficiaries? Are they genuinely making an effort to divide the spoils of economic progress between the haves and haves-not in a more balanced way than has been done so far? In the context of my fieldwork in south Gujarat, I observe a trend in the opposite direction: not a narrowing but a widening of the gap between the people at the top from those at the bottom of the heap.

The landowning elite feel neither compassion nor anxiety about the misery in which the Halpatis live. Incidents do occur, when the local landless from the colonies on the outskirts attack members of the dominant caste and their property in the village, but these are irregular mishaps that do not escalate into a kind of class war, spilling over into neighbouring localities. Moreover, the district police can be relied upon to deal firmly with the mischief makers. How could the landless in their slums challenge the social fabric from which they have been excluded? Or rather, from which they are said to have excluded themselves. Because that is how Anavil Brahmans and Kanbi Patidars tend to qualify the sub-human existence of Halpatis. Among those who are better off, the

[23] Abram de Swaan, *In Care of the State: Health Care, Education and Welfare in Europe and the USA in the Modern Era*, Cambridge: Polity Press, 1988.

received wisdom is that poverty is the result of a defective way of life. In this view, the landless have themselves to blame for remaining stuck in misery. This particular instance of blaming the victims is justified by various kinds of rationalizations, which elaborate on the indolence, irresponsibility, deceit, and malevolence of the Halpatis. These are all traits typically associated with criminality-prone lumpen behaviour. I ventured to conclude a short essay on the relevance of the doctrine of social Darwinism with the remark that the relatively low level of technology that characterized the early phase of industrialization in the West ultimately enabled the labouring masses, until then written off as superfluous, to demand gainful and decent employment:

The industrial reserve army proved to be much more than useless ballast. Schooling put an end to the combination of hidden employment and too low wages. Around the turn of the [nineteenth] century and in the early years of the twentieth century, the poor succeeded in becoming full-fledged participants in the labour process of Western societies and contributed to growth in prosperity. Greater political representation was a logical outcome of this development.[24]

That same transformation does not appear to be the course giving shape and direction to the process of change that is currently under way in large parts of the world. Globalization is not, for all those subjected to it, a path towards more and better inclusion.

Mine is a dismal account which I need to qualify on two scores. In the first place, I have not discussed what has happened to the middle ranks in the countryside of south Gujarat. My experience, based on recurrent fieldwork, is that many of these people, holding some land or other productive assets, have been able to find somewhat more room for manoeuvre. Having said that, I would like to point out that the trend of change is set by the two classes at the poles of village society: the main landowners and the landless. They are at the forefront when it comes to finding out who has won and who has lost. Besides, as I have argued, in figuring out the sum total, the interdependency of the component parts needs to be stressed. The misery of the Halpatis can be understood only by tracing the dynamics of their subordination to the village elite. A second qualification that is required concerns the tricky issue of generalization. I immediately grant that landless labour elsewhere in the south Asian subcontinent may have fared better than the segment

---

[24] See the final chapter in this volume, 'The Eventual Return of Social Darwinism'.

of this class in south Gujarat. There are more hopeful reports showing that where members of the rural proletariat were able to increase their bargaining strength by finding regular employment in the new industrial workshops or as construction workers in urban localities, farmers had no other choice but to raise agricultural wages in order to motivate at least part of the workforce to stay on. However, such success stories must also be seen in a wider perspective. They cannot be held up as a disclaimer to the outcome of my research, nor as confirmation that the regional variation is so enormous that any generalizations are untenable. My findings are not unique; they have a relevance that goes beyond the villages I have closely investigated over a long period of time.[25] Moreover, the condition of poverty on which I have focused is not caused by backwardness. Gujarat is one of the fastest growing states in the country and the landless that I have been talking about belong to the heartland of the capitalism that has come to maturation here. In a new and vibrant stage, yes, but also ferocious and predatory in its impact.

## THE RETREAT OF THE STATE AND THE URGENT NEED TO BRING BACK PUBLIC SPACE

An understated feature in my analysis of the political economy of agrarian change so far has been the role of the state. In propelling market fundamentalism, which has become the cornerstone of economic policy, the state surrendered the agency it earlier claimed as a balancing force between the interests of capital and of labour. 'Inspection *raj* has gone,' proclaimed Prime Minister Manmohan Singh, the head of what is misleadingly called the National Progressive Alliance (NPA). His rallying

---

[25] See J. Breman, *The Poverty Regime in Village India: Half a Century of Work and Life at the Bottom of the Rural Economy in South Gujarat*, New Delhi: Oxford University Press, 2007. Factual evidence backing up my reading of rural dynamics can be found in a large number of empirical studies. To name but a few: Government of India (GoI), *Report of the National Commission on Rural Labour, Vols I and II*, New Delhi: Ministry of Labour, 1991. See also, Stuart Corbridge, G. Williams, M. Srivastava, and R. Veron, *Seeing the State: Governance and Governmentality in India, Part III: The Poor and the State*, Cambridge: Cambridge University Press, 2005, pp. 219–74; Barbara Harriss-White, *India Working: Essays on Society and Economy*, Cambridge: Cambridge University Press, 2003, chapter 2; P. Sainath, *Everybody Loves a Good Drought: Stories from India's Poorest Districts*, New Delhi: Penguin, 1996; and Arun Sinha, *Against the Few: Struggles of India's Rural Poor*, London: Zed Books, 1991. Specifically on rural labour relations, see the special issue published by T.J. Byres, Karin Kapadia, and Jens Lerche (eds), 'Rural Labour Relations in India', *Journal of Peasant Studies*, vol. 26, nos 2 and 3, January–April 1999, pp. 1–358.

cry ended all pretension to insist on a minimum wage rate. The market would realize what the state failed to achieve: to raise more and more people above the poverty line. Statistics are being produced to vindicate the righteous choice made in favour of this most dogmatic brand of free enterprise. In Gujarat, the number of people below the poverty line has—in state-produced statistics—plummeted from 41.9 per cent in 1983 to 14.2 per cent in 2004–5. But on the Human Development Index, Gujarat ranks much lower than its official economic record would suggest. Travelling around urban and rural Gujarat, it takes more than mere wishful thinking to accept the government's claim that the problem of indigence is on the verge of being solved. It requires the observer not to look behind the Potemkin façade that has been erected. The statistical tally is engineered by sending instructions from the commanding heights in the state to the district and sub-district authorities not to issue new below poverty line (BPL) identity cards and to unregister households owning some durable assets, thus taking away their right to buy a monthly food ration at a subsidized price. Poverty has become a phenomenon that needs to be kept out of sight and out of the government's bookkeeping. Scaling down the size and intensity of misery, if not in reality then at least on paper, is part of the Shining India operation.

The retreat of the state in keeping a check on how the economy is run has not only resulted in a policy of deregulation aimed at repealing a host of restrictions on the free interplay of the forces of production, but has also led to an erosion of the public domain. The proponents of this approach maintain that privatization is the ultimate solution and that the state has no business in poverty alleviation. People living in that condition have to avail themselves of economic incentives that give a higher return to their labour power. In this perception, appealing to self-interest is the best route to upward mobility and the reward for heeding that message is crossing the poverty line. Nevertheless, in the face of immense misery due to underemployment, low wages, failing health, or old age, by no means is everyone convinced by the logic of the free market and its supposed benevolence. In the NPA which held power at the central level until Spring 2009, Congress has been put under pressure to generate employment by carrying out public works, introduce social security benefits for the more than 90 per cent of the total labour force working in the informal sector of the economy, and upgrade labour standards in order to safeguard workers against hazards to health and well-being. One of the measures suggested under the latter scheme, put forward in a report of the National Commission for Enterprises in the Unorganized Sector (NCEUS), is the introduction of a minimum wage.[26] The proposal seems to acknowledge that the unbridled working of the market needs to be tamed by public action. It is rather naive, to put it mildly—after having given in to the strong pressure for a thorough informalization of the economy and endorsing the verdict that the formalization of employment is the root cause of sustained poverty—to suggest that the consequences of this policy can be repaired with state-sponsored regulations that are in stark contrast to the spirit of market fundamentalism. Paying lip service to the rights of workers and the promise to provide security for them at times of illness or old age may very well be an electoral ploy. One wonders if the political will does exist to restore the public domain and bring the state back into the promotion of social welfare.

My strong reservations about such an emancipatory course of action taking place in south Gujarat are, in the last instance, based on the fact that the devolution of political power has not been able to break through the closed front of vested interests. In my long-standing fieldwork experience, it has remained an exercise in pseudo-democratization. The landowning elite, working hand-in-glove with the local state bureaucracy, has consistently frustrated attempts to include the rural poor. In a report on one of my field trips a quarter of a century ago, I described what had become of the *Gram Majur Kalyan Kendra* (Rural Workers' Welfare Centre) set up by the government a few years before.[27] These centres are still there, as ineffective as before, and the new welfare schemes are meant to be launched from these nodal points of social action for poverty alleviation. Going by their past performance, it is not so difficult to predict that the outcome will again be negative.

* * *

My conclusion is that, if space is not provided for political empowerment of the rural poor, their inclusion in mainstream society is bound

---

[26] National Commission for Enterprises in the Unorganized Sector (NCEUS), *Report on Social Security for Unorganized Workers*, New Delhi: 2006; NCEUS, *Report on Conditions of Work and Promotion of Livelihoods in the Unorganised Sector*, New Delhi: Academic Foundation, 2008.

[27] See Breman, *Wage Hunters and Gatherers*, chapter 4. In 2006, when I paid a visit to one of these centres, located close to Chikhligam, I found that nothing had changed at all. Window dressing is the best way to explain why they have not been closed down.

to remain a mere figment of the imagination, nothing but an illusion which may well turn into a fascist nightmare. The doctrine of market fundamentalism and an ingrained ideology of social inequality are a deadly combination. The upshot of that reactionary regime is that the landless caste–class should not be included. From the vantage point of the well-to-do, they get no less and no more than what they deserve: exclusion from a decent existence, leading their lives on the village out-skirts, and on the margins of the economy. In the previous pages, I have expressed my scepticism that a reversal in the trend towards exclusion is in the offing. But, what about the long-term perspective for emancipa-tion of the rural underclass? One needs a historicizing mindset to remain hopeful. A definite step forward was when the Halpatis managed to find redemption from age-old bondage half a century ago. Mere blinking at an egalitarian mirage was how D.A. Low summed up the outcome of the populist interlude in India and other Third World countries during the second half of the twentieth century.[28] Indeed, for large parts of mankind living in decency and dignity is a faraway dream. But, have the landless in south Gujarat lost all hope that such a day will come? Monitoring the milieu at the bottom of the village economy in the past decades at close quarters, I have found no symptoms of an internalization of subordination and a passive acceptance of the doctrine of inequal-ity. The mood in the rural slums is sultry, inspired more by sullenness, resentment, and anguish than by docility. To be sure, those feelings are not converted into concerted action. However, isn't it only after the event, in retrospect, that the turning point from disguised resistance to open and more sustained revolt can be identified?

[28] D. Anthony Low, *The Egalitarian Moment: Asia and Africa 1950–1980*, Cambridge: Cambridge University Press, 1996.

# II

## Leaving the Village Behind

# 3

# Coming to Kolkata

## Pathways to a Better Life or Lost in Dead-end Alleys?*

### FIELDWORK IN AN UNMAPPED TERRAIN

This review essay discusses the research findings reported by Ananya Roy in her recently published study, *City Requiem, Calcutta: Gender and the Politics of Poverty.*[1] In the title, the author has listed the main dimensions of her investigations on the southern outskirts of Calcutta (henceforth Kolkata). She began her fieldwork from a cluster of makeshift huts along the railway line at a short distance from a suburban station. Here, she found people who had drifted in from the rural hinterland to try and claim a niche in the urban economy. From this point of entry, Roy made her way to several settlements that became sites for data collection. All of them were inhabited by migrants who had trickled in from their villages of origin in search of a livelihood somewhat less precarious than the one they were left with at home. But, how do you make your way in the new habitat? By starting out on a winding and sloping path with every chance of not being able to take the next step or, having managed to climb a bit higher up, of sliding back to where the journey began, that is, in the fringe zone where city and countryside merge.

Roy points out, quite rightly, that most micro-studies on life and work at the bottom of the urban economy have been carried out in

---

* Originally published as 'Coming to Kolkata: Pathways to a Better Life or Lost in Dead-end Alleys?', *Economic and Political Weekly*, vol. 38, no. 39, 2003, pp. 4151–8.

[1] Published in the series *Globalization and Community, Vol. 10*, Minneapolis and London: University of Minnesota Press, 2003.

formalized slums rather than in the new type of settlements sprawling out on the city's periphery. Migrants without prior urban contacts have no other choice than to become squatters in this nebulous zone where rurality has not yet ended and urbanity has not yet begun. They set up camp in a landscape of railway tracks, drainage canals, bridges, rubbish heaps, roadsides, and patches of vacant land that are no longer used for cultivation. The tiny shacks they build overnight are as irregular, disorderly, and temporary as the surrounding terrain. It is no man's land, or at least that is what it looks like. But the migrants, who keep a low profile by reducing their visibility in this alien and bleak territory, know that in the end they will have to move on. Their aim is to gain access to one of the bigger settlements, in which squatters tend to congregate in larger numbers. These are still transient encampments, but more regular in the sense that some basic amenities, such as water and electricity, have been made available, while the self-built tenements are less flimsy and more lasting. From this still vulnerable baseline, petty officials of various government agencies and political brokers are contacted in an attempt to secure promises to be allowed to stay.

The negotiations with the powers that be rarely result in anything more than an ambiguous acknowledgement of temporary residence. In most cases, the land on which the squatters dwell has already been earmarked for other purposes and it is only a matter of time before they are evicted by municipal authorities or private contractors. Migrants without a record of durable stay may then have to start all over again. However, those who have some kind of formal documents—a birth certificate or a ration card, for instance—to prove that they have acquired a right to domicile are eligible for removal to another site. In this context, it is interesting to note that the municipal authorities refuse to recognize squatter settlements. The author explains the reason for this strategy of avoidance by quoting an official source: 'We are concerned that studying squatters will give them a false sense of legitimacy. We cannot acknowledge their presence.'[2] However, in the tortuous process of settlement and resettlement, the migrants slowly gain in legal status and gradually dare to become publicly more visible. Having connected themselves as clients to power mongers who are at the outreach of the urban political machine, their hope is to finally arrive in one of the regularized colonies, the residents of which have established themselves more permanently—still without

---

[2] Ananya Roy, *City Requiem, Calcutta: Gender and the Politics of Poverty*, Minneapolis and London: University of Minnesota Press, 2003, p. 27.

title deeds for the plots they live on, and to that extent dependent on the favours of their patrons at the grassroots level, but now contracted as tenants with a right to occupancy and a claim to representation. At this stage, registration in the government records is sought as a weapon against arbitrary eviction. But the price to be paid for acceptance of this tentative claim to citizenship is to be subject to dues for the better in-frastructural facilities—level roads instead of rough footpaths, in-house electricity, a water tap, and a toilet nearby—which the former squatters have come to enjoy.

It must be heaven compared to the nowhere sites from which the first contact with the urban terrain was made. Looking back through the eyes of one of her informants, Nokul, one can understand why:

I came to Calcutta with my entire family ten years ago. We lived on the railway platform for a few days. At that time, no one chased us away from the platforms. Now, if you sit there for too long, some party or union will come and ask you for *chanda* (dues). I found work doing *jogar* (casual construction labor) after about ten days. When we were living on the platform, I noticed all of these shacks nearby. We began to gather material—tarpaulin, discarded plastic bags, old tires. We would often have to fight for them, sort through the piles of garbage. But we built a shack. I guess it was more of a tent than a shack. The party took care of us...

Which party? The CPI(M) [Communist Party of India (Marxist)]. They have a club nearby—over there down that street. They would come to us during elections. We all voted for them. And they promised us that they would not evict us. But then, about seven years ago, they came to us and said that we would have to move. The *sarkar* (government) was building a bridge. This one that you now see. They told us to move our shacks next to the tracks. We met with the club leaders every day. I remember this so clearly. We were scared. But they kept reassuring us. One day, a *neta* (leader) came and he told us that if we moved to this strip of land by the tracks, no one would be able to harm us. The land belongs to the railway and they had no clubs or people to evict us. And so we moved. The other side of the tracks already had older shacks. They have electricity and now the party is building toilets for them. We don't have any of this. But perhaps we will. The party is good to us, but not to all of us....[3]

Tracing her informants along this long trajectory, Roy describes how a segment of them do indeed arrive in one of the formalized colonies, contrary to many others who are not so fortunate and get stranded somewhere in between. She also devotes attention to migrants who

[3] Ibid., p. 52.

are still at the very beginning of their flight from the rural hinterland. These are the commuters who travel up and down, leaving early in the morning and returning to their place of origin every evening. They belong to the category of footloose workers who have not yet managed to find an entry point, however temporary and fragile that might be, and who reach their urban sources of livelihood after an excruciatingly long ride on trains which are overcrowded in both directions. Roy followed up some of these informants back in their home villages, to find out, at the point of departure, why and how the decision to commute is made. Her fieldwork, thus, stretched back into the rural hinterland, although her trips for this purpose were rather short.

What needs to be emphasized is that the plan of fieldwork could not be neatly laid out in advance by sampling techniques which presume the availability of data sets in which the influx of rural migrants has already been put on record with more or less detailed information on their whereabouts. That kind of information on the people moving in and out of the twilight zone between city and countryside is simply nowhere to be found. Roy's research started when she decided to just wade into what is—in terms of directions, numbers, and locations—unmapped terrain. The logic of her investigations was to link the various nodes she encountered, because these are the routes through which her informants pass. In his investigations of rural-to-urban dynamics in Southeast Asia, McGee has classified this frontier landscape as *desakota*.[4] It does not require much imagination to recognize in this spatial configuration the pauperized nature of Kolkata's pattern of urbanization in a way that is indicative of the peripheral position of many other Asian metropolises in the world system that has emerged.

## IDENTITY OF THE FOOTLOOSE MIGRANTS

Nearly all inhabitants of the settlements in which Roy has located her fieldwork come from the same district situated on the southern side of the city. They have left their villages in the South 24-Parganas during the last fifteen to twenty years. Another shared characteristic of these migrants from the rural hinterland is their background as landless labourers. Apart from a tiny fraction (barely 6 per cent), her informants did not own even a small plot of cultivable land in their native place.

[4] T.G. McGee, 'The Emergence of Desakota Regions in Asia; Expanding a Hypothesis', in N. Ginsberg, B. Koppel, and T.G. McGee (eds), *The Extended Metropolis: Settlement Transition in Asia*, Honolulu: University of Hawaii Press, 1991, pp. 3–26.

Four-fifths of them (about 80 per cent) had a homestead but the remaining category (slightly more than 15 per cent) were also landless in that respect. Rural squatters, is how Roy chooses to define at least part of this residual lot. Quite rightly so, because squatting, although much understudied in its rural manifestation, is most certainly not just an urban phenomenon.

The myth of a homogeneous peasant community, so cherished in colonial times, has long been demolished and for good reason.[5] Without flaying this dead horse, Roy argues how the urban stereotype of the village as a collectivity of owner–cultivators seems to have been restored by the agrarian reforms the Government of West Bengal had carried out in the last few decades of the twentieth century. The fixing of a ceiling on land property resulted in the final demise of the class of landlords that had already lost much of its earlier prominence. The policy of dedifferentiation in the higher echelons of the rural economy was, however, not accompanied by a similar attempt to reshape the sharply unequal class composition at the broad bottom of agrarian society. Roy's own findings, together with her discussion of a number of relevant studies that have been conducted on the outcome of redistributive policies in the recent past, allow us to conclude that the large majority of the landless underclass, which make up a very sizeable part of the total population in the Bengal countryside, remained in most, if not all, villages firmly excluded from ownership of the surplus land that became available.

Urban politicians and policymakers show themselves unaware of the lack of access to the primary means of production for a significant portion of all rural households. In their mind, all migrants belong to an undifferentiated category of peasants who own some cultivable land which is or should be the main source of their livelihood.[6] Roy sides

---

[5] I have myself reported on this myth in several earlier publications. See J. Breman, 'The Shattered Image: Construction and Deconstruction of the Village in Colonial Asia', *Comparative Asian Studies No. 2*, Dordrecht: Foris Publications, 1988; J. Breman, 'The Village in Focus', in J. Breman, P. Kloos, and A. Saith (eds), *The Village in Asia Revisited*, New Delhi: Oxford University Press, 1997, pp. 15–75.

[6] I encountered the same type of wishful thinking at the outbreak of the financial crisis in Asia in 1997. The standing argument in policy circles was that the footloose labour, now declared redundant in the urban economy of Greater Jakarta, had gone back to their villages in the rural hinterland of Java, where they would weather the recession by living on the yield of the land owned by them. See J. Breman and G. Wiradi, *Good Times and Bad Times in Rural Java: Case Study of Socio-Economic Dynamics in Two Villages Towards the End of the Twentieth Century*, Leiden: KITLV Press and Singapore: Institute of Southeast Asian Studies, 2002.

with studies maintaining that the backbone of agricultural production is the middle peasantry with not very substantial holdings, usually less than five acres, who have been the main beneficiaries of the Left Front's tenancy reforms. The economic and political dominance of this class overshadows the much more precarious living made in the village economy by the landless proletariat. As far as the urban based power elite are concerned, the agrarian question has been settled with the creation of a more or less equitable property structure. The strong belief in a homogenized peasantry is, from Roy's point of view, a neo-populist construction that helps to justify the hostile attitude among state officials and party bosses towards the reserve army of migrants drifting into the outskirts of Kolkata. Their preconceived idea is that these people are a burden on the city's economy and would have been much better off by not abandoning what they basically were supposed to be: self-employed peasant producers in the Bengal countryside.

The widespread ignorance about the plight of the landless in the agrarian economy is a reflection of their muted voices on the platform of rural politics. In the life histories told by them, there is nothing to indicate that the Left Front is willing to protect and take care of these people. As a matter of fact, it is striking, according to Roy, how state and party have left the fates of the poorest of the rural poor untouched. Their interests are hardly represented in the local councils that are controlled by the middle peasantry eager to appropriate the development resources channelled downwards. This is by no means a feature specific to the state of West Bengal. The elite of the villages in south Gujarat, which I have extensively investigated, may be even more adamant in opposing the fair and proportionate participation of the class of agricultural labourers in the decision-making process.[7] They are forced to keep a low profile in the panchayat and the devolution of political power to the grassroots level has tilted the balance further in favour of small and middle landowners. A recently published case study of a

---

[7] For this recurrent theme in my own fieldwork accounts, I refer to J. Breman, *Patronage and Exploitation: Changing Agrarian Relations in South Gujarat*, Berkeley: University of California Press, 1974; J. Breman, *Of Peasants, Migrants and Paupers: Rural Labour Circulation and Capitalist Production in West India*, New Delhi: Oxford University Press and Oxford: Clarendon Press, 1985; J. Breman, *Beyond Patronage and Exploitation: Changing Agrarian Relations in South Gujarat, India*, New Delhi: Oxford University Press, 1993; J. Breman, *The Labouring Poor in India: Patterns of Exploitation, Subordination and Exclusion, Part I*, New Delhi: Oxford University Press, 2002.

village in Burdwan, also, documents the relative absence of the rural proletariat from the political process.[8] Roy could have strengthened her observations by elaborating on the caste hierarchy in rural Bengal. It would not be farfetched to assume that the contrasting positions in the structure of the political economy are backed up by social–cultural demarcations that articulate the divisiveness, but on this dimension, the author has chosen to remain totally silent. Nor are we informed about the caste composition in the urban settlements where the migrants try to establish themselves.

## MIGRATION AS AN ACT OF ESCAPE

Roy is more pertinent and communicative on the shrinking space for landless livelihoods in the countryside. Most important of all, the demand for agricultural wage labour has not kept pace with the growing number of households dependent on this source of income. Adequate irrigation is a chief constraint in the South 24-Parganas and, because of the prevalence of single cropping, work in the fields remains limited to three months per year, informants told her. Other local employment is simply not available. The class of large landowners has been expropriated and the small and middle peasants do not need much more labour power than supplied by members of their own households for most agricultural operations. Still, Roy agrees that she may have understated some work opportunities in the lower echelons of the rural economy. More in-depth research, carried out over a longer period, would be required to find out about such niches of employability in the village of residence or elsewhere in the countryside.

Intra-rural circulation, which is seasonal in nature, has been a standard practice for many generations of agricultural labourers in the districts of West Bengal. We know from several other studies that this pattern of mobility is still prevalent or may even have increased both in magnitude and distance. Roy gives no details on either the occurrence or the frequency of this phenomenon in the villages she visited. Contrary to the manifold reports on urban informal labour markets, there is a much greater paucity of documentation on institutions bringing demand and supply together in the rural economy. Still, all said and done, I have no arguments to challenge Roy's factual statement that the migrants she investigated are driven out of their home base because of a consistent

[8] See S. Bhattacharya, 'Caste, Class and Politics in West Bengal', *Economic and Political Weekly*, vol. 38, no. 3, 24–8 January 2003, pp. 242–6.

lack of regular buyers for their labour power. To be sure, there is the homestead plot but even having a domicile that is beyond the control of employers serves no purpose when there are no wages to be earned.

Survival at the rock bottom of the agrarian economy is, finally, endangered by the privatization of common property resources. While in the past landless households were allowed to make use of the uncultivated fields in the village for grazing a goat or a cow and for gathering firewood needed for fuel, they have been cut off from further access to land lying unproductive throughout or part of the year. This trend towards exclusion has even led some of the commuters to bring back, on their daily trip, a bundle of twigs foraged in the common that has opened up in the urban fringe zone. '...in the city, at least, one can go through the garbage of the rich and find a few things to sell to the recycling plant. One can pick up a fallen branch and take it home to light a fire. One can't do that in the village.'[9]

'Requiem for the city' is the title of Roy's book. One wonders if it would not be more appropriate to read her findings as a 'requiem for the village' from the viewpoint of the landless class. Roy found that the squatters whom she met on the periphery of Kolkata were not eager at all to talk about the life they had left behind them. Her informants, often, were quite reluctant to tell her the exact villages they came from and showed surprise or discomfort when she insisted on knowing. What did it matter? They were apt to construct their engagement with the urban milieu 'as a realm of political relationships and claims, of dealing with the *sarkar* or state'.[10] Looking through their eyes, it was framed as a transition from rural marginality to urban participation. What is there to return to? The story told by Nokul was one of many:

Every time I go back it is as if I cannot breathe. It is like a heavy hand on my heart. It is crowded here in this tiny shack with all of us—I have four children, you know—but it is not as crowded as in the village. I watched my father work as an agricultural labourer. But there was no work for me. There is only one crop a year in our village. It has been that way since I can remember. Three months of work per year and then hunger, terrible hunger. My father started migrating to Hooghly district for work during the lean season. We would not hear from him for months. He had no way of sending us money. Many of the men in our village would do this. But we remained hungry. He would usually come back with some money and we would buy some rice. When I turned seventeen, my father took me to Hooghly. We worked in villages where they

[9] Roy, *City Requiem, Calcutta*, p. 64.
[10] Ibid., pp. 50–1.

were growing vegetables. But there were so many of us. We did not always find work. And then I had a family to take care of. I left as soon as I could, fourteen years ago ...'[11]

Statistics and other quantified data sets can bring out the underlying dynamics but thick descriptions like this one are a powerful way to demonstrate why even a loose foothold in the city, with all the qualms this choice entails, is seen as opting out of a dreadful habitat which holds no promises for a better future.

In an essay analysing the images held by Gandhi, Nehru, and Ambedkar on the village, Jodhka points out that the first two had major differences of opinion.[12] While the father of the nation insisted that the inhabitants had joint interests, the first leader of post-colonial India, Nehru, spoke of internal differences in the basic unit of society that, in his perception, crystallized in the divide between landlords and peasants. However, it was only Ambedkar who realized that, from the point of view of the rural underclasses, the village was an area of darkness in which, from generation to generation, many of them had been forced to live at the margins or were even held in a state of captivity. Rejecting Gandhi's scheme for revival of the lost community, Nehru's vision led him to stress the need for a restructuring of the outdated relations of agrarian production. He added, however, the proviso that such a plan of reform was bound to fail without a clear-cut policy of industrialization and urbanization. Only then would it be possible to reduce the pressure on the prime sector of the economy. In this scenario, people redundant in agriculture should be encouraged to leave the village and to settle down in the city. This was also in their own best interests since, as industrial workers, they were going to enjoy a much better life than before.

In close correspondence with the various perceptions of the village economy in past and present, there are also strong differences of opinion about the dynamics of migration. Against those who argue that pull factors are of determining importance in the decision to go somewhere else, there are others who claim that push is the main motivation for people to leave. Ideological stances often play an important role in such debates. A more fruitful perspective would be to look at migration as a differentiated process. Roy, in my opinion, quite correctly, contrasts

[11] Ibid., p. 51.
[12] S.S. Jodhka, 'Nation and Village: Images of Rural India in Gandhi, Nehru and Ambedkar', *Economic and Political Weekly*, vol. 37, no. 32, 10 August 2002, pp. 3343–53.

earlier streams of migration with the one on which she has focused in her fieldwork. While, until the recent past, out-of-state migrants were able to qualify for employment at industrial worksites in Kolkata and Bengal, and middle peasants succeeded in reaching the regularized slums situated closer to the city's inner core, the squatters and commuters traced by her are kept at bay in a footloose condition on the outskirts of the metropolis. They have left the village, but whether they have arrived in the city is a debatable issue. Coming back to the notion of mobility as a differential process, my conclusion bears out the finding of a study which was published many years ago: migration starts from a situation of inequality at the point of departure and leads to further inequality at the point of destination.[13] When members of the subaltern classes in the villages of West Bengal start their journey towards the city, they are equipped with neither physical nor social capital assets with which to pave their way to regularized shelter and work. Are those vital markers of a life in human dignity the ultimate harvest of their wandering in unmapped terrain? I shall come back to this question in a later section.

## A GENDERED PERSPECTIVE

As the subtitle of the book clarifies, Roy has highlighted the role of women in the process of migration. This choice is not only understandable but also a felicitous one in view of the masculine bias in many studies on labour mobility, including my own. The author would like to see her work discussed as a contribution to feminist ethnogeography. In the way she tells the story, there is nothing wrong with that banner and it would certainly be misconceived to label it as an expression of undue partisanship. Males are present and accounted for, but mainly through the eyes of their wives, mothers, or daughters, not as the main providers of food and care for the households to which they belong. I have one minor critical note on this gendered perspective: we do not learn an awful lot about the various kinds of work in which the men of the squatter settlements are engaged. Jogar—casual labour, usually at construction sites, together with a wide range of odd jobs—appear to be the occupational statuses that they have in common. Invariably, female employment is inferior to whatever males do and, moreover, yields lower wages. Even in the rare cases that both practise the same trade, women

[13] See J. Connell, B. Dasgupta, R. Laishley, and M. Lipton, *Migration from Rural Areas: The Evidence from Village Studies*, New Delhi: Oxford University Press, 1976.

are at a disadvantage. A clear example is the vegetable vendors. The men in this petty business either grow the vegetables themselves, and get a bigger margin when they sell the product, or they team up to buy the goods in a village and share the transport cost to the city by jointly hiring a van. Women, on the other hand, are unable buy from the village markets because they do not have enough capital to do so and can only afford to buy small quantities at one of the urban wholesale outlets.

Many female squatters or commuters work as maids in middle-class households. Like most informal sector jobs, this type of employment has become subject to feminization as well as casualization. While in the past the majority of domestic servants in Kolkata used to be males, it has become, of late, a female occupation. My observation is that a similar trend can be noticed in, for example, Bombay (henceforth Mumbai) and Delhi. The same can be said for another shift to which Roy draws our attention: replacement of live-in by daytime workers, accompanied by a transition from monthly wages to piece-rate payment. So many rupees for so many chores, and her informants have to rush from one boss to the other in order to scrape together their meagre earnings. There is, however, a category of domestic help that is still engaged day and night, and without even a break once a week, because their employers need to be constantly attended to in the running of their households. These are very young girls who are sent off to work in Kolkata by their parents in the village when they are six or seven years old. The jobs done by these youngsters, who have not yet reached the age of adolescence, are known as *khao porar*, that is, service which provides food and shelter. This term neatly sums up the arrangement. The girls have stopped being a burden to their parents, who come once a while to the city to collect the wages earned by their daughters. The money thus saved, an appallingly low sum, is meant to be put aside for paying the dowry at the time of marriage. But there is, of course, every possibility that it has already been spent earlier on more urgent priorities. In a few sentences, Roy sums up the alienation from life at home by one of these girls who started her working life when she was seven:

For Noyon, her employers are family. For the last ten years she has known no other. She can barely find her way around when she visits once a year and she has lost touch with most of the families there. In fact, when visiting her parents she is eager to return to the city, worried about how her other family is faring.[14]

[14] Roy, *City Requiem, Calcutta*, p. 102.

A striking finding is the sharply unequal participation of men and women in the labour process. In defiance of National Sample Survey (NSS) statistics that suggest high rates of urban unemployment and underemployment for both men and women, Roy insists that, among the migrants and commuters she has investigated, female work participation peaks at an extremely high level, much above the percentage of males in the same categories. In many families, women turn out to be the primary earners on whom the other members depend for their daily subsistence. A better employment record, however, is no guarantee for redemption from misery. Because of the much lower wage paid to this most vulnerable segment of the workforce, female-headed households, in particular, tend to live far below the poverty line. While male informants were inclined to present themselves as ideal husbands and are eager to spin tales of harmonious domesticity, they spend quite a large portion of their irregular and fluctuating incomes on their own consumption. Women, on the other hand, are steadier and more frugal, as well as less egoistic, in handling the lower earnings they have made for longer hours of work. Roy joins the incisive criticism, often expressed in micro-level studies, of poverty line constructions that fail to take into account the unequal distribution of resources within the household. The uneven spread in the gratification of basic needs within this unit of cohabitation results from a structural imbalance that is gender based. This is why income aggregated at the household level is, in the opinion of Roy and others who share her insights, a problematic issue.

Wives do not hesitate to express their scorn for husbands who are unwilling to go in search of work. More is at stake here than only lack of employment opportunities. Many men in the squatter settlements shirk responsibility for family care—and not occasionally but all the time. Roy suggests that, in contrast to women who are invariably driven into commuting out of deprivation, for at least a number of male commuters, the decision to go to the city stems from choice behaviour. Illustrative is the explanation given by a young vegetable vendor as to why he opted out from his native place:

I was bored in the village. I am sure there was work, but I wasn't interested in looking for it. I wanted to come to the city. Here, I can have as many wives as I want to. If one has only one wife, one's life is over. I am free. I earn money and I spend it all. On whatever I want.[15]

[15] Ibid., p. 98.

This portrayal of footloose men as free riders comes back repeatedly in Roy's report and, it seems, for good reasons. Poverty, of course, creates tension between people living together in that condition and their willingness to share, justly and fairly, what is not enough for all should not be taken for granted. But the greater vulnerability of women, burdened with the charge of reproduction, leaves them without the room for manoeuvre, which men claim in looking around for a better deal than they have at the moment. What can be defined as ongoing unemployment could also be seen as deliberate idleness. It is an attitude which comes close to surrender, to go on an indefinite strike of sorts, rather than to struggle for a better life. In that sense, women tend to give up less easily, even if only because there are dependants to be looked after. Their anger at male abandonment, husbands who do come back to the village for brief visits in order not to leave their second wife alone in the city, makes life for them more strenuous than it already is. The sense of betrayal is certainly not inspired by spite that others will now benefit from whatever the labour power of the unfaithful companion yields. As one of the deserted women commented: 'I guess his livelihood is that he now lives of two women. I come to the city to fill my children's stomachs. He comes in order to have rest and fun. He has become a *babu*, just like those whom I work for—they are all *babus*.'[16]

The household is also rife with conflicts between the generations. While adolescent sons are blamed for taking their fathers as role models, growing-up daughters who go out to work are considered to be more loyal in supporting their mothers in the ungrateful task of keeping the household going. The tide turns, however, when they also start to keep back part of their wages to buy clothes and other items of individualized consumption. Roy gives us glimpses of the importance of feminized kinship networks for rallying support and solidarity. I wish that she had further elaborated on this antidote, more covert than overt, against masculine domination in the village setting as well as in the squatter localities.

## MACHINE POLITICS

The way in which Roy has framed her study implies a labour division operating between women and men, under which the former are engaged in scraping together income needed for family maintenance, while

16 Ibid., p. 84.

the latter have made it their business to negotiate access to urban shelter by entering masculine networks of political patronage as clients. What outsiders would regard as a pastime is, according to the men concerned, a proper job and one that requires their full-time commitment. It is, they insist, regular and profitable work, with the only disadvantage that it is not paid in cash but in promises—assurances that if they remain loyal to their leaders, it will eventually result in admittance to one of the formalized settlements as full-fledged citizens. Sudarshan's account is exemplary:

When I moved here fourteen years ago, the settlement faced constant demolitions and evictions by the port authority. Strongmen would come and loot our belongings. The police would come and beat us up. We would live cowering in our shack. But then I along with the others repeatedly asked the CPI(M) party office for help. The local councillor, Moni Sanyal, was a great man. He protected us. He promised us water. He turned the police into our friend... I remember those days clearly. I would spend all afternoon and evening at the party office. I would go to every single meeting and rally. It wasn't easy. At times we had fights with boys from other parties...

The party does not pay me. But I mobilize people. During rallies and brigades, I gather them up and ensure high attendance. When the leaders come to the settlement, I organize meetings. And I maintain the club. Do you think that this is any easy task? Running the club is like running a *panchayat*.[17]

The club is a meeting place in the neighbourhood, not only for mates but also for their opponents who owe allegiance to other cliques. In other words, it is a highly fluid front where clientship is auctioned, and livened up by clamour and brawls. At the same time, it is also a communal platform for keeping the ranks closed against challenges to male supremacy coming from outside or inside.

We keep the neighbourhood peace. We maintain unity. We don't let women attend our meetings. They would only create trouble. Just like my wife. She is always complaining. But we call them in if they are part of some conflict. Just the other day, some of the young girls of our settlement were becoming too friendly with boys from the club near Durgapur Bridge. We called them in and gave them a good beating.

We raise money on a regular basis—whatever people can afford—to organize celebrations and festivals. May Day, *Durga Puja*. This is the soul of our community. We keep everyone together in this way. If it weren't for the club, this whole place would fall apart...

[17] Ibid., pp. 108–9.

You are categorizing me as *bekar*, unemployed, huh? Well I am *bekar*, and proud of it. All of the men who work and earn a few pennies. They would not be able to live here without men like me.[18]

Club and party office are crucial points of social and political control along the frontier that stretches and expands on the urban outskirts. But the party office is the site where the men belonging to the same fold come to ask for favours or to register their complaints and from where the local bosses liaise with the higher ups in the political hierarchy. Roy explains why and how:

It is the party office that mediates state intervention, as in the provision of infrastructure. It is the party office that establishes rights to the informal use of electricity, drawing lines from electrical poles to individual houses. It is the party office that distributes ration cards, creating official identities recognized by the state during elections. And it is the party office that establishes committees to draw and redraw boundaries, regulate the selling of plots with appropriate commissions, and moves families at random from colony to new colony, from settlement to resettlement.[19]

The promises of favours given so easily do not carry much weight since the political brokers themselves are ill informed about the contenders for urban space higher up and do not know when and between whom disputes will be settled. Their clients act as tough gatekeepers who pretend that by hanging around at the club and party office they can facilitate or deny access to those who call the shots. The participation of squatter men at the tail end of patronage politics does not result in urban citizenship but is more a show of manhood, a demonstration of assertion and defiance against the exclusion in which they are being kept. But their toughness has no substance and is turned around into meekness since they do not dare to stand up against the political patrons. The women are well aware of the failure of the men to get things done and have bitter comments on the poor performance of their partners. 'In order to win the favours of the party, our husbands have to be *goonda*s. But many are too weak to do even that. They are too lazy to even grovel.'[20]

The fluid and contested boundaries between settlements, the fights between slum bosses and their gangs, the raids carried out by corrupt officials, and the inroads made by estate developers, all contribute to

[18] Ibid., p. 109.
[19] Ibid., p. 150.
[20] Ibid., p. 118.

the criminalization of politics on the urban outskirts. This whole set of interaction has been affected, in recent years, by a policy of neo-liberal restructuring which aims at urban expansion by the privatization of assets owned or appropriated by the government. It is clear that those who have no capital do not rate high in the allocation of public land. Withholding or granting permission to settle down, if not indefinitely then at least for the time being, is the prerogative of the state. The struggle to convert residential status from illegal to legal is a long-drawn-out, costly, and violent business. Vested with claims and counterclaims, the battle is fought in a rugged landscape which has all the features of a war zone with politicians in the role of warlords. Clients suspected of wavering in their steadfast support risk losing protection from all quarters. Negotiating is the game that patrons are supposed to play but not their followers. Even when the mapping of land into the books of formality is finally done, it does not mean that the squatters are entitled to the documents that would testify to their full-fledged urban citizenship. And they know why. 'They will never give us *pattas* (land titles). If they did, we would no longer have to depend on them for everything, every single day. If they gave us pattas, the game would be over. Whose lives would they play with then?'[21]

Roy's analysis of the role of machine politics in the squatter settlements of Kolkata is a strong indictment of the Left Front's record. She extends her diatribe to other political parties operating in West Bengal's major city, but her main criticism is directed against the CPI(M) for having betrayed the interests of the poorest segment of society: in the first place, by not catering justly and fairly to their needs in the rural hinterland; and then also, for keeping them footloose as migrants at the base of urban society. Without qualifying her harsh conclusion, I still feel inclined to point out that the achievements of the Congress party in Gujarat in reducing the vulnerability of the subaltern classes, announced as the first priority in every election held for half a century, has been even more dismal. Clearly, an explanation with a wider reach and depth is called for in order to come to terms with the state of exclusion imposed on a major segment of the total population in the South Asian subcontinent.

## PERSISTENT POVERTY

The study under review questions the strongly held notion that departure from the village is a significant step forward towards a better life and

[21] Ibid., p. 162.

above all, economic advancement. Time and again, it has been suggested that the worldwide trend of diversification, the earning of incomes from work in other sectors of economic activity than agriculture, is a major cause of decreasing poverty levels. In that cherished image, the trek from the rural hinterland opens up new sources of employment that combine better pay with higher skills. 'Deruralization' is how Wallerstein[22] has summed up this process, which has drastically changed the composition of the global economy in the last half century. According to him, a vast labour army, liberated from their state of captivity in agricultural production, has reached the cities where they become absorbed in the informal economy before moving on to the formal sector.

Even where there are large numbers of persons who are technically unemployed and deriving their income, such as it is, from the informal economy, the real alternatives available to workers located in the barrios and favelas of the world system are such that they are in a position to demand reasonable wage levels in order to enter the formal wage economy.[23]

Wallerstein's script goes on to characterize the informal sector in the urban economy as a waiting room, a transitional entry point from where, after a certain time, rural migrants succeed in climbing up to more dignified work in the city by upgrading their skills and strengthening their bargaining position. In the accounts of my own research in south Gujarat, I have pointed out that large contingents of the land-poor and landless underclass pushed out from agriculture are forced to remain on the march between town and countryside, as well as between different economic sectors and various employment modalities.[24] Footloose labour is the term I have used to highlight the nomadic work and life patterns of this reserve army, which has left home but is unable to find a new habitat immediately or even after many years and has most certainly failed to pave its way to the formal sector of the urban economy. The most fortunate segment among these migrants do, in the end, manage to settle down in one of the regularized colonies, referred to in their

---

[22] I. Wallerstein, 'Globalization or the Age of Transition: A Long-term View of the Trajectory of the World System', *International Sociology*, vol. 15, no. 2, 2000, pp. 251–67.

[23] Ibid., p. 262.

[24] See J. Breman, *Wage Hunters and Gatherers: Search for Work in the Urban and Rural Economy of South Gujarat*, New Delhi: Oxford University Press, 1994; J. Breman, *Footloose Labour: Working in India's Informal Economy*, Cambridge: Cambridge University Press, 1996.

language as *desh* or homecoming. But still, having finally become eligible
to urban citizenship, they remain the clients of the dominant party with
all kinds of restrictions on their freedom of movement. One could argue
that marginality in the world system is more essentialized in the fringe
zone of Kolkata than by the people and sites in the city's heartland.

Also, in Kolkata, as Roy has shown, the large majority of squatters
who are in various stages of settling down remain drifting around
at the bottom of the work hierarchy because they lack the skills, the
social connections, and the money to pay the bribes needed to qualify
for regular jobs which would give a higher and more stable return on
their labour power. The outcome of her study challenges Wallerstein's
assumption that arrival in the city marks for these migrants of the
last resort—and there must be an awful lot of them spread over the
South Asian subcontinent—the hopeful beginning of their way out of
*abhab*, deprivation or scarcity. Roy has omitted to back her portrayal of
persistent and abject poverty bordering on destitution with information
on features other than lack of employment and inadequate income.
Many of her informants appear to suffer from minor or major health
problems but there is no indication of how this impinges on the
household budget, apart from total or partial inability to work. She has
also not clarified whether children are, or indeed can be, sent to school.
The impression one gets, however, suggests the absence of the minimal
investments required to embark on the road to a better life even in the
next generation. Nor does she discuss the role of indebtedness, arising
from the need to sell labour power in advance for a price even below the
already depressed daily market rate for casual jobs, as a crucial factor in
the perpetuation of life in poverty. For these most vulnerable people,
lack of access to low-cost credit plays an important role in the creation
of relationships of dependency. In this sense, footloose does not mean
to be free of restraint in making choices about where and when to go or
what to do. Such restrictions have a lasting impact.

The kind of locations in which Roy has carried out her fieldwork
can be found in and around the urbanizing landscape throughout the
country. A recent account draws attention to the precarious housing
conditions in one of the 'unrecognized' settlements in Lucknow.

Most poor urban neighbourhoods, or 'notified slums' are recognised by local
governments and receive basic city services including water, sewage processing,
garbage removal and, in most cases, electrical connections. The most precarious
of the informal settlements, however, are located on land that is either owned
by government or by a private individual or organisation that has no interest in

using or developing the site. The residents of these neighbourhoods, or bustees, have no legal right to their home sites, though they have often paid a significant fee to a neighbourhood leader for squatting privileges. The urban poverty study team visited an unrecognised settlement in Lucknow that has been in existence for nearly 25 years, though the city authorities still record the site as unoccupied land. Located on the banks of a *nalla*, or drainage ditch, it had no source of clean drinkable water until residents were able to gather the money to tap (illegally) into a city water main and establish a public tap. Now, about 95 families use this one water source, and most of the friction in the community is said to arise over the water queues. There are no latrines; all residents use the canal for defecation. There is also no public school in or near the bustee, but a NGO [non-governmental organization] has hired a teacher to instruct 25–30 of the children for a few hours a week. In many unrecognised bustees, however, none of the children are in school. Their parents recognise that without basic literacy, these children will not be able to break out of deep poverty. However, no public schooling is provided for unrecognised settlements and bustee residents cannot afford public school fees.[25]

Would it be farfetched to assume that the field visit, on which this profile rests, was facilitated by the same NGO which had also arranged for the modicum of schooling introduced in this particular settlement? Towards the end of her study, Roy tells us about an informant who remarked: if one is a citizen, one can't be homeless. Paraphrasing this quotation, I feel tempted to observe that homeless people are rarely eligible for notification in national surveys: if one is homeless, one can't be recorded. I do wonder whether it is normal procedure for data collectors authorized by the state to be instructed to visit the unmapped settlements of, for example, Valsad, Surat, and Ahmedabad, all towns and cities of Gujarat where I have located my urban studies for many years. To the best of my knowledge, few if any representatives of formal sector agencies such as health or labour inspectors have ever been seen around at these unrecorded sites. It would indeed come as a surprise to me if NSS field investigators prove to be an exception to this rule of official myopia.

Roy has carefully avoided a description of her informants as trapped in 'a culture of poverty'. Although sympathetic to the idea of Kolkata as the periphery of the world system, where the trend has been more towards deindustrialization and informalization than the other way

---

[25] Reproduced from V. Kozel and B. Parker, 'A Profile and Diagnostic of Poverty in Uttar Pradesh, Poverty Reduction in 1990s', *Economic and Political Weekly*, vol. 38, no. 4, 25–31 January 2003, p. 394.

around, she insists that the city's outskirts should not be written off as a site of powerlessness. All qualifications notwithstanding, the migrants are apt to insist that there is more space available and accessible in the city than in the village. This induces her to translate their narratives as a transition from being mere victims of structures to being political agents. Against all odds, both men and women do not hesitate to show defiance and to assert themselves as stakeholders in the terrain through which they are made to travel in illegality and without the entitlements that go together with citizenship. An example of the agency exercised by female commuters is the anger which they express when caught riding without tickets on the trains to and from Kolkata. Found out, they refuse to be cowed down.

Let them arrest us all. There is not enough space in the hold for all of us…

When she came to fine me I said, take off your coat and give it to me so that I'll have your job. Then only will I be able to afford the fine…

You want to arrest me? First get my children from the village. We'll all stay in your jail and you can feed us.[26]

## DIFFERENT INTERPRETATIONS OR DIFFERENT REALITIES?

I have already observed that there are close similarities between Roy's research findings in the margins of Kolkata and my own fieldwork-based reports on labour migration in south Gujarat. Our conclusions are out of tune with the prevalent and policy-friendly view that, despite incongruencies across various indicators, the incidence of poverty has recently fallen sharply in Gujarat and West Bengal, as well as in most other states of India during the last decade of the twentieth century.[27] A common reaction to the kind of empirical micro-studies we have produced—based on a broader conceptualization of poverty than only material deprivation, further narrowed down to consumption expenditure and food intake in particular—is either to ignore them without further argumentation or to imply that they deal with situations and

[26] Roy, *City Requiem, Calcutta*.

[27] For a recent overview, see the collection of papers solicited for a workshop held in January 2002, which was jointly sponsored by the World Bank and the Planning Commission. The contributions—under the title, *Poverty Reduction in India in the 1990s: Towards a Better Understanding*—were reproduced in *Economic and Political Weekly*, vol. 38, no. 4, 25 January 2003, pp. 295–412. For one more macro assessment for the same period, see K. Sundaram and S.D. Tendulkar, 'Poverty in India in the 1990s: An Analysis of Changes in 15 Major States', *Economic and Political Weekly*, vol. 38, no. 14, 5–11 April 2003, pp. 1385–93.

instances which are a-representative. To Roy, such comments must be as offensive as they are to me. In the mid-1980s, I accepted the invitation to participate in a workshop in which economists and anthropologists discussed their different methods in conducting research on the multidimensionality of poverty.[28] Our deliberations were meant to be the start of an ongoing dialogue but the goodwill generated among the members of the disciplines who came to the meeting did not lead to much further interaction after the event. A few years ago, I expressed my discomfort at this lack of follow-up.[29]

The inspiration for the workshop held in 1985, came from the difference in disciplinary perspective on monitoring the trend of rural poverty. Although the same discrepancy can be discerned again, this time economists seem to find much more ground for optimism than anthropologists do. Almost two decades ago, it was, interestingly enough, just the other way around. While drawing attention to the disjuncture between macro-optimism and micro-pessimism, Roy quite rightly argues that divergent evaluations on trends of rural and urban poverty should not be simply interpreted as a contrast between, on the one hand, macro/quantitative/economistic and, on the other hand, micro/qualitative/anthropological studies. I could not agree more and, also, share her reservations about survey techniques that imply that researchers are already familiar with what they are going to find out. This is actually what I meant when I wrote to be wary of 'registration techniques with a formal sector bias and which are insufficiently adapted to the concrete situation we are addressing: life and work in a state of poverty'.[30] Criticism of yet another kind has been raised by Krishna, who quotes NSS field staff confessing that it is impossible to fill up the schedules item-by-item and that what looks like meticulously detailed information is really a matter of guesstimates and founded on the common sense of local-level investigators.[31]

[28] Our meeting resulted in a volume edited by Pranab Bardhan, *Conversations Between Economists and Anthropologists: Methodological Issues in Measuring Economic Change in Rural India*, New Delhi: Oxford University Press, 1989.

[29] The occasion was the Sukhamoy Chakravarty Memorial Lecture delivered at the Delhi School of Economic Growth on 11 November 2001. The lecture was republished as part of a longer essay, 'Urban Poverty in the Early 21st Century', in Breman, *The Labouring Poor in India*, chapter 7.

[30] Breman, *The Labouring Poor in India*, p. 241.

[31] A. Krishna, 'Falling into Poverty: Other Side of Poverty Reduction', *Economic and Political Weekly*, vol. 38, no. 6, 8–14 February 2003, pp. 533–42. One of his recommendations is to undertake community-based interviews in order to capture

The study of poverty is, nowadays, considered to be the business of economists. Or at least, of those among them who are engaged full-time in the practice of econometrics and statistics. They do not easily accept that the classical literature on the subject of human deprivation has been produced by political economists, sociologists, anthropologists, and historians. Taking this knowledge on board is not what preoccupies them. They are satisfied with grounding their analyses in what one of my colleagues participating in the same workshop provocatively called, 'the ideology of measurement'.[32] Since this first round, the tribe of economists confessing to that school of thought seem to have closed shop and prefer to talk to each other on monitoring and evaluating poverty measurement in India.[33] I, for one, feel strongly inclined to dispute the wisdom and appropriateness of relying on the NSS as the sole source for poverty measurement, a hegemonistic claim fervently endorsed by prominent contributors to the poverty debate.[34] A second round of

---

the poverty track of households. He concedes that the research techniques favoured by him do not yield the type of numerical estimates that statisticians more commonly utilize for their analyses. 'But measuring poverty more precisely (against some common global standard) and dealing with poverty more effectively (in some particular local setting) are not necessarily the same objective' (ibid., p. 535).

[32] The comment was made by A. Appadurai in the workshop and elaborated upon in his contribution to the volume edited by Bardhan, *Conversations Between Economists and Anthropologists*, pp. 252–82. T.N. Srinavasan responded in similar spirit, strongly criticizing non-quantitative techniques of data collection (ibid., pp. 238–49).

[33] The widespread good news about the poverty decline in the era of liberalization is, at times, difficult to credit to other than mere wishful thinking. Thus, Bhalla insists in a recent article that it is 'almost incontrovertible' that poverty in India has dropped from 45 per cent in 1983 to less than 15 per cent in 1999–2000. His imaginative deconstruction of NSS, moreover, inspires him to conclude that there has been no further rise in inequality, that the share of the poor in consumption has gone up, and that a growth in real wages of agricultural labourers—the poorest of the poor in India—has been a major factor in the trend towards more equity, a trend distilled by few others than him. As far as Gujarat is concerned, a state generally claimed to be at the apex of the liberalization and flexibilization package, I disagree with him wholeheartedly on all counts. S.S. Bhalla, 'Poverty Reduction in India: Towards a Better Understanding', in *Poverty Reduction in 1990s, Economic and Political Weekly*, vol. 38, no. 4, 25–31 January 2003, pp. 338–49.

[34] See, for instance, K. Sundaram and S.D. Tendulkar, 'NAS-NSS Estimates of Private Consumption for Poverty Estimation: A Further Comparative Examination', in *Poverty Reduction in 1990s, Economic and Political Weekly*, vol. 38, no. 4, 25–31 January 2003, pp. 376–84.

interaction across the disciplinary boundaries, hopefully more than a single workshop, might help to sort out differences in the definition and assessment of poverty at both micro and macro levels. Such an initiative could result in meaningful insights into how to make a living in the lower echelons of the globalized Indian economy and, more importantly still, to come forward with recommendations on what needs to be done to include those who are excluded from mainstream society.

# 4

# How to Find Space, Shop Around, and Move Up in the Informal Sector*

## THE INFORMAL WORLD OF INDUSTRIAL LABOUR

Geert de Neve's book is a fascinating case study of work and life in the informal sector of the industrial economy.[1] His ethnographic monograph is based on stints of solid and prolonged anthropological fieldwork carried out towards the end of the twentieth century in Bhavani and Kumarapalayam, located alongside the Cauvery river in the central cotton belt of Tamil Nadu. In the introductory chapter, de Neve situates the outcome of his research in the body of literature on the informal sector, made up of the large part of economic activity that is neither registered nor controlled by the state. His interest in this vast and highly diverse terrain of employment and labour relations is focused on textile producing workshops in two rather small but rapidly growing townships. While the author has investigated the different worksites in minute detail, he follows up his rich ethnographic analysis by discussing the role of kinship, religion, and state action in the sphere of relationships of production. These non-work domains, which are often neglected in reporting on the world of industrial labour, enable him to contextualize his findings in the wider cultural and political dynamics of the social fabric.

Class and caste, de Neve concludes, should no longer be seen as mutually exclusive forms of identity but as identities that are truly composite in nature. A second major argument concerns upward mobility as a

*Originally published as 'How to Find Space, Shop Around, and Move Up in the Informal Sector', *Economic and Political Weekly*, vol. 40, no. 25, 2005, pp. 2500–6.
[1] Geert de Neve, *The Everyday Politics of Labour: Working Lives in India's Informal Economy*, New Delhi: Social Science Press, 2005.

striking feature of the industrial activity under scrutiny. He concedes that labour is remarkably immobile between sectors of the informal economy and, even more so, between the informal and the formal sectors. However, climbing up in the hierarchy of employment within one and the same sector of informal textile production turns out to be anything but exceptional. The trajectory from casual worker via the intermediate position as a jobber or sub-contractor to owner or merchant–manufacturer is certainly not an easy one and, for those who manage to move up all the way, it usually takes several generations. Nevertheless, the success story, as told by de Neve, is undeniable and contrasts with the stereotyped notion of the informal sector workforce that may be floating around within or between sectors of activity but remains, by and large, stuck as a reserve army of labour at the bottom of the economy. The author finds that the most fortunate ones who have moved up to halfway positions and, finally, 'made it' as workshop owners, quickly transform their financial capital into human capital (through education) in order to free their children from industrial work altogether.[2] This, then, is the ultimate yardstick of success, to be able to qualify the next generation for work and income in the formal sector of the economy.

The second chapter elaborates on the different branches of textile industry that have emerged in the two locations of fieldwork. Of long standing are the small-scale handloom workplaces in Bhavani, with a history dating back to the first quarter of the nineteenth century, initially known for the manufacture of saris and bedsheets and were later, from the 1920s to 1930s onwards, converted to carpet weaving workshops. The units, 130 in all, are split up into three social layers: the owner–merchants; the master weavers, who are either owners or leaseholders of looms; and the ordinary workers, who have or do not have looms themselves. Members of the traditional weaving communities dominate among the owners and they also have the largest workshops, while most of the common weavers are relative newcomers to the industry. Loom-less weavers constitute the bottom class and many of them used to work as labourers in the surrounding villages before taking up their new occupation in the expanding textile industry of Bhavani town. Some of their workmates are the victims of downward mobility whose parents owned the tools of production, looms which were sold, lost, or simply too few to provide work for all the children. Nowadays, two-thirds of the total workforce hails from a single rural caste, with an occupational

[2] Ibid., p. 18.

record as agricultural labourers. They are placed low in the ritual hierarchy but not so low that there were barriers to their employment in the work sheds often attached to the owner's house.

The restructuring of production started in the first half of the twentieth century when, in response to the growing demand for carpets, the original owner–merchants built bigger workshops in which they installed more looms than they earlier controlled. Labourers belonging to the local weaving communities were in short supply and the search for new hands resulted in the influx of workers from the nearby countryside. The newcomers entered the occupation of weaving as wage workers, pure and simple, but after some decades, a section of them managed to acquire leasehold or ownership over looms and work sheds. Their upward mobility—first, as dependent weavers, who at least owned the looms they operated; next, as master weavers; and finally, as industrial producers in their own right—was the consequence of steadily increasing labour militancy to which the owner–merchants reacted by distancing themselves from their active involvement in the manufacturing process. Scale enlargement, thus, went together with a more complex organization of production, lengthening the distance between bottom and top of the enterprises.

A striking feature of this particular branch of textile industry is that women constitute two-thirds of the handloom workforce. The overwhelming presence of females nowadays follows on the exodus of male workers who were lured away by the much higher wages that the power-loom and dyeing workshops, set up in large numbers since the 1950s, started to pay.

## POWERLOOM PRODUCTION: THE PRODUCTION PROCESS

Powerloom production is mainly concentrated in the neighbouring town where it has replaced handloom weaving to the extent that the old technique has almost entirely vanished. The explosive growth of Kumarapalayam is directly related to the introduction of powerlooms in the second half of the twentieth century. Migrants from the immediate vicinity flocked to the burgeoning industrial centre to operate the mechanized equipment in a multitude of newly established workshops. Those who came from outside were not only labourers but also owners eager to invest their capital, coming out of agriculture, in the new business. De Neve found about 25,000 looms running, spread over an estimated 1,200 workshops (50 per cent more than the 800 registered in the municipal books). Ranging from five to fifty machines per unit,

## COLLECTIVE ACTION

Next on the agenda is the arsenal of weapons on which industrial labour in Bhavani and Kumarapalayam relies to resist the practices of exploitation and subordination by the owners of the small-scale workshops. It is again a complex issue and, moreover, highly specific to the politics of production in the three branches of textile industry on which de Neve has concentrated his investigations. He begins this part of his study by pointing out, in chapter 5, that the existence of a trade union since several decades in the artisanal handloom units is at odds with the notion of 'low classness' in the milieu of informal sector workers. Collectively organized resistance, the author suggests, should, therefore, not be proclaimed as a defining feature of formalized economic activity. He is, of course, quite right in arguing that it is often craft workers in smallscale workshops and not the industrial proletariat in large mills who are the most militant and best organized workers. Finally, de Neve comments on the marginal position of women, the majority of handloom workers, in the trade union and shows himself in agreement with the statement criticizing the working class as a masculine construct.

Long before the handloom workers set up their own union, the owners and employers took collective action to safeguard and promote their interests in an association of their own. The Bhavani Handloom Weavers Union dates back to 1942 but became active only in the mid-1970s to fight for the conversion of a yearly bonus in kind to one in cash. The memory of the struggle is still alive: 'Imagine, we only got a *vesthti* and a towel as bonus ... we were still treated as *kottadimai* (bonded labourers, slaves) in the villages who were also paid in cash'.[5] It was an important initiative in the pursuit of honour and dignity. A couple of years later a strike broke out—although business was booming and profits went up as never before, the rise in the paltry wages had remained stagnant— that ultimately resulted in the reluctant acceptance of the Labour Officer as the official mediator in the process of collective bargaining. It was a major victory of labour over capital, which brought the state in as a party to industrial relations, and one which motivated the owners to lease or sell their looms and work sheds to former workers and henceforth, capitalize on their mercantile role. The union's record is all the more impressive in view of the workman's background of its leadership. The frontmen were and remained weavers themselves. However, a major blemish on this proud record of organized collective

[5] Ibid., p. 146.

action is that women have been excluded from active involvement in union business although they are the backbone of the workforce and do not hesitate to make their presence felt inside the handloom sheds. But while women are accepted as union members, which most of them indeed are, their interests remain unrepresented. This explains why the wages they get are lower than those of male weavers.

Since the beginning of the twentieth century, the organization of production has drastically changed in the powerloom sector due to a process of proletarianization. While in the past the weavers were self-employed and independent artisans who worked at home and had their own tools of production, today, nine out of ten are dependent or loomless workers employed as daily wage earners by a master weaver or an owner in charge of the manufacture which goes on in a separate and larger work shed. In the transition to the new mode of production, they became increasingly aware of the state of exploitation to which they were exposed. What used to be 'customary' and part of a 'tradition' was no longer acceptable to them because they lost out in the restructuring of power between capital and labour. But, as de Neve astutely comments, a common experience of miserable work conditions is a necessary but not a sufficient condition for collective action to arise. What triggered off their joint assertion along class lines was charismatic leadership, a sense of unity based on caste membership (two-thirds of them hailed from the same community), and, last but not least, a shared occupational identity which made them stand in opposition to the owners of capital but which was, maybe in equal measure, fuelled by the much higher respectability granted to powerloom workers. Craft consciousness, de Neve argues, can manifest itself as class consciousness when it is based on shared experience of artisanship, a set of similar work conditions, and demarcation in a localized setting. This insight leads him to conclude that it need not really surprise us that the rise of such consciousness is seriously hampered or pre-empted by deskilling, mechanization, and strategies of sub-contracting and outsourcing that keep workers fragmented and separated from each other.

## CLASS CONSCIOUSNESS

The absence of collective action in the powerloom units, which is the substance of chapter 6, is an interesting elaboration of this point of view. When powerloom sector started to boom in the early 1970s, the owners, many of whom were also newcomers to this branch of industry, were badly in need of a stable workforce. To solve this problem, they decided to give a cash advance at the moment of recruitment. It was the same practice by which farm labour used to be fixed into debt bondage by the well-to-do peasantry. This similarity inspires de Neve to suggest that the new industrialists did not only come with their agricultural capital but also fell back on employment modalities already known to them: 'It seems that they are now transferring and reintroducing this previous model of agricultural labour recruitment into an expanding industrial and urban environment'.[6] Although the labour markets in the towns of Bhavani and Kumarapalayam became interconnected around this time and the skill required to operate the machines could be picked up fairly soon, the expansion went so fast that the growth of the powerloom workforce lagged behind the demand for it. Moreover, not all hands willing to join were acceptable to the bosses. Since the production was organized in small shops inside or attached to the house of employers, members of harijan castes remained excluded from the very beginning.

To keep their looms running seven days a week for twenty-four hours and to realize maximum profits, the new owners competed with each other by raising the *baki,* the monetary advance, to unprecedented levels. Initially, the amount paid seldom exceeded 100 rupees, but advances of 10,000–15,000 rupees were not exceptional when de Neve did his fieldwork. To lure workers away from the local producers, the up-and-coming entrepreneurs had no other choice than buying the labour power they needed for opening a workshop. The loom operators are not supposed to gradually work off their debt and the boss actually prefers them to keep the baki, which is interest free, as long as they are willing to work for him. But on termination of the contract, the labourers are obliged to return the total amount advanced to them. It basically means that they have to find another employer willing to put up the money required to release them. Asking for baki by mortgaging their labour power is the only way for loom operators to cope with the high cost of illnesses, festivals, and life-cycle rituals.

Do the workers feel bound, caught up in a 'voluntary' contract that they have to honour indefinitely? Compliance in dependency is exactly what the employers are willing to pay for. The loom operators, and also the middlemen who are likewise held in captivity, know this and describe themselves as being bonded in the same way the permanent farm servants (*pannaiyal*) were in the past. But, is bondage the correct term for their labour status? That term seems to be justified in at least some respects.

[6] Ibid., p. 175.

The new class of powerloom producers with a rural background does not refrain from using abusive language, harsh treatment, and even physical violence to coerce its workers to either return the advance received or to keep faithfully working for it. De Neve finds, however, that such attempts to control and discipline fail as much as they are successful. Workers these days have no respect anymore for their employers and also lack the work ethos which gave such high profits in the past, is the bitter complaint often vented by the producers. In their perception, 'the labour problem' that has arisen can be summed up as absence of commitment and loss of morality on the part of the workforce.

The employers have come to realize that the total amount of advances outstanding not only represents a huge waste of capital but also did not achieve what they wanted: a steady and docile workforce. The sharp competition going on among the producers means that loom operators can always try and tap another source of credit to which they then shift, for the time being, their loyalty. Who has trapped whom? Producers claim that they are the ones who are bonded. As one of them observed:

The situation now is such that the owners fear dismissing a labourer since they first of all might not be able to find another one, and secondly, if they want to dismiss the labourer, the latter might simply say: if you dismiss me now, I cannot pay back the advance.[7]

The politics of immobilization are an outright failure. The telling comment of de Neve is that the loom operators did not strike him as being unduly bothered by their attachment. This, he adds, is maybe precisely because they have devised their own strategies to escape from bondage. For sure, saving from their regular wages to get out of debt and be free from all bonds is, for most of them, next to impossible. Much more prevalent is transferring to another factory by finding an employer who is willing to settle accounts with the previous owner. There are various reasons for leaving the job: a dispute with the owner but also quarrels with fellow workers or the supervisor. Baki notwithstanding, labour is indeed footloose. The rotation of this proletariat around the powerloom sheds undermines the strategies which the employers apply to control and discipline their workforce.

## THE ROLE OF KINSHIP
Do the owners of production in this branch of textile industry succeed in tying down their labourers in lasting bonds of dependency? All said

[7] Ibid., p. 192.

with an average of barely twenty, the size is characteristic for this petty, commodity mode of production. Typical for this branch industry, also, is that production goes on day and night in two shifts of twelve hours each.

The work hierarchy is again spit up into three interconnected tiers with the owner–merchants at the top, in the middle the job workers as dependent producers—they lease or own the looms, often have their own workshops but produce under the control of owner–merchants—and at the bottom the loom operators hired by their direct employers as piece-rated wage labourers. In the early stage of this branch of industry, there were only owners who themselves supervised the workers. In striking similarity to the bosses of the handloom units, they relinquished their former role as employers when the size of the workshops as well as the number of looms started to increase. They encouraged, among their employees, the most trusted ones to take charge of the production process as sub-contractors. Master weavers in the handloom sector and job workers in the powerloom sector emerged as linkmen because the first batch of industrialists withdrew from the workfloor once they realized that more substantial profit was to be gained from the trade of yarn and finished cloth. In their case as well, it was, however, more than only a matter of business acumen and avoidance of risk caused by the fluctuating demand for the commodity. Getting out meant, above all, that they did not need to bother any longer about the labour problem. 'Many owner–merchants simply felt incapable of disciplining labour. They saw the transfer of production to job-workers or sub-contractors as the only way out and many admitted that getting rid of their looms was a great relief.'[3]

As has already been observed, a very high proportion of both owners and labourers happened to be newcomers to Kumarapalayam. Large numbers of well-to-do peasants belonging to a dominant caste in the region entered the powerloom industry as factory owners and, within a relatively short time, they managed to get control over one-fifth of the installed capacity. The powerloom operators are from a more humble background and many of them were employed as agricultural labourers in the villages around before they joined the footloose army of industrial workers in the urban informal sector. De Neve does not inform us how and by whom they were initially recruited, that is, before they managed to establish a bridgehead of their own which helped to

[3] Ibid., p. 68.

pave the way for the entry of 'latecomers' from their community. Is it too farfetched to suggest that the bosses for whom they used to work in the fields are the same ones who brought them to the factories? After all, as new industrial employers, these erstwhile peasant–owners had to find their way around in a rapidly expanding labour market and fresh hands from the rural hinterland were badly needed. Another telling detail is that in the transition from handloom to powerloom production, not all former owners had the capital needed to consolidate their privileged position. A sizable segment was left behind as loomless workers and their downward mobility forced them to accept employment as casual hands in workshops belonging to their more successful caste mates.

The enormous increase in textile production also gave a boost to dyeing as an ancillary industry. In the beginning, this activity was still an integral part of the powerloom sector but later on, weaving and dyeing were separated and new units were established for colouring the grey cloth. It is dirty, polluting, and demeaning work that, for this reason, is handled by members invariably belonging to low castes. Among them can be found members from the same community with a record as agricultural labourers who became handloom and powerloom workers. Making up not less than 70 per cent of the total workforce, they even dominate this new type of industrial employment. While the original owners have largely lost their interest in the dyeing workshops, the next generation of manager–producers started their occupational career as ordinary workers, then moved on to become sub-contractors, and are now, in increasing numbers, the proud owners of these industrial enterprises.

It will have become clear that the rapid expansion of the textile industry has led to a thorough restructuring of the relations of production in the handloom, powerloom, as well as dyeing units with, as a noticeable feature in all branches and at all levels, the arrival of newcomers. Women and children (at least for some specific tasks) form a growing part of the total workforce but it is only in the handloom sector that they outnumber male weavers. A new category of industrial entrepreneurs has bought their way into ownership (of powerlooms) with peasant capital. In addition to this type of inter-sectoral mobility, and even more remarkable than those success stories, are the many cases of ordinary workers who, from a modest background, managed to join the ranks of independent owner–producers. But the boundaries of upward mobility are neatly demarcated. De Neve comments:

None of the people I knew in Bhavani or Kumarapalayam had ever managed to obtain jobs which were secure in the formal sector of the economy, either locally or further away. Yet, both individuals, and castes as a whole, have been surprisingly successful in improving their position within the boundaries of the informal world.[4]

## EVERYDAY POLITICS

In the third chapter, the author discusses how everyday politics in the workshops got shaped and in doing so, he makes a distinction between relations of production and in production, a distinction that does not make much sense to me. In his analysis of the interaction between and among workers on the one hand, and managers–owners, on the other hand, de Neve shows how class, gender, and caste relate to each other on the shop floor. It comes as no surprise that the division of labour in all branches of the textile industry is quite simple. Still, skill formation is required and is achieved, as in nearly all sectors of the informal economy, by training on the job. Learning by doing, in the shadow of experienced relatives, neighbours, or friends, does not take longer than a couple of months. In the handlooms, wages are paid at the end of each and every day and since these are on piece rate, the pace of work increases when this moment draws nearer. The actual payment is not restricted to a cash transaction but is livened up by negotiations. The weavers confront their boss in loud voice with their life of misery and extol on the merits of their boss as a generous man. The role of the employer as moneylender and the resulting financial dependency on him underscore his authority in the workplace. These forms of patronage, de Neve says, belong to the essence of capitalist production itself and should not be considered as the remnants of a feudal type of labour relations. The flight of men from this manufacture has left behind a workforce that is predominantly female and, as far as the employers are concerned, this trend will further continue. They find that women are more hardworking, less troublesome, and more committed then men, now brandished by the owners as lazy and undisciplined.

The work process in the powerloom units, as already noticed, has become more complex with the appearance of *maistries* as intermediaries. Although instructed to supervise the workers, the owners have not delegated much real power to these linkmen and their main role is to ensure that the looms are running continuously. The intermediate role

[4] Ibid., p. 80.

is an uneasy one. Coming from the ranks is good enough reason to side with the workers but the man-in-between is supposed to represent and promote the owner's interests. The solution found for this ambiguity is to keep a low profile in the management sphere and to stress technical competence, that is, the ability to handle machines rather than their operators. The room for manoeuvre afforded to middlemen is highly context specific with, as major variables—seasonality versus perennial production, recruitment of either local or migrant workers, and management practices that do or do not stretch all the way to the work floor. Surely, the jobber remains a fascinating figure in the industrial landscape. In the process of formalization, he (yes, with rare exceptions they are men) has been either co-opted in the managerial hierarchy or driven back into the ranks. But with the changing of the tide, the drift towards informalization of economic activity, brokers who know how to bridge demand for labour and supply of employment are of pivotal importance.

How does labour resist and challenge the control and discipline to which they are exposed? In the first place, by trying to maximize a sense of comradeship in the workshop. As the title of chapter 4, 'Here we can be jolly', demonstrates, the solidarity that cements the day-to-day relationships between the workers is expressed in joking and teasing. While women are expected to behave with strict modesty in public space, they 'play the game' in the sheds with remarkable freedom. They dare to criticize and ridicule men and do not shy back from sexual innuendo, thereby signalling the shift in the gender balance of power that has been going on inside the sheds. The relaxed atmosphere colouring the interaction among workers is underscored by the use of kinship terminology. But, de Neve warns, in addition to feelings of intimacy and reciprocity, such language of affinity can also express relations of authority and hierarchy. Social interaction is much more difficult to maintain in the powerloom units if only because the incessant noise and the pace of work—the looms dictating the drive of men rather than the other way around—make it difficult for the operators to communicate, other than by gestures and shouting. De Neve does not forget to mention the other side of sociability on the shop floor. The pent-up frustration about the control and discipline imposed from above seeks an outlet in lateral antagonism or downright victimization of the most vulnerable ones who lack all power to resist. What is experienced as favouritism or, conversely, boss-pleasing behaviour can lead to a breakdown of solidarity, erupting in quarrels and open fights among workmates.

this process of restructuring, caste associations are of pivotal importance and the author situates this phenomenon within the framework of civil society. It is a postscript as he himself observes and, indeed, what then follows is much too short to do justice to the complexity of the issue. Civil society is usually understood as the public sphere of joint action, solidified in various forms of association and institutions, in which individuals engage voluntarily. De Neve points out that the concept is often discussed in normative terms and, essentially, as the realm of non-government organizations trying to promote development for the underprivileged, social upliftment, and good governance. Disillusionment with ineffective and biased state performance, he warns, has led to the facile assumption that caste associations, political parties, and other forms of civil activity per se result in more democracy, freedom, and equality. We are reminded that so-called civil society initiatives are all too often motivated by caste, sectional, and business interests. Giving in to such lobbies may well lead to a reproduction and consolidation of inequalities and social boundaries that remain parochial. His reference in that context to literature demonstrating the inability of civil society to curb practices of corruption that harm the poor is well taken.

In the final chapter, de Neve brings together the major arguments presented in the course of his study, and in highlighting them, I shall give my own comments. In the first place, the author quite rightly points out that informal industrial sectors are mushrooming not only as a consequence of deindustrialization but, to a large extent, also in response to rising consumption demand and burgeoning export markets. He fails to explain, however, why this enormous expansion has been going on outside the formal economic sector. The closing down of large-scale mills is the direct outcome of industrial policies favouring petty commodity production and employment regimes that enabled workshop owners to disregard the protection and rights of labour which, on the basis of collective action, had become standard practice in the formal sector. The study reads as a success story of informality, a confirmation of what lately has become the received wisdom: that informalization of production and employment is the solution to rather than the problem of economic development. All said and done, de Neve has strong empirical evidence to back up his critical reappraisal of stereotyped notions about the informal economy.

I have no qualms about his challenge of statements made that the technology applied is invariably poor, that mechanical knowledge is low, and that skill levels are adequate for the mode of production. At the same time, I am more sceptical about the merits and quality of the level of skills obtained on the job and wonder if mere informal training will ultimately not impact negatively on production and productivity. Further, the carefully recorded and documented gains made by many, owners as well as workers, are persuasive in correcting the idea of the informal sector as a circuit of work and labour with little or no prospect for improvement. Finally, de Neve argues that the widely shared notion of 'low classness' is untenable and needs to be revised in view of the collective action which the handloom weavers in Bhavani were able to resort to with success. He resolutely maintains that fragmentation and segmentation notwithstanding, resistance to exploitation does emanate, also, from primordial types of social awareness and, moreover, can be discerned as well in more individualized counterstrategies to domination. Subaltern consciousness and agency are, thus, not necessarily related in any fixed or obvious way. Still, I would not go as far as de Neve does by suggesting that collective action and individualized strategies are basically two sides of the same coin and should be clubbed under a single umbrella as acts of resistance, an arsenal of weapons from which workers take their pick for reasons of their own. In my opinion, agency then is an article of faith that hardly needs further empirical substantiation. An assessment in these terms would make it possible to refer to nearly all instances of silence, avoidance, and clientelist behaviour as shrewdly constructed practices of contest. In similar vein, caste and class can indeed be seen as mutually constitutive forms of social identity. I am puzzled, however, by the author's conviction that at least among the weavers in the handloom industry of Bhavani town, caste solidarity has facilitated the growth of class awareness. I only need to repeat his personal reservation about the exclusion of female workers, constrained in their public behaviour by a puritan caste code, from the union's activity. More acceptable from my point of view is the conclusion that kinship and caste (and I would add economic status) are neither necessarily uniting nor necessarily dividing principles of social action and identity.

## UPWARDLY MOBILE

De Neve discusses his findings in three branches of the textile industry which have their own rationale as far as everyday labour politics are concerned: trade unionism, debt bondage, or practices and discourses of kinship. The variations, I would like to submit, are too neatly demarcated in separate settings, each with its own model of bargaining: respectively, handloom establishments, powerloom workshops, and dyeing units.

Expression of horizontal solidarity does not exclude acknowledgement of vertical dependence (example, handloom weavers addressing their employer in the language of patronage) and the other way around (namely, debt-bonded powerloom operators who refuse to behave as a captive workforce unwilling to join hands). Similarly, joint and personalized strategies of interest representation are not so easy to disentangle. To end my critical remarks on the assertion (or not) of solidarity and consciousness, I do believe that lack of sustained and organized resistance is characteristic for 'low classness'. But this does not mean a total absence of collective action as the frequently signalled appeal to refuse to work or the pressure to slow down the pace of production demonstrates. Unfortunately, de Neve has omitted to pay attention to the many but unregistered wildcat strikes—of short duration, highly localized, and 'spontaneous' in nature—which are typical for labour militancy in the informal sector milieu.

The study persuasively opposes the notion of the informal sector workforce as a huge reserve army stuck at the bottom of the economy and roaming around in desperate search of jobs without much hope to get out of the misery that has always been their fate. De Neve strongly emphasizes that for many more people, life and work in the informal sector has become better than it used to be. There is ground for optimism but what the author underlines as well is that absence of permanent and secure jobs giving rise to bouts of unemployment, together with low pay rates, means that a very large segment of the workers continue to live in never ending dependency and dire poverty. A case in point is the condition of the powerloom operators who are the best paid in the textile industry. The politics of baki, the practice to accept a cash advance at the moment of recruitment that is equal to six or more monthly wages, keeps them tied to their boss. But it is the only way for them to pay for the cost of life-cycle events, festivals, and health care. They are driven into debt because most families, de Neve writes, do not succeed in making ends meet. Borrowing on these occasions from their kin is next to impossible because most relatives are equally poor. I agree with the author that what we have here is not the kind of debt bondage as it existed in the past. In his observation, powerloom workers have an instrumental view about such credit arrangements. It seems to come close to what I myself have called neo-bondage, that is, impersonal and short-term bonds of imposed immobility which do not stretch beyond the sphere of work and which in the mindset of the labourer do not entrap him forever at the worksite. However, de Neve is right in concluding that baki represents an institutional form of bondage. To escape from one boss is possible but, for all practical purposes, only if this act of defiance is followed by reattachment to another one. Entrapment, he argues, seems to be as much the outcome of poverty as dictated by the choice of the worker to bank on the unwillingness of his employer to dismiss him when the debt amount is too high.

## ABSENCE OF THE STATE

I have more problems with the decision de Neve took not to go into the relationship between the state and the workers because of a lack of direct contact between these actors. In this part of the study, the emphasis is exclusively on the representations and perceptions of the owners of production and managers in their busy interaction with government officials. The shift in the focus away from the workers to employers and sub-contractors is a regrettable one in the sense that de Neve has not problematized the non-presence of the state in the landscape of informal sector labour. This has not always been the case. As a matter of fact, the author reports in his study how in the trade union movement which came up in the handloom industry—the only clear and also successful example of classical class action found by him—collective bargaining came about with the mediation of the labour officer. Since the early 1980s, this figure seems to have faded away or even totally disappeared. Although a broad range of government inspectors make frequent 'raids' on informal industrial establishments, their task does not include monitoring of work conditions or employment modalities. The remarkable lack of state action in the implementation of labour regulations and laws that do exist, until today, also for the multitude of informal sector workers—on minimum wages, labour migration, practices of sub-contracting, etc.—should have inspired de Neve to elaborate on this issue instead of totally neglecting it. On the other hand, I warmly welcome in the monograph, the discussion at length of the diversity of tactics and strategies followed by both workers and owners in the promotion of their interests. His detailed narrative succeeds in demonstrating that the complexities of the informal sector can be further unravelled by the structural divide between owners or controllers of means of production and the vast armies which are in their casual as well as intermittent employ. De Neve has decided not to raise the policy relevance of all this.

The reservations made so far do not detract from a major conclusion which de Neve has brought to the forefront in his book: the scope and done, no, says de Neve, but the rider he adds is an important one: 'the powerloom workers appear successful in escaping individual owners whom they do not like, yet fail to escape structures of subordination that keep them tied to the employers as a group'.[8] Rather than in collective action, labour resistance in the powerloom sector remains expressed in more indirect and individualized ways. Can we really conclude, as the author does, that the absence of jointness has resulted in stagnation in the growth of a proletarian consciousness? Indeed, the nature of the work process itself testifies to the fragmentation rather than the coming together of workers in collective action. But, if overt and organized acts of solidarity are few and far between, does it really mean that the assertion of rights of labour is left to individual spontaneity? In my view, the weapons of the weak are more sophisticated than that.

In chapter 7, de Neve quite rightly sets out to rectify the 'black box' treatment of culture in many studies of industrial labour and work by drawing attention to the role of kinship in structuring relations of employment. His case in point is the appeal made by factory owners to family morality to instil commitment and discipline in the workers they have recruited. The focus here is on the yam dyeing enterprises that developed as an ancillary industry around the handloom and powerloom units in the area of research. The work process in these manufacturing establishments is very erratic due to sharp fluctuations in the demand for the yam. The employers maintain a small core of regular workers who help in the recruitment of temporary hands whenever there is a need for them. The number of working days is season specific and even then, shows an enormous variation. An average of about a fortnight per month can actually go down to barely more than one week. The owners' strategy to hire and lay-off labour instantly has to be understood against the background of an intermittent and unpredictable pattern of production.

The way in which employers attempt to overcome the labour problems caused by the uneven rhythm of production is to assuage their on-and-off workers that their help is much appreciated. They tell them that like good relatives it is their duty to turn up whenever their presence is required and to work according to the need of the moment for a few hours only or deep into the night. 'We are all kinsmen', is how the bosses try to create an atmosphere of mutual dependency and reciprocity. Relatedness goes beyond the circle of blood relatives and

---

[8] Ibid., p. 200.

also includes forms of adoptive relations and fictive kinship stretching to friends, neighbours, and caste mates. Why are employers so keen to downplay the contractual side of employment and pretend that their workers are like members of their family? They do this because such phraseology enables them to invoke kinship morality with its implied qualities of intimacy, trust, and reliability. It is in that language which combines hierarchy with closeness that they ask their core hands to be at their beck and call, to mobilize additional helpers on busy days, and to accept being laid off in times of slackness.

Clearly, the workers do not accept the jargon of affinity and friend-ship. When publicly invited to do so, they are apt to react to such appeals with embarrassment, silence, or muted consent at best. Playing along with the boss, at least not openly resisting him, is usually a safe bet. Obligation and duty are, however, not always based on fictitious closeness. In this branch of small-scale industry, the owners are from the same social background as their workers and ties of real kinship are, therefore, not exceptional at all. Even then, brothers or cousins do not hesitate to shift their loyalty to another employer either because he provides more regular employment or offers higher wages and better work conditions. The owners worry about the footloose behaviour of workers but fail in their strategy to realize indefinite labour commit-ment by resorting to a morality of relatedness. Their eagerness to present relations in these terms stands in sharp contrast to their inability to offer anything more than short-term and highly erratic employment. Still, it is important not to antagonize the current boss and to honour bonds of kinship with him, real or constructed, since upwardly mobile workers may need his support to establish their own petty workshop.

## PUBLIC BENEVOLENCE

'Festivals, patronage and community', is the title of chapter 8 in which de Neve discusses how relations shaped inside the workshops extend into the neigbourhood and town. And the other way around of course, one would immediately add. Festivals held in Kumarapalayam and Bhavani have an integrative function. Both workers and employers partake in the same celebrations and, in doing so, create a community atmosphere. But such occasions also give rise to public display of gains made on the economic ladder. The festivities are, therefore, arenas of dispute since it is during these events that the new class of industrial producers competes as 'big men' with each other and with the older established merchants–traders for prestige and power. In the opinion

of the author, the mixed social composition of workforce and owners has contributed to the formation of a community which transcends the boundaries of caste and class. The ritual roles specified in accordance with caste hierarchy are being reshuffled and upward mobility leads to conspicuous spending on festivals in which all are supposed to participate because they belong to the same collectivity.

Economic advancement and political empowerment have dignified the social status of erstwhile agricultural labourers who, in the past few decades, have managed to become industrial workers, sub-contractors, and producers. It is but natural that they now are eager to upgrade themselves in the ritual ranking as well. What I find rather remarkable is that the accumulated wealth is not only spent on individual comfort but also on schools, hospitals, and other welfare institutions. Such investments in the common good, de Neve observes, are inspired by a morally felt duty to share on the part of a few of the most prosperous and powerful textile magnates. These acts of public benevolence, of course, stand them also in good stead as generous patrons in their business. They face fewer problems in attracting skilled weavers and their reputation as good employers helps them in the disciplining and control of workforce. De Neve claims that the corporate strategy of industrialists is to promote a sense of community that encompasses the whole town.[9] I am not convinced that what he describes is an instance of civic behaviour that knows no boundaries and is all inclusive. Earlier in this chapter, he speaks of a strong bias against women in the religious sphere and this gendered exclusion, as demonstrated in other sections of the book, has other dimensions as well. His claim to the construction of a community identity seems to be further undermined by the segregation of harijans not only in the workshops but also from other than a stigmatized participation in religious festivals and their exclusion from public space in general.

'Let's unite around wages and not caste!', is the catchy title of chapter 9. The first part is an elaboration on the perception the workshop owners and sub-contractors have about the state. The mass of weavers and dyers do not figure in this narrative since they lack direct interaction with official agencies, de Neve adds. His unequivocal statement contrasts with the promise made in the introduction to investigate labour politics and workers' consciousness in the informal sector within a much wider context and to include state action in the analysis. I shall come

[9] Ibid., p. 272.

back to this shift in focus, from labour at large to industrialists, in my later comments. The owners and managers of the textile industry consider the government bureaucracy to be counterproductive to their interests. De Neve shows how the 'big men' in town avoid, stall, and otherwise sabotage all attempts to regulate business and clean up the environment because, according to them, such measures are inspired by caste discrimination. They complain about the rigid enforcement of regulations as demonstrations of official ill will because they do not fit the bill of respectability. Bribing government agents and committing fraud are then the only solution to fight what, in their perception, is undue interference in their private domain and, for that reason, morally wrong. The resentment has not led to an ideological rejection of state interference, nor to sustained forms of militant protest and the author sums up his comments with the mild conclusion that the relationship with the state is more one of miscommunication than of hostility. I think that more is at stake than just that.

The owners of production, and also the sub-contractors, have organized themselves by setting up associations for the representation of their interests. To overcome the caste bias which has remained a strong feature in promoting collective action, the leader of one of these associations appealed to unite, not around *jati* (caste) but around *kuli* (piece rates). What he really meant to say was that producers should team up and establish a common front when facing demands for higher wages. The spokesmen of class unity perceive jati as the main problem. Quite rightly so, since through the establishment of associations, corporate caste identities are consolidated and antagonisms along these lines of segmentation reinforced. The caste content of public behaviour continues to feed rivalry and to undo solidarities of class. In sum, joint action revolves around the interests of social groups based upon primordial loyalties that are the organizing principle of associations with guild-like characteristics. Thus, caste and class remain separated as well as overlapping zones of collective identity but as opposite ends of structuring work and life, they become intertwined in their day-to-day operation.

## CIVIL SOCIETY

Caste, however, is not what it used to be. In the second part of this chapter, de Neve explains how the traditional meaning of caste has been transformed. What used to be hierarchically ranked groups are increasingly blocks in competition with each other along lines of interaction that articulate political power more than ritual status. In for upward mobility in the informal sector ᴄ the economy. In view of the rich empirical evidence, this important ᴵding cannot so easily be gainsaid. Large numbers of farms servants as well as their erstwhile masters have managed to find access to the textile industry in the rapidly growing towns—towns of Bhavani and Kumarapalayam. These migrants from the rural hinterland are much better off than before. Besides, the well-to-do peasants often brought with them capital taken out of the agricultural economy to set up powerloom units of their own. Their eagerness to invest in industrial production shows that expansion of informal-sector activity is possible on the basis of surplus that is already there and need not be extracted from other sources. An even more impressive success story is the manner in which, from the rank of ordinary workers, a substantial minority has moved up in the work hierarchy. They first were appointed to intermediate positions such as master weavers and supervisors and next, made themselves semi-independent as job workers and sub-contractors before rising to the top by taking over the ownership of the same or another workshop. Such cases ranging from minor to major upward mobility are not few but many.

## DOWNWARD MOBILITY

I accept all this good news and the optimism shining through it but would like to draw attention to the reverse side of the same phenomenon on which de Neve is much less informative: downward mobility. In the first place: the workshops in the locations of fieldwork are booming, last but not least, because of the collapse of textile industry in the formal sector of the economy. De Neve does not forget to mention this economic and social drama (incorrectly discussed by him as deindustrialization). But while his praise for the vitality and dynamism of petty commodity production is understandable, the other side of the coin is that these small-town niches creating employment and profits for newcomers opened up because of the policy of informalization in which an established class of industrial workers lost their formal sector job, which included time-rated wages, and their dignified existence. In the second place, there are not only winners but also losers in the petty workshops. Self-employment, which used to dominate in the handloom shops, was replaced by a new form of production in which the independent weavers were squeezed out, sometimes also because of economic adversity or misfortune. Many more, however, seem to have lost their looms to bigger owners. They either became loomless workers in the same branch of industry or transferred themselves to the bottom of the powerloom sector. Also, in that branch of industry, not all artisans could afford to buy new looms, the author tells us in passing, and were forced to seek employment with one of their fellow caste members. In the third place, excluded from chances for upward mobility were, of course, the female workers and also, the harijans who, if at all tolerated on the workfloor, had to keep a low profile and did not qualify for appointment to the lower managerial ranks. Finally, there must have been movement of workers who climbed up the ladder but failed in their supervisory post or who went bankrupt as job workers. Such up-and-down cases are not discussed at all.

In the final balance, I have much praise for de Neve's study. His monograph is a fine contribution on a subject which, as he himself comments, still belongs to the least researched part of India's economy. The 'thick description' makes for interesting reading, the findings and the framework in which these are interpreted shed new light on a variety of issues that are central to the debate on how to understand and policy-wise handle 'the informal sector'. The book is well produced with tables, figures, maps, and illustrations by a rather new publishing house specializing on social science literature. It is a new addition to an already impressive series of publications.

# 5

# Slumlands*

Our epoch is witnessing a world-historic shift in human habitat: for the first time, more than half the global population will soon be city dwellers, in one form or another. The small-scale settlements that have been the cradle of peasant work and life for many thousands of years—the myriad villages, compact or dispersed, spread out across the countryside—are no longer home to the majority of mankind. The massive expulsion of labour from agriculture, accelerating over the last half century, has been accompanied by an exodus from the villages. At present, 3.2 billion people are congregated in towns and cities. Their number is expected to grow to 10 billion in the middle of this century. This gigantic shift is mainly taking place in the southern zones of our planet: within the next two decades, metropoles such as Jakarta, Dhaka, Karachi, Shanghai, or Mumbai will each have 25 million inhabitants or more.

Urbanization is not, of course, a new phenomenon. The push out of agriculture and the trek from the countryside are well-known themes in nineteenth and twentieth century western history. Up to the mid-twentieth century, however, that migration resulted—if not immediately, then within a relatively short space of time—in regularized employment in the mills, docks, construction industry, public-sector enterprises, or other large-scale and labour-intensive worksites, or else, in domestic service. Another route out of village life was through emigration to countries that were still struggling with under-population. Economic refugees fleeing from Europe were welcomed as colonists in these settler states, reputed for their perseverance and enterprising spirit.

* Originally published as 'Slumlands', *New Left Review*, vol. 40, July–August 2007, pp. 141–8.

They brought to these 'empty' territories the labour power required to valorize vast new tracts of natural resources. Up to thirty years ago, the assumption was that this transformation from a rural–agrarian to an urban–industrial mode of production would be duplicated in the 'backward' parts of the world. But the notion of industrialization as the handmaiden of urbanization is no longer tenable. This goes a long way to explain why huge numbers of the new arrivals to the city are slum dwellers, and are likely to remain so throughout their lives.

How and why this is happening is the story graphically told in Mike Davis's new book, *Planet of Slums*.[1] While many case studies have described what it means to reside in a *favela, basti, kampung, gecekondu*, or *bidonville*, Davis provides a properly global portrait, setting such shanty towns in comparative perspective. And, whereas urban specialists have focused on questions of space and land use in their discussions of slums, and developmentalists on the issue of their 'informal' economies, *Planet of Slums* commands our attention as a broader historical synthesis of the two. Drawing on the 'global audit' provided by the 2003 United Nations (UN) *Challenge of the Slums* report, Davis outlines the scale of world urban poverty today: Mumbai, with 10–12 million squatters and tenement dwellers, is the global capital of slums, followed by Mexico City and Dhaka, with slum populations of 9 or 10 million, and then, Lagos, Cairo, Karachi, Kinshasa–Brazzaville, Sao Paolo, Shanghai, and Delhi, with around 7 million each. If the largest mega slums—contiguous zones of urban poverty—are in Latin America (an estimated 4 million living in Ciudad Nezahualcoyotl, Chalco, Iztapalapa, and other southeastern *municipio*s of Mexico City; over 2 million in the Caracas shanty town of Libertador, or the EI Sur and Ciudad Bolivar districts of Bogota), the Middle East has Baghdad's Sadr City (1.5 million) and Gaza (1.3 million), while the corrugated iron shacks of Cité Soleil, in Port-au-Prince, and Kinshasa's Masina district, each hold half a million souls. India has nearly 160 million slum dwellers, and China over 190 million. In Nigeria, Pakistan, Bangladesh, Tanzania, Ethiopia, and Sudan, over 70 per cent of the urban population lives in slums.

The laudable ambition of *Planet of Slums* is to propose a historical overview of the global pattern of these settlements; one that will provide, as Davis puts it, a periodization of the principal trends and water-sheds in the urbanization of world poverty in the post-war period. Broadly speaking, he discerns an initial acceleration of Third World

[1] Mike Davis, *Planet of Slums*, London and New York: Verso, 2006.

urbanization in the 1950s and 1960s, with the post-independence lifting of colonial pass laws (especially in sub-Saharan Africa), the 'push' of civil war and insurgency (Latin America, Algeria, post-partition India, Southeast Asia), and the 'pull' of employment opportunities offered by import substitution industrialization policies (Latin America, South Korea, Taiwan). Davis documents what he terms the 'treason' of Third World states in failing to provide housing for their new urban workers, as post-independence governments (in Africa and South Asia) or dictatorships (in Latin America) abdicated responsibility for the poor to rule in the interests of local elites. But the 'Big Bang' of urban poverty comes after 1975, with the imposition of International Monetary Fund (IMF)–World Bank Structural Adjustment Programmes (SAPs) which devastated rural smallholders by eliminating subsidies and pushing them to sink, or swim, in global commodity markets dominated by heavily subsidized First World agribusiness. At the same time, the SAPs enforced privatization, removal of import controls, and ruthless downsizing in the public sector. And they were accompanied by the 1976 switch of IMF–World Bank policies—under the joint influence of Robert McNamara and former anarchist–urbanist John Turner—to 'self-help' slum improvement schemes in place of new house building, representing, in Davis's words, 'a massive downsizing of entitlement'[2], which soon hardened into neo-liberal anti-statist orthodoxy. The net result has been a gigantic increase in urbanization decoupled from industrialization, even from development per se.

As Davis documents, the relentless waves of *homines novi* pouring into the cities are far in excess of the demand for their labour. The combination of lack of work plus ultra-low wages leaves this foot-slogging infantry of the global economy deprived of the basic means of human subsistence. One cannot enter the colonies populated by these people in Latin America, Africa, and Asia without being struck by the acute poverty that prevails there. Increasingly, today's slums are not to be found in the inner cities, as used to be the case in the West, but are situated on their outskirts, in an extensive belt where urban zones gradually give way to the surrounding countryside. This in-between landscape can also be found in Eastern Europe, where the Second World has been dissolved within the Third—with the proviso that the eclipse of the 'post-capitalist countries' has, by definition, also pre-empted the concept of a Third World. One consequence of this is the urgent

[2] Ibid.

need to revise the developmentalist jargon that was en vogue during the second half of the twentieth century; that short era has disappeared, without leaving a lasting imprint behind. Although the lobby of non-governmental organizations (NGOs) continues to advocate the ideals of development, this form of private initiative has often, under the guise of empowerment, aided and abetted the surrender of their constituency to free market forces.

In official literature, such as the UN *Challenge of the Slums* report cited by Davis, it is the physical features rather than the socio-economic dimensions of slums that are foregrounded. In this definition, a slum is an overcrowded settlement consisting of poor, informal housing with inadequate access to safe water and sanitation, an intolerably high density of habitation, and an absence of drainage, levelled roads, and waste removal. Title deeds to land plots, and whatever is built on them, are non-existent. Tenements are usually self-built in successive stages, resulting in a motley collection of properties, varied in size and shape, which often serve a double purpose as living space and worksite, without neat demarcation of either sphere. The blurred nature of these flimsy constructions is underscored by their materials: crude bricks; corrugated iron; scrap, wood, cement, or mud blocks; flattened tin plates; plastic or canvas cloth; straw, asbestos sheets, gunny sacks, cardboard; and other waste products, recycled for essentially unsustainable usage.

Nor are the occupants of such shacks necessarily their owners. Slumlords–moneylenders, pawnbrokers, shopkeepers, policemen, low-ranking officials, traders in drink and drugs, bucket-shop or gambling operators, vehicle owners, or gang bosses rent out the housing space they have appropriated; not all slum dwellers are impoverished. Rather, capital is generated by raising legal and illegal dues from the poor. Following these flows of labour and capital makes it clear that the slums are not a separate circuit of production, distribution, and consumption, but are well connected—if subservient—to mainstream economic practices. At the same time, criminality of all sorts is rampant, originating both inside and outside the slums, but with their inhabitants largely playing the role of victims rather than perpetrators. To live and work in poverty entails a systematic exposure to violence. The hierarchy of deprivation has its parallel in the gradations of vulnerability: topping both lists are women, children, the elderly, the chronically ill, and the disabled.

The life cycle of a slum begins with the arrival of the first batch of squatters. If these pioneers are not instantly thrown out, their number soon increases, and their makeshift shades are gradually upgraded to somewhat better forms of shelter. Davis sketches a typology: urban core or peripheral, informal or formalized settlement; for what follows, once the squatters are established, are efforts to regulate their homes. It may take many years but, in the end, city authorities will usually acquiesce in the existence of the settlement and hand out papers saying so; generally in exchange for votes, and without any reciprocal obligation to provide basic facilities such as drinking water, access roads, or electricity, let alone public health or schooling. As Davis documents in his chapter, 'Haussmann in the Tropics', evictions can still occur, often justified by the argument that the space occupied is needed for formal urban expansion, or simply as a show of brute force: the removal of people who appear a nuisance to mainstream city perceptions or whose presence keeps land prices low. Building contractors, in collusion with the strong arm of the state, drive through a *mise-en-valeur* operation, their bulldozers demolishing in a morning what many hands had painstakingly constructed over months or years. Those who are driven out have to start all over again somewhere else.

The ceaseless rotation of this footloose proletariat in the nowhere land between city and countryside makes it hard to produce reliable estimates of the slum population. Official statistics deliberately undercount the number of squatters trying to carve out a niche in these hermaphroditic zones—desakotas in Indonesian. Governments try to keep the teeming mass out of public view, if only to pre-empt future claims of rights in the wake of settlement registration, while established urban property owners aggressively collude in the non-acceptance of these hordes of migrants as citizens. Census figures, therefore, need to be read as conservative appraisals. Yet, the slum population estimates cited earlier may be set in comparative perspective: while in the developed regions of the world, a mere 6 per cent of the urban population are slum dwellers, this proportion escalates to more than three-quarters of all urban inhabitants in what are still, despite all evidence, known as 'developing' countries. The cancer of slums is spreading even more rapidly than the growth of cities.

While citing the effects of SAPs, Davis does not elaborate on the crisis of the countryside and the reasons why increasing numbers of people are unable to sustain a rural way of life. Arguably, the fortunate few who manage to find a fixed abode and regular, long-term work are genuinely better off in the city's mega slums. The lot of the millions roaming in the twilight zone where the countryside ends and the city begins, is more debatable. In addition to these floaters or drifters of the extended urban periphery, who have left but not arrived, there are even more who cannot be defined as one-way migrants, a term which suggests at least an extended departure from the countryside. Doing fieldwork, both in Java and in Gujarat, I was struck by the phenomenon of ongoing labour circulation, which pulls people out of their rural habitat for part of the year but pushes them back again when the seasonal employment comes to an end. This pattern of constant movement to and fro has become an important feature of the informal economy. The upshot is that the nowhere landscape is populated with nowhere people, who are absorbed and expelled again, according to the need of the moment. A further development has been the rapid rise in village slums, inhabited by a landless underclass that has become redundant in the agricultural economy but lacks the cash and the contacts to venture outside its own segregated locality. This is an urgent problem, but one in which policymakers and politicians have no interest whatsoever. They prefer to keep preaching the UN's 'millennium goal' of cutting poverty by half within fifteen years, despite the fact that seven years have already elapsed since the mission statement was adopted with the trends all moving in the wrong direction.

How, then, do slum dwellers support themselves? Davis tackles this issue by analysing labour relations and conditions in the 'informal economy'. This container concept, which applies to roughly four-fifths of the total workforce, was coined in the early 1970s to point out that the masses of peasants flooding into the cities are not employed in factories or other structured and regulated workplaces, but make their living from a wide range of unskilled and low-paid casual jobs without being able to claim any form of security or protection. They obtain occasional work either as waged labourers or in self-employment: some at home, others tramping the streets, or locked in small-scale sweatshops. Their labour power is disseminated across all sectors of the economy: industry and crafts, petty trade and transport, construction and services, or a combination of all these. Sometimes they own their tools or other means of production, sometimes these are hired out to them, or provided by employers or their agents. It is a form of organization lauded by the apostles of market fundamentalism as the best strategy for poverty alleviation. In the writings of Hernando de Soto and others, the huge masses of informal sector workers are characterized as petty entrepreneurs, excluded from the supply of formal credit as a consequence of the unregistered nature of whatever property they own. Microcredit extended to them by banks on commercial terms would, according to this line of reasoning, enable them to increase their productivity and thus, help them to get out of their precarious existence.[3]

It is a Baron von Münchhausen model of self-upliftment, as Davis phrased it, and he rejects this solution as a myth, created and propagated by the World Bank and its protagonists to hold the have-nots accountable for the misery in which they continue to live and work. Large segments of informal sector workers constitute a reserve army of labour, hired and fired at will. The conditions of employment are not negotiable. They include an extreme extension of the working day, alternating with long and erratic periods of unemployment; dragooning children and the aged into the labour process; the subjugation of women and other dependants to the diktat of the head of the household, all for the lowest possible remuneration. It is, in short, a regime of relentless flexibilization from which, in line with neo-liberal doctrine, public authority has disappeared as a regulatory force and given up even the fiction of balancing the interests of capital and labour. Privatization and the retreat of the state have evacuated the public sphere, which used to offer some counterweight to the unbridled discipline of the market.

In what ways do the slum dwellers themselves articulate and assert their interests? The traditional imagery, after all, is of slums as smelting volcanoes waiting to erupt. There are indeed myriad streams of resistance, as Davis writes, but a preliminary survey shows that these do not amount to much. Davis correctly points out that slum populations support a bewildering variety of responses to structural neglect and deprivation, ranging from charismatic churches and prophetic cults to ethnic militias, street gangs, neo-liberal NGOs, and revolutionary social movements. The ranks of the slum dwellers are not closed but divided along lines of religion, caste, clan, and tribe, or plain regional identities. Possibly even more obstructive is the fragmentation of labour across an enormous span of makeshift occupations and forms of casual–contractual employment, which frustrate the formation of a consciousness based on social–class unity. And lastly, there is the state, which condemns every desperate act of rebellion against oppression and exploitation as a breach of law and order. Explosions of dissatisfaction do occur—for example, when the price of bread or bus fares is raised—but these are generally

[3] Hernanado de Soto, *The Other Path: The Invisible Revolution in the Third World*, New York: Harper and Row, 1989; and Hernanado de Soto, *The Mystery of Capital: Why Capitalism Triumphs in the West and Fails Everywhere Else*, London: Bantam Press, 2000.

quite spontaneous, short lived, and localized rather than organized and sustainable, appealing to vertical loyalties rather than horizontal solidarity.

What are the geopolitical implications of a planet filling with shanty towns? Fed by the doomsday scenarios of 'the coming anarchy' by authors such as Robert Kaplan, the notion of *une classe dangereuse* in a globalized shape has come to stay.[4] The richer countries aim to protect themselves against this threat by closing and fencing their borders. Mass migration to 'empty' or cleaned-out territories is no longer an option for societies wanting to get rid of people who are a drain rather than an asset to productivity. Economic refugees nowadays reach the shores of the promised lands as boat people, or climb the fences and walk through the desert hunted by the state or private gangs. Comparably, the run-of-the mill migrants who end up in an urban slum in their own society are also represented as posing a threat to global security. Davis draws a telling parallel between the brutal tectonics of neo-liberal globalization since 1978 and the catastrophic processes that shaped a '"Third World" in the first place' during the era of nineteenth century imperialism that he explored in his 2001 work, *Late Victorian Holocausts*. At the end of the nineteenth century, the forcible incorporation into the world market of the great subsistence peasantries of Asia and Africa entailed the famine deaths of millions and the uprooting of tens of millions more from traditional tenures. The end result (in Latin America as well) was rural 'semi-proletarianization', the creation of a huge global class of immiserated semi-peasants and farm labourers lacking existential security of subsistence.

Structural adjustment, it would appear, has recently worked an equally fundamental reshaping of human futures. [Thus] instead of being a focus for growth and prosperity, the cities have become a dumping ground for a surplus population working in unskilled, unprotected and low-wage informal service industries and trade.[5]

It could be added that the new liberal revolution has also seen the return of a form of neo-social Darwinism in the world at large. In the earlier version, not poverty but the poor themselves were stigmatized as

---

[4] R.D. Kaplan, *The Ends of the Earth*, Peter Smith Pub. Inc., 1996, reprinted 2000; and R.D. Kaplan, *The Coming Anarchy*, New York: Vintage, 2000.

[5] *The Challenge of Slums: Global Report on Human Settlements*, UN-Habitat, 2003, pp. 40, 46.

defective: if they led miserable lives, it was because they were incapable of taking control of the circumstances in which they were forced to maintain themselves. The instinct among 'civilized people' to sympathize with these wretches, so the warning went, offered them unwarranted support and protection; by tempering the natural play of social forces, modern society had burdened itself with a parasitical underclass. In his epilogue, 'Down Vietnam Street', Davis cites writings that suggest a return to favour for this late-nineteenth century line of reasoning, accompanied by the tacit recognition that current economic and social policies will make it impossible to solve the problem of mass poverty.[6] As in Victorian times, 'the categorical criminalization of the urban poor is a self-fulfilling prophecy, guaranteed to shape a future of endless war in the streets'.[7] From the mid-1990s, US military theoreticians have been urging preparation for 'protracted combat' in the nearly impassable, maze-like streets of poor Third World cities. As the *US Army War College Quarterly* described in a 1996 article entitled, 'Our Soldiers, Their Cities':

The future of warfare lies in the streets, sewers, high-rise buildings, and sprawls of houses that form the broken cities of the world. Our recent military history is punctuated with city names—Tuzla, Mogadishu, Los Angeles [I], Beirut, Panama City, Hue, Saigon, Santo Domingo—but these encounters have been but a prologue, with the real drama still to come.[8]

The names are those of the cities, but the real danger lurks in their vast slums where alienated and seething masses dwell. In the opinion of researchers operating from state-run American think tanks, security forces should address the sociological phenomenon of excluded populations. Davis backs up this documentation with quotations from Pentagon sources that argue the case for contingency plans in support of 'a low-intensity world war of unlimited duration against criminalized segments of the urban poor'.[9] Quite rightly he concludes that this mindset reveals the true 'clash of civilizations'.

[6] Davis, *Planet of Slums*, pp.199–206.

[7] Ibid., p. 202.

[8] Ralph Peters, 'Our Soldiers, Their Cities', *Parameters: US Army War College Quarterly*, vol. XXVI, Spring 1996, p. 203.

[9] Davis, *Planet of Slums*, p. 205.

# III

## The Urban Economy and its Workforce

# 6

## Industrial Labour in Post-colonial India

### The Early Beginnings*

## CONSTITUTING LABOUR

In post-colonial India, labour began to signify work in *industry*; the 'worker' worked in the modern economy, towards which development would be rapid. The rural–agrarian order would soon be replaced by an urban–industrial one; labour economics was consequently closely associated with industrial employment, and the authors of authoritative textbooks on the shape of the working class and the trade union movement[1] felt that they were able to largely ignore the vast majority of the working population. The National Planning Committee (NPC), set up in 1940 by the All India Congress Committee and chaired by Jawaharlal Nehru, formulated policies that would be executed after independence. The Gandhian doctrine of small-scale village development was completely ignored. One of its working groups was on 'labour', but the only subjects it discussed were concerned with *industrial* relations, and the regulations it proposed were modelled on those already in the industrialized world. One major reason for this circumscribed

---

* Originally published as 'The Study of Industrial Labour in Post-colonial India: The Formal Sector', in J. Parry, J. Breman, and K. Kapadia (eds), *The World View of Industrial Labour in India*, New Delhi: Sage Publications, 1999, pp. 1–41.

[1] For example, H.A. Crouch, *Indian Working Class*, Ajmer: Sachin Publications, 1979; S.C. Pant, *Indian Labour Problems*, Allahabad: Chaitanya Publishing House, 1965; S. Sen, *Working Class of India: History of Emergence and Movement 1830–1970*, Calcutta: K.P. Bagchi & Co., 1977; R.R. Singh, *Labour Economics*, Agra: Sri Ram Mehra & Co., 1971.

focus was the fact that only the industrial sector had an established trade-union movement.

Even more important than the unions was the leading role which the state would play in the transformation to come. A modern industrial infrastructure would require huge investments which could not be mobilized by private businesses alone. The active participation of the state in restructuring the economy was therefore essential, and met with the unreserved approval of private enterprise.[2] Public and private sectors would reinforce rather than compete with each other, and the strategic role of the state would facilitate the public regulation of the terms and conditions of employment in the new and modernized sectors of national economy. The labour legislation that was soon introduced gave the government considerable power over industrial procedures and dispute settlement, and this led to the creation of a massive bureaucracy charged with its policing.

At the start of the post-colonial era, India had fewer than 10 million industrial workers, of whom considerably less than half worked in factories (in 1950, a mere 2.5 million, according to Ornati).[3] But even on the higher figure of 10 million, industrial labourers formed less than 6 per cent of the total workforce; of the non-agrarian sector, it was barely 17 per cent.[4] This small minority was nevertheless regarded as prototypical of the labour force that would determine the future.

...their importance does not lie in numbers... (but) because growth and expansion of the economy depends, to a large extent, upon its attitude towards industrialisation. It being the only section where labour organisation exists and can grow easily, it can influence the pace of change. It is this section which along with its problems will grow with the progress of industrialisation.[5]

But attention was focused on industry not only because of its future dominance but also because of its political significance. The post-colonial economy would be planned and socialist in orientation; industrial employment would shape a future in which employers, workers, and the state would accommodate their separate interests for the common good.

[2] R.K. Ray, *Industrialisation in India: Growth and Conflict in the Private Corporate Sector, 1914–47*, New Delhi: Oxford University Press, 1979.

[3] O.A. Ornati, *Jobs and Workers in India*, Institute of International Industrial and Labour Relations, Ithaca: Cornell University Press, 1955, p. 9.

[4] Pant, *Indian Labour Problems*, p. 12.

[5] Ibid.

Even when the industrial breakthrough failed to materialize, when planning became far less significant in policy execution, when the goal of a socialist ordering succumbed to other interests, and the emphasis shifted from public to private-sector expansion, 'labour' retained its connotations of employment in the organized sector of the urban economy. The implicit assumption was that a social system would eventually emerge similar to the West. K.N. Raj, the economist, referred approvingly to a statement made before independence by Zakir Hussain, the future President, to the effect that Indian capitalism would differ little from that of the West.[6] Little thought was given to the way in which local and historical conditions had shaped the working class in that part of the world; and it was the evolutionary schemes which dominated the social-science theory of the time which provided the point of departure, rather than the more recent exceptionalism of Chakrabarty,[7] whose critique of the universalist view of working-class dynamics elaborates on the specificities of the Indian case.

The accelerated migration from the countryside to the cities seemed to herald the approaching transformation. Between 1901 and 1961, the urban population rose from 4 to 18 per cent of the total. But still, only a tiny portion of the working population was employed in modern factories, and little consideration was given to how the much larger remainder managed to earn a living, to the huge number of labourers who worked for big industrial enterprises in the rural hinterland. Mine workers and plantation coolies constituted a far bigger workforce than that of the factories of Bombay (henceforth Mumbai) and Calcutta (henceforth Kolkata). Among the exceptions were Mukherjee[8]—who discussed working conditions in mining and the plantation corporations—and Chandra.[9] But neither of them paid any attention to waged labour in agriculture.

The preoccupation with industrial employment diverted attention not only from the large segment of the urban population that earned

---

[6] K.N. Raj, 'Unemployment and Structural Changes in Indian Rural Society', in T.S. Papola, P.P. Ghosh, and A.N. Sharma (eds), *Labour, Employment and Industrial Relations in India*, Presidential Addresses, The Indian Society of Labour Economics, New Delhi: B.R. Publishing Corp., 1993, p. 211.

[7] D. Chakrabarty, *Rethinking Working Class History: Bengal 1890–1940*, New Delhi: Oxford University Press, 1989.

[8] R.K. Mukherjee, *The Indian Working Class*, Bombay: Hind Kitab, 1945.

[9] B. Chandra, *The Rise and Growth of Economic Nationalism in India: Economic Policies of Indian National Leadership, 1880–1905*, New Delhi: People's Publishing House, 1966.

its living in other ways, but even more from the social relations of production in agriculture. Iyer was one of the few who specifically drew attention to agricultural labour as a separate social formation, commenting at the start of the twentieth century on the miserable plight of the landless.[10] Post-colonial policymakers only very slowly came to realize that agricultural labourers constituted the largest single section of the labour force.[11] Nation-wide investigations in the early 1950s showed that this rural underclass included roughly one-quarter of the agrarian population. The industrial proletariat, even in its broadest definition, was far smaller in size. This systematic neglect had begun in the colonial era and was related to the stereotyped image of the rural order as made up of fairly homogeneous communities of independent peasant producers. Case studies, such as that of Lorenzo,[12] were barely noticed.

Reacting to the received wisdom in nationalist circles, represented by writers like Patel,[13] who saw the growth of a class of landless labourers as the product of the break up of the old village community of peasants and artisans under alien rule, Kumar[14] was able to establish its significant presence in early colonial times; to show that this class was overwhelmingly made up of people of low caste and was subjected to servile labour arrangements based on bondage. Widespread use was later to be made of indebtedness in recruiting rural workers not only to coal mines and tea plantations but also to harbours and factories. The classic thesis that industrial capitalism only comes about when the transition to free labour has occurred—in the dual sense of workers detached from the ownership of means of production and able to decide for themselves how and where to sell their labour power—is not applicable to the colonial situation.[15] But in various publications, I have argued that the

[10] Ibid., p. 762.

[11] D. Thorner and A. Thorner, *Land and Labour in India*, Bombay: Asia Publishing House, 1962, p. 173.

[12] A.M. Lorenzo, *Agricultural Labour Conditions in Northern India*, Bombay: New Book Co., 1943.

[13] S.J. Patel, *Agricultural Labourers in Modern India and Pakistan*, Bombay: Current Book House, 1952.

[14] D. Kumar, *Land and Caste in South India: Agricultural Labour in the Madras Presidency During the Nineteenth Century*, Cambridge: Cambridge University Press, 1965.

[15] J. Breman, *Of Peasants, Migrants and Paupers: Rural Labour Circulation and Capitalist Production in West India*, New Delhi: Oxford University Press, 1985, p. 59; see also, P. Robb, *Dalit Movements and the Meanings of Labour in India*, New Delhi: Oxford University Press, 1993.

neo-bondage of contemporary industry is fundamentally different from the bondage of the old agrarian order.

For present purposes, the point to stress is that in the post-colonial literature on labour, the focus of attention was not on the rural economy per se, but on the labour surplus that had accumulated in it and would have to flow towards the real poles of economic growth. But did these supernumerary rural masses match the requirements of modern industry?

## A DEFICIENT WORKFORCE

The emphasis on the rural origins of the working class dates back to the colonial period and was coupled with the notion that early generations of factory hands refused to sever their ties with the hinterland. The industrial worker as peasant *manqué* was a principal motif of the *Report of the Royal Commission on Labour in India*,[16] which reiterated the conventional view that economic necessity forced the migrants out of their villages, to which they remained socially and emotionally bound.[17] This explained the lack of enthusiasm with which they subjected themselves to the demands of the industrial regime. Their disappointing quality was shown by their slovenly work pace (loitering was an ever-recurring complaint), the ease with which they changed jobs, and their high rates of absenteeism which were linked with their perfidious habit of returning to their villages and of staying away indefinitely. At heart, they were still peasants and their labour discipline was seriously defective. Moreover, the suspicion grew that this was not a transitory phenomenon that would be corrected as workers grew accustomed to their new world.

This image was reinforced by the social-science literature of the 1950s and 1960s on the modernization process. The capacity of non-western peoples to internalize the behavioural norms required by an industrial way of life seemed at issue. For Feldman and Moore, as for Kerr, industrialism imposes a set of conditions that must be met before economic transition can be considered complete. The key question was therefore, how, as economic development progresses, the obstacles that hamper the quantity and quality of labour could be overcome.[18] Ornati spoke

---

[16] Government of India (GoI), *Report of the Royal Commission on Labour in India*, London: HMSO, 1931, p. 26.

[17] Ornati, *Jobs and Workers in India*, p. 36.

[18] C. Kerr, 'Changing Social Structures', in Moore and Feldman (eds), *Labor Commitment and Social Change in Developing Areas*, New York: Social Science Research Council, 1960, pp. 351–2; W.E. Moore, *Industrialisation and Labour*,

of a dislike for factory work and doubted that the industrial worker, in the proper sense of the term, exists in India. Violations of industrial discipline, including damage to goods and machinery, protracted inertia, and other forms of 'unsuitable behaviour' were persistent. Shows of defiance were symptomatic of the worker's inability to adapt to the new working conditions.

Occasionally, the worker leaves the factory not to return to the village but to rebel against being forced into what might be called the 'factory norms': time discipline, the limitation on leisure, the confines of the machines, the toil of learning, and the like.[19]

It was their peasant background which explained why workers preferred the more irregular and risky, but less self-disciplined, existence of the self-employed. The life of the 'peasant entrepreneur' was, in social and psychological terms, more attractive.

In 1958, the American Social Science Research Council sponsored a conference on how to motivate labour to perform non-customary tasks as a precondition for economic growth. Moore and Feldman edited the subsequent volume, *Labor Commitment and Social Change in Developing Areas*. 'Commitment,' as they defined it, 'involves both performance and acceptance of the behaviours appropriate to an industrial way of life.'[20] Kerr's contribution distinguished successive stages, culminating in the willingness to conform, permanently and unconditionally, to the demands of the new mode of production;[21] while Myers had elaborated on the conditions necessary before one could speak of a stable and dedicated labour force:

… when workers no longer look on their industrial employment as temporary, when they understand and accept the requirement of working as part of a group in a factory or other industrial enterprise, and when they find in the industrial environment a more adequate fulfilment of personal satisfactions than they enjoyed in the village or rural society.[22]

---

Ithaca: Cornell University Press, 1951; W.E. Moore and A.S. Feldman (eds), *Labor Commitment and Social Change in Developing Areas*, New York: Social Science Research Council, 1960.

[19] Ornati, *Jobs and Workers in India*, p. 47.

[20] Moore and Feldman (eds), *Labor Commitment and Social Change in Developing Areas*, p. 1.

[21] Kerr, 'Changing Social Structures'.

[22] C.A. Myers, *Labour Problems in the Industrialisation of India*, Cambridge, Massachusetts : Harvard University Press, 1958, p. 36.

Indian factory workers were, at best, only partially committed. Though keen to have fixed employment, they had few scruples about deserting the job in order to visit their village. They want, as Myers put it, 'to have their cake and eat it too'.[23] To protect themselves against such unpredictable desertion, the factories set up a reserve pool of casual labour on which they could draw when necessary. James saw in this provision of *badli* (substitute) labour, the good sense and tolerance of the employers. Recognizing that their workers found it difficult to adjust to an industrial existence, and drawing on long experience, they refrained from harnessing their permanent workforce too tightly.[24]

The high rate of absenteeism was not the only reason why Myers placed Indian factory workers so low on the ladder of commitment. 'Commitment to industrial employment implies more than the presence of workers on the job, however. It involves also their acceptance of industrial discipline and the performance of tasks under supervision.'[25] The self-discipline of committed workers was required if they were to keep up with the tempo of the machines. But it is important to remember that they operated machines which were not owned by them; and it is possible that their resistance to machinery might have been due to their rejection of the property relations intrinsic to the industrial mode of production. As Moore and Feldman[26] recognized, we must therefore ask about their ownership notions. Until we are informed about these, it seems premature to pontificate about their capacity for, or commitment to, modern machine production.

Lack of commitment narratives slide seamlessly into complaints about lack of discipline. Workers are reported to be unwilling to accept managerial authority, in particular the control of shop-floor supervisors. What is initially explained as non-internalization, soon becomes a question of the employers' failure to gain an adequate grip on the behaviour of their subordinates. Loitering and leaving machines unattended are the most innocent examples of behaviour which shades into sabotage, physical violence against management agents, such as timekeepers, or *gherao*ing company offices.[27]

[23] Ibid., p. 45.

[24] R.C. James, 'The Casual Labour Problem in Indian Manufacturing', *The Quarterly Journal of Economics*, vol. 74, no. 1, 1960, pp. 100, 104.

[25] Myers, *Labour Problems in the Industrialisation of India*, p. 53.

[26] Moore and Feldman (eds), *Labor Commitment and Social Change in Developing Areas*, pp. 19–26.

[27] Myers, *Labour Problems in the Industrialisation of India*, p. 48.

What seems to be forgotten in these discussions is that commitment
to industrial work and commitment to managerial practices are not the
same thing. Rather than inadequate engagement, much labour unrest
can equally and perhaps more justifiably be described as an index of
the opposite. What is more, the lack of commitment is always that of
the working class. Kerr is explicit that it does not apply to the management[28]—a diagnosis flatly at odds with the findings of research in a West
Bengal factory where supervisors charged with disciplining the workers
did not themselves have the necessary discipline to fulfil their task.[29]
Invariably, the problems are *with* labour not *of* it—not those it experiences but those it causes. With Myers, this bias seems to be closely
connected with the way he did his research. He held discussions with
management and his Indian research associate reported on the unions.
In addition to 125 officials in forty-nine enterprises, he spoke to leaders of employers' organizations and trade unions, government officials,
academics, and representatives of international agencies (including
the International Labour Organization (ILO) and American technical
missions). Workers? It is not clear that he met any.[30]

## REJECTION OF THE COMMITMENT CONCEPT
Morris's historical study of labour and the growth of cotton mills in
Mumbai, supplemented by briefer and less detailed research into
the development of the Tata Iron and Steel Company (TISCO) in
Jamshedpur, brought him to conclusions that were, in many respects,
diametrically opposed to the prevailing orthodoxy. In response to
the thesis that urban industry had initially suffered from a lack of
labour, Morris showed that it had never been difficult to recruit workers
for the textile factories, although the distance they came from increased
over time. Simultaneously, however, a working class evolved which
closely identified with Mumbai's industrial sector and had renounced
its roots in the rural milieu.[31] Workers were not irredeemably mired in

[28] Kerr, 'Changing Social Structures', p. 358.
[29] G. Chattopadhyay and A.K. Sengupta, 'Growth of a Disciplined Labour Force:
A Case Study of Social Impediments', *Economic and Political Weekly*, vol. 4, no. 28,
1969, pp. 1209–16.
[30] Myers, *Labour Problems in the Industrialisation of India*, p. xvi.
[31] M.D. Morris, 'The Labour Market in India', in Moore and Feldman (eds),
*Labor Commitment and Social Change in Developing Areas*, pp. 173–200; M.D.
Morris, *The Emergence of an Industrial Labour Force in India: A Study of the Bombay
Cotton Mills, 1854–1947*, Berkeley: University of California Press, 1965.

traditional institutions or incapable of cutting their umbilical ties with the village.

So, why the vast army of migrant labour? To understand it, we first have to distinguish between large- and small-scale industries, between enterprises that produce only seasonally and those that produce the whole year through. In short, circulation between city and village was a product of the nature of economic activity rather than of the ingrained habits of workers.[32] In the end, Mumbai's cotton mills got the workers that they wanted: temporarily employed and dismissable without notice; and their productivity remained low because of a lack of investment in training and management:

These practices made it possible to use very large amounts of minimally trained labour, precisely the sort that was easy and cheap to obtain in Bombay. But the work schedule also made it necessary to employ enough labour to permit workers to take breaks while the machines were running, to develop what in effect amounted to an informal shift system … There is no question that employers could have initiated a tighter and more precise system of labour utilisation and discipline had they so wished. But such an approach would have required more expensive supervision than could be obtained from the jobbers … .[33]

The psychologizing interpretation of writers like Kerr and Myers were well off the mark. Industrial work did indeed subjugate the workforce to fairly rigid rule-by-the-clock, but there was no question of a sharp break with the labour regime to which workers on the land were accustomed; and, in fact, the majority of factory workers had no contact with machines.[34] Nor did labour unrest indicate a lack of commitment. Willingness to strike meant just the opposite—adaptation to the industrial way of life.

Again, Lambert—a sociologist who, in 1957, had investigated the origins and identity of the workforces of five factories in Pune—reported that he had found no confirmation of the 'recruitment-commitment problem'.[35] Some of the workers he interviewed (a stratified random sample of 856 chosen from a population of 4,249) said that they would probably return to the countryside when their working life had finished. But one-third of his respondents had been born in Pune, an unspecified

[32] Morris, 'The Labour Market in India'.
[33] Morris, *The Emergence of an Industrial Labour Force in India*, p. 203.
[34] Morris, 'The Labour Market in India', p. 188.
[35] R.D. Lambert, *Workers, Factories and Social Change in India*, Princeton, New Jersey: Princeton University Press, 1963, p. 6.

percentage in other urban localities, and the majority were certainly not recent rural migrants. Further, three-quarters of his respondents could be classified as 'committed' in Moore and Feldman's sense of the term.[36] But Lambert was clear that he found little utility in this modish concept.

Notwithstanding that scepticism, he was clearly also dubious about the transformative effects of the urban–industrial system. The transition from tradition to modernity had been very partial; and factory organization had features derived from the social institutions of caste and the village. In particular, the *jajmani* system gave members of the local community the *right* to a job and a livelihood which the patron could not unilaterally abrogate. Employer–employee relations in the factory were based on the same principle. The worker regarded his job as his property, of which, he assumed, his employer could not deprive him as long as he behaved as a duly deferential client and fulfilled all sorts of obligations that had nothing to do with work performance. As far as the latter was concerned, it may have been better if the workers were less committed to the secure niche to which they believed themselves entitled, irrespective of their competence and work discipline. In the early phase of industrialization, the employer's only escape from these claims was to use labour contractors and jobbers who profited from a constant rotation of workers. When those practices disappeared, the factory job became a more permanent form of property. Employers reacted to this limitation of their powers to discipline and dismiss their workers by making it more difficult to obtain fixed employment. They did so by forming a pool of reserve workers who were available when needed and who had far fewer rights than permanent employees.[37] In India, the transformation from *Gemeinschaft* to *Gesellschaft* still lay in the distant future.

More nuanced was Sheth's study of labour relations in a modern industrial enterprise in Rajnagar, a fictionally named medium-size city in western India. No confirmation was found for its working hypothesis: that traditional institutions like the village community, the caste system, and the joint family had obstructed progress towards industrialism.[38] What Moore, Kerr, and others had characterized as 'industrial society' was actually an ideal–typical construct for a great variety of social formations

[36] Ibid., pp. 83–4.
[37] Ibid., pp. 91–4.
[38] N.R. Sheth, *The Social Framework of an Indian Factory*, Manchester: Manchester University Press, 1968.

which did not, in reality, approximate to it at all closely. It was equally impossible to reduce the 'pre-industrial' society to a single uniform type. Neither were the two types of society polar opposites and nor did the new technology preclude continuity with the traditional social system. Moore[39] was in error to suggest that sluggish economic development was to be blamed on the tenaciousness of traditional social patterns, of which idea the commitment concept was simply a development. There is no radical rupture between relations in industry and those in the wider social environment; and factory managements make use of ascriptive and particularistic norms in their dealings with the workforce. Was that not also characteristic of Japan? Between the tradition-oriented social life of the worker and his rationality-based work in the factory, there was no conflict. What we have rather is 'a coexistence of the two sets of values and neither seems to hinder the operation of the other'.[40]

Sheth's study had affinities with Lambert's. Both denied that industrial employment is a watershed in the worker's attitudes and behaviour. Neither discussed the social life of the workers or the way in which they spend their income and leisure time outside the factory gates. On the other hand, Sheth points out that his methods were different from Lambert's, who had focused on questionnaire data and had paid no attention to interpersonal relations in the factory. But even more than Lambert, Sheth failed to give the pool of casual labourers (in both cases, about one-fifth of the total factory workforce) the strategic significance that the industrial reserve army undoubtedly deserves.[41]

Other authors rejected the commitment thesis on other grounds. Sharma, on the basis of socio-psychological research on the attitudes and behaviour of workers in a car manufacturing plant in Mumbai, set out to test the thesis through 262 in-depth interviews. The factory appeared to prefer educated, urban born workers with industrial experience over illiterate, rural born labourers with no experience or with a background in non-industrial occupations.[42] But workers of rural origin had *better* attendance records than those who had grown up in the city (and trade union members were less likely than non-members to be absent). There was apparently no evidence of alienation and anomie to which

[39] Moore, *Industrialisation and Labour*, p. 124.

[40] Sheth, *The Social Framework of an Indian Factory*, p. 203.

[41] Lambert, *Workers, Factories and Social Change in India*, pp. 94–104; Sheth, *The Social Framework of an Indian Factory*, pp. 56–7.

[42] B.R. Sharma, *The Indian Industrial Worker: Issues in Perspective*, New Delhi: Vikas Publishing House, 1974, p. 14.

the labourer from the countryside stereotypically would fell prey in his new environment, and of which, lack of discipline was an important symptom. The conclusion was that:

> ... traditional Indian culture appears to present no serious obstacles to the workers in either accepting factory employment or in becoming committed to industrial work. Moreover, the commitment of workers seems to be influenced not by their traditional backgrounds but by work technology within the factory.[43]

The last point is clearly important. Commitment varies according to the nature of the industry, the technology used, and the demands regarding training and skills made at the time of recruitment.

Holmström's monograph[44] on industrial workers in Bengaluru was based on more anthropological methods of data collection. His fieldwork concentrated on workers in four factories, two in the public and two in the private sector; his focus was on the residential milieu rather than the factory itself; and the findings were based on case studies of 104 workers, selected to provide a cross-section of them—educated and uneducated, young and old, members of diverse castes, and so forth. Holmström's point of departure was that the significance and impact of urbanization should not be confused with those of industrialization and that it was senseless to assume a simple linear dichotomy between tradition (rural–folk society) and modernity (urban–industrial society). His principal questions concerned the social identity of the factory workers and what distinguished them from the majority of city dwellers who had not found access to modern and large-scale industrial enterprises. And, how did members of this industrial vanguard think about their work and careers? The commitment issue was bypassed as largely irrelevant to the workers he studied.

In an overview published in 1977, Munshi concluded with a devastating judgement on the utility of the whole concept, again rejecting the opposition it postulates between modernity and tradition and the implicit assumption that industrialization would follow the path that it had followed in the West. Failure to do so had come to be seen as the inability of the working masses to meet demands dictated by the logic of industrialism and a lack of awareness of the strategic significance of a

---

[43] Ibid., p. 48.
[44] M. Holmström, *South Indian Factory Workers: Their Life and Their World*, Cambridge: Cambridge University Press, 1976.

management style attuned to industrial relations in American industry.[45] As Holmström later summarized it:

Foreign writers, and some Indians, wanted to find the formula for successful industrialisation, the ingredients missing from the traditional society which must be added to make India an industrial country: entrepreneurship, efficient management, changes in social values, 'achievement-orientation' or a committed labour force. The problem of supplying the missing ingredient or ingredients was believed to be common to non-industrial countries which lagged behind, at various points, on the great highway of development marked out by the west and Japan.[46]

But, at least the new variant of the old colonial dogmas acknowledged that non-western peoples did have the ability to follow that highway. The bad news, however, was that this was likely to be a slow process since the industrial mentality took more than a generation to instil.

Kalpana Ram was one of the first to attempt to put the discussion on a new footing by drawing attention to the ways in which the capitalist work process manifests itself in India. Its specific nature, she argued, lies in the interconnection between rural and industrial labour. In the coal and iron mines of West Bengal, Madhya Pradesh, and Orissa, for example, workers did not have the chance to cut their ties to their villages of origin. This also applied to many migrants who found more permanent employment but had neither the accommodation nor the income that would allow them to maintain their family in their new location. The migration system 'allows employers to transfer the costs of reproducing and maintaining workers' families, and even of providing for the worker himself in times of illness and old age, on to the villages'.[47] It also results in an extremely unequal distribution of work between the sexes. The Indian pattern of industrialization and urbanization has largely been based on women's exclusion from industrial employment; and Ram rightly points out that the theoretical literature has paid much

[45] S. Munshi, 'Industrial Labour in Developing Economies: A Critique of Labour Commitment Theory', *Economic and Political Weekly*, vol. 12, no. 35, 1977, p. 82.

[46] M. Holmström, *Industry and Inequality: The Social Anthropology of Indian Labour*, Cambridge: Cambridge University Press, 1984, p. 28.

[47] K. Ram, 'The Indian Working Class and the Peasantry: A Review of Current Evidence on Interlinks between the Two Classes', in A.N. Das, V. Nilkant, and P.S. Dubey (eds), *The Worker and the Working Class: A Labour Studies Anthology*, New Delhi: Public Enterprises Centre for Continuing Education, 1983, p. 182.

too little attention to the very biased gender composition of India's industrial economy.

## FACTORY WORKERS AS A DOMINANT CLASS IN THE URBAN ECONOMY

The growth of India's modern proletariat was largely an urban phenomenon. The new towns and cities, as well as existing urban centres, became the sites of a great diversity of industrial enterprises. Jute and cotton mills had long been of vital significance to Kolkata, Mumbai, and Ahmedabad. Of much more recent origin was the emergence of heavy industries in the public-sector economy, in particular the manufacture of iron and steel for the production of capital goods—for machine and construction workshops, petro-chemical enterprises, cement factories, the manufacture of cars and other forms of transport, military equipment, shipbuilding, etc. The Second Five Year Plan, implemented in 1956, had prioritized the expansion of the industrial infrastructure.

The new public sector industrial workforce soon acquired a distinct character. The benefits of jobs within it included security of employment and various social provisions—like housing, health and education which were often the envy of workers in private enterprises. It is therefore hardly surprising that such workers became the reference point in the collective actions of industrial labour at large; while the relations of production initiated in these new government enterprises helped to give labour a new dignity. The 1969 *Report of the National Commission on Labour* elaborated on the characteristics of this new type of factory worker: The social composition of labour is undergoing a change. Labour is not restricted to certain castes and communities... [S]ocial mobility today accounts for the emergence of a mixed industrial work force. While in traditional industries this change is slow, one cannot escape noticing it in sophisticated employments such as engineering and metal trades; oil refining and distribution; chemicals and petro-chemicals; machine tools and machine building; and synthetics and in many white-collar occupations. The background of the intermediate and lower cadres in the latter industries is overwhelmingly urban: their level of education is higher. They come from middle or lower middle classes comprising small shopkeepers, petty urban landlords, lower echelons of public service and schoolteachers and professional groups. They have a pronounced polyglot character.[48]

---

[48] GoI, *Report of the National Commission on Labour*, New Delhi: Ministry of Labour, 1969, pp. 33–4.

In what follows, I will look, in turn, at the recruitment, mode of employment, and the social composition and lifestyle of this segment of the working class.

## Recruitment

According to the colonial stereotype, the workforce which flowed straight from the villages to the factory gates had little if any direct contact with management. Workers were recruited by jobbers who were, frequently, also charged with control on the work floor. Combining the functions of recruitment and supervision, the middleman was sometimes also responsible for housing and feeding his workers. The physical, economic, and social gap that had to be bridged was so crucial that the jobber is justifiably described as the midwife of India's industrialization. But one of the first changes to occur, starting around the turn of the century, was the transfer of recruitment from the hinterland to the factory itself. Increasing pressure on subsistence resources as a result of population growth and land alienation accelerated the flow of poor farmers and non-agrarian workers to the cities where industrial employment gained new impetus during and after the Second World War. The role of the jobber declined. From being an intermediary between worker and management, leader of a gang of workers whom he had himself brought together, he became a foreman charged with implementing orders from above. 'The hiring of workers is becoming the responsibility of the employment office, and the "labour officer" is beginning to take over the welfare and service activities of the sirdar.[49]

The decline of the jobber went hand in hand with the introduction of new rules which obliged major industrial enterprises to professionalize their personnel practices, and which eventually led to his disappearance.[50] But, if selection procedures become more impersonal, can we infer that qualities based on individual achievement—experience, training, social skills—have replaced those based on ascription? Economic logic and the interests of the employer would suggest that they should. Thus, Papola[51] dismissed the suggestion that caste, religion, custom, or tradition might be crucial. But, in fact, it is clear that they continue to play a very large

---

[49] Ornati, *Jobs and Workers in India*, p. 40.

[50] T.S. Papola and G. Rodgers, 'Labour Institutions and Economic Development in India', Geneva Research Series, International Institute for Labour Studies, 1992, p. 27.

[51] T.S. Papola, 'Economics of Labour Market', in V.B. Singh (ed.), *Labour Research in India*, Bombay: Popular Prakashan, 1970, p. 182.

part. From the employer's point of view, recruitment mediated by existing workers helps to stabilize performance in daily production.

Recruitment through present employees continues to prevail. According to the
evidence before us, employers prefer this method to improve the morale of
workers. In some companies, labour-management agreements specify entitlement to a percentage of vacancies to close relatives of senior employees. In a few
cases, both the employer and the union maintain rosters of people so eligible
for employment. Recruitment through advertisement is restricted mainly to
supervisory and white-collar employments and is being increasingly used to tap
skilled labour. For occupations which do not require skills, an arrangement by
which workers appear at the factory gate in the hope of getting employment
still operates.[52]

The widespread use of relatives, neighbours, and friends in order to
influence those who have jobs to bestow testifies to the enormous
disparity between supply and demand. So great is the latter that
applicants without such contacts stand no chance at all.[53] Some authors
have seen the vitality of such particularistic mechanisms as a carry-over
from the traditional prescriptions of kin solidarity; and Sheth noted the
continuity between the patronage found in the factory and the values
of the world outside it. But in any event, it is now hard to believe that
particularism can be simply equated with an 'earlier' or 'lower' stage in a
unilinear transformation along a continuum that eventually culminates
in a universalistic and globalized civilization. The Japanese example is
instructive. Rather than emphasising its continuity with older social and
cultural forms, others—myself included—would see such behaviour
in more universalistic terms as a common response to a situation of
extreme scarcity which prompts people to put pressure on kin who are
more favourably placed. But whichever way it is, the facts are not in
doubt. Papola summarized a series of studies from different parts of the
country as follows:

In over two-thirds of cases, the workers got information about the availability
of jobs from friends, relatives and neighbours. Employment exchanges were
the source of information to a very small extent ranging from 1.5 per cent in
Bombay to 10.6 per cent in Coimbatore, though 20 per cent of the workers

---

[52] GoI, *Report of the National Commission on Labour*, p. 70.
[53] Holmström, *South Indian Factory Workers*, pp. 42–54; U. Ramaswamy,
*Work, Union and Community: Industrial Man in South India*, New Delhi: Oxford
University Press, 1983, pp. 18–19.

in Ahmedabad and 25 per cent in Poona had registered with the exchanges. Newspaper advertisements provided information about their jobs to 1.5 per cent of workers in Bombay, 2.2 per cent in Poona and 10.6 per cent in Coimbatore. Jobs were secured on the basis of recommendation or introduction by friends, relatives and persons of the same region and caste, generally employees of the same factory, in 67 per cent of cases in Poona and in 61 per cent of cases in Ahmedabad, Bombay and Coimbatore. Placement through employment exchanges accounted for 2 per cent of jobs in Poona and Ahmedabad.[54]

Many factory workers attribute their access to the coveted arena of employment, in more veiled terms, to 'coincidence' or 'good luck'. Such terminology quite incorrectly gives the impression of an unexpected windfall, a mere stroke of fortune. It is a euphemism for claims made on their more fortunate fellows for help.

## Mode of Employment

Much of the work on Indian industry has been based on survey data, questionnaires, and formal interviews. In earlier studies, there was seldom much personal contact with the workforce. On Myers[55] I have already commented; while Singer's essay on 'The Indian Joint Family in Modern Industry' was based on the family histories of 'nineteen outstanding industrial leaders in Madras City'.[56] The next generation of researchers did actually descend to the level of the workers, but their contact with them rarely went beyond brief one-off encounters. The exceptions were studies of a more anthropological nature like that of Uma Ramaswamy who lived in an area populated by factory workers during her fieldwork.[57] To my knowledge, however, no researcher has ever actually worked in a factory. What is also lacking is documentation that originates from the workers themselves—diaries, biographies, or even oral histories.

Nor has research usually focused on the workplace, often no doubt as a consequence of management suspicion combined with some scepticism about its tangible benefits to the company. The researchers too have had their prejudices and inhibitions; one reported that questions

---

[54] Papola and Rodgers, 'Labour Institutions and Economic Development in India', p. 27.

[55] Myers, *Labour Problems in the Industrialisation of India*.

[56] M. Singer, 'The Indian Joint Family in Modern Industry', in M. Singer and B.C. Cohn (eds), *Stucture and Change in Indian Society*, Chicago: Aldine Publishing Co., 1968, p. 433.

[57] Ramaswamy, *Work, Union and Community*, p. 14.

regarding trade unions were avoided 'because these excited the workers
too much'.[58] Sheth is still unusual in having managed to move freely inside the factory, to ask whatever he liked, and to observe the daily work
cycle, all on the understanding 'that I would stick to my academic business and would cause no trouble in the administration of the factory'.[59]
But the blessings of management may, of course, result in antagonism
and distrust among the workers. One told Sheth that:

It is all very well. You are doing good work which may benefit us in the long
run. But you don't know our employers' tactics! You will now write down your
report and publish it. But I am sure that if your book contains anything against
the interests of these masters, they will buy up all the copies of your book to
prevent others from reading it. And they are so rich that they can buy any
number of copies that you print. All your labour will then prove futile.[60]

That the majority of accounts of factory labour are based on contacts
with employees outside the factory explains why ethnographies of
the work process and hierarchy are still comparatively rare. The social
mobility mentioned in the 1969 National Commission on Labour
(NCL) report assumes the possibility of progress up the occupational
ladder. The picture presented by most studies, however, is one of little
task differentiation. Lambert found that, in the five factories he investigated, 75–90 per cent of all workers were rated as unskilled or semi-
skilled, and the majority were doing the same jobs as they had started
with. The unskilled category in particular, varying from one-third to
three-quarters of the workforce, was distinguished by an almost complete lack of mobility.[61] It is, therefore, hardly surprising that roughly
three in five workers did not expect any promotion and considered their
present position to be as high as they would get.

As this suggests, the idea that factory work is skilled is only true to
a very limited degree. In many enterprises, roughly one-quarter of the
workforce belongs to the supervisory and maintenance staff. The former
act as bosses on the work floor and do not directly participate in the
production process. The maintenance staff are indispensable but not
important. As cleaners, guards, messengers, or general dogsbodies, they

---

[58] W.W. van Groenou, 'Sociology of Work in India', in G.R. Gupta (ed.),
*Contemporary India: Some Sociological Perspectives*, New Delhi: Vikas Publishing
House, 1976, p. 175.
[59] Sheth, *The Social Framework of an Indian Factory*, p. 8.
[60] Ibid.
[61] Lambert, *Workers, Factories and Social Change in India*, p. 131.

occupy the lowest ranks in the factory hierarchy. Between these two poles are the production workers, about three-quarters of the total workforce, who are split into two sections: 'operators', who are assumed to be the skilled workers; and the subordinate 'helpers', who function as their less skilled sidekicks and substitutes. The progressive mechanization of production means that a higher percentage of workers than in the past now, regularly or continuously, handle machines to whose regime they have to subject themselves. But this does not necessarily mean that their work is more skilled. Much of it is monotonous and makes no demands of craft competence. In fact, induction into the factory workforce may even result in a loss of skills.

If the prospects of promotion up the factory hierarchy are limited, we might expect workers to try to realize their aspirations by moving sideways into other enterprises. But, by contrast with the lack of commitment stereotype, the great majority show extreme entrenchment. None less than Myers discovered that they tend to cling at all costs to the job they have got. Absenteeism is high, but horizontal mobility is rare—by contrast with the United States of America (USA).[62] Or, as Lambert put it in terms that will by now be familiar: '…a factory job is a form of property to the worker, … [H]e will seek to retain, but not improve it … [T]he worker's status in the general society seems not to be increased by upward occupational mobility within the factory'.[63]

While the early literature complained about lack of commitment, the problem was now defined as one of workers who behaved as though they were clients who could not be dismissed by their patrons–employers, and who showed no inclination to either work or find another job. Under-commitment had mysteriously metamorphosed into over-commitment.

Uma Ramaswamy reached a more balanced conclusion. On the one hand,

most workers expect to retire in the factories they first joined unless better opportunities present themselves elsewhere, which is unusual. They increasingly look at their jobs not only as a right but also as property to be passed on to their children through *warisu* [a hereditary transaction]. All these find their reflection in the low turnover in the work-force.[64]

---

[62] James, 'The Casual Labour Problem in Indian Manufacturing', p. 103; Myers, *Labour Problems in the Industrialisation of India*, p. 47.

[63] Lambert, *Workers, Factories and Social Change in India*, p. 179.

[64] Ramaswamy, *Work, Union and Community*, p. 145.

But she is, on the other hand, clear that this is not a simple product of the power of custom or of inescapable cultural determinism. It is rather the consequence of a quest for maximum security in an insecure world in which it is the lack of permanent employment which is the norm.[65] The attributes of factory workers in permanent employment have to be seen in the context of the very substantial labour reserve retained by most enterprises. What is striking is how many researchers have focused on this rather peripheral category of badli labour (regular substitutes who report to the factory daily), while largely ignoring the much larger numbers of floating casual workers. A United Nations Educational, Scientific and Cultural Organization (UNESCO) survey of factory employment in various Indian states unblushingly says that 'the short-tenure factory workers and the non-factory workers had to be left out'.[66] Though the presence of the badlis is required to replace permanent workers who are absent, this does not always mean that management is able to send them away again when they report at the stipulated time and there is no work. Their more or less continuous involvement in the flexibly organized work process, long beyond any reasonable trial period, is often essential to management. Their lack of formal work contracts, however, gives employers the freedom to minimize their rights. In south Gujarat, I repeatedly encountered people who had worked for the same boss on a temporary basis for more than ten years, without ever giving up hope of eventually being rewarded with a permanent job in return for their 'loyalty'.

The size of the labour reserve varies by enterprise. In the five factories studied by Lambert, 10–20 per cent of the workforce belonged to that category; in Sheth's study, almost one-fifth, although this did not include the casual workers who were hired and fired according to need. Two sub-contractors were charged with hiring these casuals. Each morning the manager gave instructions as to how many extra workers were needed that day, and the two labour contractors would admit them at the factory gates. On average, they numbered seventy or eighty men, representing another 10 per cent of the total labour force. The contractors were paid piece rates; and neither they nor the gangs under them appeared on the factory's books. First, the contractors deducted their own generous cut and then, paid their teams. This floating reserve,

---

[65] Holmström, *South Indian Factory Workers*, pp. 139–40.
[66] J.D.N. Versluys, P.H. Prabhu, and C.N. Vakil, *Social and Cultural Factors Affecting Productivity of Industrial Workers in India*, New Delhi: United Nations Educational, Scientific and Cultural Organization (UNESCO), 1961, p. 7.

completely without rights, was not only called upon for all kinds of odd jobs but also to take the place of regular labourers who had not reported for work.[67]

Holmström's Bengaluru study revolved around the idea that those fortunate enough to have found factory employment had crossed the threshold to a secure existence. The contrast was with the precariousness of life outside.

Once inside the citadel, with a job to fall back on, improving one's qualifications and getting promotion becomes a gradual process, a matter of more or less, faster or slower progress, rather than simply of having a permanent job or not having one.[68]

In my view, however, Holmström pays too little attention to the considerable and often lasting gap between temporary and permanent workers, appearing to suggest that passing from the former to the latter category is, in most cases, nothing more than a matter of time and patience. 'Even educated Brahmans will take unskilled casual factory work in the hope of permanent jobs. Once inside the citadel, a man can look around for alternatives, if he wants'[69] The idea that upward mobility is a common career pattern is not confirmed by other studies. In fact, temporary workers often get no further than the bottom of the work hierarchy. Although better off than the labour nomads beyond the factory gates, they can make no claim on the secure conditions of employment enjoyed by permanent hands, and are usually assigned the lowliest and most unskilled chores. Even when their work is the same, they are paid far less than permanent employees.[70] Further, Lambert noted a tendency to lengthen the term of temporary employment:

... [I]t does appear that the average time spent on non-permanent status is increasing in all the factories, and that the two older companies using the badli system have a non-permanent labour pool that is tending to become stabilized.[71]

I would make that conclusion dependent on business cycles. During periods of rapid growth, when existing factories expand their production and new ones are opened, permanent employment becomes more

---

[67] Sheth, *The Social Framework of an Indian Factory*, pp. 56–7.
[68] Holmström, *South Indian Factory Workers*, p. 41.
[69] Ibid., p. 137.
[70] Lambert, *Workers, Factories and Social Change in India*, pp. 99–100.
[71] Ibid., p. 102.

quickly and easily available. The reverse happens in recession. It is probably no coincidence that Uma Ramaswamy—whose fieldwork was conducted at a time when the local textile industry had just passed through a decade of massive retrenchment—described a residual category of workers who had sometimes been registered as temporary hands for over a dozen years. They were not only much cheaper, but factory management expected them to be far more tractable, which is not surprising given the following account:

There are about seventy temporary workers in our mill. They were made to give their signatures on blank sheets before being taken for work. They have to report for work ten minutes before the others and are sent out ten minutes after the shift is over. The idea is to prevent them from mixing with permanent workers. Management fear that association with permanent workers might cause discontent in them. If a temporary worker is found sitting at the back of my cycle, he would be immediately denied employment. The blank sheet with signature would be used to write out his resignation.[72]

In general, labour productivity remains low. Management publications attribute this to worker and union militancy. What with the numerous holidays and days off, this means that a quarter to almost half of all days in the year are, according to some sources, lost to production.[73] But from an entirely different perspective, low productivity is also blamed on the owners' refusal to invest. Rather than technological improvement, the emphasis is on increasing productivity by intensifying labour. Women are frequently the victims. Fearing a loss of income, they are prepared to do work that is customarily carried out by men, to allow themselves to be illegally included in night shifts, and to work overtime without extra payment.[74]

Skilled factory work remains the preserve of only a tiny portion of the total workforce. In recent times, surplus labour, which has acquired enormous proportions in the countryside, has looked *en masse* for work away from the village and agriculture. Those of this surging army of migrants who manage to reach the urban economy, for shorter or longer periods, are rarely able to penetrate the strongly protected bastions of secure factory employment. And even if they are, the security of a

[72] Ramaswamy, *Work, Union and Community*, p. 21.

[73] Papola, Ghosh, and Sharma, *Labour, Employment and Industrial Relations in India*, pp. 294–325.

[74] Ramaswamy, *Work, Union and Community*, p. 23.

permanent job is often beyond them. It is those fortunate enough to have such a job, more influential than might be supposed from their numbers, who have acquired a vital significance as a truly dominant class in the urban–industrial landscape. What are the principal social characteristics of this elite group among the working population?

## Social Profile

Rather than being rural migrants, the majority of studies show that, today, many if not most workers have lived in the city or its immediate environs for many years, if not since birth.[75] Those who have only recently settled in urban locations would, generally, be only too grateful for factory employment, but lack the experience and contacts needed to compete for it. E.A. Ramaswamy's report from the mid-1970s is by no means exceptional:

The textile industry in Coimbatore is near saturation from the employment point of view. Even with the creation of additional capacity, jobs are too few in relation to the number of aspirants, particularly considering the low skill requirement.[76]

Literacy rates among workers in large-scale enterprises are quite high. Although it is not really essential for unskilled work, practice shows that the ability to read and write is a minimum qualification for even a temporary hand. Over time, educational qualifications for recruitment to permanent jobs have been continually upgraded. Candidates without a secondary school certificate are no longer considered.[77]

The old wisdom held that the first to report for work in the modern urban industries were landless and land-poor farmers from the countryside,[78] the social complement to their economic vulnerability being their low caste. But as industrial employment gained in respectability, the higher castes also began to show interest.[79] Morris was amongst the first

[75] Holmström, *South Indian Factory Workers*, p. 28; Lambert, *Workers, Factories and Social Change in India*, p. 7; Ramaswamy, *Work, Union and Community*, p. 12; Sheth, *The Social Framework of an Indian Factory*, pp. 79–82.

[76] E.A. Ramaswamy, *The Worker and His Union: A Study in South India*, Bombay: Allied Publishers, 1977, p. 175.

[77] Holmström, *South Indian Factory Workers*, p. 38; Ramaswamy, *Work, Union and Community*, p. 20.

[78] For example, D.H. Buchanan, *The Development of Capitalist Enterprise in India*, New York: Macmillan, 1934, p. 294; Ornati, *Jobs and Workers in India*, p. 29.

[79] Myers, *Labour Problems in the Industrialisation of India*, pp. 39–40.

to reject this view, which he traced back to Weber's claim that significant part of the emerging industrial proletariat stemmed from 'declassed and pariah castes' of rural origin. In Mumbai's cotton mills, Morris found that caste was not a relevant, let alone a primary criterion of recruitment, and that untouchables were not discriminated against.[80] But,

it is interesting that this distinctive institution of caste has been almost entirely ignored in connection with Indian industrialization. No detailed study of the relation of caste to industrial work is available. In the vast array of official investigations into the conditions of industrial labour, virtually the sole reference to caste relates to caste dietary restrictions, which employers claimed prevented them from establishing factory canteens. The institution has been treated mainly by anthropologists, and almost entirely in its rural setting. Those who have studied caste have ignored industry, and those who have studied industry have ignored caste.[81]

Little of this disregard is noticeable in later research, and we now have a considerable body of data on the relationship between caste and factory employment.[82] The general conclusion seems to be that the caste composition of the workforce broadly reflects that of the urban population as a whole, though the middle and higher castes are over-represented in the higher echelons of the industrial work hierarchy,[83] while the bottom ranks have high concentrations of lower-caste workers—a correlation which is strongly affected by differences in educational levels. But, has the growing discrepancy between the limited supply of industrial work and the enormously increased demand for it led to exclusion of the socially deprived categories? Harriss, amongst others, offered evidence which pointed in that direction.[84] Moreover, in capital-intensive, technologically advanced industries, particularly corporate and multinational concerns, staff are almost entirely recruited on the basis of requirements that show a strong bias towards the

---

[80] Morris, *The Emergence of an Industrial Labour Force in India*, pp. 200–1.

[81] Morris, 'The Labour Market in India', pp. 182–3.

[82] Holmström, *South Indian Factory Workers*, pp. 32–4; Ramaswamy, *Work, Union and Community*, pp. 102–14; Sheth, *The Social Framework of an Indian Factory*, pp. 73–5.

[83] B.R. Sharma, 'The Industrial Workers: Some Myths and Realities', *Economic and Political Weekly*, vol. 5, no. 22, 1970, pp. 875–8.

[84] J. Harriss, 'Character of an Urban Economy: "Small-scale" Production and Labour Markets in Coimbatore', *Economic and Political Weekly*, vol. 17, no. 24, 1982, p. 999.

higher social classes. On the other hand, positive discrimination in public sector employment has prioritized the recruitment of candidates from the scheduled castes and tribes. But, however one assesses these contradictory currents, no demonstration that caste still operates inside the factory gates should be taken to mean that it must still retain its old ideological salience.

… [C]aste is no longer plausible as a thorough-going religious ideology, justifying all social and economic relations as parts of a divinely established hierarchy. The main public ideology—not just the language of politics and unions, but much ordinary talk—tends to stress moral and social equality. The status inequalities that count depend on jobs, income, life style, manners and education. Where these things go with caste rank, this is usually because some castes had more access to education and good jobs in the past—a situation that will not last, because effective caste job-finding networks are not stable or confined to high castes.[85]

More generally, Sharma's conclusion of thirty-five years ago seems to stand: that factories prefer 'educated workers over the non-educated, urban born over the rural born, and those with industrial experience over the ones having no experience or with a background in non-industrial occupations'.[86] But what is still missing from this profile is its gender dimension. Early studies give the impression that women were rarely found in factories. Their apparent absence prompted Kalpana Ram to comment that 'the virtual exclusion of women from the Indian industrial working class has drawn little theoretical comment',[87] particularly in the light of their far higher participation in the early industrialization of the West as well as in various contemporary Third World societies. Her formulation needs some qualification, however, in that in Mumbai's cotton mills at the end of the nineteenth and in the early twentieth century, for example, women made up one-fifth to one-quarter of the workforce.[88] Although that was far less than in the early western textile industry, it was certainly not negligible.

So, how are we to explain the fact that the steady expansion of the industrial sector brought a fall rather than a rise in the percentage of female factory workers? The primary cause reported is that factory legislation restricted the use of the far cheaper labour of women and children

---

[85] Holmström, *South Indian Factory Workers*, p. 80.

[86] Sharma, *The Indian Industrial Worker*, p. 14.

[87] Ram, 'The Indian Working Class and the Peasantry', p. 182.

[88] Morris, *The Emergence of an Industrial Labour Force in India*, p. 65.

in the first few decades of the twentieth century. More important, in
Morris' view, is that women's reproductive role causes them to absent
themselves more frequently. It is not clear, however, how this argument
squares with huge local variations in the employment of women in
textile industries throughout the country. For Morris, the marginalization of women substantiates his thesis that there was no lack of male
workers who were ultimately preferred by the industry.[89]

By the mid-twentieth century, industrial work was more than ever a
male preserve. The prototypical factory worker was a young man of no
more than 30–35 years. Official reports confirm the decreasing participation of women.

This decline has been more marked in the textile and basic metal industries. In
both cotton and jute textiles … [it] is attributed mainly to technological changes
rendering their jobs … redundant. Fixation of minimum work load and stan-
dardisation of wages in the cotton textile industry necessitated retrenchment
of women workers who were working mostly as reelers and winders where the
work-load was found to be lower … Rationalisation and mechanisation schemes
in the jute industry eliminated some of the manual processes which at one time
were the preserve of women workers. Certain occupations giving employment
to women in the jute industry earlier were found to be hazardous and are therefore closed to women now by Rules framed under the Factories Act.[90]

Rationalization of production and the weaker sex being relieved of
labour considered too strenuous for them, whatever the pretext, the fact
is that the progressive elimination of women from the workforce has
further strengthened male dominance of economic life.

In factories where machines are not only used but also made, women
seemed to disappear entirely. While Sharma at least reported that only
males were employed in the car plant he studied,[91] Sheth totally omits
any mention of the fact that the workforce of Oriental did not apparently include a single woman. Where both sexes are employed, women
are invariably in a small minority. In 1956, women formed only 11.7
per cent of the workforce in manufacturing industries in India, and were
concentrated mostly in medium-sized to large enterprises.[92] They were
present in only two of the five Pune factories which Lambert studied,
and his sample was 96.6 per cent male—which under-represented their

[89] Ibid., p. 69.
[90] GoI, *Report of the National Commission on Labour*, p. 380.
[91] Sharma, *The Indian Industrial Worker*, p. 7.
[92] Lambert, *Workers, Factories and Social Change in India*, p. 23.

average in the enterprises in question. The same applies to Holmström's Bengaluru study: 5.6 per cent of his sample were women, compared with 15 per cent of factory workers in Karnataka as a whole.[93] The bias is not unconnected with a code of social conduct which makes them less easy to approach not only by male researchers but also by male co-workers.

… [T]he one woman 'draftsman' says the men in her office treat her as a sister, but she never goes among the men on the factory floor to discuss design problems, and so she cannot get promotion. Women keep to themselves in the canteen, play a minor part in most clubs and then only in the shadow of their husbands, and take little part in the union beyond attending general meetings and voting.[94]

It is no accident that women workers have a higher profile in Uma Ramaswamy's research. They formed 15 per cent of the total workforce but their participation, in absolute as well as relative terms, was declining.[95] Again, this was part of a trend towards mechanization by which they, in particular, were victimized. At the time of the study, the output of one woman equalled that of five a few decades earlier. Their employment was falling even though their productivity was higher than that of male workers. Why? The answer boils down to the fact that, in practice, it is easier to let men take the place of women than vice versa. In addition to all manner of inhibitions connected to the employment of women, and regardless of their willingness to work night shifts, they have to be paid for maternity leave. Factory regulation had also helped to reduce the differential wage level which meant that the attraction of women as cheap labour was reduced.

'Supernumerary' women are dismissed or transferred to unskilled work with lower earnings. It is repeatedly shown that they are invariably the lowest paid workers. Insofar as they have not been completely ousted from the industrial labour process, women seem, principally or exclusively, to be assigned tasks which need no special knowledge or skill and which—thought often monotonous—require precision and alertness.

When a certain job requires, in the employers's eyes, delicate handling, or when the work is time-consuming and tedious, women are called upon to do it. Thus,

[93] Holmström, *South Indian Factory Workers*, p. 19.
[94] Ibid., p. 65.
[95] Ramaswamy, *Work, Union and Community*, p. 22.

women are favoured in the electronics industry, for jobs which require tiny parts to be handled gently and carefully, and where fine wires have to be twisted and wound. In the textile industry, women have traditionally been employed as menders, spinners, winders, reelers, folders and cottonwaste pickers. In the pharmaceutical industry, women are generally employed as packers.[96]

Far more than men, the jobs they can get keep them riveted to the bottom of the work hierarchy without prospect of promotion.

## Lifestyle

Despite their considerable social heterogeneity, factory workers in the organized sector share a number of characteristics that have to do with the industrial culture in which they work and live, and which distinguish them from other components of the labour force. The expectation that a more homogeneous lifestyle would eventually emerge prompted various researchers to investigate the effect of the urban–industrial setting on household forms. In much of the literature, the industrial worker is a man living apart from his family and leading a bachelor's existence in the city.[97] Only when thoroughly established, he would be joined by his wife and children who had been left behind in the village. But, in southern India, labour migration was far less likely to lead to family separation. The worker was either accompanied by his family or was joined by them at the first opportunity.[98] As Kerr saw it, family reunion at the place of employment marked the transition to 'commitment'. The worker,

… is fully urbanized and never expects to leave industrial life. His family is permanently resident in an urban area, and it is not unusual for the wife also to enter the labor market. In fact, one good test of the degree of commitment of a labor force is the percentage of it comprised by women. An uncommitted or semi-committed labor force is predominantly male. The committed worker depends for his security on his employer and on the state, not his tribe. His way of life is industrial.[99]

Low female participation in the industrial labour force is held, in short, to be symptomatic of low commitment. What this wholly implausible

[96] Holmström, *Industry and Inequality*, p. 227.
[97] A.N. Das, 'The Indian Working Class: Relations of Production and Reproduction', in Das *et al.* (eds), *The Worker and the Working Class*, p. 165.
[98] Holmström, *Industry and Inequality*, p. 68.
[99] Kerr, 'Changing Social Structures', p. 353.

proposition ignores is that it is not that women are unwilling to take factory work, but rather that they cannot get it. Those who do, make use of precisely the same channels of influence and personalistic links as men. This explains why factory women are frequently close relatives of a male employee in the same enterprise. The greatest favour that a worker can hope for from management or the union is a job for his wife.[100] If both work, they have an income that many middle-class households would envy.[101]

In the early literature on factory labour, the transition from caste to class—not whether but when—was widely discussed. So, too, was the break-up of the joint family given its supposed incompatibility with urban–industrial life.[102] Both caste and the joint family represented the traditional culture and social structure which would be progressively transformed by the new economy. The much smaller size of the average household in industrial areas looked like confirmation. However, faith in this theory that development would follow the same course as it was supposed to have taken in the West was gradually undermined. The realization dawned that for a very large segment of the rural population, the joint family had not been the only or even most common unit of cohabitation. Further, Singer described the preservation—albeit streamlined—of the joint family among the industrial elite of Chennai, and showed how 'the home becomes the sphere of religion and traditional values; office and factory become the sphere of business and modern values', the phenomenon which he called 'compartmentalization'.[103] 'Modernization' was a much more complex and uneven process than was often supposed; in one sphere, 'tradition' might rule, in another, the values of modernity.

With regard to the joint family, however, I find the argument unconvincing, not least because it was entirely based on the households of Chennai's captains of industry. Lambert, however, develops a similar thesis for industrial workers. Though their households were not very different from those of other segments of the city's population as a whole, they did, on an average, include more members, being frequently

---

[100] Ramaswamy, *Work, Union and Community*, p. 25.

[101] Holmström, *Industry and Inequality*, pp. 227–8.

[102] For example, W.J. Goode, 'Industrialisation and Family Change', in B.F. Hoselitz and W.E. Moore (eds), *Industrialisation and Society: Proceedings of the Chicago Conference on Social Implications of Industrialisation and Technical Change*, Paris: UNESCO, 1963, pp. 237–55.

[103] Singer, 'The Indian Joint Family in Modern Industry', p. 438.

supplemented by all kinds of relatives.[104] This seemed to contradict the supposed transition to the conjugal family form. It is by no means certain, however, that this should be taken as evidence of the persistence of the 'traditional' joint family. I would rather agree with Holmström that for the average factory worker:

...the earning and spending unit is the nuclear family settled in the city, depending on one main earner, which expands to take relatives in need and then goes back to its normal size; linked to relatives elsewhere by bonds of duty and sentiment which are sometimes expensive.[105] This alternation of expansion and contraction is based on obligations towards relatives-cramped living space limiting the possibility of housing them indefinitely, and the inclusion of additional members partly arising from the necessity of broadening the household's economic base by increasing the number of workers. To contrast the 'traditional' joint family with the modern nuclear family is to ignore the fact that the predominant working class household in the industrial-urban milieu belongs to neither. It is rather a unit of cohabitation forced into being by low earnings and by specific conditions of employment.[106]

The NCL report observed that the quality of accommodation for industrial labour had improved since the first generation of *ahata*s in Kanpur, labour camps in Mumbai, shanties in the south, and *basti*s in eastern India which, over time, had become even more miserable and congested. New urban housing colonies have been constructed, though they rapidly tend to be burdened by overcrowding. Some large industrial enterprises have their own quite respectable housing estates, but these cater to only a small fraction of the working class. The greater proportion has to make do with primitive and confined living quarters in neighbourhoods that are mostly dilapidated and sordid.

Real change is seen inside the tenement. Earthen pots have been replaced by aluminium or brass-ware; pieces of crockery are not an unusual possession. There are also items of furniture, such as charpoi, a bench or a chair and a mosquito net. Radio/transistors/watches are often the proud possessions of not a few.[107]

This list of consumer goods, now more than forty years old, would, today, include a sewing machine, a bicycle, or even a Hero Honda, a fan,

---

[104] Lambert, *Workers, Factories and Social Change in India*, p. 56.

[105] Holmström, *Industry and Inequality*, p. 274.

[106] Report of a Survey, 'Working Class Women and Working Class Families in Bombay', *Economic and Political Weekly*, vol. 13, no. 29, 1978, p. 1169.

[107] GoI, *Report of the National Commission on Labour*, p. 33.

refrigerator, and television. Most would have access to tap water and many to a toilet. The NCL report also comments on new consumption patterns in food and clothing. Regional specialities are now common throughout the nation, for which factory canteens are partly responsible. Some foods are now bought pre-prepared. Clothing and footwear have increased both in quantity and quality. Many labourers now wear overalls in the factory, and gone are the days when they went unshod and were garbed only in short baggy trousers and a vest.

A composite portrait of the average factory worker is difficult because the differentiation is so striking. The upper bracket consists of employees in capital-intensive multinational corporations who should be included in the expanding middle class, not only because of the nature of their employment but also due to their lifestyle. At the bottom is a colossal army of unskilled and semi-skilled workers in industries that lack almost any advanced technology and have far less attractive working conditions. Comparatively, these workers are not badly paid, but they are threatened by continual demands that they increase their low productivity and have more difficulty passing their jobs on to the next generation.

However great the distance between these two poles, they also share some crucial characteristics. In the first place, they are all in regular employment and the great majority receives a wage that fluctuates little. This is based on the hours they have put in, which in turn implies a clear distinction between working and non-working times. Finally, their conditions of employment—not only of appointment, promotion, and dismissal but also a great diversity of secondary provisions regarding illness, vacations, pensions, Dearness Allowance (DA), bonuses, etc.—are governed by well-defined rules laid down in legislation and partly brought about by trade union pressure. It is this combination of features which leads me to consider workers in medium-sized and large industries as the dominant fraction of the working class in the industrial sector of the modern economy. Their lifestyle, culture, and consciousness reveal their commonality.

They belong to a distinctive Indian industrial culture, with typical assumptions and expectations and tastes which cut across divisions of skill and age and origin. They share a common situation. They act, and sometimes think of themselves, as a group (if not a class) different from peasants, workers in the 'unorganised' sector or in older factories with different technologies, from casual labourers, shopkeepers, professional people and so on.[108]

[108] Holmström, *South Indian Factory Workers*, p. 27.

But they are only a small minority; and it is their high social, political, and economic profile, rather than their numbers, that makes them dominant and a model for emulation amongst other segments of the working class. Should they, therefore, be regarded as a privileged elite who—like the dominant caste in the rural–agrarian sphere—have appropriated a disproportionate share of scarce goods at the expense of other groups? Opinions differ.

Their basic wage, which increases with the number of years worked, is supplemented by a DA and other benefits. Their total earnings are significantly higher than that of other sections of the proletariat without formal labour contracts with their employers; and various social provisions—which also benefit their families—insure them against risk and uncertainty. They know that they are privileged, but are reluctant to share their advantages with the far larger mass of workers without them, realizing that their extension to others might well result in their dilution. Lowering the citadel wall, or building more entrance gates, would threaten inundation. So, according to some, this industrial vanguard has developed into a class that is solely concerned with strengthening its own interests.

> ... [I]t is the organisational strength of industrial labour that prevents the transfer of resources from urban to rural sector and thereby to agricultural labour. If the power of the industrial labour is curbed and it is prevented from exploiting its strategic location in the growth of the Indian economy, efforts can be made to improve the lot of the rural poor.[109]

Sinha here summarizes a standard argument, though his own views are different. Arguing that industrial wages have only risen in reaction to increases in the cost of living, he rejects the suggestion that capital accumulation has been delayed by draining off profits to organized sector labour for consumption. However, other authors continue to see them as a labour aristocracy whose privileged position explains why, all over India, the gap between their income and the wages paid to agricultural workers is now far greater than ever.

## THE ASSERTION OF DIGNITY

What further marks factory workers in regular employment as a special category is that they have amalgamated into trade unions to negotiate

---

[109] G.P. Sinha, 'Crisis in Industrial Relations Policy', in Papola *et al.* (eds), *Labour, Employment and Industrial Relations in India*, p. 271.

improvements in their conditions of work and to defend their rights. In both, the state has also played an important role. The labour legislation introduced after independence has operated primarily, if not exclusively, to the benefit of this segment of the working class. Nor should it be imagined that the protection of the state was prompted by pure benevolence. It was a concession to the power built up by the factorized proletariat, and the inevitable consequence of the commanding role which the state had assumed in managing the transition to an industrial order in which these workers were considered so vital. At stake in the discussions of the NPC in 1940 was the creation of industrial machinery similar to that which already existed in Europe. Coupled with this was the introduction of extensive legislation on conditions of employment, including delimitation of the working week; prohibition of child labour; provisions for sanitation, health, and safety at work; the fixing and implementation of a minimum wage; equal pay for equal work; the right to a paid vacation; maternity benefits; housing quarters; procedures for settling conflicts; and compulsory arbitration by government (necessitating the establishment of a Conciliation Board and an Industrial Court). The creation of a system of social security was also discussed.

A system of compulsory and contributory social insurance for industrial workers should be established directly under the control of the State to cover the risks of sickness and invalidity other than those covered by the Workmen's Compensation Act. Schemes for providing alternative employment to those involuntarily unemployed, Old Age Pensions and Survivors' Pensions, and also Social Insurance to cover risks of sickness and invalidity for all, should be established directly under the State. These schemes should be extended by stages, priority being given to particular classes of workers, with due regard to the relative urgency of their needs, facility of application, and to the ability of the community to provide for them.[110]

The last sentence was intended to check exaggerated expectations. During the deliberations, however, Ambalal Sarabhai, President of the Ahmedabad Mill-Owners' Association, who acted as the employers' representative, asked whether it was really intended that the entire package should be introduced in the short term. The Chairman, Jawaharlal Nehru, explained that it represented a coordinated scheme which did not allow for piecemeal selection, but was vague about the timing of

---

[110] National Planning Committee (NPC), 'Minutes of National Planning Committee', Collection of Papers in Nehru Memorial Museum, New Delhi, May 1940.

its implementation which would anyway have to wait until after the transfer of power.

The nationalist leadership realized that the mobilization of industrial workers—which had started in the colonial era and had expressed itself in strikes and other forms of protest—might gain new impetus after the liberation from alien rule, and therefore, recognized the need to pacify labour. In 1929, the number of registered trade unions in India was twenty-nine; in 1951, it was 3,987.[111] Economic policy obviously had to come to terms with this institutionalized interest. Although the unions cared for the interests of only a tiny minority of the labouring classes, that minority formed its most vocal and most militant segment. The hope was that, in exchange for special treatment, this vanguard of 'the dangerous classes' might be induced to abandon more extreme demands. Peasants and workers were *ad nauseam* told to sacrifice their own interests for the good of the nation. One member of the NPC suggested that there should be no room for industrial unrest in the planned economy. However, fear of the radicalization of the factory proletariat, whose numbers were bound to increase rapidly, was nevertheless great.[112]

Faced with this threat, the politicians adopted various strategies. First, they successfully encouraged the rise of trade unions that were linked to different political currents and whose mutual rivalry prevented the labour movement from forming a united front. Second, every effort was made to avoid or defuse direct confrontation between employers and employees. The priority given to harmony and reconciliation, with arbitration prescribed, meant that the state itself became a principal party to negotiations. Third, through the carrot of benefits and facilities, they sought to detach the industrial elite from its links with the far greater mass of workers. This enormous army of underprivileged labour was excluded from formal wage negotiations, and there was no institutionalized mechanism for the promotion of their interests. A Fair Wages Committee was given the task of finding out how much an industrial worker needed to provide for himself and his immediate family (significantly identified as a unit of man, wife, and two children):

… not merely the bare essentials of food, clothing and shelter, but a measure of frugal comfort, including education for the children, protection against ill

---

[111] Ornati, *Jobs and Workers in India*, p. xi.
[112] For example, S. Kanappan, 'Labour Force Commitment in Early Stages of Industrialisation', *Indian Journal of Industrial Relations*, vol. 5, no. 3, 1970, p. 315.

health, requirements of essential social needs and a measure of insurance against the more inevitable misfortunes including old age.[113]

The employers argued, however, that even 'a measure of frugal comfort' was too heavy a burden and that they could only grant a fair wage if labour would agree to increase production and maintain industrial peace. This was not unattractive in that the wage set was far above that on which the greater part of the working population had to survive. Until the beginning of the 1960s, the illusion was maintained that industrialization could be instrumental in the transition towards a socialist society. In addition to a fair wage and bonus policy, and the acceptance of collective bargaining, industrial socialism would also mean workers' participation in management and eventually, profit sharing;[114] but this, of course, was never achieved, nor even seriously attempted.

The class consciousness of factory workers is demonstrated by their willingness to organize, and union membership is conventionally taken as evidence of their readiness for collective action and as an index of their solidarity. In fact, by no means all workers in the formal sector became union members. Even on the grossly inflated membership figures provided by the unions themselves, less than one out of three workers were registered; and if regular payment of union dues is the yardstick, the proportion shrinks much further. The hard core of trade unionists is actually a small minority; and as we have seen, this 'vanguard' of the working class shows no inclination to join the struggle for improving the plight of the non-organized masses.

Evaluation of this rather pessimistic picture must be on the basis of empirical research on the relations between workers and unions. The best study undoubtedly remains that of E.A. Ramaswamy, already more than three decades old. This showed that Coimbatore mill workers keep a sharp eye on whether the union's cadre exert themselves in caring for their concerns; but are also acutely aware that their existence is far more comfortable than that of the great mass of workers who have no one to defend their interests. As one senior member remarked:

---

[113] P. Loknathan, 'Employment and Wages in Indian Economy', in Papola *et al.* (eds), *Labour, Employment and Industrial Relations in India*, p. 51.

[114] C. Joseph, 'Workers' Participation in Industry: A Comparative Study and Critique', in E.A. Ramaswamy (ed.), *Industrial Relations in India: A Sociological Perspective*, New Delhi: Macmillan, 1978, pp. 123–39; R.K. Mukherjee, 'The Role of Labour in Democratic Socialism', in Papola *et al.* (eds), *Labour, Employment and Industrial Relations in India*, p. 109.

There is a limit to what we can ask from the millowner. I get four times as much as my neighbour who toils in a field all day, and yet my job is easier and not very much more skilled than his. Unless conditions improve all around it is difficult to get us to ask for more.[115]

Despite Ramaswamy's title (*The Worker and His Union*), trade union membership includes women. Hastening away at the end of their shift to do their household chores, they are said to be generally quite passive in union affairs and to do no more than pay their contributions. But if their jobs are endangered, or if other problems arise, they are extremely militant. At the time of the research, they had every reason to assert themselves because women were particularly threatened by redundancy.

We have earlier seen that women are concentrated in the lowest ranks of the labour hierarchy and often get no further than casual work. Whatever their sex, casual workers have greater need than regular workers of the help and protection of a union. Not only is their unionization opposed by the employers[116] but union leaders show little zest for, and even some hostility to it. Can they be blamed? Holmström takes a charitable view, pointing out that consolidating their gains is difficult enough without having to defend the interests of a mass of workers who are far more vulnerable. Even more than the badlis, who have at least been able to join the pool of reserve labour to await their turn for a job, that vulnerability afflicts the infinitely greater masses who have not yet found their way into the waiting room.

Many unions are overwhelmingly defensive. They are there to protect jobs first, then the real value of wages against inflation, with safety and working conditions a poor third, rather than to win more than the members have already. They know their bargaining power is weak; noisy militant demands for more are a tactic to hold the line, something to be bargained away when vital interests are threatened. The union has a hard enough job protecting its own members without worrying about outsiders.[117]

Other authors, like Mamkoottam,[118] are far more critical. The leaders are manipulative and corrupt, more concerned with their own interests than in caring for those of the rank and file. Workers react by making

---

[115] Ramaswamy, *The Worker and His Union*, pp. 182–3.

[116] Ramaswamy, *Work, Union and Community*, p. 21

[117] Holmström, *Industry and Inequality*, p. 289; see also, Das, 'The Indian Working Class', p. 174.

[118] K. Mamkoottam, *Trade Unionism: Myth and Reality*, New Delhi: Oxford University Press, 1982.

their support for them contingent on the results they achieve. If these are disappointing, they have no hesitation in defecting to a rival union. It is not a question of ideology but a pragmatic choice of who offers the most for the lowest price. According to such authors, trade union bosses operate as brokers, like the earlier jobbers, and use their mandate to enter into deals with employers, politicians, and rival unions. It is perhaps not surprising that the unionization of the factorized workforce remains quite limited.

The battles which had to be fought in order to break through the employers' resistance to the formation of unions and to the first collective actions is perhaps the principal reason why the present generation of factory workers have any faith in these organizations. The memory of champions in the fight for a better life, who often had to pay a high price for their ideals and dedication, still lives on. Sheth, who concluded that the union had only marginal significance for the workforce he studied, nevertheless added the qualification that:

… workers realised that though the union achieved precious little for them, they could achieve even less in the absence of a union. Individual workers could make a comparison in retrospect between 'union days' and 'unionless days' and found that though the union got them hardly anywhere in relation to the demands it made on the management, it was necessary for systematic dealing with the management.[119]

This seems to be a common view amongst organized labour, whose lack of a more embracing sense of solidarity I see less as the product of a short-sighted aristocratic mentality than as of a quite realistic fear that the cake may be too small for all comers.

In my view, however, the Indian trade union movement has played an emancipatory role. Perlin is quite correct in pointing out that little if any improvement has been brought about in the more deplorable working conditions. In a great many enterprises, these are injurious not only to health but also to human dignity.[120] The complacent opinion of the NCL report that industrial workers become inured to such

---

[119] Sheth, *The Social Framework of an Indian Factory*, pp. 159–60; see also, B.R. Sharma, 'Union Involvement Revisited', *Economic and Political Weekly*, vol. 13, no. 30, p. 1239.

[120] E. Perlin, 'Ragi, Roti and Four-Yard Dhoties: Indian Mill Workers as Historical Sources', in M. Gaborieau and A. Thorner (eds), *Asie du sud: traditions et changements*, Paris: Editions du CRNS, 1979, p. 457.

hardships and can more or less ignore them,[121] fails to grasp the sense of resentment, ill-being, and pollution to which such conditions often give rise. But this does not alter the fact that factory workers in regular employment have made great progress, particularly in their own self-esteem, and that this has been significantly due to the protection offered by membership of a trade union. Conversely, self-esteem encourages them to organize themselves, even when this is likely to arouse the displeasure of their bosses. The NCL concluded that the industrial worker of today has acquired a dignity not known to his predecessor, while the employers perceived a greater measure of defiance on the industrial worker's part towards his superiors. The new assertiveness was based on a new awareness: 'a worker today is more politically conscious than before, more articulate of the existing order and more sensitive to his conditions and hardships'.[122] And it was the charismatic role models provided by the cadre members which induced the less active and less conscientized factory workers to assert themselves, even if only temporarily. Ramaswamy's research illustrates this well:

[They] describe in detail—with sketches of individuals and their life histories and thoughts—a world of the union activists … held together by an ideology of working-class solidarity cutting across barriers of caste and employment. By their personal example, they carry along the mass of ordinary workers who are moderately apathetic about wider issues, but still loyal enough to strike, demonstrate and perhaps vote when asked by those they respect. The union provides a service when needed; in return it sometimes asks for sacrifice and enthusiasm.[123]

Wage increases have undoubtedly been the most urgent demand of the trade union movement since its inception. Its programme of action soon broadened, however, into a more general protest against the hierarchical order, not only of industry but of society as a whole. While that hierarchy instructed labour to resign itself to its own subor-dination, the ideology of the unions nurtured the principles of equality and social justice. Corruption of those ideals was linked to everyday party politics, in which the unions were deeply embroiled; and also, resulted from contradictory currents that prevailed among the working masses, a great proportion of whom originated from a world that was by no means impervious to distinctions of caste, class, ethnicity, religion, and gender.

[121] GoI, *Report of the National Commission on Labour*, p. 35.
[122] Ibid.
[123] Holmström, *Industry and Inequality*, pp. 294–5.

It is, thus, all the more significant that 'the main public ideology—not just the language of politics and unions, but much ordinary talk—tends to stress moral and social equality'.[124] Assertions of dignity were also a denial of dependency and inequality, and were met with considerable oppression from the employers who attached great significance to the recognition of their traditional authority, and who, quite rightly, saw industrial agitation as undermining their claim to respectful obedience. Consider the following appeal with which, at the start of the 1950s, one employer called his striking workers to order:

Your illegal and indisciplinary ways distress me. I am tired and will be compelled to take action … My advice to you as your elder and wellwisher is work wholeheartedly and maintain discipline … [I]f you do not follow my humble advice you will compel the company to dismiss all those who act illegally as we have waited patiently for long …[125]

Three decades later such language would have been greeted with utter hilarity.

During the 1970s and 1980s, drastic changes took place in labour relations as a result of the restructuring of the industrial economy. Rationalization of production became a major trend, first, in private business but subsequently, also in public sector enterprises, and resulted in significant 'downsizing'. Between 1968 and 1984, the average number of production workers per factory declined from seventy-five to sixty-one.[126] Technological change played some role but many more workers were replaced by cheap casual labour than by machines. Exit policies in the guise of 'voluntary' retirement schemes reduced the size of the permanent workforce in both large and small companies. The efficiency drive met with the wholehearted approval of the state bureaucracy, which increasingly shared the employers' view that the maintenance of existing labour rights was a major obstacle to economic growth. The inevitable outcome of the 'flexibilization' of industrial work has been a contraction of production in the formal sector, and a further expansion of the informal sector economy.

In this scaling down, the job security of the permanent workforce was nevertheless reaffirmed and they may even have improved their

---

[124] Holmström, *South Indian Factory Workers*, p. 80.

[125] Ornati, *Jobs and Workers in India*, p. 15.

[126] T.S. Papola and G. Rodgers, 'Restructuring in Indian Industry', in G. Edgren (ed.), *Restructuring. Employment and Industrial Relations: Adjustment Issues in Asian Industries*, New Delhi: World Employment Programme, ILO, 1989, p. 46.

bargaining position—suggesting a direct link between the privileges granted to a tiny section of the workforce and the marginalization of a much larger segment. But, however this may be, lower manning levels meant heavier workloads for those who remained. In return for higher wages, they had to commit themselves to higher production targets.

These changes gave rise to a new type of trade union leadership, exemplified by Datta Samant in Mumbai. The style of negotiation was confrontational, demands were immoderate, and legal niceties were ignored. The leader insisted on a united front and demanded total obedience, but also promised no compromises. Direct action had only one aim: monetary gain. In this type of trade union leadership, the relationship between leader and worker is essentially contractual and does not bind them beyond the duration of the strike. The union boss is more the leader of a campaign than the head of an enduring organization. He neither bothers about the problems, complaints, and requests of individual workers, and nor is he deeply interested in ideological issues or the working-class movement at large. If the strike fails, he simply moves on to the next target, which may be a different industry. Before the start of any action, the financial standing of the company is carefully assessed in order to calculate the level at which the union's demands should be pitched. When labour costs are not critical to the total cost of production, management is much more eager to settle the dispute than in industries where wages are pegged at one-fourth or one-third of manufacturing expense. The failure of the huge textile strike in 1982–3 in Mumbai, which lasted for eighteen months and in which more than 200,000 workers took part under the leadership of Datta Samant, should be seen in this light. The defeat certainly affected his reputation, but only for a short time and not in more capital-intensive branches of industry.

Aggressive leadership of this kind stands in marked contrast to the less militant and more legalistic leadership of the conventional unions. Mavericks, like Datta Samant, are accused of luring workers away from established leaders who best know how to take care of their real interests. They antagonize employers and land workers with deals which are bound to turn sour. But, as several authors have argued, this representation does little justice to the sense of disillusionment and resentment which many organized sector workers had developed towards their erstwhile representatives. The new combination of working-class radicalism and businesslike unionism is indicative of a new stage in industrial relations in which wider solidarities are sacrificed to narrower and more short-term interests. To dismiss such behaviour as apolitical would be to misread the assertiveness and self-consciousness of these militant workers whose social identity differs markedly from the older generation of factory hands.

The traditional stereotype of the industrial worker as an illiterate low-caste migrant, pushed out of the village by unemployment, was dubious at the best of times. Now it is becoming more untrue with each passing day. Most enterprises in the organised sector would not consider for employment anyone without a school leaving certificate, and the presence of graduates and post-graduates—the blue-collar workforce has long ceased to be a novelty. For the skilled trades, a technical diploma from an industrial training institute is an additional advantage. With wages so attractive and employment so scarce, the blue-collar workforce too become[s] a polyglot mix of workers from various castes and religious backgrounds.[127]

As for management's reaction to this new radicalism, much depends on their readiness to adjust to the new times. Some took offence at being addressed in a manner which did not acknowledge their authority and superiority. Others responded in a businesslike fashion and clinched deals which still gave them the upper hand. In exchange for an increase in the wage packet, they insisted on including clauses on heavier workloads, incentive schemes, and lower rates of absenteeism. It was not at all rare for the union which had called the strike to be held responsible for the worker's fulfilment of these conditions. By allowing the likes of Datta Samant to operate on their premises, the employers not only hoped to buy industrial peace but also a more productive workforce. The other side of the story is, of course, that ever-increasing benefits were placed in the hands of ever-shrinking numbers. As Ramaswamy has astutely noted, contract work, casual labour, redundancy, and voluntary retirement schemes create the surplus that is passed on to those left behind in permanent employment. The flow is from one segment of the workforce to another rather than from capital to labour. If not from ideology, then at least from self-interest, the unions will eventually have to organize the unorganized—if they are to be left with a constituency at all.[128]

[127] E.A. Ramaswamy, 'Indian Trade Unionism: The Crisis of Leadership', in M. Holmström (ed.), *Work for Wages in South Asia*, New Delhi: Manohar, 1990, p. 170; see also G. Heuze, 'Workers' Struggles and Indigenous Fordism in India', in Holmström (ed.), *Work for Wages in South Asia*, p. 177.

[128] E.A. Ramaswamy, *Worker Consciousness and Trade Union Response*, London: Oxford University Press, 1988, p. 74.

Employers who initially did not know how to cope with the phenomenon of independent unions have grown to like them. What they want
for their enterprise is not representation by several unions fighting with
each other over the spoils, but a strong leader able to instil discipline
among his clientele. The industrialists' organization has consistently
argued in favour of the 'one factory, one union' principle.[129] That preference is strongly inspired by the perception that plant-level associations
do not have a wider agenda and are wary of joining national federations
which are hand in glove with political parties. This trend is also in line
with World Bank recommendations. In its 1995 Annual Report,[130]
negotiations at plant level are praised as the most appropriate framework
in which to achieve positive economic effects. Positive for whom? Does
the Bank's recipe for 'responsible trade unionism' take cognizance of
the vast army of casual and contract labourers moving around as wage
hunters and gatherers in the lower echelons of the industrial economy?
Their work and employment are dealt with in the next chapter.

[129] Heuze, 'Workers' Struggles and Indigenous Fordism in India', p. 185.
[130] World Bank, *World Development Report, 1995: Workers in an Integrating
World*, New York: Oxford University Press, 1995.

# 7

# Industrial Labour in Post-colonial India

## Getting Rid of Formal Sector Employment*

In the landscape of labour, industrial workers in the organized sector of the economy form a privileged and protected enclave. They are generally identified as skilled factory workers who are permanently engaged in modern enterprises equipped with advanced technology. In addition to their secure employment status, they constitute an 'aristocracy' with a high social profile and a reasonably comfortable lifestyle. Not least, those who belong to the upper bracket of the industrial workforce have a dignity that derives from their status as organized and legally protected employees. The moment one tries to specify all these characteristics, however, it becomes clear that they form an *ideal type* as understood by Weber: a compilation of traits which provides a stereotyped image in which the work and lives of only a small minority of plant labourers can be recognized.

To put it in another way, it is almost impossible to define the average factory hand. The differences among them, between and even within industries, are too great. Just as progressive variations predominate among the players in the superior league, there is no question of a clear and rigid rupture with the world of waged labour outside

* Originally published as 'The Study of Industrial Labour in Post-colonial India: The Informal Sector, a Concluding Review', in J. Parry, J. Breman, and K. Kapadia (eds), *The World View of Industrial Labour in India*, New Delhi: Sage Publications, 1999, pp. 407–31.

it.[1] The economy thus does not allow itself to be split into two sectors, one formal and the other informal, and that also applies to conditions of employment. Holmström, having abandoned his earlier model, has more recently reconceptualized his sharp dichotomy between the two sectors by a more nuanced and more differentiated chart of the labour terrain:

My image of the citadel was too simple. The organized/unorganized boundary is not a wall but a steep slope. Indian society is like a mountain, with the very rich at the top, lush Alpine pastures where skilled workers in the biggest modern industries graze, a gradual slope down through smaller firms where pay and conditions are worse and the legal security of employment means less, a steep slope around the area where the Factories Act ceases to apply (where my wall stood), a plateau where custom and the market give poorly paid unorganized sector workers some minimal security, then a long slope down through casual migrant labour and petty services to destitution. There are well-defined paths up and down these slopes, which are easiest for certain kinds of people.[2]

In abandoning the idea that the economy follows a dualist pattern, Holmström reaches the further conclusion that the world of labour cannot be divided into two sections of organized and unorganized sector workers respectively. There is no clear dividing line between them. I am in agreement with that observation, but find the lesson that he draws from it, however hesitantly, more problematic, namely: that there is only one working class with common interests and a common fate. If what Ram and others have remarked is true, that 'anyone descriptive generalisation of the characteristics of the Indian working class simply no longer seems to suffice',[3] it is perhaps more suitable to draw attention to the multiple identity of this very diverse and heterogeneous social amalgam of classes. That option forms the point of departure for the following analysis of industrial employment outside the organized sector of the economy. My particular attention will be directed towards the

[1] J. Harriss, 'The Working Poor and the Labour Aristocracy in a South Indian City: A Descriptive and Analytical Account', *Modern Asian Studies*, vol. 20, no. 2, 1986, pp. 231–83.

[2] M. Holmström, *Industry and Inequality: The Social Anthropology of Indian Labour*, Cambridge: Cambridge University Press, 1984, p. 319.

[3] K. Ram, 'The Indian Working Class and the Peasantry: A Review of Current Evidence on Interlinks between the Two Classes', in A.N. Das, V. Nilkant, and P.S. Dubey (eds), *The Worker and the Working Class: A Labour Studies Anthology*, New Delhi: Public Enterprises Centre for Continuing Education, 1983, p. 184.

working environment and to the social distinctions between the various categories of workers who depend upon it for their existence.

## MAIN FEATURES

Rural–urban migration, which started long before independence, has accelerated during the last half century. Only a small minority of that army of migrants, however, has found work in the formal sector of the economy. The greater part of the urban population, both long established and newcomers, are excluded from such employment. How, then, has this gradually increasing mass of people managed to earn a living? The answer is, with work of varying kinds which provides little stability, even if continuous and full time. Our understanding of the informal sector is still influenced by the images evoked by Hart[4] when he invented the term. His account stressed the colourful cavalcade of petty trades and crafts that may be countered in the streets of Third World cities, including those of India: hawkers, rag-and-bone men, shoe cleaners, tinkers, tailors, market vendors, bearers and porters, drink sellers, barbers, refuse collectors, beggars, whores and pimps, pickpockets, and other small-time crooks. In the 1970s and 1980s in particular, registration of this repertoire of work expanded enormously.[5] It is striking that publications on the subject did not originate among conventional researchers into labour, who were interested mainly in formal sector employment.

The contents of leading professional journals, such as *The Indian Journal of Industrial Relations* and the *Indian Journal of Labour Economics*, show that their one-sided interest did not change until recently. This neglect was due both to lack of knowledge regarding the lower levels of the urban economy and to lack of affinity with methods of research that could increase that knowledge. The informal sector included a ragbag of activities for which no statistics were available and to which customary measuring and counting techniques were inapplicable. The landscape of informal sector employment has been charted mostly by anthropologists doing qualitative rather than quantitative research. However, the existence of the informal sector was acknowledged in various earlier publications. In 1955, Ornati divided industrial employment in India into two segments: 'organized' versus 'unorganized'. His distinction was

---

[4] K. Hart, 'Informal Income Opportunities and Urban Employment in Ghana', *Journal of Modern African Studies*, vol. 11, no. 1, 1973, pp. 61–89.

[5] J. Breman, *Wage Hunters and Gatherers: Search for Work in the Urban and Rural Economy of South Gujarat*, New Delhi: Oxford University Press, 1994.

based on the enforcement or non-enforcement of a packet of employment conditions laid down in the Factories Act. The great majority of
industrial workers proved not to be covered by those regulations:

A very large group of workers finds employment in the myriad small manufacturing enterprises which produce a large variety of products for local consumption. Much of the production of shoes and leather products is conducted in
factories which, because of their size, are not covered by the Factories Act. In
addition, many workers are employed in small cereal-milling establishments,
printing firms, bangle factories, and by mica processors. Working conditions
in this sector vary considerably from region to region and from enterprise to
enterprise. Little is known about the precise number of people employed or
about the conditions under which they work.[6]

At the end of the 1960s, the same classification was used again in an
official publication, but with a different meaning given to the concept
'unorganized': 'those who have not been able to organize in pursuit of a
common objective'.[7] The same source refers to the category of unprotected labour, found particularly in larger cities. The only information
given is that 'very little is known about it and much less has been done
to ameliorate its conditions of work'.[8] The great diversity and irregularity of employment in the informal sector, and the smallness of the work
unit is noticeable: often, no more than a single household or even one
individual. Hart, in his pioneering essay, suggested that the difference
between the organized and unorganized sectors of urban employment
coincided with wage labour *versus* self-employment. Many authors since
then have been inclined to see the informal sector as a collection of
micro-entrepreneurs, people who work chiefly for their own account
and at their own risk.

Another noticeable factor is the predominance of activities in the
tertiary sector of the economy, often carried out in the open air. Apart
from the heterogeneous mass working in the service sector, however,
industrial work also forms an essential part of the informal sector
economy. This refers to a type of manufacture that is mostly, if not
always, carried out in closed spaces, that is, in small workshops or, in
the case of home workers, in premises that are also used for domestic

[6] O.A. Ornati, *Jobs and Workers in India*, Institute of International Industrial
and Labour Relations, Ithaca: Cornell University Press, 1955, pp. 64–5.

[7] Government of India (GoI), *Report of the National Commission on Labour*, New
Delhi: Ministry of Labour, 1969, p. 417.

[8] Ibid., p. 434.

purposes. Powerlooms, leather-working ateliers, and diamond-cutting workshops are all prominent examples of small-scale industry in India, responsible for a very large share of the total turnover in their particular branch of business.

The most obvious characteristics of these small-scale urban industries are: first, a lack of complexity in the production process, limited capital, and little use of advanced technology and second, there is less division of labour than in the formal sector. Low capital intensity restricts expansion. Enterprises are fairly small, employing no more than a dozen or so workers, usually managed by a single owner. Wages are low, based not on total hours worked but on the quantity produced. Piecework rather than time rate is the measure for the sum that workers receive weekly from their employers. The workplace is a small shop or shed. Although workers are employed on a continuous basis, they derive no rights from their verbal work contract. The boss is free to terminate or interrupt the arrangement at any given moment. Termination may be due to seasonal fluctuations, to a breakdown in the power supply, or to problems with the supply of raw materials or with sales of the product. Even when the industrial cycle is not unpredictable, the employer retains the right to sack his workers at will.

The practice of instant hire-and-fire indicates that workers are not protected by legal regulations. Such rules do exist but due to the state's lack of will to exercise effective control over their enforcement, they are circumvented by employers with ease.[9] There is no regulation of work conditions: of wage levels, modes of payment, working hours, vacations, or social welfare provisions. Nor are there directives to protect workers' health during the production process. The unprotected nature of informal sector labour is closely linked with the inability of the workforce in this sector to protect itself by organizing. Trade unions are rare, although there may be more of them than we know.[10] It is the defencelessness of the workforce that encourages employers to keep their enterprises outside the formal sector of the economy.

Industrial establishments, such as those described earlier, employ masses of workers who far exceed the total number of men and women engaged in the formal sector of the economy. Home workers form a

[9] J. Breman, *Footloose Labour: Working in India's Informal Economy*, Cambridge: Cambridge University Press, 1996, pp. 177–221.

[10] See T. van der Loop, *Industrial Dynamics and Fragmented Labour Markets: Construction Firms and Labour Markets in India*, New Delhi: Sage Publications, 1996.

third category of industrial workers and represent the least visible but most vulnerable part of the labour force. The lack of reliable quantitative research means that their numbers can only be estimated. One problem here is that home-based work is rarely a full-time activity; rather, it is an activity that occupies more than one household member to varying degrees of frequency and intensity. As a result, far more women and children than men are involved in home-based working. Since domestic work is the sole responsibility of women, they are often willing to accept home-based work even if it is badly paid. Because they have to combine this with their housekeeping work, home-based women workers carry a double burden. This also means that they have little time to spare for participating in workers' movements or for learning new skills.[11] Under the putting-out system—a form of work that dates back to pre-capitalist times—raw materials are brought to the home of the producer and finished products are returned to the supplier or his agent. Production requires only simple tools, if any at all. Lace and brocade, hosiery, carpets, and *bidi*s, for example, are mostly manufactured in this way; home-based workers also assemble components into final products, ranging from toys to furniture and clothing.

The degree of skill required for industrial work in the informal sector of the economy varies considerably, but in general, access to a trade is not tied to formal education. While applicants for factory work in the formal sector are expected to have at least a diploma from an industrial training institute—a long-term training that follows completion of elementary and secondary school—informal sector workers have to pick up their skills on the job. Sometimes, they are apprenticed for a few months, but usually, they learn by assisting an experienced worker. During this training phase, newcomers are paid little if any wages; if they are paid, they are expected to give part of their wage to their instructor. If skill is required, as in the case of diamond cutting, the employer only takes on apprentices who are prepared to pay for their training or who will commit themselves to long-term work after its completion. Most authors have assumed that informal sector workers do not have a high degree of skill. According to some of these writers, newcomers to the urban milieu do not need technical knowledge as much as aptitude.

…although the vast majority of the urban labour force is unskilled, urban employment may require certain patterns of coordination and motor responses

---

[11] N. Banerjee (ed.), *Indian Women in a Changing Industrial Scenario*, New Delhi: Sage Publications, 1991, p. 31.

which differ from traditional agriculture and thus influence the possibilities of commitment...There may be need for more rhythm and monotonous repetition, coordination, careful timing, and higher levels of spatial, verbal or logical conception.[12]

Discipline, we are told, is a virtue that has to be instilled in the informal sector workers. This view shows a complete ignorance of the types of demands made on workers in the rural economy, regardless of whether they own a small plot of land or are landless. In addition, it underestimates the division of work in industrial production in the informal sector and the considerable technical skill that is required to perform adequately.

Waged labour is not only central to capitalist enterprises in the formal sector, it is also central to the informal sector. The term, 'self-employment', should only be used for own-account work. Sub-contracted work and job work should not be termed self-employment, for they are indirect, that is, mediated, wage-work agreements. They are not forms of micro-entrepreneurship because they lack autonomy. Industrial contracting and sub-contracting are associated with the activities of middlemen. Such people form the link between providers of capital in the form of raw materials and sometimes, also tools, and workers. Labour brokers come in all guises. They fill a particular role: they control the labour force, ensure that a job gets done, and make payment at job completion.

Large establishments give out contracts of jobs or of particular operations, e.g., loading and unloading, to contractors on a lump-sum payment. The contractor engages his own workers. The contractor can be an individual or an establishment or even a senior worker like a maistry or a mukadam or a sirdar.[13]

Sometimes, the entire production process is broken up into a number of composite parts. What looks like a factory in the formal sector, that is, a large workplace filled with machinery and with a few hundred workers, proves, on further inspection, to be an enterprise run on a completely informal basis. This can be exemplified by the dyeing and printing mills in Surat.[14] Work gangs are led by sub-contractors who also act as labour jobbers and supervisors. The factory owner has nothing to do with recruitment of the workforce and accepts no responsibility for the conditions of employment. Jobbers have not disappeared from the

[12] S. Kanappan, 'Labour Force Commitment in Early Stages of Industrialisation', *Indian Journal of Industrial Relations*, vol. 5, no. 3, 1970, p. 321.

[13] GoI, *Report of the National Commission on Labour*, p. 418.

[14] Breman, *Footloose Labour*, p. 158.

industrial economy; on the contrary, they are still emphatically present in the informal sector where they fill a key role.

What is the social identity of industrial workers in the informal sector? The stereotypic image is of migrants who have only recently left the countryside and who have come to the city in search of a better existence. This is true to a certain extent. Many home-based workers and workers in small business originate from outside the city. Their outsider status is, in fact, an important reason why employers prefer them. A high percentage of newcomers are young males. The lack of adequate and affordable housing forces married men to leave their families behind in the village. The bachelor existence, which is characteristic for the life of many migrants, causes them to congregate in groups in shared accommodation where they also share meals. The enormous increase in urban informal sector jobs has given urban streets a strongly masculine appearance. However, the informal sector is not the exclusive domain of migrants. Many workers in the informal economy were born and grew up in the city. As in the formal sector, the work they do has frequently been handed down to them by the preceding generation.

From which castes do informal sector workers come? The diversity is great, and there is no truth in the assumption that members of higher castes avoid informal work. Nevertheless, social origins frequently determine the type of work carried out. The informal sector is not homogeneous but can be broken down into various layers. Without doubt, access to work is connected to caste membership. This applies also to the better-skilled and better-paid tasks in informal industrial work. In recruitment to such work, intermediate and 'Other Backward Castes' seem to be strongly represented. In contrast, workers who perform the most humble and miserable forms of informal sector work are mostly recruited from the lowest social ranks and are often from tribal and dalit communities.

Notwithstanding the unequal sex ratio of the urban population, women's participation in informal-sector work is far greater than in the formal sector. Child labour is also common. The nuclear family is the standard household unit. A family can only survive if both adults and children work. So the number of non-working members per household is lower than in the formal sector. However, the participation of women and children in industrial work does not signify that the balance of power within the household is more equal. The fact that a man is no longer the sole or principal breadwinner seems to have little effect on his dominance. Skilled tasks, where required, are carried out by the man. The time and effort given by his wife and children may be no less than his own, but they are remunerated at a far lower level. The wage earned by all the family members together is often paid to the man, who also decides how the money should be used. As head of the household, his role with regard to other family members may be compared to the labour jobber's role in relation to his work gang.

The notion soon arose that industrial work is intrinsically linked to urban locations; even today, this assumption seems to have lost little of its persuasiveness. If the transition from an agrarian to an industrial society was to be realized, a large part of the population had no alternative but to leave their villages and to settle in the cities. More than a century ago, in 1881, Ranade wrote:

There is a superfluity of agricultural labour in the agricultural labour market and unless that is removed from it and employed elsewhere, no remedial measure to improve the wretched condition of the agriculturalist will be productive of permanent good results. The development of agriculture and mechanical industry must be simultaneous.[15]

Spatial mobility, that is, large-scale migration leading to urbanization, was considered a necessary precondition to economic transformation. Pant estimated surplus peasant labour to be one-quarter to one-third of the total; from that he deduced that roughly 33 million workers would have to leave the countryside, together with their families.[16] After independence, scepticism regarding the inclination of rural people to migrate voluntarily caused policy advisers to suggest the setting up of migration boards which would encourage migration away from agriculture and the village.[17] Only later was it realized that the lack of rural employment could not be solved solely through an industrialization process that was urban based.

But employment in the countryside was not exclusively agricultural, even historically. Plantation production was always characterized by an industrial work regime, as was mining. The rules that governed

[15] Cited in B. Chandra, *The Rise and Growth of Economic Nationalism in India: Economic Policies of Indian National Leadership, 1880–1905*, New Delhi: People's Publishing House, 1966, p. 494.

[16] S.C. Pant, *Indian Labour Problems*, Allahabad: Chaitanya Publishing House, 1965, p. 362.

[17] T.S. Papola, P.P. Ghosh, and A.N. Sharma (eds), *Labour, Employment and Industrial Relations in India*, New Delhi: The Indian Society of Labour Economics and B.R. Publishing Corp., 1993, p. 45.

urban factory workers were also applied to plantation coolies and mine workers. The industrial organization of these large-scale and labour-intensive enterprises was the rural variant of the formal-sector economy. During the last half century, modern industrial plants have been set up throughout the countryside. For example, in the 1960s, a multinational chemical plant was set up in a rural location along the Mumbai–Surat railway line. A small township sprang up around it: high-ranking staff and skilled specialists lived there. However, two-thirds of the 4,000 strong workforce commuted daily to the plant from the surrounding small towns and villages.[18] Employment conditions here were the same as in the urban–formal sector. But these conditions have not applied to traditional craftsmen working in cottage industries in the villages. Attempts to encourage traditional forms of production, or to reactivate them according to Gandhian principles, have almost always resulted in failure. Traditional cottage industries have proved no match for the capitalist mode of production that has steadily gained ground, largely because they have not been able to compete with the cheaper mass-produced goods.

The breakthrough in agrarian production in the 1960s was coupled with the diversification of the rural economy. The decreasing significance of agriculture as the main source of livelihood was compensated for by the increase in employment opportunities in the non-agricultural sector. This included the transport, construction, and service sectors, as well as new industrial employment based on capital and entrepreneurship derived from agriculture.[19] The government's industrialization policy encouraged the establishment of both large and small industries at areas far away from the primary cities. This led to the creation of industrial estates, on the edges of secondary or tertiary urban centres, whose workers came partly from the surrounding villages. The labour regime in such enterprises was similar to that in the urban informal sector.[20] Some rural processing industries had originated in colonial and even pre-colonial times: these included cotton-ginning, jute-pressing, sugar production, and tanning. Significantly, the recent expansion of some of these agro-industries into large-scale, technologically modern

---

[18] K.M. Kapadia and S.D. Pillai, *Industrialisation and Rural Society: A Study of Atul–Bulsar Region*, Bombay: Popular Prakashan, 1972.

[19] See M.A.F. Rutten, *Farms and Factories: Social Profile of Large Farmers and Rural Industrialists in West India*, New Delhi: Oxford University Press, 1994.

[20] H. Streefkerk, *Industrial Transition in Rural India: Artisans, Traders and Tribals in South Gujarat*, Bombay: Popular Prakashan, 1985.

factories (producing, for example, sugar, paper, and conserves), has not resulted in the formalization of labour relations between employers and employees.[21]

Finally, I would like to point out that two major avenues of rural industrial employment have remained marginal to labour studies: employment in quarries and brickfields. They provide seasonal employment to multitudes of workers throughout the country. Production here is small scale, yet, during the last decade or so, their significance has grown considerably due to the enormous increase in both public works and private construction. A central feature of this industry is its seasonality. The labour force consists mainly of migrants brought in from elsewhere, often over long distances, by labour jobbers who also work as gang bosses. It is quite mistaken to assume that alien labour is imported only when there is an insufficient supply of local labour. On the contrary, local landless labourers have to migrate annually from these regions during the agricultural off-season to seek work. They work in road building, construction, and cane cutting, and also, as brick makers and quarry workers. Thus, labour circulation is the predominant pattern; this work is usually temporary and carried out in the open air.

Labour nomadism is not a new phenomenon, but its magnitude and the distances workers cover have increased greatly over time. Pant considered labour nomadism to be an expression of economic distress and a symptom of social disintegration. He concluded that it would be brought to an end by greater rural development.[22] On the contrary, I believe that such forms of migration are very closely linked to the accelerated progress of the capitalist mode of production in the countryside.[23] However, the situation of those workers who remain in the villages is becoming even worse. The agricultural wages of landless labourers have fallen even further behind. The rural poor who are most affected are those who are the most vulnerable: women, the aged, and the physically handicapped.

## STRUCTURING THE INDUSTRIAL LABOUR MARKET

There is no sharp bifurcation of the industrial labour market into a formal and an informal sector. Yet, Holmström's image of the citadel

---

[21] Breman, *Wage Hunters and Gatherers*, pp. 133–287.

[22] Pant, *Indian Labour Problems*, pp. 33–4.

[23] J. Breman, *Of Peasants, Migrants and Paupers: Rural Labour Circulation and Capitalist Production in West India*. Oxford: Clarendon Press and New Delhi: Oxford University Press, 1985.

is a persuasive one because it suggests the highly privileged nature
of a comfortable life in the protected labour sector, in an economic
context where the great majority of workers have virtually no rights
at all. Holmström found the citadel image to be one which had been
internalized by organized sector workers themselves.

> They tend to see factory work as a citadel of security and relative prosperity,
> which it is: it offers regular work and promotion and predictable rewards, as
> against the chaos and terrifying dangers of life outside. For everyone inside the
> citadel, there is a regiment outside trying to scale the walls.[24]

Although this sharply dualistic model is persuasive, I would, instead,
suggest a more graduated and varied model that draws attention to the
enormous diversity in work conditions within *both* sectors.

In the formal sector, security characterizes the lives of those factory
workers who are in regular employment. They are paid reasonably well,
are adequately skilled, protected by labour legislation, and organized,
so that their interests are safeguarded. Their modest security makes
them creditworthy, so that they are able to incur debts without any
loss of autonomy. Their style of life and work provides these industrial
workers with prestige and respect. This also explains why there is a
desperate pursuit of the few positions that become vacant annually
within the citadel. For example, in 1995, the Kerala State Public Service
Commission received 200,000 applications for sixteen jobs as low-
ranking government clerks.[25] My own research shows that well-educated
applicants are willing to pay bribes equivalent to four times their annual
wage to get secure jobs as unskilled workers at the large Atul concern
in south Gujarat. Applicants see this as a good investment because this
employment is secure and because they are paid two or three times more
in the formal sector than in the informal.

Other conditions of employment in the lower ranks of the economy
also amount to an almost total reversal of labour relations in the
formal sector. Here, workers are not in regular employment and can
be dismissed arbitrarily. The production process is irregular: its rhythm
is subjected to unexpected fluctuations, with the consequence that the
size of the workforce varies, while working times are not standardized.
Exorbitantly long hours of work are followed by days or weeks of

---

[24] M. Holmström, *South Indian Factory Workers: Their Life and Their World*,
Cambridge: Cambridge University Press, 1976, p. 136.

[25] C.S. Venkata Ratnam, 'Tripartism and Structural Changes: The Case of India',
*Indian Journal of Industrial Relations*, vol. 31, no. 3, 1996, p. 361.

inactivity. This instability gives rise to a continuous drift of labour among the numerous small enterprises. The unremitting flexibility that has to be shown by workers is due to the manner in which production is organized and certainly does not imply any lack of commitment on their part, though this is what employers have claimed in the past. This state of flux is further aggravated by the standard practice of giving preference to outsiders over local labourers. The greater vulnerability of these alien workers is a major reason why employers prefer them. Migration becomes circulation when employment is of short duration. An example of this is the seasonal workers who leave their villages, often accompanied by their wives and children, to escape the agricultural off-season by working as cane cutters or brick makers. Occupational multiplicity is their only means of survival. Their incomes are so low that all household members have to work. These temporary migrant workers are far more vulnerable than settled migrant workers and are hard put to defend themselves from the many life crises that they encounter.

It is misleading to focus solely on the contrast between the two extremes of the labour hierarchy. Instead, it is the enormous diversity, not only between formal and informal sectors but also within them, that should, above all, be stressed. The distance between skilled multinational corporation (MNC) workers in regular employment and temporary factory workers in the formal sector is just as great as that between the latter and skilled diamond cutters, who earn more than the temporary factory hands and whom I would place at the top of the informal sector. Such diamond cutters, in turn, are elevated far above brick workers who also work as agricultural labourers for part of the year. Thus, a unidimensional hierarchical stratification does not exist. Confusing heterogeneity characterizes the broad middle range. At the top of the range is guaranteed job security, at the bottom, multiple vulnerabilities.

The dignity inherent in formal sector work changes into a lack of dignity in the lower economic echelons. At the bottom of the informal sector is the mass of people who may be termed 'coolies'. Though the term is banned from official use due to the denigration it is said to imply,[26] it seems the appropriate one to describe the degrading terms that nomadic labour is forced to endure, constantly on the move as it is, and paid with wages that are often below subsistence level. In addition to intense poverty, 'coolie' life is characterized by heavy

---

[26] GoI, *Report of the National Commission on Labour*, p. 31, n. 2.

work, physical exhaustion, the odium of untouchability, and inhuman working conditions characterized by fumes, noise, stench, and filth. Such workers have to endure a living hell. Rapidly worn out by the production process, when their productivity decreases, they are discarded, as so much waste.

An absence of choice confronts workers. Incomes are low and uncertain, so that the autonomy of workers is restricted. They lack savings and have little creditworthiness. Their labour power is the only collateral they possess. Work indicating economic dependency, expressed in a debt relationship, is a very common phenomenon in the informal sector milieu. Employers present such arrangements as 'advances' on wages that will be repaid through the labour of the borrower. However, such 'advances' are solely intended to appropriate labour, whether immediately or at a later date. Neither party views the transaction as a loan that will be terminated on repayment.

Debt bondage is not a new phenomenon. In the past, it was the customary manner by which landless low-caste workers were bound to landowning households belonging to higher castes. This master–serf relationship was common throughout South Asia. My fieldwork in south Gujarat inclined me to characterize such bondage, known as *halipratha*, as a pre-capitalist system of tied labour.[27] The contract was usually lifelong, bondage continuing from father to son, and sometimes maintained for several generations. The landowner appropriated more than the labour power of his servant (and his wife and children). He demanded a broad range of services, both economic and non-economic, that demonstrated the subjugation of his *hali*. This beck-and-call relationship stressed the social inequality between the parties. The state of captivity within his master's household, forced immobility on the servant. The only way in which he could escape his subjugation was to flee. But the exercise of extra-economic control was central to the efficacy of the hali system and so, if a servant absconded, his master could count on help from the local authorities in tracing him and bringing him back.

The social context in which this master–serf relationship operated was a localized rural order whose economy was based on subsistence production. A comprehensive process of change led to the disappearance of the hali system as an institutionalized bondage relationship between

[27] J. Breman, *Patronage and Exploitation: Changing Agrarian Relations in South Gujarat, India*, Berkeley: University of California Press, 1974 (Indian edition, New Delhi: Manohar, 1977).

dominant castes on the one hand, and tribal or detribalized communities on the other. This occurred over a considerable period of time and traces of the earlier system still existed in the early 1960s.[28] My study started with the question of what kind of labour relations has taken the place of bondage. Other research had shown that a definite change had occurred. In his 1968 essay, 'The Emergence of Capitalist Agriculture in India', Thorner concluded that: '... the various forms of bondage and unfree labour services which were formerly rampant in many parts of India, have now virtually disappeared, except in States still notorious for this, as parts of Bihar and adjacent areas'.[29] I found that, although the hali system no longer existed, bonded farm labourers had not become free labourers. They continued to be indebted to particular landowners and were, therefore, unable to sell their labour power to others. Landowners continued to give advances in order to immobilize their permanent workers. Nevertheless, their relationship had undergone fundamental change. For a start, casual labour in agriculture had increased strongly. Modern farm servants differed in essential respects from the halis of pre-capitalist times.

The state of indebtedness of labourers today does not alter the fact that the exercise of power by landowners has been checked in major respects. The term of bondage is shorter and remains restricted to the work sphere, while the use of extra-economic coercion with which to ensure compliance with the agreement entered into is contrary, today, to the law of the land. Crucially, landowners are no longer able to enforce their authority. Servants are no longer captives in their employers' households. The housing of landless people in their own village quarters has reduced their dependency, while the new employment opportunities outside agriculture and away from the village have stimulated their mobility. For all these reasons, my opinion differs fundamentally from that of Brass, according to whom labourers who have incurred debts are exposed to the same unfree regime as in the past. The argument that very significant changes have occurred in the social relations of production is one that Brass forcefully rejects. This forms a focal point of his diatribe against the stance I have taken.[30]

---

[28] Ibid., p. 68.

[29] D. Thorner (ed.), 'The Emergence of Capitalist Agriculture in India', *The Shaping of Modern India*, New Delhi: Allied Publishers, 1980, pp. 236, 246.

[30] T. Brass, 'Immobilised Workers, Footloose Theory', *The Journal of Peasant Studies*, vol. 24, no. 4, 1997, pp. 337–58.

The reduced intensity of extra-economic coercion has caused me, like many others,[31] to doubt whether the term 'bonded labour' is in fact applicable to present-day farm servants. I have argued that the indebtedness of labour is caused by both the lack of work and by very low wages, and that it is not the result of total subordination of the landless to the rule of the landowner.[32] Rudra has observed that it is not the length of the labour arrangement that determines whether there is evidence of feudal or capitalist relations of production, but rather the terms of the contract. In the first case this would include a wide range of unspecified and onerous obligations, while in the second case both form and substance would be more specific.[33] I have summarized the difference between past and present as follows:

> … the present situation differs from the earlier one in that the present day worker who enters into debt repays it with labour power without subjecting himself in any other respect and unconditionally to the will of the 'master'. In comparison with the servitude of former times, the present arrangement is more restricted in nature. The employer is primarily interested in attaching labour, no less but also not much more than that. Although traces of servitude are certainly present in cases of long-term employment, the lack of freedom that formerly existed in my fieldwork villages has lost its social legitimacy.[34]

The opinion that I voiced in 1985 to the effect that indebtedness should not be equated with bondage arose from the emphasis that I wished to place on the transition from the old to the new regime that had become manifest in the agricultural economy. Without wishing to detract from the significance of the changes that have occurred, I have pointed out in various publications that '…a capitalist mode of production…by no means precludes certain forms of absence of freedom, emanating for example from the necessity to enter into debt'.[35] Indebtedness continues

[31] For example, G. Omvedt, 'Capitalist Agriculture and Rural Classes', *Economic and Political Weekly*, Review of Agriculture, vol. 16, no. 52, 1981, pp. A140–A159; A. Rudra, 'Class Relations in Indian Agriculture—part I, part II, part III', *Economic and Political Weekly*, vol. 13, 1978, pp. 22–3; and vol. 24, pp. 916–23, 963–8, 998–1004.

[32] Breman, *Of Peasants, Migrants and Paupers*, pp. 311–12.

[33] Rudra, 'Class Relations in Indian Agriculture—part II', vol. 13, no. 23, p. 966.

[34] Breman, *Footloose Labour*, p. 163.

[35] J. Breman, 'Seasonal Migration and Co-operative Capitalism: Crushing of Cane and of Labour by Sugar Factories of Bardoli', *Economic and Political Weekly*, special issues, vol. 13, nos 31, 32, and 33, 1978, p. 1350; see also, J. Breman, 'The

to be a crucial aspect of the capitalist work regime which I have defined as new or neo-bondage. It is a mode of employment that is not restricted to the shrinking category of farm servants. Similar arrangements also characterize a diversity of industrial labour in both rural and urban informal sectors. Men, women, and children recruited for cane cutting or brick making receive, through the jobber, a payment which binds this army of migrants to the place of employment for the season's duration, a period ranging from six to eight months. Payment of an advance is intended to force them to move, that is become mobile, and to prevent them from withdrawing prematurely from their contracts. To ensure immobilization of the floating workforce for the duration of the production process, payment of the wage is deferred until the season ends. More skilled and better-paid urban workers such as powerloom operators and diamond cutters can also obtain 'loans' (*baki*) from their employers, in exchange for which they lose the free disposition over their own labour power.

The new regime of bondage differs from the traditional one in terms of the short duration of the agreement (often for no longer than one season), its more specific character (labour instead of a beck-and-call relationship), and finally, its easier termination or evasion (even without repayment of the debt). The far greater risk nowadays of breach of contract discourages employers from being imprudent and generous in granting an advance on wages. It is difficult to recoup losses made in this way and it is useless to appeal to the authorities for help in punishing transgressors. Present-day bosses lack the natural superiority which, in the past, made it unthinkable that a contract should be broken. In many cases, the social identity of the employer is the same as that of the employee. The labour jobber originates from the same milieu as the members of the gang that he recruits for work in the cane fields or brickworks, while the owner of a diamond-cutting workshop often belongs to the same caste as the cutters who work for him.

Finally, I would like to draw attention to the fact that the new regime of bondage through debt applies not only to workers but also extends to employers in the informal sector. Labour jobbers are indebted to industrialists who commission them as their agents, just as owners of

---

Renaissance of Social Darwinism', Lecture on the Occasion of the Dies Natalis, Institute of Social Studies, The Hague, 1988, p. 21. Subsequently published in summarized format as: 'Agrarian Change and Class Conflict', in G. McNicoll and M. Cain (eds), *Rural Development and Population: Institutions and Policy*, New York: Oxford University Press, 1990.

powerloom workshops and diamond-cutting workshops are dependent
on traders. This shows that not only labour relations but the entire
organization of industrial production in the informal sector has a strong
mercantile capitalist tilt. The difference is that, unlike their workers,
bosses are not obliged to sell their labour power in order to redeem
their debts. Their terms of bondage are different. It is undeniable
that employers in agriculture and industry make use of pre-capitalist
mechanisms of subordination, whether or not in transmuted form, in
order to keep wage costs down in a production process that satisfies
the demands of capitalist management. While making this observation,
Ramachandran adds that the difference between bonded and free labour
cannot be reduced to a simple black-and-white contrast. Social reality is
far more complicated and thus, demands a more qualified interpretation.
This brings him to the following fieldwork-based conclusion, which is
supported by the results of my own research.

The unfreedom of workers who were neither bonded nor completely free to
choose their employers took different forms, their freedom to choose employers
was circumscribed in different ways and in different degrees. The most common
manifestation of this kind of unfreedom was what has been called the right of
first call of employers over workers.[36]

The indebtedness that prevents workers from being able to do as they
please robs them of the dignity inherent in freedom. In addition to
defending the proposition—with more obstinacy than plausibility—that
unfree labour arrangements in agriculture are increasing rather than
decreasing, Brass also opines that workers in a debt-dependency relationship have lost their proletarian status. By the 'deproletarianization'
process that he considers to be in progress, he understands 'replacing
free workers with unfree equivalents or by converting the former into
the latter'.[37] This statement suggests that present-day, debt-bonded workers would earlier, as genuine proletarians, have had freedom of choice
over the use of their labour power. Such reasoning implies that a process
of capitalist transformation is in progress in the Indian countryside in
which free labour is disappearing to make place for a regime of unfreedom. In fact, the trend is the reverse.

In a number of publications, I have drawn attention to the growing
assertiveness of landless labourers, seeing this as indicative of proletarian

---

[36] V.K. Ramachandran, *Wage Labour and Unfreedom in Agriculture: An Indian
Case Study*, Oxford: Clarendon Press, 1990, p. 252.

[37] Brass, 'Immobilised Workers, Footloose Theory', p. 348.

conscientization. Undoubtedly, labourers who work many or most days of the year for the same landowner are still frequently bonded through debt. Among the younger generation, however, the submissive attitude with which debt bondage was accompanied in the past has made way for far greater independence of mind. Does this mean that the former halis were resigned to their subjugation or perhaps, even internalized their state of dependency? The lack of contemporaneous material that is reasonably trustworthy and detailed makes it hazardous to speculate on this question. Nevertheless, there are sufficient indications that there was no lack of resistance to the claim to superiority with which landowners customarily stressed their dominance. In the context of a highly localized rural economy, however, such resistance was easily put down. But today, this is more difficult to do because of the diversification of the rural economy and its growing linkages with the outside world. Alternative sources of livelihood, modern transport facilities, and the ease with which one can leave the village for a shorter or longer period, mean that the landless are today less obliged to act in compliance with the dictates of landowners. The traditional power of the latter was founded on repressive sanctions for which there is no legal basis in the new political order. The hegemony of dominant landowners has come to an end and the landless have freed themselves from the stigma of inferiority.

One way this new mood is expressed is through resistance to any form of unfree labour that is accompanied by a debt relationship. Brass casts doubt on this growing resistance from below and also, points out that it has little effectiveness. Referring to my own writings on the subject, Brass observes: 'the "from above" power of the economic relationship invariably overrides any manifestation of "from-below" resistance'.[38] However, I do not regard the limited success of resistance to be an effective criterion with which to determine the degree of proletarian conscientization. Neither am I inclined to make the existence of that mentality dependent upon collective action that develops into class conflict. I have tried to summarize the situation that has developed as follows:

The need to accept a cash advance on wages entails the obligation to subject oneself to the orders of an employer for the direct future. Back payment has a similar binding effect. The loss of independence that adheres to such a labour contract explains why it is only entered into through lack of a better alternative.

[38] Ibid., p. 347.

That so many nevertheless have recourse to this last resort of employment indicates the enormous pressure on resources of livelihood in the bottom echelons of the economy. Even that disenfranchisement is subjected to restrictions of durability, range and intensity. The work agreement is not entered into and continued for an indefinite time, as was the case with the *hali* of former times. The neo-bondage is further strongly economic in nature and restricts the imposition of the employer's will and his claims of superiority *per se*. The behaviour of wage hunters and gatherers not only expresses their longing for material improvement but also manifests their basic unwillingness to seek security in bondage. Theirs is a type of social consciousness that might be expected from the proletarian class.[39]

This applies not only to agricultural labourers in south Gujarat but also to the industrial labourers who float around in the informal sector of the economy. This footloose proletariat adopts various ways by which to resist employers' endeavours to appropriate their labour power through indebtedness. Labourers do not hesitate to leave without notice if the employer or the work itself is found to be too oppressive, and certainly do so to work for a higher wage. Creditors today lack the power to prolong the contract until the debt has been repaid. They are no longer able to call on the authorities for their help, and employers' attempts to exclude 'defaulters' from further employment usually fail due to rivalry between employers. In brief, the loss of bonded labour's social legitimacy means that those who pay an advance are no longer assured that the promised labour power will indeed be provided. The chance that compliance with the contract will be enforced does not necessarily increase as the social gap between the two parties widens. The labour–jobber, who belongs to the same milieu as the worker, is more effective than the employer in this respect. Even more effective than the labour–jobber is the male head of household who does not shy away from using physical force to obtain control of the labour of his wife and children.

Modes of resistance show great diversity. Earlier, I have attributed occupational multiplicity to the lack of permanent employment in any particular branch of industry. Frequent changes of job and workplace, however, can also indicate a strategy by which workers avoid dependence on a single source of livelihood. Further, when a man migrates alone, this may be due to his wish to protect his family from the dependency and degradation inherent in life and labour in the informal sector. Similarly, I do not see labour circulation as exclusively indicating fluctuations in

[39] Breman, *Footloose Labour*, p. 237.

the supply of work. A refusal to continue a contract indefinitely, also, embodies a protest against a merciless work regime.

There is little documentation of resistance in the form of collective action, although this is a common occurrence, perhaps because the study of industrial agitation is restricted mainly to the formal sector. Strikes are usually of short duration and limited in range. Their spontaneity and local character indicate a lack of organizational experience. The fragmentation of the workforce, dispersed over numerous small firms, also inhibits the mobilization of greater support. Given the vulnerability of industrial workers in the informal sector and their dependency, it is not surprising that resistance is mostly on an individual basis. Resistance includes inertia, pretended lack of understanding, foot-dragging, avoidance, withdrawal, sabotage, obstruction, etc. These types of behaviour give nomadic labour the reputation of being unpredictable, impulsive, and liable to abandon work without reason. Employers make such complaints, censuring the 'lack of commitment' of wage hunters and gatherers. But seen from another angle, this evasive action is an attempt to obtain or maintain a fragile dignity. There is a degree of solidarity, but it is not based on any realization that workers all belong to an undivided working class.

Employers make use of primordial ties with which to exercise control over labour for shorter or longer time periods. Conversely, such parochial attachments are equally important for the mass of workers to optimize its resistance and manoeuvrability. Although this is not necessarily expressed in a generalized horizontal solidarity, i.e., manifest in class organisation and action, nomadic workers nevertheless show signs of social consciousness which is essentially proletarian in nature. In my opinion, their mental make-up and lifestyle are indicative of the capitalist basis of the economy, in both its urban and rural manifestations.[40]

More research into multiple identities of workers in the informal and formal sectors of the economy is urgently needed. The facile conclusion that all social formations that deviate from an unadulterated class alliance are an expression of false consciousness, does not evince much understanding of the complicated conditions that determine the changing and fragile existence of wage labour in India at the end of the twentieth century. The popular movements that increasingly manifest themselves in urban centres as well as rural hinterlands give voice, both within and

[40] Ibid., p. 21.

outside the work sphere, to endeavours to achieve emancipation and, more particularly, to deny inequality as being the organizing principle of societal structure and culture. The theory of economic dualism can be split into two variants. The first argues that both informal and formal sectors are more or less independent of each other. The second suggests a hierarchical stratification whereby the informal sector is subordinated to, and exploited by, the formal sector. The protection enjoyed by the well-organized higher circuit, including the workers employed therein, is at the expense of the far greater mass of producers and consumers in the lower circuit. Das has written a critical essay on theoreticians who defend this dualistic model.

The basic argument of such rightist attacks on the industrial workers organised in trade unions is that they are a small minority of the total population who are being paid disproportionately high wages because of the strong bargaining position they have entrenched themselves in owing to the 'monopoly of labour' which they have established in league with 'monopoly capital', and hence they are the prime villains in the process of exploitation from which other sections of the population, notably peasants, suffer.[41]

However, industrial workers in the formal sector frequently increase their wages by moonlighting. Such practices illustrate the interconnectedness between the formal and the informal sector rather than exploitation of the latter by the former. In a local level study, Harriss concludes that the different segments of the labour force are cross-cut by broader social relationships.[42] His opinion is supported by studies of labour allocation in working-class households. These show that members are active in both sectors.[43] In my analytical framework, therefore, prime place is given not to the bifurcation of the sectors but to their mutual interpenetration. In terms of industrial labour, this signifies a complex and greatly fragmented landscape in which an extensive plain of informal work is interrupted by both smaller and larger hills of formal employment. The continuing

[41] A.N. Das, 'The Indian Working Class: Relations of Production and Reproduction', in Das *et al.* (eds), *The Worker and the Working Class*, p. 171; see also, Holmström, *Industry and Inequality*, pp. 17–18; Papola *et al.* (eds), *Labour, Employment and Industrial Relations in India*, pp. 271–2.

[42] Harriss, 'The Working Poor and the Labour Aristocracy in a South Indian City', pp. 278–80.

[43] Holmström, *South Indian Factory Workers*, pp. 56, 77; Holmström, *Industry and Inequality*, p. 261; U. Ramaswamy, *Work, Union and Community: Industrial Man in South India*, New Delhi: Oxford University Press, 1983, pp. 30–5.

mobility of the workforce, the enormous crush on the routes between the plains and the hills and vice versa, further add to the confusing image offered by this terrain. The industrial labour market shows great differentiation, and is clearly in a state of flux.

The protection given to organized industrial labour dates from a period when the state attempted to accelerate growth through economic planning. But, even then, political priority was given to capital accumulation. The promotion of this factor of production demanded that industrial peace be ensured. The motivation for regulating conditions of employment through legislation was not for the existing power of organized labour but rather the anticipated increase therein in the near future. However, the stagnation which occurred in the expansion of formal employment caused a critical reappraisal to be made of the need to extend protection to ever-greater numbers of the working population. The project of encouraging a massive transition of workers to modern factories, after having given them an initial technical training in informal sector workshops, was never implemented. Further, formal sector employment could not keep pace with the growth of the working population.

What is the relative significance of the two sectors and what shifts have occurred between them over the years? Reliable statistics are lacking and estimates vary for the different branches of economic activity. In 1961, according to Joshi and Joshi, half of Bombay's (henceforth Mumbai) working population belonged to the informal sector. For industrial workers, however, the percentage was far lower, namely, about 30 per cent. Of the great majority of industrial workers who were covered by labour legislation, three-fifths were employed in the hundreds of textile mills in the city.[44] Ten years later, according to the same authors, formal industrial employment had increased but had not been able to prevent a considerable upward leap of the relative share of similar work in the informal sector.[45]

I believe these estimates of the magnitude of formal sector employment to be exaggerated. The trend is clear: a decreasing percentage of industrial workers lead a formal sector existence. Holmström states that less than half the total number of industrial workers are employed in the formal sector.[46] In my judgement, today, it is no more than 10–15

[44] H. Joshi and V. Joshi, *Surplus Labour and the City: A Study of Bombay*, New Delhi: Oxford University Press, 1976, pp. 49–50.

[45] Ibid., pp. 57–66.

[46] Holmström, *Industry and Inequality*, p. 149.

per cent. The remainder can be divided roughly into two categories: first, those who are unprotected, regular workers in small-scale workshops, under constant threat of dismissal (approximately 60 per cent of workers); and second, casual workers and nomadic labour (approximately 25–30 per cent of the total). Such sub-divisions are also evident in other sectors, example, trade, transport, and services, though the percentages differ. Formal sector employment has only a minute share in almost all important branches of the economy. It, therefore, seems obvious that future research into industrial labour relations should focus on this populous middle category of labour.

The history of industrialization suggests an evolution that finds its climax when the great majority of the working population has become factorized. This is the classic path of economic development which structured western society. However, the capitalist route followed in India, during the second half of the twentieth century, has clearly not been in accordance with this dominant model. The importance of agriculture has certainly decreased, but the labour expelled from it has not been absorbed by urban factories. The path towards industrial capitalism has taken a different route. The expansion of the formal sector has lagged far behind that of the informal sector. In fact, we clearly see a process of informalization. While the so-called 'normal' transition to industrialized society assumes the transfer of home-based work, first, to workshops and then to large-scale factories, the trend has been the reverse in many industries in India. The abrupt interruption of Mumbai's formal sector growth was caused by halting factorized textile production. Powerlooms were removed from Mumbai's mills and installed in small workplaces elsewhere, often in other cities. In these new worksites, the machines were operated by informal sector labour.[47]

Patel has investigated the consequences of the closure of cotton mills in Ahmedabad, the town that was the 'Manchester of India'. Dismissed workers today depend on the informal sector for their livelihood. They are in casual employment, earning half their former wages. They have also lost the social provisions and legal protection that gave them status.[48] Regression in the industrial work regime can go even further. In some parts of south India, bidis were produced in small factories. But

---

[47] Breman, *Footloose Labour*.

[48] B.B. Patel, *Workers of Closed Mills: Patterns and Problems of their Absorption in a Metropolitan Labour Market*, New Delhi: Oxford and IBH Publishing Co., 1988; see also, R.N. Sharma, 'Job Mobility in a Stagnant Labour Market', *Indian Journal of Industrial Relations*, vol. 17, no. 4, 1982, pp. 521–38.

factory closure and the sub-contracting of production to home-based workers occurred in one factory after a strike, and in a second factory, after the introduction of legal measures intended to improve working conditions.[49] The deregulation of industrial labour relations is not only happening in the private sector but also in the public sector. In the public sector steel cities, access to protected work is denied to increasing numbers.

… as time went on, the steel plants employed considerable and increasing quantities of labour from outside the organised sector. Having built a reserve by creating a labour duality in these locations, they went on to exploit it … Up to 20 per cent of the labour force at any time consisted of contract labour (and a far greater proportion at times of major capacity expansion). This labour was not given any of the facilities enjoyed by the permanent core. Nor was it unionised. Furthermore, the scheduled castes and scheduled tribes were heavily represented in it.[50]

Will large-scale industry make way for smaller units? That seems unlikely, given that modern industrial production demands both high-grade technology and labour specialization. A combination of various forms of industrial production, ranging from large factories via small workshops to home-based work, seems a more likely development.[51] Careful attention will need to be given to investigating the political economy of these new forms of industrial integration.

Given the globalization of the economy, it is important to keep the international context in mind when studying industrial work and labour in India. Prominent global agencies show a very considerable interest in the trajectory of industrialization in India. The World Bank has been an outspoken advocate of the dismantling of the labour legislation and social provisions that protect employment in the formal sector.[52] The

---

[49] A. Avachat, 'Bidi Workers of Nipani', *Economic and Political Weekly*, vol. 13, nos 29 and 30, 1978, pp. 1176–8,1203–5; M. Mohandas, 'Beedi Workers in Kerala: Conditions of Life and Work', *Economic and Political Weekly*, vol. 15, no. 36, 1980, pp. 1517–23.

[50] N. Crook, 'Labour and the Steel Towns', in P. Robb (ed.), *Datit Movements and the Meanings of Labour in India*, New Delhi: Oxford University Press, 1993, pp. 349–50.

[51] M. Singh, *The Political Economy of Unorganised Industry: A Study of the Labour Process*, New Delhi: Sage Publications, 1990.

[52] World Bank, *World Development Report, 1995: Workers in an Integrating World*, Washington, DC: The World Bank and Oxford: Oxford University Press, 1995.

earlier assumption that South Asia would adopt the western pattern of industrialization has, apparently, been reversed: instead, India is now presented as the pioneer of a labour regime of deregulated industrial production, which is propelling it from the periphery of the global capitalist economy towards its centre. The World Bank's reports suggest that India, by choosing liberalization, is at last taking the right path, but that deregulation should be much more rigorous. These are no gratuitous recommendations. After all, the programmes of structural adjustment provide the Bank with the opportunity to force India to take the desired course. In any case, the current employment trends of contractualization, enforced migration, and casualization, all facilitate the flexibilization of labour. I, therefore, conclude that there is little cause for optimism regarding any speedy improvement in the lifestyles and work regimes of the hugely varied groups who make up India's industrial labour force.

# IV

## THE EXODUS OF RURAL LABOUR

# 8

# The Informal Sector of India's Economy*

The term, 'informal sector', dates from the early 1970s when it was coined by Hart in a study on Ghana to describe urban employment outside the organized labour market. This category of employment includes a great diversity of occupations characterized by self-employment.[1] His essay, which was based on anthropological fieldwork, brought attention to the enormous variety of economic activities which were not registered anywhere and were often clandestine in nature or, anyway, outside the framework of official regulations, carried out by a large part of the population of Accra in order to survive. The improvised and inadequate manner whereby this took place demonstrated that these people lived mostly in poverty and were to be found at the bottom of the urban landscape.

The concept became quickly popular when the International Labour Organization (ILO), as part of its World Employment Programme, sent out missions to examine the employment situation outside the modern, organized, large-scale, and capital-intensive sectors of the economy. The first of these country reports investigated Kenya and the Philippines. These studies were followed by reports that examined the particular features of the 'informal sector' in a number of Third World cities such as Kolkata, Jakarta, Dakar, Abidjan, and Sao Paulo. To supplement these case studies, the ILO commissioned a number of more analytical essays

---

*This paper was presented at Monbusho International Symposium on South Asia under Economic Reforms, held in Osaka in 1999.

[1] K. Hart, 'Informal Income Opportunities and Urban Employment in Ghana', in R. Jolly, E. de Kadt, H. Singer, and F. Wilson (eds), *Third World Employment*, Harmondsworth: Penguin, 1973.

such as the ones authored by Sethuraman[2] and Kanappan.[3] The World Bank also joined the action and published a paper by Mazumdar.[4]

As a result of the way the concept had been framed, and the attention it subsequently drew from development economists and policymakers in particular, the informal sector became, to a significant extent, associated with the economy of the large cities of Africa, Asia, and Latin America. Most of these cases concern societies with a predominantly rural-cum-agrarian identity in which the process of urbanization began relatively recently. The dynamics of this spatial shift in settlement patterns include a declining importance of agriculture as the principal source of economic production and the expulsion from village habitats of a growing proportion of the land-poor peasantry in particular. However, this transition has not been marked by a concomitant expansion in the metropoles of technologically advanced and modernly organized industries to accommodate this newly mobile section of the population from the rural hinterland. Only a small part of the labour that reaches the urban areas manages to penetrate the 'secure' zones of regular, more skilled, and hence, better-paid work. The majority of the migrants must be satisfied with casual labour which is unskilled or pseudo-skilled, has no fixed working hours, provides a usually low income which, moreover, fluctuates significantly, and, finally, is only available seasonally.

The description of the informal sector is characterized by analytical vagueness. In order to indicate the wide repertoire of occupations, commentators often confine themselves to an arbitrary enumeration of activities which one comes across walking through the streets of the Third World metropoles. Included in this parade are market stall holders, lottery ticket sellers, parking attendants, vendors of food and drink, housemaids and market women, messengers and porters, ambulant artisans and repairmen, construction and road building workers, transporters of people and cargo, shoe polishers, and newspaper boys. Numerous occupations on the seamy side of the society are not omitted such as pimps and prostitutes, rag pickers and scavengers, quacks, conjurers and confidence tricksters, bootleggers and drug pedlars,

[2] S.V. Sethuraman, 'The Urban Informal Sector: Concept, Measurement and Policy', Working Papers, World Employment Programme Research, International Labour Organization (ILO), Geneva, 1976.

[3] A. Kanappan (ed.), 'Studies of Urban Labour Market Behaviour in Developing Areas', International Institute of Labour Studies, ILO, Geneva, 1980.

[4] D. Mazumdar, 'The Urban Informal Sector', World Bank Staff Working Paper, Washington, DC, 1975.

beggars, pickpockets, and other petty thieves. It is a colourful assortment of irregularly working people that scratches around for a living close to or at the bottom of urban society and which, in the overwhelming majority of cases, both lives and works in extremely precarious circumstances.

## ORIGINS

The division of the urban economy into two sectors can be seen as a variant of dualism theories which had gained currency earlier. Basing himself on colonial Indonesia, the Dutch economist, Boeke, voiced the idea at the beginning of the twentieth century that native producers had not internalized in their behaviour the basic principles of the *homo economicus*. Unlimited needs and their deferred gratification in accordance with a rational assessment of costs and benefits did not stand at the forefront of the peasant way of life in the Orient. Rather their way of life was determined by the immediate and impulsive indulgence of limited wants. This colonial doctrine of what Boeke referred to as *homo socialis* would return in later development studies in the image of the working masses in underdeveloped countries as people obstinately refusing to respond to the primacy of economic stimuli. The rejection of the axiom that there is a real difference in rationality and optimizing behaviour between western and eastern civilizations ended in the construction of a new contradistinction in post-colonial development economics, namely, that between the countryside and the city. This spatial contrast corresponded, more or less, with a sectoral division between agriculture and industry. Western mankind was superseded by the city–industrial complex as the dynamic factor, against which village and agriculture were seen as static and diametrically opposed.

The new dualism theory, like its precursor, was associated with the rise of capitalism as the organizing principle of economic life. While the bulk of the peasants in the villages were attributed an outlook restricted to subsistence, modern industry was expected to concentrate itself outside the agrarian sector and in the urban milieu. According to this line of thinking, the contradiction between both sectors was indeed not of a fundamental nature, but merely reflected different stages of development which corresponded with the traditional–modern dichotomy. The dualism concept in this sense was used, first, by Lewis[5] and subsequently,

---

[5] W.A. Lewis, 'Economic Development with Unlimited Supplies of Labour', *The Manchester School of Economic and Social Studies*, vol. 22, no. 2, 1954, pp. 139–91.

by Fei and Ranis,[6] with the aim of examining the outflow of superfluous labour from the rural subsistence economy and to trace the arrival of this labour in urban growth poles as part of the gradual expansion of non-agrarian production. The evolution of social transformation in developing countries is, in this scheme of interpretation, similar to the capitalist process of change that took place in the Atlantic part of the world in an earlier phase.

It is against this background that the latest version of the dualism model, now under discussion, should be understood. The urban agglomerations are not growing exclusively, or even predominantly, as centres of technologically advanced industrial production along capitalist lines. In addition to the presence of an economic circuit that fits this description, there is also a sector consisting of a plethora of activities of a completely different nature. Key terms such as 'modern management' and 'capitalist organization' appear to be scarcely relevant for this sector. The slow pace of factory-based industrialization and the presence of excess labour, as a result of increased demographic growth in combination with the expulsion from the agricultural economy, are given as the principal causes leading to a dualist system in cities of the Third World. The lower echelons in this bipolar order consist of the mass of the working poor who have a much lower rate of productivity than those in the technologically advanced section of the economy to which this rapidly increasing segment of the urban population, as yet and perhaps for ever, cannot obtain access.

Can the wide range of activities which informal sector workers have to depend on for their survival be seen as 'traditional'? This is the stereotyped notion of these modes of production in which emphasis is laid on their old-fashioned and outmoded character. They depend on fairly simple occupational skills and employ very meagre as well as inadequate tools. The sparse availability of means of production based on superior technology results in a return on labour that is almost always quite low. A consequence is that, in order to scrape together a minimum income, the working day is extremely long while the work is also so physically demanding that poor health is a common occurrence. An argument against the tendency to portray the informal sector as traditional and 'pre-capitalist' is the fact that among the enormous variety of activities that fall under this category, very many, in fact, were

---

[6] J.C.H. Fei and G. Ranis, *Development of the Labour Surplus Economy: Theory and Policy*, Homewood, IL: Irwin Publishing Company, 1964.

created by the capitalist transformation of the urban milieu. It would be misleading to suggest that the urban dualism observed is shaped, on the one hand, by a dynamic growth pole marked by advanced technology and innovative organizational management and, on the other, by a more or less static circuit of long established, miscellaneous, and stubbornly surviving but outdated pre-capitalist activities. Instead of speaking of a gradually disappearing contradiction between 'modern' and 'traditional', or capitalist versus non-capitalist, what should be emphasized is the drastic restructuring of the entire economic system whereby the interdependence between the different sectors needs to be identified as the most important element.

This conclusion is, in part, derived from an appraisal of the transformation which took place in the western world over a period of more than a century, and for which the dual process of urbanization and industrialization were of major importance. Without suggesting that the societies, which until recently were rural/agrarian, are currently experiencing a similar process of change, I would, nevertheless, like to draw attention to the fact that what is now referred to as the informal sector, characterized by many different forms of self-employment and petty commodity production, has for a long time remained a striking feature in the urban economies of the northern hemisphere as well. Research on the various forms of the informal sector in developing countries, as it has been conducted since the 1970s, is handicapped by the virtual lack of comparison with the very profound changes in the organization of work and labour which went together with the emergence of metropolitan economies elsewhere in the world in the last two centuries. This lack of historical perspective coincides with the disciplinary background of the majority of researchers, mainly development economists and policymakers, who have little affinity with the need to understand the problem stated in a time span, highlighting instead of obfuscating the continuing effects of the past on the present.

## CLARIFICATION AND DEFINITION OF CONCEPTS
One of the first ILO reports on this subject discussed the informal sector by focusing on a set of characteristics: easy entry for the new enterprises, reliance on indigenous resources, family ownership, small-scale operations, unregulated and competitive markets, labour-intensive technology, and informally acquired skills of workers. The assumption behind this description is that the opposite of all these features applies to the formal sector of the economy. In this definition, which is built

on an implicit contrast, the type of economic activity is not used as the differentiating criterion but the way it is practised. In slightly different formulations, and supplemented with new suggestions, this list of indicators is found in a myriad of later studies. It is certainly possible to question the inclusion of some of these traits. For example, highly trained formal sector professionals such as lawyers or accountants often run their business in a manner which does not satisfy the criterion of large-scale operation. And again, it is just as misleading to presume that, in the bottom echelons of the urban economy, newcomers can establish themselves without any trouble as hawkers, shoe polishers, or beggars on every street corner. Furthermore, features that were initially accorded great importance—such as the foreign origin of capital or technology, the use of mainly waged labour, the large and impersonal distance between the supply of and demand for commodities and services—appear, after closer examination, not to constitute the watershed between formal and informal. The easy answer to this criticism is that urban dualism must be understood not by assuming the validity of each and every separate characteristic but rather the total fabric in an ideal-type construction. Informal would then be the whole gamut of economic activities characterized by small scale, low capital intensity, inferior technology, low productivity, predominantly family labour and property, no training or only that obtained 'on the job', easy entry, and finally, a small and usually poor clientele. In this formulation, the emphasis lies on the sub-division of the urban economy into two independent circuits, each with its own logic, structural consistency, and dynamics.

Another form of the concept of economic dualism derives from the contrast made between activity which is officially registered and sanctioned by official legislation and that which is not. The term informal, in this case, refers to operations kept out of the sight and control of the government and, in this sense, is also denoted as the 'parallel', 'underground', or 'shadow' economy. The legal recognition on which the formal sector can rely is not only expressed in the levying of taxes but also in the promulgation of various protective regulations. The much easier access to the state apparatus enjoyed by the owners or managers of formal sector enterprises leads to disproportionate advantages in the granting of various facilities, such as credit and licences, as well as the selective use of government ordinances of what is permitted and what is not. The privileged treatment claimed by formal sector interests disadvantages or even renders criminal informal sector activities when these, for instance, are seen as forming a hindrance for traffic on the street or threatening 'public order'. Unregulated activities may also clash with the prevailing state ideology. In the former socialist regimes of Central and Eastern Europe, producers supplemented their income with transactions on the black market both outside and during official working hours. The conversion of the party leaders in post-Maoist China to free market thinking went together with the legalization of various economic activities of an informal nature which, until then, had not been allowed or to which a blind eye had been turned. When first using the concept, Hart did not omit to draw attention to the criminally inclined nature of some of the activities he enumerated. The association of informal with subversive or illegal is partly the result of an unwillingness to recognize the economic value of the providers of these goods and services. It should also be realized that excluding this great army of the deprived from access to space, water, and electricity only encourages them to make clandestine use of these services and to contravene public health instructions. Yet, the authorities are not slow to conduct large-scale campaigns against such violations of the law. In any case, it is clear that the government is not absent in this milieu but, on the contrary, actively concerns itself with disciplining the sector.

Furthermore, the dividing line in the two-sector model has to be drawn very differently when it comes to the observance of legislation and official regulations. The tendency to conceive of the informal economy as an unregistered, unregulated, and hence, untaxed circuit ignores the ease with which power holders, particularly the personnel in government agencies responsible for implementing formal regulations and laws, see this unregulated industry, once it has been made invisible, as their private hunting ground. Moreover, it would be a great distortion of reality to dissociate certain phenomena, such as fraud, corruption, demands for the payment of speed and protection money and bribes, and, more generally, the conversion of public resources into private profits, from transactions in the formal sector economy where they primarily occur. This goes a long way in explaining why not only the legal income of politicians and policymakers, who are part of the elite, but also the basic salaries of many low-ranking health care workers, police constables, and teachers lag far behind their income of an 'informal' nature.

The third and last variant of the formal–informal sector dichotomy is related to the existence of bifurcated labour markets. A first feature to be discussed is the degree of the division of labour. Formal sector labour is usually performed in a complex work organization that consists of a set of specific tasks which are interrelated to each other but are hierarchically and differently valued and which, to differing degrees, require previous training. The small-scale operation, in combination with the low capital intensity of informal sector employment, implies very little or no task differentiation and requires skills and knowledge which are picked up in daily practice.

There is little known about the size, origin, and composition of the working population in the informal sector due to a lack of accurate and ongoing or periodical data collection. The labour statistics which are maintained are mainly restricted to the supply and demand of permanent workers, who are recruited and dismissed on the basis of objectified criteria, in the higher echelons of the urban economy. This registration is a result of, as well as a condition for, greater control of the economy by official regulations. It is, therefore, not very surprising that studies of employment and labour relations have focused primarily on the upper segment of the urban order. Given the above mentioned characteristics, the alternative name for the informal sector as the zone of unorganized or unregistered labour is understandable and just as clear is a third synonym, the unprotected sector. There are simply no legal rules concerning entry nor the conditions and circumstances under which informal sector labour is put to work. If some elementary standards have been introduced—such as the fixing of a minimum wage, the ban on labour which is deleterious for health and the environment, and the prohibition of child labour or practices of bondage—a machinery is lacking for their enforcement. The organized, registered, and protected character of formal sector labour is in diametrical opposition to this situation. In terms of organization, there is another advantage enjoyed by formal sector workers, namely, the possibility to set up their own associations in order to defend their common interests when dealing with employers or the government. This form of collective action increases the efficacy of the existing protection and is, at the same time, a means of extending this protection. In the informal sector landscape, trade unions are only rarely encountered. This absence contributes further to the maintenance of low wages, the social vulnerability, and the miserable conditions of employment.

The introduction of the concept, 'informal sector', has irrefutably drawn attention to the jumbled mass of activities—unregulated, fragmented, and infinitely diverse—whereby a large part of the working population manages to survive, usually with a great deal of difficulty. Research on urban employment in the past was almost always restricted to labour in factories and other modern enterprises with, as recurring themes, the rural origin of the new working population, its adjustment to an industrial lifestyle, and the labour relations in these large-scale enterprises. With the shift in focus from the formal to the informal sector, an end has been made to the long fostered idea that the large mass of workers who have not been incorporated, in a regular and standardized manner, in the labour process should, in fact, be seen as unemployed. But, on the other hand, the discussion on the informal sector has begged more questions than it has answered. This is the result of a lack of precision in the definition, among other things, which amounts to everything being categorized under the concept 'informal' that is not regarded as belonging to the formal sector. This assumption, made very early on, gives a distinctly tautological slant to the difference made between the two sectors.

The dualism that has been discussed relates sometimes to the labour market, sometimes to the economic circuits with different modes of production, and, in other cases, to permissible versus clandestine or plainly criminal economic activities. There is often a combination of all these variants with the implicit or explicit suggestion that the different criteria of the dual division run parallel with each other. I fundamentally disagree with this idea. One of the definitional problems arises precisely from the discordance between the different dimensions of the dualism concept. For example, it is simply not true that informal sector workers produce goods for and perform services to only, or even principally, clients in their own milieu, just as, the other way round, many formal sector commodities find their way to informal sector consumers. Furthermore, formal sector regulations are often avoided by transferring some or even all business activities and industrial production to the informal sector. These are only some arbitrarily chosen examples, amongst many, of the interdependence of the two sectors.

It is significant that, particularly, authors who base their work on empirical research are often critical of the formal/informal conceptualization. From my own long experience of studying rural and urban labour relations in western India, I conclude that the concept is useful in an idea-typical sense only. In my opinion, the informal sector cannot be demarcated as a separate economic circuit and/or a segment of the labour force. Attempts to persist with this strict demarcation, hence, create innumerable inconsistencies and problems which will become clear later. Instead of a two-sector model, there is a much more complex differentiation of the urban economy which should be the point of departure for structural analysis. The reduction to only two sectors, one capitalist and the other, non- or early capitalist, does not reflect the reality of the much greater complexity of work and production. A final objection of perhaps greater importance is that, by assuming a dualist system, the interrelationships between the various components of the economy threaten to be lost from sight. In place of splitting up the urban system into two sectors, I want to emphasize the fragmented character of the total labour market. In place of seeing the separate fragments as mutually exclusive, the connection between them is central to my analysis.[7]

## SIZE AND DYNAMICS

Estimates of the size of the informal sector are not very precise. The figures which have been reported for various countries or cities differ greatly, a variation which does not necessarily signal real differences in economic structure or developments over time. The most frequently cited estimates used to fluctuate between 30 and 70 per cent of the urban workforce. This very broad range is indicative of the serious lack of terminological clarity. Since the first use of the concept, a trend of upwards correction has become apparent—both of the total number of all workers and the proportion accounted for by the informal sector. Virtually, all recent studies on this subject assume that at least half of the population in large Third World metropoles can be categorized as belonging to the informal sector, while this proportion is even higher for the smaller-sized cities and towns. The changing criteria used—including the nature of the work (industry, trade, transport, or services); the scale of operation (more or fewer than ten workers for each enterprise); use of other production factors than labour (energy and technology)—virtually exclude a systematic comparison of the estimates for different places and years. Based on the official statistics, derived from the requirement to register formal sector labour, Visaria and Jacob estimated that, in 1972–3, 18.8 million of the total of 236.7 million working people in India belonged to this category. In 1991, their number had increased to 26.7 million out of a total of 343.5 million. Hence, in both the first and last year, formal sector employment came to less than 8 per cent of

---

[7] J. Breman, *Wage Hunters and Gatherers: Search for Work in the Urban and Rural Economy of South Gujarat*, New Delhi: Oxford University Press, 1994; J. Breman, *Footloose Labour: Working in India's Informal Economy*, Cambridge: Cambridge University Press, 1996.

the total workforce.[8] I may add here that I have little confidence in the completeness and reliability of the figures on which these estimates are based. Moreover, it should be realized that the data banks on employment and labour relations collected by international organizations such as the ILO and the World Bank are not much better.

A serious methodological problem is that on both sides of the dividing line, the working population is constituted very differently. Use of the term 'economically active' is of problematic significance even for the informal sector. Women, but also the elderly, minors, and the less able often participate in the work process, although their labour power is neither always used nor fully used. This applies to the labour power of able-bodied male adults at the peak of their physical strength as well. The ratio of earners to non-earners in homogeneous, informal sector households is higher than that in the pure formal sector households. However, on the other hand, the working members of formal sector households are more permanently employed. But to estimate that: of the working members of informal sector households, only one in eight is a female, as Papola calculated on the basis of research in Ahmedabad, seems to indicate significant under-registration in terms of gender.[9] Similarly, until recently, there has been a systematic underestimation of the extent of child labour. The information to be found in the same source that children constitute only 8 per cent of the workers in the non-registered hotels and restaurants is highly unlikely. The actual proportion of these young 'helpers', between five and fourteen years, must be at least double this figure.

The length of the working day in the informal sector is considerably greater than that of the formal sector and work often continues into the night. There are also no days off in the week, while annual festivals are celebrated much less or not at all. On the other hand, there are much greater seasonal fluctuations in the annual work cycle. The net effect of all these factors on the size and intensity of the labour power in the formal and informal sectors is difficult to ascertain. In order to obtain insight into the living conditions of the poor masses, empirical research at the level of the household deserves priority. Only by assuming that a large part, if not all members of households at the bottom of

[8] P. Visaria and P. Jacob, 'The Informal Sector in India: Estimates of its Size and Needs and Problems of Data Collection', *Working Paper Series No. 70*, Ahmedabad: Gujarat Institute of Development Studies, 1995, p. 14.

[9] T.S. Papola, *Urban Informal Sector in a Developing Economy*, New Delhi: Vikas Publishing House, 1981, p. 122.

the urban heap—regardless of age, sex, or degree of physical ability—are, or want to be, partially or completely incorporated in the labour process, is it possible to understand the relative elasticity with which unemployment, greatly fluctuating income, and other adversity is countered.

The specific nature of work arrangements in the informal sector seems to suggest a gradual continuum from employment to non-employment rather than a sharp break. The consequence of this peculiarity is that permanency and security are not marked features of informal work performance and that, instead, irregularity and vulnerability dominate. This particular trait of the informal sector makes an analysis of the labour market an extremely arbitrary and even disputable matter. The attempts to subject work, which is not standardized and is performed irregularly, to quantitative analysis in terms of exact measures and clear counts might stem from a research methodology which is based on formal sector notions. The recurrent complaints from researchers about the chaotic appearance and the lack of transparency in the informal sector should be seen in this light. This explains why sociological and economic analyses of the labour market are so strongly distorted in favour of data collection on formal sector enterprises. Of course, the small size of this sector does not at all justify this bias. The contrast between the top and bottom of the urban economy is easy to describe. In the broad social spectrum between these polar ends, however, where informal and formal labour merge into each other, there is no clear dividing line. Consequently, I conclude that the image of a dichotomy is much too simple and can better be replaced by the idea of a continuum.

The first studies of the informal sector concept created the impression that this segment of the urban economy functioned as a waiting room for a rapidly increasing stream of migrants pushed out from the rural economy. It was merely meant to be their first 'stay' in the new environment. The work that they performed provided them with craftsmanship and stimulated them to develop their talents as micro-entrepreneurs. Those who completed this apprenticeship successfully would, in the end, cross the gap which separated them from the formal sector. The promise of social mobility expressed by this optimistic scenario, however, appears, in practice, to be fulfilled for only a tiny minority. Time and again, the results of numerous investigations show that a very considerable part of informal sector workers are born and raised in the city and, at the end of their working lives, they haven't come much further than where they started—at the bottom of the heap.

A completely different dynamic, in an institutional and not an individual sense, arises from the idea that the informal sector is nothing more than a transitory phenomenon caused by the massive expulsion from the rural–agrarian economy. Given that the growth of formal sector employment is slower than would be necessary to accommodate, fully and immediately, the size of this exodus, there is a temporary excess of people in the lower layers of the urban system. As economic growth accelerates, the need for and significance of employment in the informal sector declines and eventually little or nothing of this 'buffer zone' will remain. In my conclusion, I shall show that this representation is nothing more than hopeful expectation.

## AN URBAN PHENOMENON?

One of the shortcomings in the debate on the informal sector is the unflagging preoccupation with the urban economy. It is difficult to sustain that there is dualism in the urban order but that the countryside is, in contrast, characterized by homogeneity. To be sure, the peasant economy *in toto* demonstrates a number of features which are very similar to informal sector activity. This is true both for the way production takes place as well as reflected in the pattern of employment. On the other hand, it is not so far-fetched to classify plantations, mines, or agro-industries in the rural areas as formal sector enterprises as they possess most of the dominant characteristics. Why is attention in the majority of studies on this subject, then, focused on the urban economy? This preoccupation appears to originate in the misplaced supposition, first, that the countryside is the almost exclusive domain of agriculture, which is, second, performed by a virtually homogeneous peasant population. We are concerned here with a monolithic image which does not allow a sectoral division in terms of formal and informal. Moreover, this three (one rural and two urban) compartment model suggestively indicates the direction of social dynamics: peasants migrate to the city where they find work and an income in the informal sector before making the jump to the formal sector of the economy. Against this line of reasoning, inspired by wishful thinking, I maintain that, regardless of the reservations that one can have about the validity of the informal sector concept, it is both theoretically and in practice impossible to declare that this concept is exclusively applicable to the urban domain.

There are some other researchers who share this critique and focus attention on dualist features manifest in the organization of agrarian production.[10]

Analyses based on the comprehensive totality of economic activities, irrespective of whether they are located in the urban or rural areas, emphasize the small volume of formal sector employment in India. As mentioned earlier, for example, Visaria and Jacob came to a figure of not more than 8 per cent. According to them, this extremely skewed division is primarily caused by the dominant position of the agrarian working population that consists almost exclusively of informal sector workers. The ratio of 92:8 is so highly uneven that it cannot be considered as a sound basis for sectoral analysis This leads me to exclude agriculture, both in terms of production and labour, and to employ the formal–informal dichotomy as a framework of analysis for all other branches of the economy together; in other words, not divided according to city or countryside. It is a point of departure which takes care of my objection that there is a tendency to see the informal sector only as an urban phenomenon and helps to highlight the magnitude of informal non-agrarian employment in the rural economy. Skilled crafts of all sorts, trade and transport, as well as services in differing degrees of specialization have always been important occupations in the past as well as the present. The size and importance of this non-agrarian work, performed either as the worker's main activity or as a sideline, has increased significantly in many parts of India in the recent decades. Table 8.1 illustrates the shift in the composition of the workforce in the last twenty years—the declining importance of employment in agriculture in face of the growth of, particularly, informal sector activity in other economic sectors.

Even taking into account all possible criticism of the accuracy of the given figures, which are derived from government statistics, they are still sufficiently robust to provide insight into the trend of economic transformation in the long term. First, agricultural employment declined from 74 per cent in 1972–3 to 65 per cent fifteen years later. In the same period, non-agricultural labour rose from 26 per cent to 35 per cent. The number of people employed in non-agriculture increased from 61.8 million in the first year to 113.6 million in 1987–8. According to another source, non-agricultural work was the main

---

[10] N.V. Jaganathan, *Informal Markets in Developing Countries*, New Delhi: Oxford University Press, 1987.

TABLE 8.1    Agricultural and Non-agricultural Workers (in millions), Classified According to Formal/Informal Sector, India, 1972–3 to 1987–8

| Branch of Industry | 1972–3 | | | 1977–8 | | |
|---|---|---|---|---|---|---|
| | Formal | Informal | Total | Formal | Informal | Total |
| Agriculture | 1,1 | 173,8 | 174,9 | 1,2 | 189,7 | 190,9 |
| Non-agriculture (a) | 17,7 | 44,1 | 61,8 | 20,0 | 57,9 | 77,9 |
| Total | 18,8 | 217,9 | 236,7 | 21,2 | 247,6 | 268,8 |

| Branch of Industry | 1983 | | | 1987–8 | | |
|---|---|---|---|---|---|---|
| | Formal | Informal | Total | Formal | Informal | Total |
| Agriculture | 1,3 | 206,3 | 207,6 | 1,4 | 209,7 | 211,1 |
| Non-agriculture (a) | 22,7 | 72,5 | 95,2 | 24,3 | 89,3 | 113,6 |
| Total | 24,0 | 278,8 | 302,8 | 25,7 | 299,0 | 324,7 |

*Source:* National Sample Survey (NSS), as cited in Visaria and Jacob.[11]
*Note:* (a) This category includes mining and quarrying, manufacturing, construction, electricity, gas and water, trade, hotels and restaurants, transport, storage, and communication and services.

source of income for one out of four men and one out of six women in all rural households in India at the end of the 1980s.[12] The growth indicated by these figures is principally propelled by activities which fall under the informal sector. The annual rate of increase in this sector is 4.9 per cent, which is more than double that of the formal sector. It is important to observe that acceleration in the diversification of the rural economy does not correspond with an increasing formalization of employment. One example concerns the emergence of a major agro-industry in the south of the state of Gujarat: for the large-scale harvesting and processing of sugarcane, each and every year, huge armies of migrant labourers are mobilized from nearby Maharashtra and other catchment areas. At the end of the campaign, they are made to leave the area again.[13] As will appear in the conclusion, this stagnation of formal sector employment is a more general phenomenon which goes far beyond the city–country contrast, and hence, must be understood in a broader context.

[11] Visaria and Jacob, 'The Informal Sector in India', pp. 17–18.
[12] G.K. Chadha, 'Non-Farm Employment for Rural Households in India: Evidence and Prognosis', *The Indian Journal of Labour Economics*, vol. 36, no. 3, 1993, pp. 296–327.
[13] Breman, *Wage Hunters and Gatherers*, pp. 133–287.

## EMPLOYMENT MODALITY

Self-employment is described, in a large part of the literature, *as* the backbone of the informal sector. When introducing the concept, Hart mentioned this *as* the most significant feature. The distinction between formal and informal income opportunities is based essentially on that between waged labour and self-employment.[14] Subsequently, many authors expressed themselves in similar vein. A quite arbitrary example is Sanyal, who, in an analysis of informal sector policy, states, without any reservation or empirical evidence, that the majority of the urban informal sector population lives from the income gained from self-employment.[15] This is, of course, the well-known image of the army of odd-jobbers and Jacks-of-all-trades that travels around in the open air or survives from put-out work performed at home, but always does this on their own account and at their own risk. In such descriptions, emphasis is laid firmly on the ingenuity, the stamina, and the alert reaction to new opportunities demonstrated by these small-scale, self-employed workers and last, but certainly not least, the pride they show of being their own boss. Some authors speak of these workers as mini-entrepreneurs and tend to describe the informal sector as a breeding ground for more sophisticated entrepreneurship which, as it is larger scale and capitalist, can only be developed in the formal sector. Not only trained in practice but hardened in the struggle for daily existence, one can recognize here the profile of self-made men who started small but once mature, were able to develop into true captains of industry.

Another and more critical school of thought is represented by authors who describe and analyse the informal sector in terms of petty commodity production. In these writings, the emphasis is on the limited room for manoeuvre in which the self-employed have to operate, their dependence upon suppliers who lumber them with poor quality or overpriced products, moneylenders who charge extortionate rates of interest for short-term loans, street vendors who are easy prey for the police, sex workers who are in the hands of their pimps, slumlords who demand protection money, home-based workers who can offer no resistance in the face of the practices of contractors or agents who commission their work, etc.

---

[14] Hart, 'Informal Income Opportunities and Urban Employment in Ghana', pp. 66–70.

[15] B. Sanyal, 'Organizing the Self-Employed', *International Labour Review*, vol. 130, no. 1, 1991, p. 41.

What is portrayed as own-account work carried out at the risk of the producer is, in fact, a more or less camouflaged form of waged labour. There is a wide diversity of arrangements which actually show great similarity with tenancy or sharecropping relationships in agriculture, where the principle of self-employment is so undermined in practice that the dependency on the landowner is scarcely different from that of a contract labourer. This is true for many actors operating in the informal sector such as the 'hirers' of a bicycle or motor taxi who must hand over a considerable proportion of their daily earnings to the owner of the vehicle, or for the street vendors who are provided their wares early in the morning on credit or commission from a supplier and then in the evening, after returning the unsold remainder, learn if and what they have retained from their transactions. The facade of self-employment is further reinforced by modes of payment which are often associated with informal sector practices. For example, the sub-contracting of production to home-based workers is a common occurrence. Piece rate and job work suggest a degree of independence which is different to the relationship between regular wage workers and employers. In the latter case, the time worked is the unit of calculation of the wage, while the wage is also paid regularly: per day, week, or month. The actual payment of this regular wage confirms the status of the worker as a permanent employee. Putting-out and one-off jobs, on the other hand, are in this aspect much closer to self-employment.

Last but not least, there is no valid reason to describe waged labour as a phenomenon that is inextricably bound with the formal sector. The informal sector landscape is covered with small-scale enterprises that not only make use of unpaid labour, requisitioned from the household or family circle, but even more of personnel that is hired for a special purpose. This does not, however, always take the shape of an unequivocal and direct employer–employee relationship. There are different intermediaries—those who provide raw materials and then collect semi-finished or finished products from home-based workers, or jobbers who recruit and supervise gangs of unregistered workers—who function as agents for the ultimate patron. In all these cases, it would be incorrect to construct a sharp contrast between self-employment and waged labour corresponding to the informal–formal sector divide.

Such a division would also conflict with the occupational multiplicity which is characteristic for casualized labour. The bulk of these workers are continually in search of sources of income and perform a wide range of odd jobs within a relatively short time period—a week, a day, or even a few hours. These activities sometimes appear to be characterized by self-employment, sometimes waged labour, and sometimes a combination of both. For those involved, the nature of and the manner in which they perform is not of importance but, primarily, what it will pay. The necessity not to specialize in one occupation but to show interest in a multitude of diverse activities arises from the seasonal fluctuations which are inherent to the informal sector economy. The alteration between the dry and the wet season, summer and winter, corresponds with the uneven annual rhythm of a great deal of these open-air occupations. Much less use, and sometimes no use at all, is made of the services of building and road construction workers, quarrymen, brick makers, street vendors, itinerant artisans, and other street workers during unsuitable seasons. But, significant fluctuations throughout the year also occur in the demand for labour for numerous activities which take place in roof-covered and enclosed spaces. In their case, not the climatic conditions, but the changing demand in the annual cycle of certain commodities and services is the main factor. The months preceding the wedding season are a period of peak production for the manufacture of embroidered *saris*, while religious festivals also give a great but temporary incentive to associated industries. The same applies for the great variety of workers in the tourist industry. Cessation of production, or perhaps a sudden spurt, can be determined by stagnation in the supply of raw materials, cuts in the electricity supply or availability of transport, price falls or rises.

It is characteristic for informal sector employment that the use of labour, in size and intensity, is seen as derived from all these market imperfections of a structural or conjunctural nature. In other words, the business risk is passed on to the workers. They must remain available for as long as there is need of their labour, not only in daytime but also in the evening and at night. Periods of overemployment are then followed by shorter or longer periods of enforced idleness. However, they can derive no rights from this pattern of irregular or suddenly changing working hours in the form of wage supplements or continued payment of wages for hours, days, or seasons that work was stopped or declined in intensity. The excessive subjection of labour to the highly variable demands made by the production process arises from the presence of an almost inexhaustible labour supply, if not actually, at least potentially. This reserve army consists of men and women, young and old, who differ from each other more in the degree of previous experience and suitability than in the preparedness to make the required effort for the lowest possible price. To speak of super exploitation of waged workers by employers in the informal sector but then to regard the self-employed as responsible for their own degree of exploitation gives, in my opinion, an exaggerated picture of the differences between both categories and ignores the similarities, also in this aspect.

The standardization of the conditions of employment in the formal sector of the economy—in terms of wage scales, length of the working day, security, and social benefits—equally applies to obtaining access to the sector. This observation implies that recruitment and promotion are subject to fixed rules related to training, seniority, and other objectively determined qualities of the workforce concerned. Conversely, access to industry in the informal sector is characterized by much greater coincidence and arbitrariness. This difference is, of course, consistent with the more permanent employment in the formal sector and the much more casual and shorter lasting jobs which dominate in the lower zones of the labour hierarchy. Without wanting to contest that access to employment in both sectors can be differentiated on the basis of these criteria, I would like to add that these differences become blurred with increasing pressure on the formal sector labour market. When supply also exceeds demand in this sector, the standardized rules make way for more subjective considerations in the selection policy. Formalized labour arrangements then appear to be anything but free of arbitrary, personal preferences and prejudices which are more often used to describe practices of recruitment and dismissal in the informal sector.

The conclusion that I draw from the previous pages is that the diverse modalities of employment do not confirm the image of a dualist but of a fragmented labour market. The distinction made between the two sectors is further complicated by the manner whereby the occupiers of formal and informal labour positions try to build fences and barriers in order to guarantee access to the conquered niche of employment for candidates hailing from their own circle, with maximal exclusion of 'outsiders'. The latter are those who do not belong to the same kind, to which close family members, neighbours, and friends, and also a little further away, members of the same caste, religion, tribe, linguistic group, region, or ethnicity are counted. Of vital importance for the organization of the labour market is a pronounced state of fragmentation which is expressed in the innumerable compartments of employment, of which some assume a fluid form while others are demarcated by quite hard partitions, in both the higher and lower levels of the economy.

## SOCIAL IDENTITY

The very broad spectrum of activities grouped together under the concept of the informal sector are performed by just as heterogeneously composed categories of working people. Despite the wide diversity, there are still a number of common features in the social profile of these masses. In the first place, these workers have little or no formal training and the majority is even totally illiterate. Second, they are completely, or virtually *so*, without any means of production, which implies that they have no other source of income than the earnings from their own labour. Even the acquisition of the most simple tools—such as a shovel and basket or bowl for carrying earth in the case of road workers; a barrow, oil lamp and scales for a street vendor; a little wooden box with polish and brush for shoe polishers—represents an investment which beginners cannot afford out of their own savings and for which they have to take out a loan. The moneylenders operating in this sector charge a high interest rate even for the small amounts and short-term repayments which they grant.

The acute lack of credit worthiness of informal sector workers is closely connected to a third feature: the extremely low wages which they receive for their strenuous efforts. It is precisely the paltry returns that force informal sector workers to make use of all hands, big ones as well as nimble fingers, which are available in their household. Or, in the case of migrants, to leave behind 'dependent' family members who no longer or not yet able work to an extent that would at least compensate for the extra costs needed for their maintenance. In this weighing up of pros and cons, a role is also played by how much of the income should be spent on housing. In order to keep this expenditure item as minimal as possible, seasonal migrants, in particular, make do with a very primitive roof over their heads, improvised from waste material that happens to be available, or they even set up a bivouac under the open sky. Migrants who establish themselves for longer periods far from home, sometimes, may hire living space together, in the case of single men, or attempt, if accompanied by wife and children, to find their own accommodation preferably with water and sanitary facilities, however primitive, in the immediate vicinity. A fourth feature has been implied by the above discussion. The rural and urban zones in which informal sector activities are concentrated have not only more labour migrants than in the sector of formal employment but can also be identified by the occurrence of a much higher percentage of one person units, each of which is separate, or tend to cluster into larger gangs.

Finally, informal work has a low status. This is partly the sum of the features mentioned above in combination with the substitutability and irregularity of the work, and partly, the result of the socially inferior origin of this workforce; in India, the large majority of them are members of backward or untouchable castes. Although the word 'coolie' is no longer fashionable, the derogatory connotation implied by its use in the past covers quite well the lack of respect that is associated with this sort of work. The strenuous physical effort that is often demanded goes with sweat, filth, and other such bodily features which bear the odium of inferiority and subordination. Besides being tainted with the stigma of pollution, these characteristics also undermine the health of the workers in a way which leads to their being prematurely worn out. In addition to all these hazards, women and children are further exposed to sexual harassment. Female and child domestic servants are at risk from their employers and such members of work gangs, from the foremen. Lack of dignity results from their inability to cope with misfortune, for example, illness, or to save for the considerable expense which cannot be avoided for important life-cycle rituals which have to be observed at birth, wedding, or death. By taking an advance on these occasions, they try to meet their social obligations even though it leads to a form of labour attachment, to their employer or an intermediary, which restricts even further their already limited room for manoeuvre.

Does it follow from what has been just stated that informal sector workers have a style of living and working in common with each other which could categorize them as belonging to one homogeneous social class? In comparison with the labour aristocracy employed at the top of the formal sector economy—permanently employed; well educated; with a daily rhythm in which work and free time are sharply marked; reasonably well paid and hence, creditworthy; living in reasonable comfort and consequently, aware of their social dignity and respect—the many times greater army of workers without all these prerogatives forms one uniform mass. But a closer examination reveals that there is not a simple division into only two classes. At the very broad bottom of the economic order, there are striking differences between, for example, migrants forced to wander around various sites of employment in the open air and labourers who operate powerlooms or other simple machines in small workshops. It is true that the textile workers go every day to work for the same boss, at least for the time being, but they cannot derive from their regular employment at the same site any claim for decent treatment or even the right to a minimum form of security.

In an earlier work, I proposed to classify the informal sector workers into three classes.[16] First, a petty *bourgeoisie* which, besides the owners of mini-workshops, self-employed artisans, small traders, and shopkeepers, also include those who earn their keep as economic brokers or agents, such as moneylenders, labour contractors, intermediaries who collect and deliver piecework and home work, rent collectors, etc. Compared with the lower ranks of formal sector labour, the income of this category is not, infrequently, on a much higher level. In reports which tend to value the informal sector as a breeding ground for entrepreneurs, the emphasis lies on the right type of behaviour. Those who belong to this social category set great store by their relative autonomy—they exhibit a need to avoid subordination to others in general and an aversion to wage dependence in particular—and show by good bourgeois attributes, such *as* thrift and hard work, that they are striving to improve their individual position within the social hierarchy.

Second is the sub-proletariat, which subsumes the largest segment of informal sector workers, consisting of a colourful collection of casual and unskilled workers who circulate relatively quickly from one location of temporary employment to another. It includes both the labourers in the service of small workshops and the reserve army of labour which is recruited and dismissed again by large-scale enterprises according to the need of the moment, itinerant semi-artisans who offer their services and (paltry) tools for hire at morning markets, day labourers, home-based workers, vendors, and the long parade of occupations practised in the open air, including the unavoidable shoe polisher and messenger. They differ from the residual category by having, if not a permanent, at least a demonstrable form of accommodation; by keeping a regular household even if all the members are not always able to live together as a family; by a labour strategy that is based on a rational choice of options which are time and place bound; and by attempts to invest in education, health, and social security, even though the irregularity of their existence and the inability to accumulate consistently, be it at a low level, excludes any firm plans for the future.

Although the misery is great (from which many often escape into drunkenness), these workers are still distinguished from the category of the last resort, which I am inclined to describe as paupers. These are the *lumpen*, the dregs of society with criminal features, whose presence nobody values. They are the declassed who have often broken contact

---

[16] Breman, *Wage Hunters and Gatherers.*

with their family or village of origin, who have no fixed accommodation, and who maintain no regular contacts with other people in their immediate environment These people not only lack all means of production but also do not have the labour power and stamina needed to be able to meet their daily minimal requirements in full. Thus alienated even from the means of consumption, they easily fall into a state of pauperization and form a ragbag of crushed, broken-spirited rejects—single men, widows or divorced women with children, children without parents, the mentally or physically handicapped, and the superfluous elderly.

A comment that I want to make is that this classification does not mean that an unambiguous, clearly hierarchical formation of three discrete social strata has crystallized. A household can consist of members who have been absorbed in the labour process in various ways; it is not always the case that all members of one household work in either the formal or informal sector. A consequent lack of consistency in terms of class position and associated lifestyle is, however, rectified by part of the household sometimes breaking away or pushed off to form a new household. The fluidity in the transition between the different social classes, as well as shifts in the proportional distribution among them, that occur over time under influence of contraction or expansion of the economy, mitigate against a division which is either unduly rigid or too static. It is, hence, empirically not easy to delimit the largest segment of the working population, the sub-proletariat, from the other collectivities. Upward and downward mobility are both possible, in theory, and occur in practice at all levels to some degree, although it is very exceptional for this mobility to apply for one individual all the way from the bottom to the top or vice versa. In most cases, mobility is limited to much shorter movements.

## REPRESENTATION AND PROTECTION

One of the most common criteria for the operationalization of the formal–informal sector dichotomy is whether or not labour has managed to get organized. The protection enjoyed by workers in the large-scale and capital-intensive enterprises is the result of action taken by them for the collective promotion of their interests, including wage levels, rules for recruitment, promotion and dismissal, and hours of work, as well as secondary terms of employment. Not all who have found a niche in the formal sector are, in fact, a member of such a trade union. On the other hand, it is even less common for workers in the informal sector to join together in an effort to improve their position. Still, this has actually occurred in a limited number of cases and it is interesting to observe that these initiatives arise from or focus on very vulnerable groups. This applies, for example, to the Self-Employed Women's Association (SEWA) which is based in Ahmedabad. In Kerala, both within and outside agriculture, different trade union-like organizations have been established with the explicit objective to reinforce the rights of informal sector workers.[17] Becoming acquainted with the occasional successful experience is relevant for answering the question: how the emergence of trade unions can be facilitated in the lower echelons of the economy? There is hardly any difference of opinion concerning the urgent need of such a course of action. With a few exceptions, why are they absent then in the informal sector landscape?

The explanation must be sought, first, in the subaltern identity of these working masses and the manner in which they are absorbed in the labour process. The workers concerned are mostly young men and women who belong to the lowest levels of the social hierarchy, who can often neither read nor write, and who have arrived in an alien environment as migrants. They manage to survive with casual and irregular work which often gives them the appearance of being self-employed. The work performed is not connected with a fixed location but is subject to constant change. Besides having to move from place to place looking for employment, they also need to engage themselves in a variety of different activities in intervals of one year, season, week, or even day.

This profile of occupational multiplicity demonstrates how difficult it is to bring together, in an organization, these casual, unskilled, itinerant, fragmented, and poverty-stricken masses on the basis of their common interests. Furthermore, any attempts at unionization made in the separate branches of informal sector industry in practice come up against barriers thrown up by employers and their agents, such as intermediaries and labour contractors. This resistance is sometimes expressed in the form of intimidation or instant dismissal of workers who not only try to press for their own interests but also for those of others. Even worse, it can come to actual violence or the terrorizing of labour activists by gangs of thugs or hired killers whom the employers don't hesitate to use.

[17] K.P. Kannan, *Of Rural Proletarian Struggles: Mobilization and Organization of Rural Workers in South-West India*, New Delhi: Oxford University Press, 1988; S.M. Pillai, 'Social Security for Workers in Unorganised Sector: Experience of Kerala', *Economic and Political Weekly*, vol. 31, no. 31, 1996, pp. 2098–107.

Are the existing trade unions, established by and for formal sector labour with a permanent job, better trained and usually higher paid, aware of the miserable state of the masses crowding in the lower zones of the economy? And, more important still, can they be persuaded to see these irregular workers, with a low social visibility and fragmented into unconnected, fluid segments, as potential members of their organization? No, or at least hardly at all. This disinclination arises partly from all sorts of practical problems as, for instance, the difficulty involved in mobilizing such an amorphous and floating multitude on the basis of shared interests. The task set is further complicated by the necessity to promote these differing and diverse interests in a bargaining dialogue with a very great number of micro-employers. This effort requires large overhead costs which would be impossible to finance for members who belong to the most vulnerable economic categories. Furthermore, experience shows that the needs and problems of informal sector workers are quite different from labour arrangements in the formal sector of the economy. These differences in needs demand a type of organization and promotion of interests of which conventional trade unions have little experience, many of them none at all. Even more important, the union leadership is not prepared, in the light of these much wider aims, to reformulate its mission and to operationalize the new agenda into a concrete plan of action.

In the final analysis, the trade unions close ranks to restrict access. The miserable lot of informal sector workers is not seen as a challenge but as a threat to the much better deal—the outcome of a long-lasting struggle for a reasonable degree of security, prosperity, and dignity—enjoyed by labour in the formal sector. The strategy of fending off of the mass of excluded workers explains why, conversely, the latter feel little affinity with the recognized trade union movement. Both the union leadership and members do not appear to unduly worry themselves over the question of how they could contribute to improving the lot of the informal workers and instead tend to see them as scabs. With scorn they regard the reserve labour army as supplying the strike breakers who unscrupulously accept the jobs, temporarily made available, of formal sector workers who have gone on strike in the hope of being able to occupy them permanently.

Only in recent years, and under the pressure of stagnating or even declining levels of employment in the formal sector, have the established labour organizations dropped their indifferent or even hostile attitude. At the initiative of the International Congress of Free Trade Union

(ICFTU), a conference was held in 1988 on the transformation of the international economic order and the concomitant trend of informalization of employment modalities. It had become clear to insiders as well as outsiders that the trade union movement was threatened with marginalization by its exclusive concentration upon a relatively small elite engaged under formal terms of employment. The leadership finally realized that a large part of the working masses did not recognize the trade union movement as an ally in the struggle against deteriorating working conditions. The unions that were members of this international federation were urged to make the informal sector issue a high priority. A report that appeared only a year later described, as a first aim, the formalization of the gigantic army of unprotected and unorganized workers. They should enjoy the same legal protection as employees in the formal sector. It will be clear that this demand is characterized by a woefully inadequate sense of reality. Moreover, at the same time as it was made, it demonstrated a very poor understanding of the dynamics of the informal sector. The formula to achieve this new goal was confined to the suggestion to accelerate what, according to conventional wisdom, would be the predictable result of the process of economic development. It was a naive supposition and after this recommendation, very little has happened in the routine practice of trade union activities.

The lack of support from the established trade union movement does not mean that the informal sector workers passively accept the labour regime forced upon them. Many make efforts, often repeatedly *so*, to combat the insecurity and miserable conditions of employment by trying to negotiate a somewhat better deal with their particular employer. They do this by emphasizing their subordination and loyalty to their patron for which, in exchange, they appeal to his discretionary power to grant favours. In turn, employers are bent upon reducing even further the already small space in which the massive army in search of work must operate, given the abundant supply and limited demand for labour. The employers make use of all sorts of arrangements which lead to a curtailment of their employees' room for manoeuvre. Mechanisms to tie the worker further to the employer such as providing an advance on salary or paying in arrears show similarities with forms of unfree labour which occurred in the past,[18] but differ from them by a more articulated contractual and capitalist slant. Against this background,

---

[18] J. Breman, *Beyond Patronage and Exploitation: Changing Agrarian Relations in South Gujarat*, New Delhi: Oxford University Press, 1993.

it is understandable why much labour resistance assumes the shape of sabotage, obstruction, avoidance, and other deeds of covert protest, summarized by the term, 'weapons of the weak'.[19]

Despite the severe sanctions which are particularly brought to bear on attempts to form a common front and thus, openly express latent feelings of solidarity, such collective signals of resistance are the order of the day in the informal sector. Reasons which were elaborately discussed earlier explain why, for example, strikes 'suddenly' break out, rarely spread to the whole branch of the industry, and also, relatively quickly die out. The weak capacity to resist makes it understandable why these actions are usually spontaneous, local, and short in duration. But there is also, in part, an underreporting of some forms of resistance as they occur much less or not at all in employment modalities under formal conditions. The registration of labour resistance has been unduly focused on the nature and course of the social struggle in the formal sector. Proto-trade unions, such as those that existed in Europe's pre-industrial past, could be an interesting point of departure for comparison with the manifestation of labour unrest and industrial action in the informal sector of the economy of today.

The protection enjoyed by formal sector workers arises from a gradual shift in the balance of power between capital and labour for a period of roughly one hundred years. The introduction and implementation of separate legislation for protecting labour, in the same way although not to the same extent so that the rights of capital were also safeguarded, would be inconceivable without the intermediary role of the state. What has been the role of national and local government in regulating the informal sector of the economy? For one thing, the impression often created that there is absolutely no official interference is incorrect. Where there is universal suffrage, which is actually exercised in reasonable freedom in India since independence, the political system cannot afford to ignore completely the working masses which make up the majority of the electorate. This consideration is of relevance for explaining why minimum wages have been fixed for landless labourers, why the practices of illegal labour contractors are restricted, why various ordinances regulate the movement of migrants, and why violations of the prohibition of bonded labour are punishable by law, to mention just a few examples.

---

[19] J.C. Scott, *Weapons of the Weak: Everyday Forms of Peasant Resistance*, New Haven: Yale University Press, 1985; J.C. Scott, *Domination and the Arts of Resistance: Hidden Transcripts*, New Haven: Yale University Press, 1990.

In many states of India, in particular, there are detailed rules regulating employment for a great many occupations, even for casual labour that is limited to particular seasons of the year.[20] What is lacking, however, is an effective machinery to implement these regulations as well as the appointment of an adequate number of officials responsible for their enforcement. Civil servants who are allocated inspection responsibilities, moreover, in practice make use of their mandate to obtain extra income. It is an example of the abuse of public authority for private advantage which occurs at all levels of the bureaucracy.

## POLICY AND GLOBALIZATION OF THE LABOUR SYSTEM

After the 'discovery' of the informal sector, amazement was expressed in many publications that such a large part of the population survived or even thrived on it. The reaction of the authorities gave evidence of the need felt for regulation. At the same time, the way in which this took place made clear that this involvement was not motivated so much by the desire to improve the lives of these workers but arose largely from irritation over their escape from government control. In this negatively coloured assessment, the informal sector was seen as a conglomerate of activities which were inconvenient and caused trouble. The parasitic or openly criminal features attributed to these workers reinforced the tendency of the government to protect the public and the economy from these useless, unhealthy, or downright dangerous elements. Bicycle taxis and perambulatory vendors were driven from the streets, while 'unfavourably' located slums, in so far as they were not razed to the ground, were removed from public view by enclosures. City beautification was the slogan in many countries which was supposed to justify this persecution and banishment.[21]

The plea for a more positive attitude, first made by the ILO in particular, was the beginning of a new direction which at least promised to make an end to the open hunt on informal sector workers and their trades. The argument in support of this policy was that the returns from these activities not only provided a living for those involved but were also of genuine use from a more general economic perspective. In order to increase the efficiency and effectiveness of this sector, an extensive package of supportive measures were recommended, varying from better

---

[20] Breman, *Footloose Labour*.

[21] J. Breman, 'The Bottom of the Urban Order in Asia: Impressions of Calcutta', *Development and Change*, vol. 14, no. 2, 1983, pp. 153–83.

training and more credit, with improved accessibility, to expansion of the markets for informal commodities as well as services and, finally, greater tolerance in issuing government permits. The question whether these proposals should be understood as reflecting a policy of formalization remains unanswered as most of them were never implemented. A scenario with which policymakers felt more at ease was to not involve themselves with the informal sector, in either a positive or negative sense. The persecution and unbridled mania for regulation by bureaucrats at all levels was discontinued but without switching over to active protection. A well-known and influential advocate of this formula, with a very strong neo-liberal leaning, is de Soto, who has created great enthusiasm for it among leading politicians and international agencies.[22] This is understandable as the policy of non-state intervention he advocated tends to leave the existing relations of deep-seated inequalities in the distribution of property and power untouched and goes on to legitimate a situation which guarantees the domination of formal sector interests, of both capital and labour.

I have already indicated earlier that in populist inspired interpretations of the informal sector phenomenon, attention has been focused, to a significant extent, on self-employment as an important element in the definition of the sector. To suggest that these workers operate for their own account and at their own risk leads to an analysis focusing on micro-entrepreneurship with all its positive features: ingenuity, versatility, boldness, industriousness, and flexibility. This is also an image that pleases these neo-liberal politicians and policymakers because in their perception, success or failure is purely an affair of the actors themselves as individuals. They feel no need to look for the causes of this success or failure in the structure of the society, of which informal sector workers form such a major segment, nor in the unequal opportunities which are inherent to it.

The continuous formalization of employment in the urban and rural economy did not materialize in the end. In most cases, including India, there has even been a reversal of the trend: a chipping away of the formal conditions of employment which are being replaced by casual and short-term labour arrangements as part of an overall change in the organization of industrial production. An example is the

[22] H. de Soto, *El Otro Sendero*, Lima: Free Enterprise Institute, 1986 (English translation, *The Other Path: The Invisible Revolution in the Third World*, New York: Harper & Row, 1989).

closure of textile factories in Mumbai and Ahmedabad from which the powerlooms for the manufacture of rayon were transferred to thousands of small-scale workshops in new urban growth poles such as Surat.[23] The new international economic order demands the addition of more capital to the industrial process, but this takes place in a manner which guarantees the availability of abundant labour, the payment of very low wages, and provides employment only when needed. The pattern of employment still runs along informal sector lines to the extent of becoming, in recent decades, an ideological maxim, a credo. What is heralded as the 'flexibilization of production' is actually contracting out of work, replacing time wage with piece rate and permanent with casual workers. This trend implies not only deterioration in the working conditions of formal sector workers but also undermines the role of the trade unions which have promoted the interests of this privileged section. The further implementation of the recent policy calls for the dismantling of the existing labour legislation. In addition to a considerable drop in wages, the inevitable result is cutting back the social security benefits that have been built up over many years and, in the end, also a reappraisal of perceptions of dignity and self-esteem. The decline in quality of workers' lives has been exacerbated in many developing countries by the simultaneous introduction of structural adjustment programmes. These schemes, imposed by the World Bank and the International Monetary Fund (IMF), have included a drastic reduction of subsidies which kept food and transport prices low, and of expenditure meant to facilitate public access to education, health, and housing.

*Labour in an Integrating World* is the title of the 1995 World Bank Annual Report.[24] According to this document, the dualism that determines the organization of the labour market arises from the unjustified preferential treatment of formal sector workers. In this view, the labour arrangements in the informal sector are not perceived as a problem, as modalities of employment which contribute to the perpetuation of poverty, but are sooner recommended as a solution to the situation of immense deprivation suffered by such a large part of humanity. The argument made for the withdrawal of state involvement in the labour system, for the repeal of existing protective legislation, and for the abolition instead of more effective enforcement of minimum

---

[23] Breman, *Footloose Labour*.

[24] World Bank, *World Development Report 1995: Workers in an Integrating World*, New York: Oxford University Press, 1995.

wage regulations is part of a political economic doctrine founded upon the unfettered freedom of the market as the guiding principle. The organization of economic production, in a period of growth characterized not by a lack of labour but of capital, benefits the latter at the cost of the former. The providers of work, under these conditions, pay the lowest possible price after the rejection of social security rights which, directly or indirectly, require wage supplements. The crumbling away of the welfare state where it had previously existed, as well as its halting development where it had only just begun to come into sight, can be seen as confirmation of a trend in which the slowly advancing emancipation of labour in recent decades appears as if it is being reversed into its opposite—subordination and insecurity. The progressive polarization of social classes accompanying these dynamics has given rise in Europe to a debate which concentrates on the inclusion–exclusion contrast. It seems to mark the return of the old dualism concept in yet another form.

## REFERENCES

Aziz, A., *Urban Poor and Urban Informal Sector*, New Delhi: Ashish Publishing House, 1984.

Banerjee, B., *Rural to Urban Migration and the Labour Market*, Bombay: Himalaya Publishing House, 1986.

Banerjee, N., *Unorganised Women Workers: The Calcutta Experience,* Occasional Paper, Calcutta: Centre for Studies in Social Sciences, 1978.

_____, 'Indian Women in a Changing Industrial Scenario', Indo-Dutch Studies on Development, *Alternatives*, no. 5, New Delhi: Sage Publications, 1991.

Bienefeld, M., 'The Informal Sector and Peripheral Capitalism: The Case of Tanzania', *Institute of Development Studies Bulletin*, vol. 6, 1975, pp. 53–73.

Bose, A.N., *The Informal Sector in Calcutta Metropolitan Economy*, Geneva: ILO, 1974.

Breman, J., *Of Peasants, Migrants and Paupers: Rural Labour Circulation and Capitalist Production in West India*, Oxford: Clarendon Press, 1985.

_____, 'Labour, Get Lost; A Late-Capitalist Manifesto', *Economic and Political Weekly*, vol. 30, 1995, pp. 2294–300.

Bromley, R. and G. Gerry (eds), *Casual Work and Poverty in Third World Cities*, New York: John Wiley & Sons, 1979.

Gerry, C., *Petty Producers and the Urban Economy: A Case Study of Dakar*, World Employment Programme: Working Papers, no. 8, Geneva: ILO, 1974.

Holmström, M., *Industry and Equality: The Social Anthropology of Indian Labour*, Cambridge: Cambridge University Press, 1984.

International Congress of Free Trade Union (ICFTU), *On Organising Workers in the Informal Sector*, 1989.

ILO, *Employment, Incomes and Equality: A Strategy for Increasing Productive Employment in Kenya*, Geneva, 1972.

_____, *Sharing in Development: A Programme of Employment: Equity and Growth for the Philippines*, Geneva, 1974.

_____, *World Employment Programme: Research in Retrospect and Prospect*, Geneva, 1976.

Jaganathan, N.V., *Informal Markets in Developing Countries*, New Delhi: Oxford University Press, 1987.

Joshi, H., H. Lubell, and J. Mouly, *Abidjan: Urban Development and Employment in Ivory Coast*, World Employment Programme, Geneva: ILO, 1976.

Joshi, H. and V. Joshi, *Surplus Labour and City: A Study in Bombay*, New Delhi: Oxford University Press, 1976.

Kannan, K.P., 'Labour Institutions and the Development Process in India', in T.S. Papola and G. Rodgers (eds), *Labour Institutions and Economic Development in India*, International Institute of Labour Studies, Research Series, no. 97., Geneva, 1992, pp. 49–85.

Lis, C., J. Lucassen, and H. Soly (eds), *Before the Unions: Wage Earners and Collective Action in Europe. 1300–1850*, International Review of Social History, Supplement 2, Cambridge: Cambridge University Press, 1994.

Lubell, H., *Calcutta: Its Urban Development and Employment Prospects*, Geneva: ILO, 1974.

Mathew, P.M. (ed.), *Informal Sector in India: Critical Perspectives*, New Delhi: Khama Publishers, 1995.

Mazumdar, D., *Labor Issues in the World Development Report: A Critical Assessment*, Unpublished paper, Centre for International Studies, University of Toronto, 1995.

Noronha, E., 'Liberalisation and Industrial Relations', *Economic and Political Weekly*, Review of Labour, vol. 31, 1996, pp. L14–L20.

Oteiza, E., *The Allocation Function of the Labour Market in Latin America*, International Institute for Labour Studies Bulletin, vol.8, 1971, pp. 190–205.

Papola, T.S. and G. Rodgers (eds), *Labour Institutions and Economic Development in India*, International Institute of Labour Studies, Research Series no. 97, Geneva, 1992.

Safa, H. (ed.), *Towards a Policy of Urbanization in Third World Countries*, New Delhi: Oxford University Press, 1982.

Schaefar, K., *Sao Paulo: Urban Development and Employment*, World Employment Programme, Geneva: ILO, 1976.

Sethuraman, S.V., 'Urbanisation and Employment: A Case Study of Djakarta', *International Labour Review*, vol. 112, 1975, pp. 191–205.

_____, 'The Informal Sector in Developing Countries: Some Policy Implications', *Social Action*, July–September 1977.

Singh, M., *The Political Economy of Unorganised Labour: A Study of the Labour Process*, New Delhi: Sage Publications, 1990.

Stedman Jones, G., *Outcast London*, London and New York: Oxford University Press, 1971.

Tom, I., *Women in Unorganised Sector: Technology, Work Organisation and Change in South India*, New Delhi: Usha Publications, 1989.

Van der Loop, Th., *Industrial Dynamics and Fragmented Labour Markets: Construction Firms and Labourers in India*, Netherlands Geographical Studies 139, Utrecht/Amsterdam: Institute for Social Geography, University of Amsterdam, 1992.

Wertheim, W.F. and G.H. van der Kolff (eds), *Indonesian Economics: The Concept of Dualism in Theory and Policy*, The Hague: W. van Hoeve Publishers, 1966.

# 9

# Labour Migration from Rural to Urban China*

## ACCELERATION OF ECONOMIC GROWTH IN THE LAST QUARTER OF A CENTURY

China's first steps towards forging a prominent place for itself in the global economy in the early 1980s were marked by a new economic policy. That policy included the designation of Special Economic Zones (SEZs) as focal points for industrial development. The urban centres around which these zones were clustered have since expanded to become extensive agglomerations, and have experienced explosive population growth. The economic transformation that took place was founded essentially on the transition to a neo-liberal mode of production financed by private capital, much of which came from abroad. This sea change put a stop to far-reaching government intervention in the economy. The closure of state-owned enterprises (SOEs), which were inefficient and suffered from low productivity, led to mass redundancies. The change, of course, meant that the urban population no longer enjoyed the right to employment and therefore, lost the security of a permanent job, which may have paid low wages but offered a range of social provisions such as medical insurance, a pension, and public housing benefits.

Although the new economic policy destroyed much of the existing economic activity, it also created a lot of new work, though it was organized along different lines: not by the government but by private entrepreneurs or by encouraging people to become self-employed. It

---

* This paper was presented at the Agrarian Change Seminar, School for Oriental and African Studies (SOAS), London, on 5 November 2009.

was a radical change in the system of industrial relations, which led to many older workers being made redundant (with the necessary support and benefits) and the relocation of the younger segment of the labour force. Central to this operation were special job centres, which helped arrange training and counselling, mediation, and the payment of benefits for a period of three years. Those who failed to qualify for other work were entitled to a benefit to cover their minimum subsistence costs. In 2004, the reforms were considered to have been completed and those who were too old or too inflexible to meet the demands of the new economy crystallized into an underclass of urban poor who remain almost invisible.

Seeking new jobs for the working class already active in the urban factories took place against the background of a much more radical restructuring, the arrival of an enormous army of workers from the countryside. The influx was largely the consequence of a mass exodus from the agricultural sector. When decollectivization took place at the end of the 1970s, agricultural land was allocated to peasant households for them to farm on their own or by tenants. The reform made it clear that a large proportion of agricultural households were redundant. Initial attempts to transfer this surplus to other sectors in the rural economy, by setting up cooperative Town and Village Enterprises (TVEs), were, in the end, not as successful as had been expected. This was partly because the World Trade Organization (WTO) refused to accept anything less than full privatization of all economic activity. The growing interdependence in the global system meant that accepting this demand was inevitable if the country wished to attract foreign capital.

The reshaping of the rural economy, and of agriculture in particular, gave rise to a massive wave of migration. The mobilization of this enormous army of reserve labour broke through the long-standing divide between city and countryside. The *hukou* system of household registration, introduced in 1950, institutionalized the policy of compartmentalization which as good as precluded spatial relocation. Registration was based on place of birth and it was difficult to acquire permission to move elsewhere. The division of the working population into peasants in the villages and factory workers in the cities, with any transition from the first to the second thoroughly blocked, was at odds with the needs of the new economic regime. It was now the order of the day to encourage people to leave the countryside, rather than prevent them. The figures given in Table 9.1 show the extent to which migration to the cities has accelerated.

TABLE 9.1   Estimated Size of Rural-to-Urban Labour Migration, from the
1980s until the End of the First Decade in the 21st Century

| | |
|---|---|
| Up to 1995 | 80 million |
| Up to 2003 | 98 million |
| Up to 2005 | 120 million |
| Up to 2008 | 150–200 million |

*Source*: India–China Joint Seminar on Labour Markets in China and India, 'Experiences and Emerging Perspectives', held at New Delhi, 28–30 March 2007.

The end is by no means in sight. According to an official source from 2001, the plan was to reduce the size of the rural workforce by 350 million, 70 per cent of the total. Only then would the countryside be liberated from the reserve army of labour for which there was no place in the agricultural sector, which was largely founded on small-scale economic activity. Achieving this aim does not in any way mean that the remaining population would be reduced to the status of a residue. It is expected that, with an increase in spatial mobility, the share of the urban population would rise to 55–60 per cent of the total by 2020.

## THE TRANSFORMATION OF XIAMEN INTO A GROWTH POLE

The ongoing transition in economy and society demanded substantial infrastructural improvements, such as building roads and bridges and modernizing the transport system. The resulting loss of agricultural land is especially visible in the vicinity of the large cities, where property has been expropriated to be annexed by the urban agglomeration. Extensive industrial complexes and new residential districts have led to a considerable expansion of the total built-up area. This transformation of former towns and cities into metropolises is especially noticeable in the east of China. In the province of Fujian, the port of Xiamen was designated as an SEZ as early as 1980. The urban area that was initially designated, covered little more than 2.5 square kilometres, but in 1984, this special status was extended to cover the whole island on which the city lies, an area of 135 square kilometres. For the city and its surrounding area, this was the start of an enormous economic leap forward, which was also reflected in the explosive growth in the number of inhabitants. From a population of 300,000 in 1980, the city has doubled in size every decade since, reaching a total of 2.97 million in 2008. Of this, 1.68 million are permanent residents, while the other 1.29 million are registered as belonging to the 'floating population'. With a migratory population of 43 per cent, Xiamen is not an exception; in cities like

Shenzhen and Guangzhou, outsiders can account for more than half of the total population.

Statistics and reports on the situation in China as a whole show how the process of migration has developed, which provinces migrants come from and go to, and what changes have taken place in the kind of jobs held by the working population. The economic and social dynamics of the macro situation need, however, to be complemented by micro-studies that offer an insight into the impact of the large-scale movements of people on their places of origin and destination. My study shows what impact the influx of migrants from the hinterland has had on a city on the east coast of the province of Fujian and how the migrants themselves have fared. During both of my earlier visits to Xiamen—the first time in 1992 and again, in 2001—I kept a field diary. These rough notes describe the radical upscaling experienced by this urban centre and the area around it over the past quarter of a century. Because my special interest lies with the mass of migrants from the hinterland, during a new round of fieldwork in the summer of 2008, I visited what are known as 'urban villages', distinct neighbourhoods of newly built, compact residential blocks on the edge of the city inhabited by newcomers who are not accommodated in the dormitories in the industrial areas. I also went on short trips to the hinterland where the migrants originate from, to obtain a brief impression of the effects of this large-scale exodus at the point of departure.

The urban landscape has changed drastically. In 1992, I saw mainly low-rise apartment blocks no more than four or five storeys high. The streets were not overfull, residential districts had basic services and small, largely traditional local shops. The first department stores had opened near the harbour, which attracted a lot of window shoppers, but few paying customers. The threat of a military confrontation with nearby Taiwan had until then hampered the expansion of Xiamen and the coastal zone around it. Today, Xiamen has the allure of a major urban centre, with skyscrapers of twenty to thirty storeys throughout the entire city. Flyovers carry the major traffic arteries through the middle of the city, making the various neighbourhoods easily accessible. This cosmopolitan impression is reinforced by the shopping malls filled with branches of foreign chain stores, like Wal-Mart, McDonalds, Benetton, and Kentucky Fried Chicken. The feeling of rampant consumerism is reinforced by enormous billboards. An excellent network of public transport and explosive growth in the number of cars guarantee a busy road system that becomes very congested during the morning and evening rush hours. The large number of bicycles which were so conspicuous in my earlier visits has since declined. Mobility is facilitated by wide footpaths and a noticeable attention to greenery. The city is part of a large network of bus and train connections. The small airfield that ensured that Xiamen was also accessible by air in the past has now been replaced by a large airport, clearly built to cater for more than domestic flights. The improved relations with Taiwan, separated from Xiamen only by a very narrow strait, has reinforced expectations that the city will be a major intersection in the flow of goods and people that is sure to develop. Both trade and capital have already started to act on these expectations, before they have been realized.

Economic growth is very much typified by the informality which characterizes the labour system as a whole. The nature of employment is not very different from what I have encountered in India and Indonesia during my fieldwork in past decades.[1] I have outlined these features in a series of publications: employment on the basis of a verbal agreement rather than a written contract; casual work rather than steady jobs (although this does not mean that the relationship may not become more regular at some point), sub-contracting that can take on the character of self-employment; lengthening of the working day (up to twelve hours or more) and working week (with free days limited to one or two days a month), with a lot of shift work and variable, rather than constant, working hours; primarily low wages paid on a piecework rather than time rate; a lack of social provisions and other labour rights; and an absence of collective action, sometimes enforced by an official ban on trade union membership.

China's truly impressive growth is illustrated by a sevenfold increase in gross national product since 1981. This great leap forward has largely occurred in urban growth poles like Xiamen. It is important to note,

---

[1] See, among others, J. Breman, *Wage Hunters and Gatherers: Search for Work in the Urban and Rural Economy of South Gujarat*, New Delhi: Oxford University Press, 1994; J. Breman, *Footloose Labour: Working in India's Informal Economy*, Cambridge: Cambridge University Press, 1996; J. Breman, *The Making and Unmaking of an Industrial Working Class: Sliding Down the Labour Hierarchy in Ahmedabad, India*, New Delhi: Oxford University Press, 2004; J. Breman and Gunawan Wiradi, *Good Times and Bad Times in Rural Java: A Study of Socio-economic Dynamics Towards the End of the Twentieth Century*, Leiden: KITLV Press, 2002; and Hein Mallee, 'Migration, Hukou and Resistance in Reform China', in Elizabeth Perry and Mark Selden (eds), *Chinese Society; Change, Conflict and Resistance*, New York: Cambridge University Press, 2000, pp. 83–101.

therefore, that my account does not apply to the many areas whose inhabitants have been left behind. Although there is something of a spill-over effect, the contrast between town and countryside, and between the west and east of the country, has become even more marked than before. The situation in the central part of the country is more complex because some provinces have experienced the same growth as the coastal zones, while in others, people are primarily leaving to seek work elsewhere. The macro statistics across the board suggest a rapid fall in employment in agriculture (from 77.2 per cent in 1975 to 62.4 per cent in 1985 and to 44.8 per cent in 2005). Remarkably enough, after an initial increase in industrial employment (from 13.5 per cent in 1975 to 23 per cent in 1985), the share of this sector levelled out, reaching only 23.8 per cent in 2005. The expansion of the service sector (from 9.3 per cent in 1975 to 16.8 per cent in 1985 and 31.4 per cent in 2005) suggests that there are no grounds for assuming that nearly all migrants are engaged in industrial work.[2] My own observations show that this also applies to newcomers in Xiamen. The notion that China is becoming the world's factory does not mean that the other economic sectors remain unaffected by the new dynamics.

## DENIAL OF FULL CITIZENSHIP

The migrants are indispensable as labour in the city but the majority of them are denied citizenship. Their hukou status remains linked to their place of origin in the countryside and means that they are seen as outsiders and that their temporary residence entitles them to no rights. Looked upon as a floating population, they have no access to work in the formal sector of the economy, they are not permitted to engage in collective action to improve their terms of employment and working conditions, and they may not do jobs for which there are sufficient local workers. Nor are they eligible for social provisions that entitle them to free health care and pension benefits. They have no right to low-rent housing or public education, which is only free to those with hukou status in the city. In brief, they are second-class citizens who have come to the city to work for an unspecified period and who are not expected to settle permanently. I will examine the profiles of these labour migrants and the distinct place they occupy in the living and working environment of the city in which I conducted my field research on the basis of six sub-themes.

[2] The 2007 India–China Joint Seminar on Rural–to–Urban Labour Migration.

## Housing and Neighbourhood

The following description of my findings is based on semi-structured interviews with respondents in the agglomeration of Xiamen, supplemented with information from case studies by researchers in other cities. I generally selected the respondents on the basis of introductions that, in most cases, enabled me to inform them of my interest in meeting them in advance. I was able to ask them about their backgrounds, work, and lives—in lengthy and sometimes repeated conversations—without creating the impression that their answers were intended for anyone other than myself. Of the twenty-two households on which I collected data, seven of the respondents were single, nearly all of them sharing the household with others, while the remaining fifteen cohabited with a partner (mostly as married couples with or without children). It would be inaccurate to deduce from this that the majority of the migrant population is living together as members of composite households. A substantial proportion of the urban newcomers are young men and women who are still unmarried and who do not make their own living arrangements. In the first years after their arrival in Xiamen, they have no other choice than to live in accommodation provided by their employers. However, after they have been in the city for a longer period, they start to prefer their own living space.

I gathered most of my data from visits to neighbourhoods where migrants have found independent accommodation. One of the main reasons for focusing on them is the restricted access to the men and women living in dormitories provided by their employers. Outside their working hours, too, they lack the freedom to move around as they please or to receive visitors. My requests to meet them without their bosses or guards present were often denied or remained unanswered. In addition, there is a not insignificant group of migrants who disappear into the city and become invisible because they do not live in one of the 'urban villages'. Among the first wave of migrants, there were many who used to sleep at the worksite.

Hawkers slept under tables in the markets where they sold vegetables; maids on a sofa in the employer's home, carpenters in the owner's workshop, construction workers in and around the buildings they made, cooks and waiters on the floor of the restaurant during closing hours, etc.[3]

---

[3] Y. Wang, 'Housing Reform and its Impact on the Urban Poor in China', *Housing Studies*, vol. 15, no. 6, 2000, p. 855; D. Solinger, 'The Floating Population in Cities: Chances for Assimilation?', in D. Davis, R. Kraus, B. Naughton, and E. Perry

Such practices are less prevalent now, also, because of the close supervision by the municipal authorities. Still, I met with migrants who try to arrange for their own accommodation for sleeping at, or at short distances from, wherever they work. They rent places themselves or stay in temporary shelters, such as huts on building sites, or places that are used for other purposes during the day, such as offices or storerooms which they are permitted to sleep in but which are not intended for permanent residence/accommodation. To obtain some idea of this category, I supplemented my study in the migrant neighbourhoods with a random sample of migrants who I came across on the street in a neighbourhood specifically selected for this purpose. Expanding my database in this way could not prevent, however, that men and women from outside the city who do not work in the open air—such as hairdressers, shop assistants, or housemaids—but also do not rent a room in one of the urban villages largely fell outside the scope of the study. Lastly, I visited a new, large industrial park that is being built some distance from the urban agglomeration. The sites have been prepared for construction and the factories that have been built on them are on offer to foreign companies, from Taiwan in particular. To compensate for the loss of their fields, the inhabitants of the villages in the affected area have been given permission to build shops and housing blocks on the land that is left to them for the tens of thousands of labour migrants who will be arriving. This visit gave me the opportunity to check on the planned but uncertain progress of the new economic policy in the coming years.

The decision to focus my research mainly on the inhabitants of the 'urban villages' was founded on my assumption that the majority of the migrants do not consider themselves as temporary residents of Xiamen, returning after some time to their place of origin or seeking work in another city. The use of the term 'floating population' indicates that this is how the authorities treat the newcomers who flock to the city, but this stubbornly held belief that they are dealing with a mass of transient workers is diametrically opposed to the desire of the migrants themselves to settle permanently in Xiamen, at least for the duration of their working lives, if not for good. That is also why young people like to exchange their communal accommodation after some years for their own living space, which they rent together with a fellow worker in one of the urban villages. This desire for more autonomy and privacy certainly arises if

---

(eds), *Urban Space in Contemporary China: The Potential for Autonomy and Community in Post-Mao China*, Cambridge: Cambridge University Press, 1995, p. 134.

migrants have found a marriage partner with whom they wish to share a household.

The 'urban villages' are generally located on the outskirts of the city but, due to the expansion of the urban area, they have become an integral part of the agglomeration and are now surrounded by more expensive districts inhabited by permanent city dwellers in higher-income groups. As the city has expanded, the municipal government has expropriated land on a large scale, compensating the former owners, who were usually farmers or labourers themselves. They were given permission, and often credit, to build apartment blocks a few storeys high and rent them to migrants. Most of these tenement houses are jerry built and bring in a rent of 275–450 yuan a month for each apartment. They consist of a single room covering not much more than 15 square metres without their own water supply. Meals are cooked in the corridor and the toilet has to be shared with several neighbours. These overcrowded flats with minimal provisions are not found only in the urban villages of Xiamen. The following passage comes from a report from a field study in the city of Ningbo, which also lies on the east coast of China.

Almost all migrant households in two urban villages occupy only one room. In most households, two to three persons share a room of 10 to 20 square meters. The average occupancy rate is 2.53 persons per room, the average per capita floor space 6.76 square meters ... Most households cook in the same room where they sleep. Only 5 percent have their own bathroom, 55 percent (mostly women) have to take a bath inside the bed room with a water container ... Apart from the jam packed dwellings, there is a serious shortage of sanitation facilities. Most of the houses have no sewer connection and the toilet facilities in the villages are seriously inadequate. The almost 5,000 migrants residing in Changfeng have access to only 6 latrines with 34 toilets, the 2,000 migrants in Jinjacao only 2 latrines with 16 toilets. The ratio of 54 households per toilet is far below UN Habitat standards (not more than 2 households sharing one toilet). Almost half of the migrants have to queue for a toilet for 10 to 20 minutes in the morning rush hours, another 35 percent wait for 5 to 10 minutes.[4]

Living units which do have their own toilet, washing, or kitchen space, and even two or three rooms, are obviously let for a much higher rent (from 500 yuan onwards). They are inhabited by households that are not

[4] Qi Changqi and He Fan, 'Informal Elements in Urban Growth Regulation in China: Urban Villages in Ningbo', India–China Joint Seminar on Labour Markets in China and India, 'Experiences and Emerging Perspectives', held at New Delhi, 28–30 March 2007, p. 11.

only better off, but usually have more members. This does not mean that the one-room apartments are occupied only by one person. The tenants are married couples, with or without children, or young men and women who have met at work and often come from the same place or area. I only met one person—a twenty-four-year old seamstress—who did not share her single room. Building labourers often sleep in communal sheds on site. Married couples do not have their own place to sleep, but have to share it with others. These construction workers lead a nomadic existence and move to another site when a project is completed. The temporary accommodation is, however, not always demolished after a project is finished. A large proportion of the migrants are given accommodation by the company they work for, together with many other employees. It consists of a bunk bed in a large or small communal dormitory. Each has a small cupboard for their clothes and other possessions, but they do not hold much. More than the lack of facilities, this absence of private space in which to spend their free time alone or with a few workmates is incentive enough, after some time, to move to a room in a nearby urban village, and to separate their work from their living arrangements.

These neighbourhoods are densely populated as the apartment blocks are built very close together. The streets between them are very narrow, making them look more like alleyways. Public space is scarce. There is little in the way of public utilities such as street lighting or vegetation, and the open sewers add to the sloppy appearance of most of the urban villages. Nevertheless, the inhabitants can buy all their daily and more incidental needs in the local shops, deposit their rubbish in bins that are emptied regularly, and are obliged to keep the streets clean and orderly. The neighbourhood committees, the lowest tier of the municipality, occasionally order a clean-up campaign and the apartment owners are held accountable to carry those orders out. These neighbourhoods are not slums like those I have encountered during my research on the margins of large cities in India and Indonesia. Yet, the urban villages of Xiamen strike a sharp contrast with the comfortable and even luxurious housing in high-rise blocks and other neighbourhoods where the established residents of the city live. They bear the mark of informality and the density of the building makes them disorderly and inferior in the eyes of officialdom.

Politicians often blame urban villages as a stigma of urban development. Decision makers tend to demolish and replace them with more presentable buildings. This is, however, not an easy task, because it could very well trigger off social unrest which could stop political careers. In view of that, planners prefer to ignore such areas and leave them to remain inside the city. The urban villages clearly constitute an informal element in Chinese urban growth regulation.[5]

Nevertheless, I did not encounter in Xiamen the kind of sub-human slums described as typical of Third World cities by Mike Davis,[6] characterized by poverty, deprivation, and exclusion for the masses of migrants who flood into them after being expelled from the surrounding countryside. A United Nations (UN)–Habitat report confirms that China has succeeded in industrializing at a rapid pace without the emergence of large slums or informal settlements.[7]

## Migrant Profile

Of the twenty-two households that form the core of my database, seven have a single member (three unmarried men, three unmarried women, and one divorced woman). The other fifteen are households consisting of married couples, thirteen of whom live together in Xiamen, while two men have wives who live in their place of origin (one became unable to work after an accident on a building site, while the other stayed behind to look after their small children). The families of the fifteen households consisting of married couples are incomplete. The children are generally either sent back to the place of origin or did not come in the first place, being left behind—usually with their grandparents—to attend school and grow up. I encountered no cases of child labour during my research. Where a few young children do live with their parents in Xiamen (in eight of the twenty-two households), the main reason is that there is no one back in the place of origin to look after them. Children who become old enough to work themselves (from the age of sixteen), sometimes, join their parents in the city (in three of the fifteen households with married couples, I encountered a working son or daughter) but the shortage of living space usually means that they find shelter elsewhere in or outside Xiamen.

Two age groups are strongly underrepresented among the migrants: young children and old people. Again, the most important reason for their absence would appear to be the shortage of living space. It is difficult enough for the inhabitants of the urban villages to have their own children living with them, let alone their elderly parents. And then,

---

[5] Ibid., p. 6.

[6] Mike Davis, *Planet of Slums*, London and New York: Verso, 2006.

[7] *The Challenge of Slums: Global Report on Human Settlements*, United Nations (UN)–Habitat, 2003, p. 126.

there is the higher cost of living in the city. There is no room in Xiamen for those who are unable to work, who have no capacity to earn income. That also means that migrants who lose their ability to work—through illness, an accident, or encroaching old age—are unable to stay on in the city. My respondents were reconciled to the fact that they would eventually return to their places of origin, but took solace in the fact that they had paved the way to the city for their children. With a better education and better prepared for what was in store for them, the next generation had the chance of a better future. The majority of the migrants are adolescents from sixteen to eighteen years old, young adults between twenty and twenty-five, and more mature adults from thirty-five to forty. The proportion of newcomers declines sharply beyond middle age. Typical inhabitants of the urban villages are men and women from twenty to forty years old. Younger migrants are less visible as they tend to stay close to their place of employment—industrial sites that are usually far from the city centre—and have little opportunity to gain access to the urban domain. As I mentioned earlier, they are, therefore, underrepresented in my database.

A final notable statistic is that men and women migrate from the countryside to the city in roughly equal numbers. I was unable to determine whether this has been the case since the beginning of the migration process a quarter of a century ago or has gradually evolved. In this respect, it is also clear that women come to work and not to take care of the household. The twenty-two households on which I base this conclusion have a total of forty-nine members. Of those who work, eighteen are women and twenty-one are men. The ten who do not work include eight small children and two women, one of whom has just had a baby and is therefore, temporarily, unable to work and the other is an older woman who has come to Xiamen to care for the child of her son and his wife. I have no cause at all to believe that the households in my database are an exception to the more general rule. I consider the high degree of participation in the labour process, with thirty-nine of the forty-nine members of the sample belonging to the working population, as typical of the average migrant household in Xiamen.

My informants, most of whom I met in the setting of the household to which they belong in the urban villages, come from a wide variety of provinces. Yet, most come from regions that lie in the immediate hinterland of Xiamen, such as Fujian and the adjacent Jiangxsi. It is, however, not exceptional for migrants to come from further afield. Conversely, I suspect that, while those who leave the closer hinterland tend to migrate to the cities on the east coast of Fujian, many men and women also go to the other more northerly or southerly provinces of eastern China. I spoke to a large number of respondents with close relatives in Guangdong, Anhui, Sichuan, Henan, Jiangxsi, or Zhejiang. How did the migrants find their way to Xiamen? In most cases, it was through family, friends, or neighbours—the primary channels of kinship or other close ties. Where such contacts were already in Xiamen, they would help the newcomers to find work and accommodation. Most of the migrants came directly to Xiamen from the hinterland, though quite a number of them have also worked in other cities. Why did this latter group not stay where they first went? Loneliness or bad experiences with employers would often drive them to return home, where lack of employment or prospects would tempt them to try their luck again in Xiamen. My findings proved to apply to other growth poles as well: a case study in Ningbo, a city that also lies on the east coast in the province of Zhejiang and with a population of over 5.5 million in 2006, showed that more than half of all migrants came directly from the hinterland.

About 15% had migrated to more than three cities before they made their move to Ningbo. About half of the respondents live in Ningbo since more than 3 years, about one third between one and three years, only one fourth for less than one year. Most migrants chose Ningbo as first choice, and almost nine out of ten would like to settle down permanently as soon as they find a suitable job.[8]

The term floating population is inaccurate as only a minority—mostly young, single men—move around in search of adventure and variety. Most migrants have no other plans for the future than to remain where they are, in Xiamen.

The large majority of the migrants have been to school. The younger ones had attended at least six years of primary school before their departure and many had also completed three years at junior high school. That means that they are all able to read, write, and do basic arithmetic, and most of them can do so at a higher than basic level of proficiency. This has equipped them to find their way to and in Xiamen. A small minority, mostly older people, are still illiterate. One of these, a woman who sells telephone cards on the street, told me that when she was a child, almost forty years ago, it was much less common to attend school than now. She said that her lack of basic schooling had hampered her in

---

[8] Qi Changqi and He Fan, 'Informal Elements in Urban Growth Regulation in China', p. 10.

finding better paid and more highly valued work. This encouraged her to ensure that her own children did attend school. Only a minority of the migrants, no more than a fifth, had completed a further education. Most of those had studied for four years to acquire their senior high school certificate before seeking work, while a few had also continued on to some form of advanced education. With these qualifications, they are able to compete for jobs at a higher level in the urban economy. The large majority of the migrants, who have had only nine years schooling or less, are only eligible for unskilled work.

There is a razor-sharp division in society, in which level of education is decisive in determining social and economic status. Low educated migrants are aware of this and accept that they lack the knowledge and skills to find work in the higher echelons of the labour market. When asked why they did not persist in their studies, they reply that when they were young they underestimated the value of an education. The poverty of their parents made it difficult to send the children to school. In addition, there was little interest in schooling in their households, certainly beyond the primary level. This absence of a self-propelled drive to learn was fuelled by a lack of insight into the educational demands of the new economy that was emerging beyond the village or the small rural towns in which they grew up. But the parents I spoke to in the urban villages of Xiamen also indicated that they suffer from a lack of schooling and admitted that they do not know how to guide their own children how to get ahead, despite their belief that it will certainly require a secondary education. One man told me that he had not continued his education after junior high school because he was from the 'wrong class'. In his view, the fact that he came from a family of landlords would have prevented him from gaining access to higher education anyway, and this awareness made him satisfied with settling for a job as a construction worker. He hoped that his children or grandchildren would be free of this class stigma.

I observed that boys are given more opportunities to gain a secondary education than girls. This divergence seems to be based on the dubious assumption that girls are less expected than boys to provide for their aged parents after getting married. From the accounts of my respondents, I deduced that many migrants are convinced that they gave up their education too soon. As adults, they now realize that they have little hope of making up the lost ground. Other researchers have also noted such feelings of regret at having dropped out of school at too young an age.

Among those who had failed to continue school after nine years, or had dropped out earlier, it was common to describe this as an unfortunate event, not necessarily at the time that it happened but seen in the longer perspective of a working career and income.[9]

There are, however, exceptions. A few migrants do succeed, through self-study, in qualifying for jobs that were initially far beyond their reach. A good example that I recall is the younger sister of a staff member of the university who started her working life in Xiamen as a seamstress in a workshop and, despite living in a communal dormitory, succeeded in studying to qualify for better paid work. Her older sister was undeniably a role model, even more so when, after she had a baby, she offered to pay her sister living expenses and pocket money to come and care for the child. In this period, the younger sister took the opportunity to obtain her higher secondary school certificate and learned how to use a computer. When she returned to a regular job, she was taken on as a cashier in a production company and was later even promoted to head of personnel. This year she has enrolled at the open university as an undergraduate student. Hers is a success story that, as already noted, cannot be seen in isolation from the example set by her older sister. But her choices were, almost certainly, also influenced by her parents. As children, the sisters grew up in the main town of a sub-district, where their father had a doctor's practice. This shows that they by no means come from a regular peasant household and did not lead the usual village life.

This brings me to note that many migrants do indeed come from peasant families and, given the poverty and illiteracy common in this milieu, it is logical that they would start to work at an early age. Originating from the countryside should, however, not automatically be seen the same as living in a village and working in agriculture. My respondents also included the children of local officials, or traders, and shopkeepers in district towns. Diversification has long been a feature of the rural economy. Being born into a family whose head works outside agriculture would probably mean that a son or daughter was more motivated to acquire an education than if they were children of the regular peasant stock. In the 1970s, to relieve the pressure on the agricultural sector, the government began to encourage other branches of industry. Under the TVEs' policy, small-scale and artisanal production workshops

---

[9] Mette Halskov Hansen and Cuiming Pang, 'Me and My Family: Perceptions of Individual and Collective among Young Rural Chinese', *European Journal of East Asian Studies*, vol.7, no. 1, 2008, p. 87.

were set up to generate work and income for labourers who had become superfluous in the primary sector. Most of these small enterprises closed again in the 1980s, but it is reasonable to assume that their redundant employees were the first to seek employment elsewhere. Migrants' social and economic background, therefore, plays a pivotal role in the kind of employment they are able to find in the urban economy. But, generally speaking, young people in China's huge hinterland are forced to leave their places of origin because their inadequate standard of living leaves them not much choice. However, youngsters belonging to poor house-holds find it more difficult to get access to education and are, for that reason, less likely to migrate and send savings home which help to break through the spiral of deprivation of those who have to stay back.

Since this essay focuses on those who have left their rural homes and succeeded in finding their way to the urban economies, I would like to emphasize that the migrants are, evidently, not a random sample from the landscape of origin. Among the population in the hinterland, there are many who do not qualify for opting out, because of poverty, no or inadequate schooling, and lack of social capital that would facili-tate joining the trek to a better life. The old adagium that migration is the mother and father of differentiation—starting from a situation of inequality and leading to more inequality—is still relevant. On the basis of research carried out in the vast hinterland, Brennell concludes that 'the typical migrant was male, young and relatively well educated and there-fore little remittance income went to the neediest rural households'.[10] Many migrants who began their urban lives with little education are highly motivated to assure their children a better future by giving them a secondary education, and are prepared to sacrifice their own chances for a better life in order to make that happen.

## Work

I was unable to verify whether the government controls migration in the sense that local authorities in the hinterland decide who can leave and where they go, and mediate in finding work for them. What is clear is that their departure and their arrival in Xiamen are duly recorded, and they have to carry their identity card with them. The migrants must be able to prove where they have come from, where they are staying, how they

[10] C. Brennell, 'Rural Industrialization and Spatial Inequality in China, 1978–2006', *Economic and Political Weekly*, vol. 43, no. 52, 27 December 2008–2 January 2009, pp. 43–50.

are going to make a living, and who is going to provide them with work. Newcomers rarely arrive in the city without having made these kinds of arrangements in advance. As mentioned earlier, they find their way by making use of the social network around them. These friends, relations, and neighbours usually provide them with their initial requirements. Only after sometime do newcomers start to rely on contacts they have made themselves. And, as they gain more experience, they also have a growing desire to make their own decisions about what to do and how to go about it.

How is the migrant population distributed among the economic sectors in Xiamen? In my sample of twenty-two households, there are a total of thirty-nine working members. Of those, five men and eight women must be classified as industrial workers, six men and one woman work in construction, while ten men and nine women earn their living in the service or transport sectors. It would, in the first instance, be misleading to consider this sectoral distribution—33 per cent, 18 per cent, and 49 per cent respectively—as typical for the total migrant population in the city. My sample underrepresents young migrants who are industrially employed in production companies and workshops and live on the premises in which they work. Taking this largely invisible group of migrants into consideration means that the percentage of newcomers to the city engaged in industrial work is actually more than a third of the total. How much more is difficult to say. The available macro figures suggest that at least a quarter of the city's labour force can be classified as industrial workers. This category is probably larger among migrants than among the permanent inhabitants of Xiamen, but I consider it highly improbable that the overrepresentation of industrial occupations applies to more than half of all newcomers. Women are mostly employed in the manufacture of clothing and the assembly of all kinds of products, while men are more likely to find employment in the metal and chemical industries and where the work is heavy and physically strenuous. In construction, most of the skilled labourers (carpenters, iron bartenders, plasterers, bricklayers, and tilers) are men, while the far fewer women are employed as helpers, supporting the craftsmen by fetching and carrying sand, stones, pipes, and other materials. Men are also more common in the transport sector, working as drivers, driver's mates, and loaders. What struck me during my visits to the urban villages was the prevalence of service providers among both male and female workers. It seems that this tertiary sector is the most important in the entire urban economy.

The migrants pick up the knowledge and skills required for the work they do on the job, instructed by their workmates. They only get paid the full wage of an experienced worker after they have completed this period of training. How long it lasts depends on the demands of the work they have to do. They enter into a verbal agreement with the employer, an informal understanding which is not always sealed with a written contract, although it is obligatory to do so since 2007. Sometimes, the employer asks old hands to stand guarantee for the good behaviour of the newly recruited. Both parties feel free to end the relationship at will and, although a period of notice is normal, they can quite easily be dismissed or resign on the spot. They are not employed on the basis of a one-off or short-term assignment, but to work for an unspecified period. The main mode of employment is that of a regular job, but without it being a permanent and protected position. It is interesting to note that, although a written employment contract is supposed to be a form of security, young migrants, in particular, claim to be very attached to their freedom. From this perspective, a formal contract curtails their freedom to come and go as they please.

A contract is a way of binding workers. It is just a system to the advantage of the enterprise. If you sign a contract they will 'fry you until you drop', one young man explained. While we assumed that a labour contract would be a kind of insurance for workers, guaranteeing stable and predictable work conditions, our interviewees rejected this assumption almost without exception, and claimed that the employer was in full control once the contract was signed. By emphasising their 'freedom to come and go', workers who were bound to carry out manual labour for long hours discursively manifested themselves as subjects in power, rather than as the mere objects of misfortune, deprived of pride, opportunity and dignity—an image that dominates the official, as well as popular, discourse on migrant labourers and school drop-outs.[11]

It should be emphasized that these are the opinions of adolescents who are still unmarried. Once migrants have been in the city for a longer time, and especially after they have started a family, they increasingly feel the need for a decent job, that is, a permanent position, a steady income, and acceptable terms of employment.

Casual work, limited to temporary assignments, is the exception rather than the rule. I encountered this kind of work, primarily, in the construction sector, for example, a plasterer who is not employed by a

---

[11] Hansen and Pang, 'Me and My Family', pp. 90–1.

contractor or building company, but takes on odd jobs whenever he can find them, moving around from site to site in and outside the city. He keeps himself informed about projects where he might be able to find work through a network of workmates and sub-contractors. He earns a better daily wage than permanent employees, but that is offset by the periods, shorter or longer, that he has no work. A number of other construction workers also have no permanent employer, but they are members of a gang under the leadership of a jobber. They follow him wherever he goes and may get an advance from him for days that there is no work for them. A jobber with a gang of six male and female gardeners works on the same principle. He finds them work and they make sure they are available. Work at one's own expense and risk is also quite common. This is the case with, for example, the woman who sells telephone cards, a street vendor, and a trader in old rags and metal. I also met some people who were 'half and half', for example, a driver who owns his own delivery van and who is paid a monthly wage which includes reimbursement for use of the vehicle on behalf of the employer.

The working day of the average migrant is longer than that of the permanent inhabitants of Xiamen. They sometimes have to work twelve hours or more, because if an order has to be completed quickly, the work in garment workshops and other production companies will continue unabated, if the boss so wishes. Conversely, the working day might be shortened if there is a shortage of orders. Helpers in shops and restaurants also have to start early in the morning and remain available until late at night. In addition to the long hours, the working day tends to be unpredictable. I have often made appointments that were cancelled because the person concerned suddenly had to work. Only large enterprises that operate around the clock and whose personnel work in rotating shifts have a stricter schedule that does not permit flexibility. The majority of the migrants are not paid on the basis of the hours they work but on piece rate or for the job done. This, too, has a strong tendency to lengthen the working day. The working week is also long, with free days usually limited to one or two a month. Virtually, the only opportunity the migrants have to enjoy a longer period of rest is the New Year, which they take advantage of to visit their families in the hinterland.

Compared to the miserable circumstances in which unskilled labour migrants are employed in Indian cities, their fellows in China fare considerably better. That applies not only to the level of pay, which I will return to later, but usually to the conditions in which they have to work. Construction workers wear helmets on site, scaffolders wear protective gloves, and gardeners have dust masks and protective glasses. These and other examples show that labour has both value and dignity. I was told by employers that they found it increasingly difficult to hire migrants who were prepared to do work that they considered dirty and dangerous to health. Spending the day working in stinking fumes or with chemicals that cause skin rashes is good reason to avoid these kinds of jobs. Established and more well-to-do city dwellers whose lifestyle reflects their comfortable position complain of the difficulties they encounter in finding domestic help, maids, or minders for the children.

The majority of the migrant population earn a living doing unskilled work requiring little schooling. Their lack of education means that, for most of them, there is not much hope of upward mobility. On-the-job training does allow construction workers, for example, to offer their services to the jobber or foreman as fully qualified craftsmen. The jobbers and foremen themselves started as labourers, obtaining their positions of authority on the basis of suitability and experience. A few of my respondents succeeded in improving their lives by starting up their own businesses. One of these is the co-owner of a small garment workshop. His partner is responsible for production, for which they purchased seven sewing machines, and employ four seamstresses. He himself finds the orders and delivers the finished articles. Another man has opened a small construction workshop, where he and two helpers do work outsourced by large manufacturers. These petty entrepreneurs, who operate as subcontractors at their own risk and expense, obtained the seed capital they needed to buy machinery and rent premises by borrowing money from friends or relations. They are not eligible for credit from a bank. They also depend on contacts made during their time in employment to gain access to the market. There is certainly no lack of entrepreneurial spirit. Two of my respondents, a cook and a waiter in an eating house, have plans to start their own business. It is lack of funds rather than resolve that is stopping them from realizing this ambition.

Migrants generally stay in the sector in which they find work on arrival in the city. Construction workers are used to working in the open air and show little interest in jobs that mean they are shut up in a factory and force them to work on an assembly line. Young people seem to have less difficulty with this sort of employment, and are more likely to move from job to job than from sector to sector. Lastly, during my stay in Xiamen, I came across very few people who worked purely on a casual basis or who were homeless. The individual cases I encountered on the street were apparently people with mental disorders and I have no reason to believe that they were necessarily migrants. The striking absence of vagrants is, of course, closely related to the fact that the government keeps a close watch on law and order. Beggars and other needy people are not welcome in public spaces. I was told that, in the run-up to the Olympic Games, the authorities did everything they could to remove anything from the public eye that might have harmed the desired impression of order and discipline.

## Income and Expenditure

In mid-2008, migrants earned between 30 and 60 yuan a day, amounting to 900–1,800 yuan a month, with the majority at the lower end of the scale. What they actually earn depends on their own efforts, as they are paid on a piecework basis, but the rates for women are invariably lower than for men, and they earn less. Pay increases as workers become more experienced and with the extent to which they are prepared to work longer days. One father told me that his daughter was willing to work, but not every day. He said it was a matter of time before she became used to a more regular routine. In any case, not all employers tolerate such persistent fickleness. Most migrants strive to earn a regular income, and as much as possible, a desire that they can only fulfil by working as much and as long as possible and agreeing to do overtime, rather than rejecting the opportunity. Another basic strategy, in the interests of limiting expenditure, is to keep the number of non-working members of the household to a minimum. Fixed costs, mainly for rent and food, are estimated at around 25–30 yuan per adult per day. Incidental and variable costs include water, electricity, transport, use of the telephone, sending children to school in the city or paying grandparents or other family members to care for them in the place of origin, and medical expenses. Migrants' income is usually sufficient for them to buy all kinds of consumer goods: clothing and bed linen, a bed, a small table and chairs or stools, cooking and eating utensils, a table fan, a television, refrigerator, and mobile telephone. The room is often stuffed full with these items, many of them packed up in suitcases, bags, and boxes. They spend little money on leisure activities outside the house, largely because they have little spare time.

Real income has risen in recent years. During my first visit to Xiamen in 1992, migrants were earning around 500 yuan a month. When I returned in 2001, this had risen to 800 yuan or more. As mentioned earlier, this rising trend continued in the years that followed. Of course, the cost of living has also gone up in the same period, but my impression was that this has happened at a slightly lower pace. On the basis of a survey conducted in early 2009 among migrants working in urban localities, the large majority of them in Xiamen, Li Minghuan reported the following spending pattern of 903 informants over a period of the last three months (see Table 9.2).

TABLE 9.2    Spending Patterns of Migrants Working in Urban Localities

| Monthly Expenses | Overall % | Female % | Male % |
| --- | --- | --- | --- |
| Less than 500 yuan | 14.4 | 9.5 | 4.9 |
| 501–800 yuan | 39.2 | 19.6 | 19.7 |
| 801–1,000 yuan | 26.1 | 14.7 | 11.4 |
| 1,001–1,400 yuan | 11.3 | 5.0 | 6.3 |
| More than 1,400 yuan | 8.9 | 3.4 | 5.6 |

*Source*: Li Minghuan, 'Always Circulating between Rural and Urban Areas? A Study of Young Females in Fujian Province in the Period of Economic Downturn', Paper contributed to the Workshop on Social Security in a Comparative Perspective held at Amsterdam, 2–4 November 2009.

The favourable trend of a higher real wage rate over the years is offset by the observation that the gap between the migrants and the better-off residents of Xiamen has widened. Those at the base of the urban economy are aware of this increasing inequality, but they still have good reasons to believe that life in the hinterland is more impoverished. Most migrants are able to save 100–250 yuan from their monthly income. The money is meant to be spent in their place of origin to which they have to retire at the end of their working life. The ultimate loss of one's own labour power is an unpleasant prospect, but does not mean that working children are automatically expected to contribute to costs of maintaining their elderly parents. After all, meeting their own subsistence costs and investment in the education of the next generations receives first priority.

## Household Life in the Urban Villages

The rent for an apartment in one of the residential blocks is usually too high for one person. In fact, at least two incomes are necessary to permit the luxury of a single room. This means that unmarried migrants are only able to escape the communal dormitories on the employer's premises by moving in with a friend or colleague. Most household units consist of a married couple. Sometimes there were already married, others decided to live together after one or both of them had arrived in Xiamen. In all those cases, the women also work, because their incomes are required to cover the household costs. It is rare for a man and wife to do the same work and have the same employer, which means that they have different working hours and free days. Married couples generally want a family, but caring for a small child is a heavy additional burden on the household. The conventional solution, because it goes together with access to medicare, is to give birth in the place of origin and to leave the child with relatives. This is usually the grandparents, who bring the child up. In some cases, the parents send money to pay for the child's care.

It is primarily the women who take care of the household tasks, such as cooking, washing, and cleaning. But the men help, for example, by shopping for food and other necessities. One room is very small, especially if there is no cooking and washing space. A large part of the room is taken up by the couple's bed, leaving little room for visitors. There are a couple of stools and a low table, but the room cannot accommodate more than a few adults. It is not easy to receive friends, but they do come to share a meal. The cooking is done in the corridor, while the toilets and washing area are also shared. Taking a bucket of warm water to the room offers the possibility of taking a bath without being disturbed by neighbours waiting their turn. In the evenings or on their days off, the residents of the housing blocks escape their claustrophobic, overcrowded flats and take to the streets to walk around and chat with their neighbours.

If both man and wife have a good job and earn more, their apartment may have two or three rooms and the grandparents may come and live with them to help with the household. As their lives become more comfortable, they can do things to make their spare time more enjoyable, such as go on trips, have a picnic on a sunday, or take a walk or lounge around in the park. At work, they make new friends, who usually come from the same place or area of origin. Many migrants give high priority to taking care of their own children by sending infants to a neighbourhood creche. However, migrants' children, rarely more than one per couple, have no access to local public schools. This appeared to have changed recently in Xiamen, but the less than transparent procedures prove to be an obstacle to many parents seeking to take advantage of the relaxation of the rules. When they do have their offspring with them in the city, they attend private schools which have opened in the urban villages. I heard many complaints about the high costs and the bad quality of the teaching. The lack of a normal and regular family life is a heavy burden for the migrants. Parents try to spend their spare time with each other and their children, but that is often not possible. This is illustrated by the couple described next. They work as shoemakers and live with their fifteen-year-old daughter, but will not be able to keep that up much longer.

We got the job via an acquaintance … It is too hard, but we have no choice. Currently it is difficult to find another job … We can earn about 800 Yuan monthly together. But our living expenses are higher. We need to pay 150 Yuan for renting the room, only 10 square meters … Our daughter studies in a junior high school in this sub-district. Without local *hukou*, we need pay an additional amount contribution fee for her education here, 500 Yuan annually … She will go to senior high school next year. By that time, we can't afford for her education fee, because it is 6,000 Yuan annually. We have to send her back to our home town …[12]

How do migrants find a husband or wife? It is important that marriages are no longer arranged by parents. Far from home, however, it is difficult to find a partner, as one young man explained to me. He did not know how to meet members of the opposite sex, as he had no experience of making informal contact with others. To just start talking to a complete stranger in the street or in the bus was a farfetched idea and, moreover, he had no time to go out in the hope of meeting his life partner in the course of normal social intercourse. Work is often the best place to meet people and colleagues act as intermediaries. Friends and relations also present an opportunity to get to know a potential partner and make dates for further meetings. Exploring the possibilities of marriage, however, does not occur without the approval of the immediate family and this requires consultation. I got the impression that sisters and brothers play a more important role in this respect than parents. In most cases, the man or woman selected as a partner comes from the same place as origin and, as the relationship develops, the families on both sides are involved in discussing the arrangements. The decision about whether to go through with the marriage is, however, primarily left up to the couple themselves.

In my sample, there are three couples who do not come from the same places of origin and who met each other without anyone else mediating.

---

[12] Yuting Liu, Shenjing He, and Fulong Wu, 'Urban Pauperization under China's Social Exclusion: A Case Study of Nanjing', *Journal of Urban Affairs*, vol. 30, no. 1, 2008, p. 32.

In one case, the woman got to know her future husband through a chat site. Her elder sister found her partner after getting into conversation with him while she was living in a dormitory at the factory where she works. He was living in the dormitory of an adjoining factory. The third man was taken to hospital after having an accident and met a nurse there who he later married. All of these people come from successful migrant households, with above average jobs and incomes. When they retire, they would be expected to return to the man's place of birth, where the wife has no ties. It seems more likely to me, however, that these newcomers are determined to settle permanently in Xiamen.

Finding a partner remains difficult. One of my respondents, a twenty-four-year-old woman, remains 'unbooked', as she put it. She was the only single person I met who had rented a room for herself. Her friends and acquaintance all live with their partners, enabling them to share the costs of maintaining the household.

A sense of panic of not being able to settle down and marry in 'due time' set in at around 22–24 years of age for women and 24–26 for men. And while it was widely acknowledged that one could have 'fun' (not necessarily meaning sex) dating different people, interviewees agreed that one would certainly end up using a set of relatively clear criteria before making the final decision of whom to marry.[13]

With a shortage of women of their own age, it is quite common for young male migrants to remain single, especially those who are least educated and have the lowest paid work.

## Length of Stay

Migrants come to the city meaning to stay on for the duration of their working lives. Before leaving their place of origin, they are issued an identity card from the age of eighteen onwards. Their ultimate return to their places of origin is virtually inevitable. Residing in the city depends on earning an income. Anyone who is registered as a temporary resident on arrival and who is no longer able to work through lack of employment, illness, or old age has no choice but to leave Xiamen. Yet, returning home is not what most migrants want, in the long or the short term. On the contrary, my conversations with the members of the households in my study indicated that they consider their departure from their homes in the hinterland as the moment at which they

---

[13] Hansen and Pang, 'Me and My Family', p. 84.

decided the courses of their own lives and no longer took account of what others wanted or expected. Most of them came straight to Xiamen and never left again. The respondent who had lived in the city the longest had been there for nineteen years, while the newest arrival I encountered was a young man who had come to join his brother three months earlier. It is of little use working out an average length of time because, in this respect, too, the inhabitants of the urban villages are not typical of the migrant population as a whole.

Nevertheless, I met a lot of people who had been in Xiamen longer than five years. On the other hand, of course, my account contains no information on the number of men and women who were unable to survive in the city and returned to their places of origin. However, I have no reason to assume that they constitute a significant percentage of the total migrant population. The shortage of work and income in the hinterland requires that those seeking work have to go elsewhere and certainly offers no opportunity for return. Most migrants do not manage to settle down more permanently on their arrival in the city.

It is no exaggeration to say that once in the city, migrants continue to be on the move. With substantially higher mobility rates than local residents, they experience much more residential mobility. But such mobility is not necessarily driven by the need for tenure or even amenity. Few migrants make the transition from bridgeheaders to consolidators after years of living in a city, a trend in migrant settlement seen elsewhere in other developing countries. Instead most remain trapped in the private rental sector or staying in dormitory housing. Home ownership is yet to become attainable for migrants, and self-help housing is largely absent because of intolerance of municipal authorities.[14]

The prospect of going back has little attraction for the migrants, or is even seen with deep aversion, and not only because of the lack of economic development. Unmarried young women told me that it would mean the end of their freedom. They would have to move back in with their parents and care for their younger brothers and sisters. Many of them tend to consider life in the hinterland as backward and less civilized. Not only does the countryside lack the glamour of the big city, but the people hold on to customs and habits that they see as old-fashioned. A number of my respondents had lived in other cities before coming to Xiamen. They did not stay there for a number of reasons. Sometimes,

---

[14] W. Wu, 'Migrant Settlement and Urban Transformation in China: The Case of Shanghai', World Bank Third Urban Research Symposium, held at Brasilia, 2–4 April 2005, p. 15.

they were unable to find work or lost their jobs. A young woman who had made her way to Guangdong told me that when she arrived, she knew no one and soon began to feel homesick. Unable to find work, she decided to try her luck in Xiamen and, with the help of a neighbour, got a job in a garment workshop. Some of her workmates came from the same region and that helped her to feel at home. A small group of usually young and unmarried men seem to wander from city to city in search of adventure. They give the impression that they are driven by a desire for independence. The following observation illustrates the behaviour of this more mobile group of migrants.

In underground internet cafés in villages and small towns in Fujian we often met young male workers who were travelling around the country from factory to factory, leaving for a new place whenever they got tired of the work and location. They explained that they enjoyed this kind of 'freedom' and the opportunity to see the country, although the work in itself was uninteresting, sometimes dangerous, and wages far too low. Both men and women in this category explained that they experienced a sense of freedom because they could engage with new friends in circumstances similar to their own, have romantic relations without their parents knowing it, and make their own money, and if they got too fed up with work they would move on to a new place.[15]

I still maintain that the term 'floating population' does not apply to the majority of migrants. There are eager to turn what began as a temporary stay into a permanent one. Despite this ambition, if their capacity to work declines and they are unable to support themselves, they are no longer welcome in the city. That is why the urban villages have few elderly inhabitants, but people may also be unable to continue to work as the result of an accident or bad health. The wife of a scaffolder was injured in an accident on the worksite and, although the employer paid her initial medical expenses, it is doubtful whether she will be able to work again. She went home as an invalid almost a year ago and her husband is thinking of joining her, as he has heard that new stone quarries have recently opened in his home province and that the pay is reasonable. If that is the case, he will give up his job as a construction worker after more than twenty years. Migrants are not eligible for cost-free medical treatment in Xiamen and, if they are ill for an extended period, are forced to return to the hinterland to recover and/or be taken care of. I observed that the inhabitants of the urban villages carry on for as long

[15] Hansen and Pang, 'Me and My Family', p. 90.

as they can by self-medication, buying pills to treat their ailments. But chronic illness can be a heavy burden on the migrant household.

My son is only 5 years old. He often falls ill. Because he is a child you have to take him to see a doctor. We are different, we are adult. If we are ill, I only buy some medicine … Every time, we need pay several hundred Yuan for our son's healthcare … We are different from the urbanite. They have healthcare subsidy …[16]

Migrants try to maintain contact with their homes but cannot visit very often, especially if their places of origin are far away. Many take advantage of the usual time off from work at New Year to celebrate with their parents and families. The journey there and back is extra expensive during the festival and the presents or money they take with them makes the trip even more costly. If small children have been left with grandparents, mothers in particular try to visit them now and again in between times. This might also occur if a member of the family is seriously ill or dies. The rest of the time, they stay in contact by telephone, but that too is restricted because of the costs. A divorced woman who works as a gardener has not been home to visit her child, who lives with her ex-husband, for two years because she cannot afford the high price of a ticket. Migrants with their own accommodation sometimes receive visitors in the city, a younger brother or sister, or perhaps their parents. Those who have nothing more than a bed in a company dormitory cannot permit such displays of hospitality.

## SEGREGATION

Migrants have little to do with the city and its permanent residents and tend to keep to their own domain. They spend their working days together and in the little spare time they have, they meet each other in and around the dormitories on the company premises or in the urban villages, both of which are concentrated on the margins of the city. The official view is that this mass of newcomers, which make up almost half of the city's total population, are only in Xiamen temporarily. This status as outsiders justifies excluding them from all kinds of facilities, and in public spaces, they keep a low profile. They have no business in the municipal buildings and they are rarely to be seen in the shopping malls in the centre of the city. This segregation works both ways: the residents of Xiamen have little to do with the migrants and avoid the areas

[16] Liu *et al.*, 'Urban Pauperization under China's Social Exclusion', p. 32.

where these outside people live. The 'real' inhabitants of the city and the migrants are separated not only along lines of inclusion and exclusion, but also vertically. This hierarchy of separation is clear from the following quote from a case study of migrants in Nanjing from 2004:

We, peasants, are poor. We wear worse, and our skin looks darker, so urbanites do not want to keep in touch with us. They look down on us ... We prefer to rent a room here because the majority of people here are from the countryside. We seldom have contact with urbanites except for making a deal with them ...[17]

The social hierarchy is expressed in the use of the term *suzhi*. It is a keyword in indicating the quality that some people possess and others do not. The way to obtain more suzhi is through education. In their attempts to gain in dignity, migrants try to leave behind them a way of life that is seen as simple and backward. Parents attach such importance to education not only because it gives their children access to better and more highly paid work, but also because it permits them to adopt a more refined identity.[18] That suzhi has gradually acquired a more materialistic meaning is illustrated in advertisements suggesting that people improve their quality by buying all kinds of consumer goods.

In daily life, migrants are seen as uncivilized because of their outward appearance, the way they dress, and the dialect they speak. Their children, too, share in this denigration and discrimination. They would like to enjoy the same education as the children of the inhabitants born and bred in the city but, in the first place, they are not welcome in the public schools simply because they are outsiders. Second, the children of migrants complain about the bad treatment they suffer at the hands of their age set. They are jeered and laughed at for being stupid and retarded, as Lu Wang reports on the basis of interviews held in Xiamen.[19] As a consequence, if their parents do not send them back to live in the hinterland, the 'wild children' have to attend private schools, as long as the local authorities give permission for them to be opened. Those with a good reputation impose high fees that only a few parents can afford. The small son of a successful migrant couple—she has made her way up to become the head of personnel at the company for which

[17] Ibid., p. 33.

[18] Andrew Kipnis, '*Suzhi*: A Keyword Approach', *The China Quarterly*, vol. 186, 2008, pp. 295–313.

[19] Lu Wang, 'The Urban Chinese Educational System and the Marginality of Migrant Children', in V. Fong and R. Murphy (eds), *Chinese Citizenship: Views from the Margins*, London and New York: Routledge, 2005, pp. 31–2.

she works and he is a supervisor in a foreign-owned factory—goes to a crèche every day, which costs them 80 yuan per month. The primary school they have in mind will cost even more but they are prepared to pay it because then they will be assured that their child will have an education that is comparable to that of the local children. Such cases are, however, exceptional in the urban villages.

The worst private migrant schools were run by migrants or people who earn their living from opening such schools targeted for the needs of migrating parents with low income. Motivated by a desire for profit, these schools were normally poor in school premises and conditions and paying a very low salary to teachers who were mostly unqualified migrants who were likely to leave for better opportunities after a short period of time. They rented a few dilapidated rooms and used poor-quality desks and chairs that had been discarded by local public schools, given by various donors, or brought by students themselves.[20]

Migrants who have enjoyed some form of higher education and earn enough to buy a house on the free market can also buy their hukou status in Xiamen. The price is, however, far higher than the majority of the newcomers can afford. Furthermore, they have to pay for each member of the household individually, which sometimes makes it difficult to give more than one child the benefit of an upbringing and education in the city.[21] The handful of fortunate migrants who do get the opportunity to register themselves in Xiamen may obtain the formal status of permanent residents but this change of administrative identity does not improve their social acceptability. Among my respondents was a young man of twenty-seven years, who was one of the few to have continued education after senior high school and had a certificate from a polytechnic college when he arrived in Xiamen in 1999. His first job was as a quality controller in a factory. When his immediate superior left five years ago to set up a business specialized in land surveys conducted before the construction of large buildings, he had the opportunity of joining the new company as a manager. It is a very lucrative position that assures him of an income of 180,000 yuan a year, including a share in the profits. When he married in 2006, he was able to buy a large, expensive apartment (120 square metres with a balcony and luxury furnishings) in a three-storey block. The block is in a gated community in a park-like setting, with a spacious car park, a children's playground,

[20] Ibid., p. 37.
[21] Ibid., p. 30.

a staff of cleaners, and twenty-four-hour security. He drives his own, expensive car. In short, he has been very successful. On further enquiry, however, he expresses his displeasure at how he is treated by government officials. He remains recognizable as a migrant despite his appearance and behaviour as a wealthy businessman. When asked where he comes from, he always says that he is from another city, to explain this accent. He feels that he cannot afford to admit that he comes from the rural hinterland. He sees no other future than in Xiamen for himself and his wife, who works as a nurse in a hospital, and he expects that their children will have no difficulty in being accepted as full-fledged citizens.

The migrants, dealt with as temporary residents, are subject to a wide range of rules governing their code of conduct. The enforcers of the formal order make sure that these mass of outsiders abide by the rules. Many things are forbidden, such as competing with the city dwellers. The following examples come from a field study conducted in Nanjing in 2004. The first is told by a thirty-six-year-old woman from Shandong, who lives with her husband and two small children in a room of 6 square metres:

My husband is cleaner of this residence. His salary is 300 Yuan monthly. The low income is not enough for living expenses. So I put a booth along the street to sell vegetables, earning 5 to 6 Yuan per day. One month ago, my booth was confiscated by police. Local people (urbanites) also put the booth, they are permitted. But our peasants are forbidden to do so … I have nothing to do now.[22]

A fifty-year-old man from Anhui had a similar experience:

Several years ago, I came to Nanjing and used a tricycle to deliver goods for one restaurant. One day, on my way of delivering goods in Xijiekou area (town centre of Nanjing), police sequestrated my tricycle, and I was fined 100 Yuan. I don't know why … Local people can do, we (peasants) cannot … No other way, I can only work as a porter in a wholesale market, got a pay of 450 Yuan monthly…[23]

As I moved around Xiamen, I was struck by the large number of supervisors, controllers, guards, and other personnel responsible for ensuring order and security in public areas. These professional watchers—both publicly and privately employed—are most visible in the parts of the city populated by migrants. To visitors, China appears to be an overregulated

---

[22] Liu *et al.*, 'Urban Pauperization under China's Social Exclusion', p. 31.
[23] Ibid.

state that expects its top-down instructions to be followed to the letter. Government offices are staffed by officials who are permanent residents of Xiamen. That also applies to the office housing the street committee representing the lowest tier of government in the urban villages. The extra caution which the newcomers encounter on arrival has its roots in an attitude of denigration towards the uncivilized mass of peasants flowing into the city. The outsiders have a reputation for showing little respect for the law or the rules of decent conduct and, as footloose labour, are believed to have criminal tendencies. The suspicions mean that the treatment meted out to the migrants by the authorities can be intimidating and sometimes, distinctly hard-handed. The vulnerability of the urban underclass, forced to remain 'floating', explains why the guardians of law and order abuse the government's strict regulations to their own advantage by pocketing fines, for example, for not being able to produce a licence for street vending, charging informal taxes without being authorized to do so, and imposing sanctions that are disproportionate to the nature of the offence. On the other hand, when hiring a room in one of the urban villages, migrants are required to register themselves at the office of the neighbourhood committee. However, they often fail to do so, which means that the municipal administration is operating on the basis of incomplete or outdated information.

One evening I asked the owner of a small restaurant in one of the urban villages to serve my meal outside. At my table there was a man who had come to pick up his wife, who worked in the restaurant. While we were talking, two police officers came and told us to go inside because we were violating the laws regarding public order. Of course, we immediately did as we were told, but once we were inside, my companion started to complain about the strict regime which the government imposed on the residents of these neighbourhoods. He told me that he himself was a guard working for a private company charged with keeping the working people in order and described in derisive tones the rigour with which he had to fulfil this task. Other visitors to the restaurant joined in our conversation and told of the discriminating inspections to which they were exposed at work and in their private lives. There is great indignation among the migrants at this unfair treatment and small incidents can easily escalate, with neighbours also becoming involved. There is clearly no lack of assertiveness among the underclass. Whenever reports of such conflicts appear in the media, the authorities try to respond with a mixture of tolerant understanding and no-nonsense resolve, as the following case illustrates.

In 2003 in Guangzhou, Sun Zhigang, a college student migrant from Wuhan, died as a result of police brutality triggered by his failure to carry a temporary resident ID as he did not have a local (Guangzhou) *hukou*. This case clearly illustrates the continued vulnerability of even the well-educated 'undocumented' migrants and prompted widespread outrage in the media. The silver lining in this case was an almost immediate change in the relevant Chinese law, to curb the police's abusive power (detention and fines for those failing to produce a valid ID) and better protect migrants.[24]

Whether this attempt to appease the migrants succeeded or, more importantly, the announced reforms have had any effect, is a question that requires closer investigation. The government's response is in any case to highlight the importance of social harmony as an important dimension of statesmanship.

## ABSENCE OF CIVIL SOCIETY

I did not encounter a floating population in Xiamen; yet, the government makes sure that the migrants are not permitted to acquire the status of permanent residents. This occurs by excluding them from a wide range of facilities and services to ensure that they do not become eligible for urban citizenship, together with the rights this status entails. This is achieved not only by denying them these entitlements but also by preventing them from resorting to collective action. The migrants' terms of employment do not permit them to become members of a trade union, nor to set up organizations themselves to promote their economic, social, or political interests. The authorities, at all levels, will have nothing to do with any form of civic association as a logical means of improving the migrants' lot by collective action. Labour migrants do not belong to the segments of the population from which the Communist Party recruits its members. There is just as little interest in the opposite direction. The results of a recent survey show that youngsters in particular lack aspirations to join the Party.

Our data contain numerous stories illustrating how our young interviewees, to a much larger extent than their parents, lack trust in the Party as a collective where peasants, migrant workers and people without education can bring their concerns to the forefront and find help. Their first concern was whether or not the Party's local institutions could give them, or their family, any advantages

---

[24] Xiaogang Wu, '*Danwei* Profitability and Earnings Inequality in Urban China', *The China Quarterly*, vol. 195, September 2008, pp. 559–606; see also, Hansen and Pang, 'Me and My Family', p. 96.

or support, and nearly all of them concluded that this was not the case ... The vast majority of peasants and workers considered membership to be something for the educated, for the local officials or for the older activists in their villages, but it was not relevant for themselves. They probably realised that the Party would not really want them as members, but they nevertheless argued that they personally lacked interest in membership.[25]

The migrants lack any form of representation in the urban scene. They do have the right to vote, but only in their place of origin. Their voices remain unheard in Xiamen. The economy needs their labour power but in all other respects, they are no more than tolerated. To categorize this mass of people as a floating population is misplaced in the sense that they neither act as temporary residents, nor do they wish to be treated as such. That this nevertheless happens shows that the government is determined to maintain its policy of keeping the influx from the hinterland in limbo. Rather than being constantly on the move, the migrants are held back in an ambiguous state of transience and informality by the authorities. Their incapacity to form a united front to present themselves in society and improve their public visibility contributes to their isolation in marginality. Even if the migrants find the time and opportunity to engage in sport, they do not join or form clubs. Is this much different from participation in a more active civic activity in the rural hinterland? Not really, if we dare to generalize on the contrast to which Kannan and Pillai drew attention in their comparative study of selected villages in India and China.

... our fieldwork revealed that Kerala stands distinguished in terms of political activism and civic/associational institutional density in platforms spanning trade unions to cultural and residential associations. For example, we saw a number of village reading rooms/libraries dotting the Thalikkulam *panchayat* along side women's and youth organizations. A similar presence of such organizations was not visible during our visits to the Chinese villages.[26]

That is not to say that the younger age groups, who make up the large majority of the newcomers, see the strikingly fragmented or even atomized nature of their presence as a problem. They may share a sense of disconnectedness, but within their own small web of friends, colleagues,

---

[25] Hansen and Pang, 'Me and My Family', p. 93.

[26] K.P. Kannan and N.V. Pillai, 'Basic Socio-economic Security in Rural India and China: A Comparative Study of Selected Villages', *The Indian Journal of Human Development*, vol. 3, no. 2, July–December 2009, p. 260.

and relations, the migrants in Xiamen feel comfortable. They consider themselves fortunate to have escaped the shackles of their home environment, to not have to render account for what they are up to, and to have freed themselves from all kinds of restrictions on their daily conduct. The Confucian code, that rigorously prescribed respect for and dependence on the older generation and superiors in general, has lost much of its significance during a long period of slow erosion. The socialist values that replaced it, with their emphasis on solidarity and institutionalized in the form of mutual horizontal accountability, has also lost its social relevance in the transition to a market economy. Although these changes have also made themselves felt in rural China,[27] departure from the hinterland to the city has undeniably contributed to an expansion of the space for individual freedom in a way that would encounter greater resistance and more strictures in the migrants' places of origin. Yan speaks of an ideological vacuum and attributes it to a loss of civility leading to the growth of an egocentric consumerism. The city offers much more space to do so than the countryside, and the lifestyle the young migrants in Xiamen adopt illustrates the power with which this process of individualization is moving forward. Making their own decisions, being free to take or refuse a job, to stay or to leave again, expresses the migrants' desire for independence and to bear their own responsibility. The following passages from the report on the study by Hansen and Pang paint a clear picture of this atomistic, self-centred orientation:

The longing for 'freedom' was sometimes used either to explain why interviewees dropped out of school to work, or to account for a certain job or a certain workplace. The incense factory, for instance, was dirty, of low prestige and had low wages, but it was described by many as having the great advantage of allowing workers to come and go freely, and to work when they wanted to (because all wages were calculated on the basis of production!) … Notions such as freedom, independence (*duli*) and personal development (*geren fazhan*) were all used to express variations of the importance of being able to move—move away from and back to family, move from the village to a city, move from the familiar to the unknown, and back. It was the youngest interviewees (with little work experience and not yet engaged or married) who emphasised notions of freedom and the importance of their own personal choices.[28]

---

[27] See Yunxiang Yan, *Private Life under Socialism: Love, Intimacy and Family Change in a Chinese Village, 1994–1999*, Stanford: Stanford University Press, 2003.

[28] Hansen and Pang, 'Me and My Family', p. 89.

The researchers add that, from the age of about twenty, the migrants begin to attach greater importance to security and continuity. That change is accompanied by a willingness to restrict their own self-interest and give more priority to their obligations to others. The circle within which this greater involvement occurs is nevertheless limited to members of the immediate family, especially parents, sisters, brothers, and their children. Migrants—who find a partner in Xiamen, set up a joint household, and prepare for the arrival of the next generation—realize that their sustained exclusion from urban citizenship leaves them no other choice than to concern themselves with their close family in the hinterland. After all, young children can often not stay with their parents but have to be entrusted to the care of grandparents or other relations in the place of origin. Also, in the case of temporary or permanent incapacity to work, they have few other options than to return home. The absence of non-familial social care makes this step inevitable at the end of their working lives. Conversely, migrants commit themselves to: helping a brother or sister who wants to come to Xiamen to find work and somewhere to live; giving their elderly parents financial support if that should prove necessary; and sometimes, helping with the school fees of young relatives. Hansen and Pang explain this sense of commitment:

Our material contains numerous other examples of how young people argued that since one of their siblings performed better than they themselves did in school, they should help support his or her education, and we have examples where this also happened in practice. Most would also argue that since their parents had brought them up, they were responsible for taking care of their parents during old age. Hardly any of them expected the state to take any responsibility for the old, and they took it for granted that they would have to support the elderly.[29]

Their findings concur with my own, that migrant women are more likely to be concerned with the care of their aged parents, or family matters in general, than the men are. They even take this into account when choosing a marriage partner, assessing whether they will be allowed to provide support for their families back in the hinterland. For that reason, they may be prepared to end a relationship with a man from another province. What could be seen as inspired by genuine affection for the family—and there is certainly reason to believe that—can be interpreted from another viewpoint as enlightened self-interest. Investment in a

[29] Ibid., p. 92.

social safety net in the place of origin is advisable sooner or later, as the migrants know that because of their status as outsiders in Xiamen, there is no prospect of their being permitted to settle down in the city and that they will remain ineligible for civil entitlements. When they left home as adolescents, they distanced themselves from all social ties, but once they become adults, they can no longer afford to break their connection with what they actually hoped to leave behind them.

## GROWING INEQUALITY

There is a clear contrast between the more and less well-off inhabitants of Xiamen, almost a dichotomy that largely coincides with the division between 'locals' and 'outsiders'. Has there not been a trend over the years to suggest a decrease in what those involved themselves see as a wide gap? There are reports enough to suggest that the migrants have gradually acquired more rights. As provincial and municipal authorities have a free hand in pursuing their own policies, it is difficult to say anything that applies generally. As far as Xiamen is concerned, the expansion of access to public education has already been mentioned. Still, I noted that the municipal schools have only admitted a small number of migrant children, and that they have to meet stricter criteria and pay higher fees than local pupils.

One Xiamen primary school principal said that 80 migrant children applied to enter his school in August of 2001, but only 15 were admitted. Another Xiamen primary school principal said that more than 100 migrant children applied for her school last year, but only 20 were admitted.[30]

With housing, it is the same story. Only a few migrants earn enough to afford to buy an apartment, giving them the right to register as inhabitants of the city. This exclusion also extends to health care, with migrants not being eligible for reimbursement of their medical expenses. This, in effect, forces many of them to decide not to have medical treatment or, if their complaints are serious, to return to their place of origin and seek medical help there. In the early years of the twenty-first century, a number of provinces and large cities, including Xiamen, announced the introduction of a limited system of social services for migrants. But in 2005–6, only a small proportion of them proved to be eligible for the accident insurance, while the pension scheme barely covers 10 per cent

---

[30] Wang, 'The Urban Chinese Educational System and the Marginality of Migrant Children', p. 34.

of the migrant population. Those who are insured have to pay a substantial premium and pensions are paid out only to those who have worked in the same place for fifteen years.[31] The same source reports that, while the municipal authorities do not fulfil their promise to admit migrant children to the public schools, they have no hesitation in taking hard measures against private schools operating without a licence.

A graphic example is the destructive force used in the closing of an 'illegal' school for migrants' children in Shanghai in January 2007. Police stormed and bulldozed the compound, which had provided education for some 2,000 students who did not have the city's *hukou*.[32]

How much credence is there in reports that the requirement that households have to be registered in the place of origin has gradually been relaxed and will disappear completely in the near future? As mentioned earlier, migrants who have enjoyed a higher education and earn sufficient to pay the high price of an apartment in an expensive neighbourhood may receive permission to register as permanent residents of Xiamen. Just how limited this fortunate category is can be seen from the official figures, according to which, between 1997 and 2002—a period of five years—all the large cities and towns across the whole of the country only issued 1.39 million hukou permits.[33] The authors, who present a number of similar statistics, conclude their report on a rather discouraging note:

Despite a good deal of rhetoric in the press about the recent reforms, the reality is that these initiatives have had only very marginal impact on weakening the foundation of the system. The *hukou* system, directly and indirectly, continues to be a major wall in preventing China's rural population from settling in the city and in maintaining the rural–urban 'apartheid'.[34]

---

[31] Kam Wing Chan and Will Buckingham, 'Is China Abolishing the *Hukou* System', *The China Quarterly*, vol. 195, September 2008, p. 600.

[32] Ibid., p. 594.

[33] Ibid., p. 596.

[34] Ibid., p. 604. There is extensive literature on the division of hukou registration between the city and the countryside. See, for example, Kam Wing Chan and Li Zhang, 'The *Hukou* System and Rural–Urban Migration: Processes and Changes', *The China Quarterly*, vol. 160, 1999, pp. 818–55; Tiejun Cheng and Mark Selden, 'The Origin and Social Consequences of China's *Hukou* System', *The China Quarterly*, vol. 139, September 1994, pp. 644–68; H.W. Cheng and Y.I. Cui, 'Social Exclusion in Social Security of Migrant Workers', *Social Science Journal*, vol. 6, 2006, pp. 89–92; Zhiqiang Liu, 'Institution and Inequality: The *Hukou* System in China',

What is presented as an administrative practice is, in fact, an instrument to minimize the costs of mobilized labour and, therefore, strengthen the position of the Chinese economy on the global market. While the municipal authorities, in their desire to attract more and more capital for investment, are keen to lower the labour cost and reduce the over-head required for dealing with the migrant workforce, it seems that the leadership at the central level is more worried about the rising disparities between insiders and outsiders and the mutual antagonism caused by it. It remains to be seen if it is possible to find a solution to this contrast in policy priorities.

The suggestion to link the split between better and less well off with that between the city's permanent population and the 'floating-around' crowd needs to be phrased more carefully. Neither side of the dichotomy is homogenous, and both segments are characterized by a complexity of layers. In the case of the migrants, I have already elaborated on these differences. This mass divides into various categories depending on their social identity in their places of origin, their level of education, the kind of work they do, and under what terms and conditions of employment, resulting in highly diverse profiles. But, there is also a large degree of differentiation between that part of the working population who are born and bred in the city which seems to crystallize into different social classes. It is not my intention here to examine this hierarchy and its dynamics. However, I do wish to correct the image of increasing prosperity in which everyone, who is registered as a permanent resident, shares, and warn that the consumerism that is so overtly present in the streets of the city is only a veneer, beneath which there is substantial poverty and need. An expert engaged by the provincial government of Guangzhou stated recently that the working population of the country's largest urban growth pole had benefited little from the increase in gross domestic product (GDP) between 2000 and 2006:

Guangdong has occupied the top position in terms of GDP for more than two decades, but people here are not rich … The money has been going to the

---

*Journal of Comparative Economics*, vol. 33, no. 1, 2003, pp. 133–57; E.J. Perry and M. Selden (eds), *Chinese Society: Change, Conflict and Resistance*, London: Routledge, 2000; D. Solinger, *Contesting Citizenship in Urban China: The State and the Logic of the Market*, Berkeley: University of California Press, 1999; D. Solinger, 'Labour Market Reform and the Plight of the Laid-off Proletariat', *The China Quarterly*, vol. 158, 2002, pp. 304–26; Fei Ling Wang, *Organizing through Division and Exclusion: China's Hukou System*, Stanford: Stanford University Press, 2005.

government and business owners. Local people have not benefited quite so well from the economic development.[35]

The city department responsible for labour and social security pledged to try and secure a wage rise of 14 per cent, but this proved to be an empty promise, as it was almost immediately followed by a statement that it was only a recommendation and it would not be obligatory for the government and businesses to pay their employees more. Inequality is not only increasing between the city and the countryside but also within the urban economy. In this context, I refer to the presence in cities like Xiamen of an underclass, a segment that lost its secure existence in the transition to a market economy, was unable to adapt to the demands of a flexibilized economy, and plummeted to the bottom of urban society. Retraining failed to find the members of this residual class suitable work and they have to survive with an extremely low level of financial support. This tail end of impoverished, often older people, who have always been part of the urban system and are victims of the transition of the economic regime, also remain out of sight.[36] This underclass was in such great need that the authorities in the metropolis of Dongguan, in the Pearl river delta, decided to give all residents (excluding migrants of course) with a monthly income between 400 and 600 yuan, a one-off payment of 1,000 yuan. In another city, the authorities dared not make the list of beneficiaries public for fear that rejected applicants would resort to public protest.[37] The urban poor have to struggle on out of sight and out of mind of China's policymakers, blamed for not being able to live up to the opportunities to find work and generate income in the flexibilized economy.

By 2002, a new class of urban poor had emerged, estimated to be about 15–31 million, or 4.8% of the urban population.[38] Chinese official statistics placed the number of registered unemployed in October, 2008 a 4% unemployment rate, on the eve of the world economic downturn.[39]

---

[35] *China Daily*, 22 July 2008.

[36] See, among others, the study based on field research by Liu *et al.*, 'Urban Pauperization under China's Social Exclusion', pp. 23–5, 27–30.

[37] *China Daily*, 22 July 2008.

[38] Jun Tang, 'Selections from Report on Poverty and Anti-poverty in Urban China', *China Sociology and Anthropology*, vol. 36, nos 2 and 3, 2003, p. 4.

[39] *Asia News*, 'China Facing Rising Unemployment', 2008, available at http://www.asianews.it/index.php?=en &art=136038&size=A.

The heterogeneity of the permanent residents of Xiamen, therefore, makes it impossible to reduce the social order of the city to a simple dichotomy. Having said that, I maintain that the nuances and complexity of the urban system should not prevent us from drawing a dividing line where it is most evident and rigid, between permanent residents and migrants, who move in different circuits and who interact on the basis of a relationship of superiority and subordination. If there is a clear division, it is especially visible in the contrast in the living and working conditions of those who live permanently in Xiamen and are therefore considered full-fledged citizens, and the migrants who, as temporary residents, remain excluded. As a yardstick for this wide gap, I refer to the skill level of the migrants, which is generally lower than that of the permanent inhabitants, while the latter earn, on average, a higher income than the migrants although their work is less demanding. The evidence for this in my own research is supported by the findings of a survey of 7,100 households conducted in 2006, in a large number of cities and districts throughout the country. Table 9.3 shows the differences in income.

Opinions vary as to the impact of labour migration on the changes that have occurred in the make-up of society. The assessments of researchers based on field studies also vary. In the conversations I had with migrants during my stay in Xiamen, they showed that they were fully aware of their exclusion from the urban system. It would be incorrect to ignore the fact that there has been clear improvement in some areas. The migrant population have experienced an increase in purchasing power, resulting from a real rise in their wages levels. Nevertheless, this mass of newcomers does not succeed in getting access to urban citizenship. Not being allowed to settle down is a serious obstacle to improving their own situation and that of their children. They remain excluded from all kinds of services and rights which the permanent residents of the city take for granted. I encountered more resentment than understanding for this systematic deprivation among my respondents. Other researchers, for example, Liu *et al.* are also critical in drawing up the balance of their field research in Nanjing. The comments of a woman who has just lost her job are telling:

We are peasants, so the [urban] government does not take care of us at all. They only care for urbanites, nobody thinks of our life and death. If urbanite is laid off, he [or she] can get living subsidies. Also, the urban poor can apply for the *dibao*, we [peasants] have nothing ... We have been accustomed to these things

TABLE 9.3 Differential Employment Status of Migrants and Urban Citizens

| Percentage of skill level in migrants & urban citizens | | | Percentage of monthly wage in migrants & urban citizens | | | Percentage of working week in hours in migrants & urban citizens | | |
|---|---|---|---|---|---|---|---|---|
| High | 14 | 3.5 | > 2000 yuan | 13 | 3 | < 20 hours | 2 | 2.5 |
| Reasonable | 35 | 13 | 1,501–2,000 yuan | 11 | 4 | 21–40 hours | 16 | 44 |
| Semi | 31.5 | 43 | 1,001–1,500 yuan | 22 | 14 | 41–60 hours | 48 | 39.5 |
| Unskilled | 19.5 | 40.5 | 501–1,000 yuan | 37 | 52 | 61–80 hours | 26 | 10 |
| | | | < 500 yuan | 17 | 27 | > 80 hours | 8 | 3 |

*Source:* Li Peilin and Li Wei, 'The Economical Status and Social Attitudes of Migrant Workers in China', India–China Joint Seminar on Labour Markets in China and India, 'Experiences and Emerging Perspectives', held at New Delhi, 28–30 March 2007, pp. 3–4.

In countryside, we get few concerns from the government. So in cities, we do not expect these any more ...[40]

It is interesting to note that this respondent says that it is not only at the hands of the urban authorities that she and her fellows are subjected to exclusion. She suggests that peasants are just as unlikely to find themselves faced with a benevolent government in the countryside. This experience can only have tempered her hope for better treatment in the city. Are these realistic expectations perhaps the reason why the arrival of such a large mass of men and women in search of a better life in the city has not led to widespread social unrest?

Why, ask Li Peilin and Li Wei, does this migrant mass, which receives such low wages for its work, lives in rather miserable conditions, and is treated so unjustly, not rebel against its exclusion? Their research project, 'Social Harmony and Stability', conducted in 2006, was intended to provide clarity about the absence of what, given the inferior quality of the migrants' lives, should have happened: social unrest on a large scale. One finding that surprised the researchers was that workers among the well-settled urban population proved to be more discontent than the newcomers, who experienced less stress and conflict. The researchers gave three reasons for this striking difference. First, the migrants were aware that their deprivation was caused by their lack of education and low level of working skills. This awareness went together with a belief that they could overcome their setbacks through a combination of hard work and more education. Second, the migrants have less social awareness. They are more docile because they have a less developed sense of justice and a lower level of political participation. The researchers summarize this as a deficit of democratic consciousness. Third, the migrants do not only compare themselves to the permanent residents of the city. They also tend to compare their situation to that of those they left behind in their places of origin. They can then reach no other conclusion than that the move to the city was a step forward, and not backward. It is a point of view endorsed by Li Minghuan on the basis of her conversations with migrants who had gone back to their place of origin.

... no matter how little improvement they have realized, they would regard it as testimony of their correct decision and personal ability. Chinese traditional culture has greatly highlighted individual's 'face', which is a public image of the person or even of the whole family. My earlier research in some villages

---

[40] Liu *et al.*, 'Urban Pauperization under China's Social Exclusion', p. 32.

in the hinterland during the Chinese New Year period shows that, among the returnees, many would like to chat with each other about the 'successful stories' in working area but not the suffering. Some might complain about the greedy boss, but often the story would be ended with their success.[41]

Her statement, and that of Li Peilin and Li Wei, are backed up by the findings of a recent field study among migrants in the city of Ningbo:

Over half of the respondents indicate good economic opportunities or better livelihoods in Ningbo as their major reason for migration. On average a rural household can make 1,000 to 2,000 Yuan (100 to 200 Euro) a year from farming activities, while in urban areas migrants earn this amount in one or two months.[42]

Still, while recognizing the huge difference in the average level of incomes between city and countryside, I am sceptical about the plausibility of the argument, which I consider to be very close to what can be regarded as politically correct thinking, that is, social harmony. They seem to have too easily ignored the discontentment that is continually expressed by the urban migrants, outbursts of displeasure that seem to be attracting more and more attention from the media. Equally important is that both lower and higher tiers of government are also expressing their concerns about these mass protests.[43] The caution with which the authorities acknowledge such ripples of the public order does not prevent them from, at the same time, responding to them resolutely or sometimes brutally. Even more important is the unease which seems to take hold of the government when it comes to averting an escalating expression of unrest. Calls to remain calm and gestures of tolerance are accompanied by measures intended to track down and neutralize the suspected ringleaders—who, after all, must exist—of the unpredictable outbursts of public anger. This attitude of rejection is founded on the stubborn belief that the migrants are a wayward and intrinsically subversive mass set on eroding the established order, instead of understanding their resistance as an expression of their desire to be accepted as part of that

[41] Li Minghuan, 'Always Circulating between Rural and Urban Areas?', p. 17.

[42] Qi Changqi and He Fan, 'Informal Elements in Urban Growth Regulation in China', p. 10.

[43] Kwan Lee Ching and Mark Selden, 'Inequality and its Enemies in Revolutionary and Reform China', *Economic and Political Weekly*, vol. XLIII, no. 52, 2008, pp. 34–5; Robert Weil, 'A House Divided: China after 30 Years of "Reforms"', *Economic and Political Weekly*, vol. XLIII, no. 52, 2008, pp. 67–8.

order. The media regularly reports on incidents between police and migrants which escalate into rioting. From these, I have selected the following two as typical. The first incident took place in Zhejiang; and the second, in Guangzhou.

Hundreds of migrant workers attacked and injured three policemen after an argument over registration of a migrant as a temporary resident turned violent … people have flocked to meet with local leaders with their complaints, which have ranged from illegal land seizures and judicial injustice to non-payment of salary and village officials' corruption.[44]

The rioters overturned a police van, and raided a police station and the office of the village committee in the town of Yuanzhou. The incident was sparked by a dispute over the death of a motorcyclist surnamed Ouyang from Hunan province. His family claimed he was beaten to death by security guards following a row over a 'protection fee', but police said he died in a traffic accident.[45]

The official anxiety about unrest in migrant quarters can sometimes take almost hilarious form; in the run-up to the Olympic Games, for example, serious consideration was given to removing the 'floating population' from Beijing temporarily, to ensure that there was no trouble during the tournament.[46] Even in Xiamen, where I was staying at the time, there were rumours that the authorities were preparing to rid the city of all elements that could have a negative impact on the public image of modernity, prosperity, and progress. The periodic 'clean-ups', or the threat of them, are based on the fear that there is a lumpen element within the reserve army of labour at the bottom of urban society that refuses to behave as a 'floating population' and which is prepared to break the law to strengthen its position or simply to be provocative. It is the classical spectre of the *classe dangereuse* that haunts the permanent population and the authorities charged with protecting it. The idea that the flood of migrants mobilized to provide the new market economy in the cities with an ample supply of labour pose a threat to public security, and that this risk would eventually become even more serious if they became superfluous when the work dried up, dates back a number of years. Wang Shan warned as long ago as 1994 that '… an anti-society psychology might be with everyone joining the flow for a long time'. He expressed the fear that '… if large-scale social unrest happened in China

---

[44] *China Daily*, 16 July 2008.
[45] *China Daily*, 19–20 July 2008.
[46] Chan and Buckingham, 'Is China Abolishing the *Hukou* System', p. 603.

the migrant workers who did not find jobs in cities would be the active ones thus becoming the most destructive force'.[47]

There are, fortunately, also indications of a willingness to close the gap that has developed between city and countryside by giving migrants the just treatment they have always been denied. In this context, a department has recently opened in the Ministry of Human Resources and Social Security which, in the interests of promoting social harmony, has been given the task of ensuring that the floating segment of the population is given fairer treatment. In an interview, the new head of this department referred to the need to give the newcomers the same rights as the permanent population. 'And for long they have been treated unfairly, Liu said. "Even after working in cities for years, most of them don't enjoy an urban resident's status."'[48]

This opening headline was followed by reports on the inside pages describing in detail recurrent abuses in the employment of migrants and the evasion of rules intended to protect them. Having voiced this criticism, some recent signs of improvement should also be put on record. As Li Minghuan reported in her paper:

… in Xiamen, the peasant workers who have worked in Xiamen for more than one year can send their school-age kids to Xiamen public school without paying extra tuition. At the beginning of 2009, Xiamen municipality starts to buy 'natural disaster insurance' for all Xiamen people, including the peasant workers who have worked in Xiamen longer than three months and their kids who have lived in Xiamen longer than three months. Also, in Xiamen's People's Congress, peasant workers have their representatives, although only a few. All these new policies are worth admiring. However, it is far from enough and the radical reform is still needed.[49]

## PROSPECTS OF AN UNCERTAIN FUTURE

Thirty years ago, a process started that would bring about a radical change in the relationship between the countryside and the city. The restructuring developed at a rapid pace and on an increasingly large scale. The strong decline in the importance of agriculture and the expansion of industrial production, construction, transport, trade, and services has resulted in an economic system with a working population

---

[47] Wang Shan, *Looking at China with the Third Eye*, Taiyuan: Shanxi People's Publishing House, 1994, pp. 62–3.

[48] *China Daily*, 22 July 2008.

[49] Li Minghuan, 'Always Circulating between Rural and Urban Areas?', p. 19.

that has had to find its way in a wide range of new occupations and which have meant leaving the countryside *en masse* for the growth poles of employment, the large urban agglomerations concentrated on China's east coast. The dynamic development of Xiamen, which is the focus of my case study in the province of Fujian, has to be seen in this context. However, is it feasible to assume that the turbulent growth that the city has experienced in the past quarter of a century will continue?

To acquire a greater insight into the ongoing transformation, I visited another county in Fujian but at some distance from Xiamen. The local authorities decided in 2005 to build a large industrial park. The park covers an area of around 13 square kilometres and has a full infrastructure, including roads, sewers, and a water and electricity supply. A large number of commercial premises have been built to be leased or sold. The emphasis will be on the manufacture of electronics, sports goods, and textiles. Capital investors and entrepreneurs are being encouraged to come and set up shop in the park. Most attention is being focused on Taiwanese businessmen or, more generally, overseas Chinese. Many of them have their roots in Fujian and they are being invited to strengthen their ties with their place of origin and breathe new life into it with their entrepreneurship. I asked the staff of planners and technicians in charge of the daily running of the project to tell me about how it has progressed since it started three years ago. After they gave me a short guided tour of the entire area, I started to make enquiries about the project without my official guides being present.

I first visited the villages where the inhabitants, until recently, earned a living tilling the fields. Their agrarian existence came to an end when the land they worked was expropriated. As happened elsewhere, each household received compensation depending on the area of land they operated (between 1 and 2 *mu*[50]) and the number of members. This amounted to something between 150,000 and 200,000 yuan. They used the money to build blocks three to four storeys high to accommodate the migrants who would soon be flooding into the area. The compensation only covered a quarter, at most, of the building costs, which could amount to as much as 800,000 yuan. For the remainder of the construction costs, they arranged a bank loan, with the help of the authorities. The ground floor of the block could be fitted out as shops to give the owners a supplementary source of work and income. The

[50] 1 *mu* is 0.15 hectare.

five villages in the zone were provided with paved streets, sewers, and other facilities. This gave them a more urban appearance, an upgrade that was emphasized by giving the inhabitants hukou status with all the associated rights, including health care, access to public education, etc. These changes offered the prospect of a much better life than farm work had provided. But were these expectations fulfilled?

Not in all five villages. Far fewer enterprises and businesses are located in the zone than had been foreseen in the plans and many of the production units built to attract entrepreneurs are still empty. That means that tens of thousands of migrants, for whom there would be work and accommodation, did not arrive. There is industrial activity in about one-third of the zone, concentrated mainly around two villages. These areas are undeniably crowded with migrants. They live in the one-room apartments in the housing blocks, buy their noon meal for 5 yuan a day in one of the newly opened eating houses, shop for their daily needs in the early evening in the village centre, and spend their free time walking around the streets or playing snooker. The village committee runs a large apartment block with 194 rooms and hires out twenty-four shops on the ground floor, including a supermarket with a Taiwanese manager. The other villages have met with less success so far. The land around them lies fallow, because it cannot be used for farming anymore and the industry it awaits is still to come. Since there is no work for labour migrants, the housing blocks remain half built. The income the ex-farmers expected to earn from them has not materialized and, to minimize the costs, they have not yet made use of the bank loans, which they also need to pay for the cost of their own housing. Often there is only a concrete shell, within which the owners have made a makeshift shelter. A number of shops are already open, some filled with goods. The owners sit there all day but have no customers.

Lastly, the factory jobs that the younger generation were hoping for have also not materialized. According to the company managers, this is because the young peasants are unskilled and only eligible for the simplest manual labour. A few local people have found work as guards or cleaners. The young people themselves will not work on assembly lines as it pays less than 1,000 yuan per month and the working hours are too long. They prefer to earn a living in the service sector, working as waiters in the eating houses, renting out a snooker table, or hiring their motorcycle as a taxi. The latter means spending a lot of time hanging around at road junctions, waiting for the few passengers who need a ride. Some of the older villagers grow vegetables in small fields, without asking for permission, for sale in markets in the city. This earns them very little and, more importantly, their sons and daughters think farm work is too degrading to waste their time on.

There is time enough to talk about everything that has happened and their expectations for the future. The villagers leave no doubt about their dissatisfaction. Their disappointment about the lack of progress is understandable. And, they have no qualms about airing their displeasure about the fraud and corruption that accompanied this great change in their lives. They accuse the members of the village committee of having pocketed much more in compensation, allocating themselves larger building plots, and building much bigger apartment blocks with more storeys than others were permitted to build. These kinds of practices are also common elsewhere, as Hansen and Pang report from their own field study.

The village was only a few hours from Xiamen, and much of the arable land had been bought up for industrialising purposes. Practically all local families took part in the elections and attended numerous meetings where people gathered to discuss, even argue, with the officials who were held responsible for selling out the land too cheaply years ago, and for have benefited personally from the sale … Local young people whom we interviewed and watched taking part in meetings were outraged; they expressed a very high degree of distrust in the officials' motives. They normally did not care much about the village as a community and they did not support attempts to collect money from common public goods in the village, but in this case issues of family property were at stake, and this engaged everyone.[51]

In my view, with this sketch, Hansen and Pang show clearly that there is little truth in the assumption that political awareness is not very developed in the countryside. The striking assertiveness of the villagers demonstrates that the officials at all levels have little authority and command even less respect. It makes one think of the alienation that has developed between the leaders of the state and the general population. The resistance that the government invokes in many segments of society raises doubts about the legitimacy of the regime, if not of its tenability.[52]

No longer peasants but not yet factory workers—that is how I would like to summarize my visit to the industrial park at some distance from Xiamen. The slowing down of the rate at which the new economy

---

[51] Hansen and Pang, 'Me and My Family', pp. 95–6.

[52] You-tien Hsing, 'Land and Territorial Politics in Urban China', *The China Quarterly*, vol. 187, September 2006, pp. 575–91.

expands over a steadily widening area is, perhaps, not so exceptional and need not be a cause for concern in the somewhat longer term. The golden years of turbulent growth may be over, but if development continues in the same direction, it simply takes longer than before. There are, however, signs that contradict this optimistic projection and point to the possibility of stagnation in the trend towards development. The reason for this is seen to be increasing labour costs, to a level that is impacting on China's competitive position. This is exacerbated by the rising prices of raw materials, which makes it more difficult to sell products on the international market. It has even reached a point at which factories in Fujian are closing and being relocated to Vietnam, Cambodia, and other low-income countries, which can produce the same goods more cheaply. There is, in short, good reason for the government to be concerned about the scope for continuing with its policy of encouraging superfluous farm labour in the countryside to seek a better future in the large urban growth poles.

I could have concluded the report on the findings of my research in Xiamen at the end of the summer of 2008 with an assessment along these lines if, in the months that followed, there had not been an even more abrupt crisis in the economy. It does not seem an exaggeration to speak of a dramatic turn of events in the light of the first reports on the impact of the recession that spread around the world in the final quarter of 2008. How has the migrant population in particular, extremely vulnerable because of the informal nature of their employment, managed to cope with the setback in view of their inability to make any claim to protection or financial support? Initial reports were less than optimistic, referring to mass redundancies as a result of factories closing down or at least reducing their working hours, a form of wage cutting made even worse by the drastic reduction of the already minimal rates for piecework. The return to their place of origin at the end of January 2009 to celebrate the Spring Festival has been less than festive for the migrants this time. They did not take the usual presents for those back at home, as a sign of their success in the big city, and their empty hands must have raised suspicions that they were back to stay.

According to official statistics, as many as 20 million migrant workers lost their jobs, an estimated 15 per cent of the entire floating population. In accordance with the expectations of subversive behaviour expected of these 'labour nomads', the government was concerned about the possibility that serious outbreaks of social unrest might take place and the army was given orders to use violence in responding to embryonic demonstrations and riots. The tone of this prior reaction confirmed the authoritarian nature of the state. The early reports of a severe malaise fortunately turned out to have been overly alarmist. Certainly, there was a fall in wage rates and hours of work, a loss of employment leading to a drastic rise in the cost of living. While reporting these ominous findings, Li Minghuan also came to know that the majority of migrants still wanted to continue working in the urban economy. They were able to do so because, in an impressive recovery of the economy, the urban job market was already booming again by mid-2009.

A more definite solution of the problems of poverty and labour redundancy cannot be left to the workings of the free market. A policy of economic stimulation cannot be limited to continuing on the same course: encouraging the mass of superfluous labour to leave the villages and head for the cities, while giving priority to employment in all other sectors than agriculture. The subordination or even neglect of this primary sector of economic activity must come to an end. In view of the strongly increased pressure on agrarian sources of subsistence, the expulsion of large quantities of labour is inevitable. This should not, however, be allowed to occur in a way that condemns the redundant working population to a state of persistent mobility which marginalizes them as a footloose mass in mainstream society. The lesson Li Minghuan draws from what has happened and to whom it happened bears repeating. Looking back on the trajectory of development, she concludes as follows:

... in the last three decades, millions of peasant workers in China had sacrificed their lives to push China to realize its economic miracle. The cheap Chinese production has been made possible because of peasant workers' lower income, longer working hours and no social security protection. And the whole world has benefited from their sacrifice. If getting the peasants out from absolute poverty was Chinese government's most important duty during the early periods of the reform, which had shown a great success, now is the time to develop an equal and just society by bridging the institutional gap between the rural and the urban. It is unfair to ask millions of peasants to keep making sacrifice but benefiting only little. Also, millions of peasants won't accept such a status as a new generation is growing up and the sense of justice is becoming stronger.[53]

[53] Li Minghuan, 'Always Circulating between Rural and Urban Areas?', p. 19.

# V

# THE DYNAMICS OF EXCLUSION

# 10

# Social Exclusion in the
# Context of Globalization*

## THE NOTION OF EXCLUSION

The point of departure of this essay is the concept of exclusion, defined as the lack of access to full participation in mainstream society in economic, political, social, and cultural terms. Exclusion, therefore, conveys a sense of denial or loss. The emphasis here is on the relationship between globalization and exclusion: to what extent is globalization instrumental in overcoming or, alternatively, aggravating situations of exclusion? In order to reach meaningful answers to this question, it is necessary to understand both phenomena in a historical perspective. Exclusion is certainly not of recent origin and cannot only be related to the acceleration of the process of globalization over the last quarter of a century.[1] At the same time, the structure of inequality at the transnational level can only be understood by analysing the historical trajectory of globalization.

The condition of exclusion under which people work and live is often operationalized in terms of poverty and inequality. The first dimension refers to lack of assets. Given the absence of means of production such as land or other forms of capital through which they can acquire income, large segments of the economically active population have to sell their labour to make a living. Poverty becomes particularly acute if: (i) the

* Originally published as 'Social Exclusion in the Context of Globalization', Working Paper No. 18, Policy Integration Department, Geneva: International Labour Organization (ILO), 2004.
[1] J. Breman, 'Work and Life of the Rural Proletariat in Java's Coastal Plain', *Modern Asian Studies,* vol. 29, no. 1, 1995, pp. 1–44.

price of labour is close to or even below the level of reproduction; and (ii) unemployment or underemployment is rampant because the supply of labour is structurally much higher than the demand. It often happens that these two factors are interdependent. Exclusion from means of production can lead to exclusion from means of consumption. In those cases, marginality and vulnerability take the form of a pauperized existence.

There are various dimensions to exclusion which do not necessarily overlap. In an economic sense, exclusion refers to the inability to be engaged in gainful employment which yields enough income to satisfy basic requirements. In political terms, exclusion implies a lack of access to sources of power and the inability to participate meaningfully in decision-making processes from the household level upwards. In a social sense, exclusion is equal to denigration, the loss of respectability and dignity in one's own eyes, as well as those of others. Discrepancies between these three dimensions provide room for interventions that might help to bring about inclusion. Suffrage, the one-person-one-vote principle, which became universalized after decolonization in South and Southeast Asian societies, increased the political leverage of social classes which in previous generations had remained without voice. To that extent, the introduction of democracy increased the room for manoeuvre of underprivileged people, for instance, agricultural labourers in India, stuck at the bottom of the rural economy and society. Experience has shown, however, that a democratic framework is not a sufficient condition for inclusion.

When the various dimensions of exclusion reinforce each other, a pattern of accumulated exclusion arises which is difficult to tackle. Just like the category of the super- or ultra-poor, which has been distinguished in recent literature, it might make sense to identify an underclass of the super- or ultra-excluded. The characteristic of such situations is that the various dimensions of vulnerability conflate in a state of segregation, or in other words, a kind of separation from mainstream society that also has a spatial connotation.

Poverty is not necessarily identical to exclusion. People may suffer from deprivation, but if they are not in a position to relate their own circumstances to conditions in which other people live, there is no reason for them to feel excluded. Globalization as a process has certainly helped to extend social horizons and increase aspirations. The new means of communication that have emerged make it easier for people to relate the (inferior) quality of their own life to the (superior) standards enjoyed by others, nearby or far away. Relative deprivation is, thus, of enormous significance in the definition of exclusion. In the same way, inequality is not a sufficient condition for being trapped in a situation of exclusion. Of course, social systems in which hierarchy is the organizing principle are characterized by a skewed distribution of property, power, and prestige. But can people positioned at the bottom of such societies automatically be characterized as excluded? In the earlier literature on caste order in South Asia, the conventional opinion was to define such categories in terms of exclusion: the outcasts, all those living beyond the pale, etc. In sociological terms, however, these categories were very much included, since their presence, as well as the economic services they performed, were required for the higher castes to retain their purity.

The meaning of exclusion is to be denied value, to have no constructive role to play in economic or non-economic terms, to be in excess to demand. Social systems based on the norm of equality, on the other hand, do not easily tolerate exclusion. If, for some unforeseen reason, people have stopped being included, the prevalent reaction is to facilitate their return to the fold of the included. In the world at large, and this also has to do with the process of globalization, there seems to be a trend of moving away from exclusion towards inclusion, if not in practice, then at least as a social ideal that deserves universal promotion. Exclusion, in the sense of being denied the right to have access to inclusion, may have lost whatever legitimacy it once had.

The juxtaposition of exclusion and inclusion is detrimental to our understanding of both. As in all variations on the concept of dualism, focusing on the contrasts help us to understand that in real life the essence is what lies in between. It would help to look at the exclusion–inclusion divide not as a fixed polarity, but as a continuum, a sliding scale that is subject to changes over time. What also needs to be added here is that awareness of exclusion, or for that matter of inclusion, is dynamic, not static. The questions that arise are not only exclusion from what and by whom, but also since when. Finally, as important as the perception of exclusion by those who are excluded, is the perception of exclusion by those who are included. What are the overt and covert scripts for keeping the excluded portion of humankind from becoming visible?

## GLOBALIZATION AND THE PROMISE OF INCLUSION

### A Critical Reappraisal

Wallerstein's[2] seminal work on the emergence of the world system addresses many biases in the interpretation of globalization as a recent phenomenon. For all his criticism, however, this sociologist seems to agree that the development path followed in the Third World is essentially a repetition of the transformation process that took place in the Atlantic societies during the nineteenth and the first half of the twentieth century. His analysis suggests a transition over the past few decades from rural–agrarian economies to urban–industrial economies. His scepticism mainly concerns the sustainability of the capitalist mode of production at the global level.

His point of departure is the liberation of growing quantities of labour from their captivity in agriculture and their subsequent influx into other economic sectors. With reference to this ongoing trend, Wallerstein speaks of deruralization, which over the past half century in particular has dramatically changed the earlier composition of the global economy. A much greater part of humankind, also outside the first and already highly developed part of the world, has been pushed out from the primary sector of production.[3] The shift that has come about should not be understood, in my opinion, as basically indicating a repetition of the same process of urban–industrial restructuring which occurred in an earlier epoch in the North Atlantic basin.

The exodus from the village economy in the Third World does not mean that the swelling numbers of migrants are succeeding in settling down in urban locations. Although, in terms of sheer population size, the big cities have grown more rapidly than ever before, large contingents remain on the march between town and country, as well as between different economic sectors. Such patterns of labour circulation are irrespective of distance, sometimes linking place of origin and destination within one country, or stretching, in other instances, across continental boundaries. The incessant flow and perpetual rotation are related to employment regimes marked by either own-account work or waged labour, which in the latter case is more often based on casual than on regular contracts. The need for highly flexibilized labour market

---

[2] I. Wallerstein, 'Globalization or the Age of Transition: A Long-term View of the Trajectory of the World System', *International Sociology*, vol. 15, no. 2, 2000, pp. 249–65.

[3] Ibid., pp. 261–2.

behaviour coincides with payment for tasks that require little or no skills and schooling. Such are, in sum, the conditions characteristic of a wide range of activities in the informal sector of the economy.

The optimistic statement made by Wallerstein is that the fact of becoming accustomed to this non-agrarian work, regardless of the variable demand for it that results in bouts of unemployment, in the end leads to a higher wage level. For the labourers engaged in this mode of existence, the experience thus acquired provides a take-off point for their subsequent transfer to the formal sector of the economy:

Even where there are large numbers of persons who are technically unemployed and deriving their income, such as it is, from the informal economy, the real alternatives available to workers located in the *barrio*s and *favela*s of the world system are such that they are in a position to demand reasonable wage levels in order to enter the formal wage economy.[4]

Is his conclusion also justified for the workforce that has become mobile in the towns and country areas of the region in India on which my fieldwork has increasingly been concentrated over the years?

My negative answer has been extensively documented in *Footloose Labour: Working in India's Informal Economy*.[5] Although the income of informal sector workers outside agriculture indeed tends to be somewhat higher than the wages earned by agricultural labourers, a clear majority of the households concerned still have to survive on an income of less than one US dollar per capita per day. This means that the people dependent on informalized employment are, in most cases, firmly stuck below the poverty line. According to a somewhat more lenient definition of deprivation, which allows not only for bare subsistence but also for the cost, for example, of housing, medical care, education, and a modicum of leisure, this level is fixed at an income of at least two dollars per capita per day, not incidentally but regularly. Such existence in 'comfort' is quite exceptional outside the realm of the formal sector.

The 'discovery' of the informal sector in the urban economy at the beginning of the 1970s went together with the assumption that this zone functioned as a waiting room in which the army of migrants originating from the hinterland could adjust themselves to their new habitat before making their way up to the formal sector, where they would find higher qualified, better-paid, more secure, and protected jobs. On the basis

---

[4] Ibid., p. 262.

[5] J. Breman, *Footloose Labour: Working in India's Informal Economy*, Cambridge: Cambridge University Press, 1996.

of my recurrent empirical and local investigations in both India and Indonesia, I conclude that cases of such upwardly mobile trajectories are difficult to find.

A series of policy reports in the 1970s and 1980s, commissioned mainly by the International Labour Organization (ILO), drew attention to what was called the informal sector problem, suggesting measures and regulations to upgrade the working and living conditions of the working poor in the Third World countries. The same type of analyses and the remedial schemes that accompany them are still being written. This benign strategy, however, has been gradually replaced by the opinion that labour markets in poor countries are in need of more and not less flexibilization. This is at the origin of the suggestion that what is called the unfair and unjust privileging of labour in the formal sector of the economy should be abolished. The protection of a small but powerful vanguard of the workforce should stop and, for the sake of stimulating employment growth, governments are being urged to facilitate the free interplay of market forces. According to the same line of thinking, there is no room for introducing state-initiated schemes of social provision.

These were the recommendations made by the World Bank in a major policy document.[6] I have discussed the substance and recommendations of the *World Development Report 1995* in a critical review.[7] A similar argument maintaining that the informal sector is the solution rather than the problem holds that what looks like poverty, defined as lack of property, is on closer inspection a misrepresentation of the capital formation that does, in practice, take place on an impressive scale in the informal sector of the economy. I strongly disagree with this appraisal, which is partly exaggerated and partly misleading.[8]

I now return to the analysis of Wallerstein, based on the assumption that world capitalism is in an acute and even terminal state of crisis. The ongoing expansion of this mode of production is, according to this sociologist, frustrated by an economic reversal caused by a substantial fall in profit margins. The resulting pressure implies a squeeze on the accumulation of capital, which has always been the organizing principle

---

[6] World Bank, *World Development Report, 1995: Workers in an Integrating World*, Washington, DC: The World Bank and Oxford: Oxford University Press, 1995.

[7] J. Breman, 'Labour Get Lost: A Late-capitalist Manifesto', *Economic and Political Weekly*, vol. 30, no. 37, 1995, pp. 2294–9.

[8] J. Breman, 'A Question of Poverty', Valedictory Address to the Institute of Social Studies, The Hague, 25 October 2001.

of capitalism. The investments needed to broaden and deepen markets are drying up. The first of the three factors responsible for the economic turn around has already been mentioned: rising wages all over the world, which make it impossible for capital to 'run away' to still 'underdeveloped' regions where the cost of labour is much lower. Capitalist entrepreneurs can no longer adhere to their tested strategy of the continuous relocation of production, but have to confront directly the demands from informal sector workers for more reasonable incomes. The catchment zones of reserve labour in the globalized hinterland, which until now had seemed so inexhaustible, have at last been incorporated into the market economy and, after passing through a phase of being socially uprooted and in political disarray, have finally managed to strengthen their bargaining position vis-à-vis capital and to exert upward pressure on wage levels. From the point of view of labour interests, this is a fairly optimistic assessment which I find it difficult to tally with the sustained poverty of the lower strata in rural and urban India. To an even lesser degree have I seen these people entering the formal waged economy, as suggested by Wallerstein.[9]

Do the profit levels of capital show a declining trend because of the two other factors that he discusses? These relate, on the one hand, to the rising inability of private companies not to include waste removal and cleaning up the environment in their price of operation and, on the other, to the increase in taxation needed for public expenditure. To start with, the first source of pressure, the emergence of the ecological movement would imply that firms themselves nowadays have to bear the cost of the purification of land, water, and air. In the areas of my research in South and Southeast Asia, such a decisive swing to private accountability is extremely difficult to discern. The strategy of free enterprise to externalize the costs of pollution seems, as yet, to be going on unabated. The reluctance of the average state in the Third World to take strong action against environmental degradation signals, in my opinion, the raw and untamed nature of capitalism in the global periphery. In those large parts of the world, consumer organizations and other non-governmental agencies have been able to build up much less space to exercise public pressure than in the prosperous core zones of capitalism on which Wallerstein seems to rest his case.

Another source of pressure lies in the steady intensification of taxation. Capital is subject to the demand for public security and is, moreover, no

---

[9] Wallerstein, 'Globalization or the Age of Transition', pp. 261–2.

longer in a position to continue to blatantly deny popular claims for better education, health care, and lifetime insurance. In Wallerstein's judgement, the urge to make these concessions stems from the need to legitimize state action for the as yet underprivileged segments of the population and the concomitant realization among the more well-to-do that such gestures are unavoidable for the sake of further political stability.[10] Again, in the course of my empirical research in west India over the past four decades, I have not come across the fear, either among politicians or the bourgeoisie, that the lower social strata pose a serious threat to law and order. Living up to their reputation, gained in an altogether different setting, as *les classes dangereuses*, the denigration of the labouring poor, which is the dominant attitude in mainstream society, is not tempered by the idea that there is a hidden repository of countervailing power down below waiting to be mobilized against intolerable exploitation and exclusion.

Nor is there any sign of growing support for a more rigorous system of public taxation, or a shift in the balance of power leading to a more equitable distribution of wealth. The intensification of tax collection by the state does not mean that the better off are now under closer surveillance insofar as their space to produce and consume is concerned. Indeed, their ability to maximize their private interests has increased. For the masses on the vast subcontinent of South Asia, the opposite could be argued, as the states in question are both unable and unwilling to appropriate a reasonable portion of the value added to capital in the process of production, or even to exercise adequate control over the ways in which capital is spent. Consequently, no social safety nets are introduced which would help to minimize the vulnerability of poor people, and expenditure on public housing, education, and health care are much lower than what is minimally required to substantially improve the living standards of informal sector workers.

My conclusion is that the squeeze of capital in the global economy, operationalized by Wallerstein in sharply falling profit rates, has not been taking place in the setting of my sociological investigations over the past forty years in India. Nor have I found evidence of stagnation in the accumulation of capital. In my view, it would be easier to argue the contrasting thesis, namely, the acceleration of capital formation that remains outside the reach of national or transnational governance. Capital has become significantly more volatile between countries and

[10] Ibid., p. 263.

continents, but the ways in which it is moved have not been accompanied by growing control or even transparency. To give one example, there is a serious dearth of information on the scale of private financial transfers to many regions in Asia and, conversely, from these to other parts of the world.

The freeing of capital from official regulation is paralleled by a concentration of the surplus, resulting in a progressive tilting of the balance between the haves and the have-nots. I would reject the suggestion that my findings have no other validity than for the sites of my fieldwork in Indonesia and India. Indeed, Wallerstein is very much aware that the trend towards polarization has not really halted. The record of 'postrevolutionary' regimes is that they have not been able to reduce worldwide or even internal polarization to any significant degree, nor have they been able to institute serious internal political equality. They have, no doubt, accomplished many reforms, but they promised far more than reforms. And because the world system has remained a capitalist world economy, the regimes outside the core zone have been structurally unable to 'catch up' with the wealthy countries.[11]

In view of this unequivocal statement, his prediction of a terminal crisis is all the more surprising. Without rejecting the term as such, I would like to give it a meaning that is different from the one that he has put forward. In my perception, the true crisis of world capitalism seems to be the stubborn and pernicious unwillingness to enable a very substantial part of humankind to qualify, both as producers and consumers, for full and fair participation in the regime of capitalist activity. The formalization of labour, in the sense of higher wages, job protection, and social insurance, all of which are essential ingredients for a more dignified lifestyle, remains absent. The inevitable result is that the much needed improvement in bargaining power for the labouring poor, which is a precondition for structural rather than conjunctural market expansion, has not materialized.

Mine is an uncomfortable observation which, moreover, does not square easily with the notion that capitalism, more than any other mode of production, is based on the logic of rationality. Are prosperity and democracy for a minority of the world's population in the long term really compatible with the exclusion from these 'goods' of a larger part of humankind, which is condemned to live in dire poverty and subordination? In a comprehensive socio-historical analysis, de Swaan

[11] Ibid., p. 265.

has elaborated on the reasons why and the lines along which the national elites in the North Atlantic basin ultimately decided to admit the labouring poor to mainstream society. At the end of his treatise, the warning comes that the processes of collectivization and civilization which shaped this societal transformation, for a variety of reasons, but to a large extent also because of the reduced role played by government, may not be repeated on the basis of a similar process at a global scale.[12]

Quite rightly, Wallerstein has pointed out that people everywhere in the world are taking back from states the role of providing for their own security.[13] My comment is that this trend of not surrendering the right to exercise violence may have more to do with aggressive than defensive purposes. In other words, such an inclination could find its inspiration, not in the fear of the unruly behaviour of the poor, but rather in the determination of the elite to resort eventually to untamed brutality in order to consolidate the individual or collective gains made, and even to widen the gap further by not giving to, but taking from the poor. After all, a major trend in the process of globalization is not the alleviation of misery at the bottom end, but progressive enrichment at the top end.

I disagree with Wallerstein's assessment of a terminal crisis of the world capitalist system. It may indeed be concluded that a crisis is occurring, but the one I discern has not so much to do with falling rates of business profitability, but with the hesitancy of capitalism to deepen markets by increasing the purchasing power of the segments of humankind living in poverty and, in so doing, helping to put an end to their state of exclusion in terms of both production and consumption.

## COLONIALISM AS FAILED DEVELOPMENT

From the late eighteenth until the mid-twentieth century, colonialism held a large part of the people in the conquered territories captive in an rural–agrarian mode of production, which remained largely non-capitalist in nature. In more general terms, it could be argued that the global economy, as it emerged in the colonial era, became structured in terms of severe and increasing inequality. While in the industrializing and urbanizing West, the hierarchical shape of society lost legitimacy with the waning of the traditional rural–agrarian order, colonialism was the expression of new patterns of inequality at the transnational level,

---

[12] A. de Swaan, *In Care of the State: Health Care, Education and Welfare in Europe and the USA in the Modern Era*, Cambridge: Polity Press, 1988, p. 257.

[13] Wallerstein, 'Globalization or the Age of Transition', p. 265.

founded on principles of discrimination and racism. The Indian sociologist, André Béteille, drew attention to the paradox that western societies were acquiring a new and comprehensive commitment to equality at precisely the juncture in their history when they were also developing, in their fullest form, the theory and practice of imperialism.[14]

Due to population growth and as a result of colonial policies, a huge mass of land-poor and landless rural workers became congested at the bottom of Asian economies. In the countries of South and Southeast Asia, which are the focus of my essay, the landless segments varied from little less than one-fifth to not much more than one-third of the total rural population. Did late colonial policy cause a greater concentration at the foot of the agrarian hierarchy? It is clear that the gradually increasing population density, which became noticeable towards the end of the nineteenth century and continued during the first half of the twentieth century, was of direct influence on the diminishing size of peasant enterprises. It is more difficult to establish whether there was a mass dropping down the agrarian ladder with numerous landowners being degraded, first to tenants and then to landless labourers.

During the last century-and-a-half of colonial rule, the variety of sources of employment in the rural economy probably increased very little or even decreased. The latter is said to have occurred in particular in the regions of South Asia where, according to the deindustrialization thesis (the loss of artisanal production organized as home industry), pressure on employment in the agricultural sector increased further. At any event, a reverse trend showed little if any progress. In other words, there was little sign of any advance by industrial capitalism, which had absorbed the surplus proletariat made redundant in the European rural economy. Insofar as new industries were established in the colonial metropoles of Asia, rural labour was admitted only on a partial and conditional basis: that is to say, non-working family members had to remain in the village and the labourers themselves were only tolerated in the urban milieu for the duration of their working life. This also applied to the army of landless people who were recruited as coolies for the mines and on plantations in the Asian hinterlands, who were even shipped overseas. Once the contract period had expired, most of them were sent back home or to a destination that passed as such.[15]

[14] A. Béteille, *The Idea of Natural Inequality and Other Essays*, New Delhi: Oxford University Press, 1983.

[15] J. Breman, 'Labour Migration and Rural Transformation in Colonial Asia', *Comparative Asian Studies 5*, Amsterdam: Free University Press, 1990.

The compression at the foot of the agrarian economy cannot have escaped the notice of the colonial authorities. In general, however, they made little effort to redistribute land ownership in order to free peasant production from its perpetual stagnation. An exception to this non-interventionist policy was the introduction, not of a ceiling, but of a floor in access to agrarian property in a region of Java just before the 1920s. Under that reform, land was taken away from marginal landowners and added to acreage in the hands of their better equipped co-villagers. The stated objective of this experiment was to strengthen the position of the established peasantry. Transition from the marginal to the landless class, so ran official opinion, would enable those who had thus been totally liberated from the means of production to become more flexible on the labour market. Since their tiny plot of land had in any case been inadequate for their subsistence, the measure was said to have been taken for their own good.[16] In this respect, the opinion of the colonial authorities appeared to run parallel to the suggestion made by Kautsky, among others, that marginal subsistence farmers were actually worse off than free wage labourers.[17] This apparently plausible assumption is not confirmed by my own research based on fieldwork in the rural areas of west India and Java. On the contrary, my findings show that the owners of even a small plot of land have a major advantage over landless households when migrating away from the village and agriculture to find additional employment and income elsewhere.

A survey of conditions in late colonial Asia suggests that it was the combination of economic and demographic change, in particular, that led to progressive land impoverishment. To put it in another way, land ownership at the village level continued to be concentrated largely among a fairly small upper class and a growing proportion of the agrarian population was denied access to holdings other than as tenants or sharecroppers. The landless class increased further. It is difficult to come by adequate and reliable statistics to support this quantitative shift in the class structure of the agrarian population. In practice, moreover, it is problematic to distinguish between the class of small landowners

[16] J. Breman, *Control of Land and Labour in Colonial Java: A Case Study of Agrarian Crisis and Reform in the Region of Cirebon during the First Decades of the Twentieth Century*, Dordrecht: Foris, 1983, pp. 39–71.

[17] K. Kautsky, *On the Agrarian Question* (1899). Reprinted by Zwan Publications, London, 1988 entitled *The Agrarian Question*.

and that of agricultural workers. With regard to the latter, Daniel Thorner commented in his well-known analysis of the agrarian structure in India in the mid-twentieth century that families in this class may indeed have tenancy rights to the soil, or even property rights, but the holdings are so tiny that the income from cultivating them or renting them out comes to less than their earnings from field work.[18] His observation shows clearly that, to understand the process of (pseudo-) proletarianization in rural Asia, it is imperative not to suggest a sharp divide between the land-poor and the landless, but to see them as extensions of one another. Indeed, in the densely populated regions of agricultural production at the end of colonial rule, they together comprised between half and two-thirds of the rural workforce. Speculations, with all their uncertainty, about the quantitative shift in agrarian stratification under colonial rule must not be allowed to divert attention from the qualitative change that occurred in the social relations of production. In other words, at the end of colonial rule, life as an agricultural worker had become moulded along new lines. That change, and the increasingly capitalist nature of the rural economy in the post-colonial era, had significant repercussions.

## THE TRANSITION TO A CAPITALIST REGIME

The rural development policies adopted following independence in the mid-twentieth century were characterized by a growing trend towards capitalism in agriculture. The much discussed Green Revolution, which gained momentum towards the end of the 1960s, and which amounted to the systematic introduction of a modernization package consisting of high-yielding seed varieties, fertilizers and pesticides, credit, new technology, agricultural extension services, and better water management, is illustrative of that approach. In contrast to East Asia, immediately after the Second World War, the transformation was not preceded by a drastic redistribution of agrarian resources. Where large landed estates still existed, they were abolished and tenancy relationships were reformed, with the objective of promoting the capitalist stature of a well-established class of owner–cultivators in India, usually members of locally dominant castes. This class, in particular, was charged with increasing production and productivity, as described by a long series of

---

[18] D. Thorner, *The Agrarian Prospect in India*, 2nd edition, Bombay: Allied Publishers, 1976.

commentators.[19] Hardly surprisingly, these analyses also point out that the shift in the rural balance of power, which accompanied the development strategy, caused a further deterioration in the already existing vulnerability of sharecroppers and agricultural labourers. Myrdal, who saw no other solution to the agrarian impasse, which in his view characterized the Asian drama, advocated a restrained form of rural capitalism. The idea he propagated was:

To give a small plot of land—and with it a dignity and a fresh outlook on life as well as a minor independent source of income—to members of the landless lower strata. Even in the most densely populated countries of the region it would be possible to give the landless at least small plots on acreages that are now uncultivated waste. In some cases land is available for the landless in the vicinity of existing holdings. The existing pattern of cultivated holdings need not be seriously disturbed—in some places it would not need to be disturbed at all.[20]

As we now know, little if anything of this modest recommendation has been put into practice. Resources held in common, insofar as these still existed, were rapidly privatized and usually came into the hands of the landowning elite. In Indonesia, when pressure increased for the new Agrarian Law to be implemented, which was finally adopted in 1960 as a consequence of the political climate of populism in earlier years, the military coup of 1965 put an end to efforts initiated from below to introduce some structural improvement in the position of marginal and landless rural workers, who included the majority of people living in the rural areas of Java.[21]

My conclusion is that the capitalist-directed agricultural development policy executed in the post-colonial era has further exacerbated the vulnerability of life at the bottom end of the rural economy. Although the initial sombre reports of the massive expulsion of labour as a result of rationalized and mechanized cultivation methods proved untrue, the expansion of agricultural employment as a net effect of the Green

---

[19] To mention just a few: T.J. Byres, 'The New Technology, Class Formation and Class Action in the Indian Countryside', in J. Breman and S. Mundle (eds), *Rural Transformation in Asia*, New Delhi: Oxford University Press, 1991, pp. 3–76; G. Myrdal, *Asian Drama: An Enquiry into the Poverty of Nations* (3 vols), New York: Pantheon, 1968; W.F. Wertheim, 'Betting on the Strong', in *East-West Parallels: Sociological Approaches to Modern Java*, The Hague: W. van Hoeve, 1964, pp. 259–77.

[20] Myrdal, *Asian Drama, Vol. II*, p. 1382.

[21] Breman, *Control of Land and Labour in Colonial Java*.

Revolution has not kept pace with the growth of the Asian rural population. The *World Labour Report*, published annually by the ILO, shows that self-employment in agriculture is gradually but steadily making way to wage labour. It would be premature to explain this trend purely as a sign of progressive proletarianization. The replacement of own-account or family labour by hired workers is also due to the emergence of a different lifestyle, causing even middle-sized landowners to prefer to exercise supervision over agricultural work for which outside help is hired. This trend has been a contributing factor to the creation of a rural labour market in the capitalist sense.

The continuing and abject poverty of the great majority of the landless is due to the fact that the supply of labour far exceeds the demand for it. The scenario devised by national policymakers following independence anticipated the outflow of the surplus proletariat towards the urban economy, there to be absorbed into the army of industrial workers. In the former colonial countries of Asia, however, the expansion of large-scale industry has been far slower and, above all, far less labour intensive than had been planned. Opportunities to escape to the cities are therefore limited, as will be discussed later, while emigration overseas is an equally unrealistic option. People are quite ready to leave their home country, but for the Asian rural surplus, there is no New World in which they can settle, as had been the case for the proletarianized mass from Europe a century earlier. Potential emigrants nowadays carry the label of 'economic refugees', a term whose strongly negative connotation signals that this ballast in the home economy is not welcome anywhere else in the world. My concluding observations are, first, that Asia's rural proletariat emerged from the colonial era as a class of far greater size than in rural Europe, when agriculture still formed the most important source of employment; and second, that the sluggish course followed by the industrialization process since the mid-twentieth century, in combination with a population growth that has only recently started to decline, has drastically intensified the pressure on life at the bottom end of the rural economy.

It would be incorrect, however, to deduce from the developments just outlined that the nature of landless existence actually signifies a continuation of the labour regime that began to take shape towards the end of colonial rule. Capitalist dynamics subsequently became of dominant significance in the countryside, causing drastic changes in the social relations of production. The transformation derives from three interconnected processes. The first is the diversification of the rural economy.

Agriculture has lost much of its significance in the employment pattern in rural areas due to the growing demand for labour in other sectors, such as agro-industry, infrastructure works (roads, canals, houses, and other construction activities), trade, transport, and all branches of the service sector. Such diversification has naturally not occurred everywhere to the same degree, but the trend in that direction is unmistakable. Sometimes this is employment of the last resort, in an effort to seek redress for the growing underutilization of labour in agriculture. Greater than the desperate flight away from agriculture, however, is the stimulating effect of the real growth in rural production on other branches of the economy. In the villages of west India where I did my fieldwork, these dynamics have had the result that the majority of the landless can no longer even be classified as agricultural labourers. In these localities, as well as in the state of Gujarat at large, working in the fields is no longer the predominant source of employment and income for the landless. Work at the bottom of the rural economy is characterized by occupational multiplicity. From being an agrarian proletariat, this class has remoulded itself into a more general rural proletariat.

Economic diversification has been accompanied by the large-scale mobilization of labour. Work away from agriculture usually also signifies work outside the village. Although the drift towards towns and cities has become far greater than in the past, the majority of migrants have little chance of settling there. They accumulate in the informal sector, which is the greatest reservoir of employment in the urban economy. The formal sector has shown hardly any expansion and absorbs little, if any, of the unskilled labour which continues to move in from the rural hinterland. The informal sector is not a transit zone towards a better and settled urban life, but functions as a temporary abode for labour, for which demand fluctuates strongly and which, when no longer needed, is pushed back to its place of origin. It is not departure and arrival that define the migratory chain, in a way that underlines the division between two separate economic circuits, but a continual to and fro of transients which seems to characterize not the rupture, but the linkage between rural and urban labour markets. There is no lack of willingness on the part of this circulatory workforce to engage unconditionally in an industrial way of life, as E.P. Thompson seems to suggest, at least for the initial phase.[22] It is much more a question of sheer impotence,

---

[22] E.P. Thompson, *Customs in Common: Studies in Traditional Popular Culture*, London: Penguin, 1991.

caused by lack of economic and physical space, which prevents the army of newcomers from establishing themselves as permanent urbanites, working their way up to becoming full time rather than incidental and floating industrial hands.

Labour not only circulates for shorter or longer periods between villages and towns. It also does so, and often in far greater numbers, within the rural milieu in search of work either in or outside agriculture. I have devoted a number of publications to this phenomenon of intra-rural labour mobilization, stressing the connection between long-distance seasonal migration on a truly massive scale and the breakthrough towards a more pronounced capitalist mode of production.[23]

Diversification of the rural economy and strongly increased labour mobility are, in turn, related to a third change in the essence of landless existence which has far-reaching consequences, namely, the casualization of employment. The agricultural economy shows a tendency for permanent farmhands to be replaced by daily wage labourers, or more generally, employment for an indefinite period has been replaced by short-term labour contracts based on the hire-and-fire principle. This modality also facilitates the replacement of local workers by migrants, with the advantage for employers that workers coming from elsewhere are usually cheaper and more docile, submitting more readily to treatment as a commodity. Moreover, they can be engaged or dismissed according to momentary fluctuations in supply and demand. In contrast with earlier practices, labour is paid principally or even exclusively in cash, and payment in kind in all types of goods, not only for the labourer but also shared by household members, has come to an end. Another important factor is that, rather than paying their workers per day or per year, based on time rates, employers now much prefer to pay for piecework or to contract out the task that needs to be done.

Does this mean that production relations have been cleansed of precapitalist elements? To some extent, but not completely. After all, the prerogative of labour to hire itself out at any moment and for the highest possible price is subject to many restrictions. For example, acceptance of a cash advance frequently entails a contract, which immobilizes labour power, while employers also defer wage payment as a tool for ensuring

---

[23] J. Breman, *Of Peasants, Migrants and Paupers: Rural Labour Circulation and Capitalist Production in West India*, Oxford: Clarendon Press, 1985; J. Breman, *Wage Hunters and Gatherers: Search for Work in the Urban and Rural Economy of South Gujarat*, New Delhi: Oxford University Press, 1994.

that the required labour, until the moment of dismissal, continues to be supplied. Nevertheless, the lack of freedom caused by such bonding mechanisms differs essentially from servitude, which characterized the coercive regime to which agricultural labour was subjected in the past. 'Neo-bondage' is the term that I recommend for the practices used by present-day employers to assure themselves of sufficient cheap labour power.

Having dealt with the historical features of the state of exclusion in which large segments of the rural population came to live and work under colonial rule in South and Southeast Asia, two case studies are presented in the final part this essay which examine how, in a context of globalization, increasing vulnerability can result in a situation in which people are excluded from the employment and income necessary for a life of minimal stability and dignity. Both are local profiles based on anthropological research carried out between 1997 and 2002, and both illustrate that exclusion can be a process in which people are sliding down from a better position that they occupied previously in the economy and society at large. The first report discusses what has happened to rural labour in west Java as, in the aftermath of the Asian financial crisis, their level of employment and income has fallen. The second profile is of urban labour in the city of Ahmedabad. The closure of more than fifty corporate textile mills led to the dismissal of about 100,000 workers who used to be employed in formal conditions. Following the loss of their jobs, they had to find a new living in the informal sector of the economy as self-employed or casual wage labourers. These two profiles, one rural and one urban, are intended to show where, how, and why poverty turns into immiserization and takes the form of exclusion.

## DYNAMICS OF EXCLUSION IN RURAL JAVA

The crisis which hit the economies of Southeast Asia in 1997–8, and Indonesia more than any other country, gave rise to instantaneous and fierce debate. Early on, an alarming increase in impoverishment and unemployment was predicted. The Minister of Manpower then in office went on record as saying that 22 per cent of Indonesia's total workforce would be unemployed by the end of 1998. Backed by official statistics, produced by the Central Statistics Agency (*Badan Pusat Statistik* [BPS]) on the basis of calculations that had never before been disputed, the ILO Regional Office for Asia and the Pacific estimated that the combination of wage stagnation and high inflation might cause 37 per cent of the population to fall below the poverty line by mid-1998, with a further spurt to 48 per cent before the end of that year. In comparison with the all-time low of 10.1 per cent reported for the period before the start of the monetary crisis (*krismon*, in local parlance) in mid-1997, this implied a three to fourfold jump in the incidence of poverty. This was an acceleration that threatened to undo much that had been achieved in raising the standard of living of all and sundry since the mid-1970s. The ILO further argued that the lack of improvement in household incomes and the likelihood of more price rises might even result in two-thirds of the population dropping below the poverty line in 1999.

Other international agencies produced more conservative appraisals or forecasts, vehemently rejecting the ILO's doom scenario. In February 1998, the World Bank conceded that absolute poverty might eventually rise to 17 per cent. A year later, a study commissioned by the World Bank reported that the poverty rate had gone up, but only marginally. Subsequent reports suggested that the lower income classes, in particular, had actually been quite successful in coping with the crisis. The received wisdom was that krismon had had a sharper negative impact on the urban than the rural economy; second, it had hit the better off harder than the poor; and third, it had reduced waged work in the formal sector of the economy, while employment in the informal sector had expanded. My opinion differs on almost all these scores. For a start, official statistics on economic growth and equity prior to mid-1997 underestimated the magnitude and intensity of the poverty that still existed throughout the country. I would agree with the assessment that a quarter of the population of Indonesia were unable to meet basic needs even before the crisis. Second, krismon has caused not only much more misery and loss of employment, but has further widened the divide between the poor, whose numbers swelled rapidly, and the non-poor. Third, the coping mechanisms with which people who have sunk below the poverty level can deal with life's vicissitudes have been exaggerated out of all proportion. Fourth, notwithstanding some signs of improvement in terms of employment and poverty levels, the crisis is by no means over.

The impression that deprivation under Suharto's New Order regime had become a residual problem found in rather remote pockets of the archipelago, which essentially persisted because these backward areas happened to be beyond the reach of government programmes, was in line with the late colonial myth which suggested that poverty was closely bound up with so-called 'minus areas'. In contrast to such geo-ecological exceptionalism, I would posit that poverty remained widespread in

Suharto's Indonesia, including rural Java. Without a shadow of doubt, the land-poor and landless have managed to dignify their lifestyle, and these gains have been reflected in a better quality of housing and the possession of consumer durables. However, the existence of working class households has always remained precarious. The dynamic ratio between productive and non-productive members has made all the difference between living slightly above or below the poverty line. A category of supra-poor could be identified even before krismon began to have its impact. These were the people who had no labour power or were unable to use it fully: the old, the physically or mentally disabled, and widowed or divorced female heads of households responsible for young children. The New Order regime kept a great deal of misery carefully hidden behind its propaganda statistics. The incidence of poverty was also understated in the reports of the World Bank and other international agencies. Major segments of the working classes living close to or in a state of poverty shared only marginally in the benefits of economic growth. In fact, the gap that already existed between the elite and the subaltern classes in East Cirebon and North Subang, the two villages of my anthropological fieldwork, has widened further. Contrary to the cherished policy view of rural society in Java as a communal-oriented social order based on patronage and reciprocity between strong and weak, my perception of the processes at work is that emphasis should be placed on polarization and exclusion.

Similar stark contrasts in levels of welfare can, however, be found in rural areas. More noticeable than the reduction of deprivation in the land-poor and landless milieu is the newly gained wealth of the rural elite. This affluence is expressed in the conspicuous lifestyle of a fairly small cluster of notable households, among whom most of the village capital assets, both agrarian and non-agrarian, are concentrated. Little light has been shed on the size and identity of the *orang kaya baru*, a privileged social formation owing the elevation of its members to their role as local agents of the New Order regime, which has consistently opted for a 'betting on the strong' development policy. The old colonial myth of 'village elders' who acted as representatives of the people with no voice of their own, the *masih bodoh*, became a lever to create a basis of legitimacy for the exploitation and suppression of subaltern classes in rural areas. Progressive landlessness in the recent past has not merely been a consequence of the ever-increasing demographic pressure on agrarian resources, but also of the fact that many households were excluded from cultivating land. The Basic Agrarian Law introduced in 1960 was never implemented. In fact, this effort to ensure a more equal distribution of land by imposing a ceiling on ownership became a bone of contention, which ended in the military takeover of 1965. It is against this background of a progressive divide between rural rich and rural poor that it is necessary to understand the impact on Java's village of the economic crisis which occurred a few years before the end of the last century.

In both villages covered by the fieldwork, the search for livelihood opportunities outside the locality became inevitable over the last quarter of the twentieth century. The solution was not found in leaving the place of origin to settle down in other rural areas or in urban destinations. The structural, rather than seasonal, redundancy in the rural economy led to large-scale labour nomadism. This is a pattern of migration that has required young males, in particular, to leave home for variable periods, unspecified in advance, but lasting for several weeks or months. They usually go to a wide range of worksites in or close to urban growth poles.Greater Jakarta and its satellite townships, Jabotabek for short, act as magnets for a massive army of circulatory workers from far and wide in the hinterland of Java. Only a few men and women from both villages have managed to gain access to the formal sector of employment in the urban economy. This is true even of the simplest form of factory work, which may not offer much in the way of protection against the vicissitudes of fate, but at least provides relatively fixed employment with regular working hours and a reasonably steady income.

Most of the migrant labourers from the two villages are unskilled and therefore, have little chance of finding regular, reasonably well-paid work. Because they are only employed as cheap and casual labourers, they cannot bring their families to settle permanently in the city. The costs of even the most minimal accommodation and subsistence would simply take up nearly all of their earnings. A state of flux is not, therefore, a first stage in the transition from rural–agrarian to urban–industrial employment, but is more structurally inherent to the conditions under which they continue to live. They are destined to shuttle back and forth interminably, leaving their families in the village. These circular migrants are concentrated in a number of occupational niches. The majority of the men who migrate, work as unskilled labourers in the building industry, while others make a meagre living as petty traders and street vendors. Of late, it has become quite common for young women to sign up with recruitment agencies for two-year contracts to work as maids in Saudi Arabia or Malaysia.

Most members of the new generation have turned their backs on agriculture, not only because of its declining importance in the village economy but also because of a clear preference for an urban–industrial way of life. The prospects of attaining this cherished lifestyle more fully in the near future have largely been frustrated by krismon. Young people from the better-off households prepared themselves for the leap forward into the formal economy by obtaining a secondary education and vocational training. Even in earlier, more prosperous times, only a few were successful in finding regular and well-paid work in the somewhat elevated echelons of the economy outside the village. Now that the chance of acquiring such work has as good as disappeared, these youngsters seem even more hesitant to join the labour process. So far, parents have shown remarkable restraint, especially where boys are concerned, in accepting this unwillingness on the part of their children to earn a living. The reluctance is, in effect, a protest by these educated young people against having to perform work for which they consider themselves to be overqualified on the basis of their actually quite modest level of formal schooling.

Their contemporaries from the land-poor and landless households that constitute the large majority of the village population cannot allow themselves such luxury. Economic distress forces them to seek paid employment from an early age. Any aspirations they themselves or their parents may have had for the continuation of their education after primary school often have to be abandoned in the face of shrinking household budgets. Consequently, the new generation will not have the opportunity to raise the status of their working life above that of their parents. It is almost a foregone conclusion that they will end up joining the lowest echelons of the informal sector in the rural areas and in the city, performing low-paid and irregular work for a constantly changing series of short-term employers. The prospects of any improvement in the lot of these migrant workers give rise to greater pessimism than optimism, even now that the worst of the recession is over.

There can be no denying that the large segment of circular migrants from both villages, who constitute the floating mass of working people at the bottom of the urban economy, have been hit heavily by krismon. At the end of 1997, practically all building activity in Jabotabek came to a halt and the *kaki lima*, the street vendors operating at their own cost and risk, not only lost their customers, but the sharp increase in the price of their raw materials reduced their profit margins. Having become redundant in the informal sector, many were forced to leave.

This led to an exodus of the army of labour nomads that had flocked to the cities in the heyday of the Asian miracle, but who had failed to establish themselves permanently in the urban environment. Many of these sojourners instantly dismissed from their casual jobs have been unable to reintegrate fully or even partially into sectors of employment at home. They have responded to their structural redundancy in the village economy by continuing to undertake sorties to the city areas with which they had grown familiar to search for work, with varying degrees of success.

Other segments of the working population in the rural hinterland that continued to depend on agrarian and non-agrarian means of subsistence have also suffered, particularly households with few or no means of production of their own. According to my calculations, loss of work and welfare resulted in a contraction of by at least a quarter of the gross village product of East Cirebon and by at least one-sixth in North Subang between mid 1997 and 1999. There have been some indications of a slight economic recovery from mid-2000 onwards, but this good news seems to be based more on the success of efforts to control inflation than an increase in employment or a rise in real wages. For the time being, there is not much factual evidence of recovery in the substantially diminished standards of living.[24]

There is little thorough empirical or comparative inter-sectoral research to support the conclusion that workers in the formal economy have suffered more from the crisis than those in the informal economy. It is founded on the assumption that elasticity is one of the most striking features of informal economic activity and that the men and women who are forced to eke out a living in this sector will, therefore, continue to do so during hard times. From this viewpoint, the informal sector expands and contracts like the tide. The reassuring message given out is that the enormous reserve army of labour itself knows best what it should do and where it should go, in terms of both location and sector, in response to a temporary surplus in some or all areas of economic activity. This theory does not, however, hold up in practice. After being sacked on the spot, most circular migrants from East Cirebon had little other choice than to retreat from their employment niches in the metropolitan economy. The same was true for labour nomads

---

[24] J. Breman, 'The Impact of the Asian Economic Crisis on Work and Welfare in Village Java', Dies Natalis Lecture, The Hague: Institute of Social Studies, 2000; Reproduced in *Journal of Agrarian Change*, vol. 1, no. 2, 2001, pp. 242–82.

from North Subang. Back in the village, their plight can be described as a state of limbo, characterized by a mixture of concealed and open unemployment.

I also contest the oft-voiced claim that krismon has had the greatest impact on the prosperity of the non-poor, and that the position of those without property has not worsened to any significant degree. Once again, there are insufficient reliable and comparative figures to defend or dispute this biased assertion. On the basis of my fieldwork, I conclude that, as a consequence, first, of loss of employment and second, of the rising prices of basic necessities, poverty did worsen after the outbreak of the crisis, expanding to embrace two-thirds of the inhabitants of both villages by the start of 1999. I estimate that the households with no or very little property that make up this large majority receive only one-fifth of all the income generated. Of particular concern is the advanced degree of exclusion in which the underclass of the ultra-poor, around a quarter of all the inhabitants, find themselves.

The expulsion, for the time being, of many migrant labourers from the lower echelons of the urban economy following the outbreak of the crisis expressed the failure on the part of the state to provide basic support to this industrial reserve army. With political unrest gathering momentum, policymakers and politicians were afraid that this redundant mass was about to fulfil its historic destiny as les classes dangereuses. Its expulsion from the urban environment was justified by the argument that, once back in their villages, the migrants would be able to benefit from the traditional mechanisms of social solidarity that had tenaciously survived in the rural–agrarian milieu. During my fieldwork, I found no evidence to support this brand of wishful thinking, which is so popular among politicians and policymakers. There is no reason to assume that the situation that I encountered in North Subang and East Cirebon, namely, advanced monetization of the local economy and the hegemony of contractual relations, is an exception from a general pattern in which the organic principles of what is obstinately referred to as the traditional Javanese culture can still be identified.

I found no evidence that the wealthy upper class households were prepared to spend even a minor part of their surplus to mitigate the misery of their less fortunate fellow villagers. Nor are there any collective arrangements designed to counteract the (increasingly) unequal distribution of wealth. Contractual relations have gradually replaced the former patron–client transactions, in which the wealthy would pledge assistance and protection in exchange for the labour and loyalty of the poor. Under the New Order, the elite no longer needed the dependence inherent in the system of patronage to bolster their superiority. The orang kaya baru themselves, however, increasingly became 'clients' of those in authority at the district and sub-district levels. In exchange for their support in preserving a social order based on social inequality and political exclusion, they were rewarded by their patrons in the form of preferential drawing rights on the resources of the state.

Would it be possible to detect a culture of shared poverty among the people coping for survival at the congested base of rural society, in an effort to distribute the available work and income as equally as possible, through collective action and mutual solidarity? In neither of the two research localities did I find institutionalized arrangements for house-holds to tie in their fate with others in similar circumstances. As we have seen, during the New Order era, there was no social and political space in which an awareness of common interest could develop among the land-poor and landless classes. The sustained strategy of fragmentation is most probably one of the main reasons why the outbursts of protest that accompanied the deepening crisis did not develop into open and violent class warfare.

In my view, another reason why this did not occur was the increasing opportunity for escape to the urban growth poles. The rapid expansion of employment niches, at shorter or longer distances from home, helped to lower the pressure building up in the rural economy. Large masses of migrant labourers flocked to these growth poles from the hinterland of Java without making a definite break with their milieu of origin. As a result, the bond with the village has remained intact, but it has been weakened. The constant mobility of these circulatory workers, most of whom belong to the subordinated classes, has made them less susceptible to the economic and social power of village elites. This is expressed in a recalcitrance that is a source of irritation to both rural employers and officials. Having become streetwise in the urban economy, the labour nomads enjoy a reputation for being demanding and less malleable than their colleagues who remained stuck in the villages. In mobilizing opposition from below in support of the process of political reform, greater account will have to be taken of the 'floating mass' of the people, and in a much more literal sense than when the term was coined by those in power under the Suharto regime.

The very many households that play a marginal role in the eco-nomic process have little more to fall back on during times of crisis than their own resilience. They, of course, ask for and receive help from those around them, particularly close kin and immediate neighbours. But, given the fact that this assistance comes largely from other poor households, such transfers are limited in scale, regularity, and substance. To alleviate the economic distress of those most severely affected, the government could not ultimately avoid introducing what it had consistently tried to neglect, namely, a social safety net. This scheme, intended as a temporary solution only, produced little in the way of concrete results. Even the emergency food relief and public works projects, aimed at the poorest of the poor, largely benefited persons outside the ill-defined target groups. The local authorities in North Subang and East Cirebon defended their decision to distribute the emergency provisions to all the villagers by saying that everyone had equal rights to government support. It is my conclusion that this argument was also a logical consequence of the political and bureaucratic myth of the village as a community.

The crisis in Indonesia has stopped being a purely monetary–economic recession and has escalated into the far-reaching disruption of society as a whole. The political instability and the threat to national unity may jeopardize all chances of economic recovery for many years to come. Reforms will only have the desired effect if, at the same time, the people are given more say in all matters relating to the quality of their lives. Proposals to shift the focus of political and administrative activity from the national to the regional level must be assessed in this light. These plans are at an advanced stage and their implementation has already been initiated. Without guarantees that the very weak bargaining position of the rural poor will be strengthened, the devolution of political and executive power will result only in legitimizing the informal supremacy of the district and village elites. It is the old principle of 'betting on the strong' that has always been at the forefront of Indonesia's development model.

The colonial theory of dualism saw an irreconcilable opposition between two economic systems in rural Java, caused by the penetration of the capitalist forces of production and their clash with a static pre-capitalist society. The main criticism of this dichotomy of stagnation versus dynamism was that it had its origins in foreign domination. Later versions of the same dualistic model, first, of the city versus rural areas and then, the formal and informal sectors in the urban economy, proved to be just as much a product of their age, enjoying popularity in analyses of the development process in the second half of the twentieth century.

The current debate on inclusion and exclusion within the context of the globalization of the political economy can be seen as a new variant of the old theme of dualism. The scale of enlargement in terms of production, consumption, and distribution has a strongly differential impact on the social classes that become, actively or passively, involved in the global transformations. Since the fall of Suharto, Indonesia has taken the first hesitant steps towards the transition to a civil society based on a democratic order. The progress made on this route will depend largely on whether the far-reaching social exclusion of the subaltern classes takes a turn for the better at the start of a new century![25]

## THE PROCESS OF INFORMALIZATION IN AHMEDABAD

The majority of the workers, dismissed from their permanent jobs when more than fifty corporate textile mills closed their gates during the last quarter of the twentieth century, ended up in the informal sector of the city's economy. These 'new poor' have come to join the already enormous army of workers who have never known a different kind of life. How many people actually suffered a genuine deterioration in their quality of life? The various publications come up with different figures for the number of mill workers who had secure jobs and lost them. My own estimate is that this happened to approximately 85,000 workers who were sacked from the early 1980s onwards. Already, in the decade before the mill closures, the management of these enterprises had reduced the size of the workforce in permanent employment. Casual hands who never qualified for full protection under the labour legislation were not generally hired on a more permanent basis to replace labourers who reached the age of retirement. Some tasks in the production process were also contracted out to jobbers who had to bring their own work gangs, which remained unregistered in the factory records. Of an estimated total of 85,000 workers with regular contracts who were dismissed during the last two decades of the twentieth century, somewhat more than 10 per cent may have left the city after being made redundant. Wherever they went, usually back to their place of origin, they only rarely succeeded in gaining access to similar jobs in the formal sector of the economy. Their future was as dark as for the large majority who decided to stay on in Ahmedabad. Another 10 per cent, most of them

---

[25] The full survey has been published as a monograph by J. Breman and G. Wiradi, *Good Times and Bad Times in Rural Java: A Study of Socio-economic Dynamics Towards the End of the Twentieth Century*, Leiden: KITLV Press, 2002.

belonging to the technical or administrative staff in the mills, were able to find jobs of more or less equal income and skill. Apart from this small segment, which somehow managed to consolidate their formal sector status, all the others, according to my calculations no fewer than 75,000 workers, were eased out into the informal sector, a transfer that implied a dramatic downturn in their fortunes.[26]

If the composition of the household is taken as a basis for determining the impact of the mass redundancies in Ahmedabad, it may be said that, at a conservative estimate, at least 300,000 people, the workers themselves and the members of their households, were directly affected by the dismissal of their main breadwinners from the secure jobs they held in the textile mills. And, in addition to these main victims, petty trade, services, and transport in the mill localities suffered from the drastic loss of income of the mill households, which constituted a major part of their client base. With the total population of the urban conurbation of Ahmedabad rising from 2.5 million in 1981 to 3.3 million in 1991, the mill closures directly affected no less than one-sixth of the city's inhabitants, an undeniably significant proportion. And even that was not the end of the story. As a result of the influx of households expelled from the formal sector, the already fragile existence of workers in the informal sector came under greater pressure than it had already experienced. It is clear that competition for work has led to much tension and conflict, both in residential areas and in relation to work.

For the former mill workers, the initial refusal to accept that the mills had closed for good was replaced by the realization that there was no other option than to look for work elsewhere. The search for new employment was driven by the need to provide for their families, and this period of transition was marked by great insecurity. There was no time and little financial breathing space to recover from the loss of their jobs at the cotton mills. Many could not keep their heads above water without borrowing money from relatives or moneylenders, or asking for credit from shopkeepers. They did this in the belief that, if the mill did not reopen, at least they could look forward to the payment of their savings and the other sums owed to them by their former employers, including their redundancy pay. Those among them who did finally

---

[26] J. Breman, *A Turn for the Worse: The Closure of the Ahmedabad Textile Mills and the Retrenchment of the Workforce*, Wertheim Annual Lecture 12, Centre for Asian Studies, Amsterdam School of Social Science Research: University of Amsterdam, 2001.

receive their money, considerably less than what they were entitled to, had to use it to payoff the loans and other debts they had run up to survive the period of unemployment.

Slightly fewer than one-third of the ex-mill workers considered themselves unemployable after their dismissal. Half of them gave their age (over fifty) as the main reason for not going back to work, while one-fifth put it down to failing health. The rest said that they were willing to work but were unable to find a job. It would be a mistake to take this difference in motivation for their actual behaviour too literally. Age and ill health may be valid arguments for stopping working, but few people who find themselves suddenly unemployed at the bottom of the economy can afford this luxury. It is only possible if other members of the household compensate for the loss in income. In nearly all cases, this proved to have been the case and was the reason why those who claimed to be still seeking work in vain could continue to do so. Unemployment is therefore a flexible concept, determined by what is considered suitable work at any given moment. The final choice, and whether this, in turn, is eventually revised in the last resort, depends on the balance between the availability of work, conditioned by such factors as the nature of the work and how heavy it is, its regularity, pay, and the other terms of employment, and the extent to which the obligation to acquire income for the household can be delegated to other family members. The starting point in the search for other work was always the same: the desire to find a job that, insofar as possible, offers what the mill provided. The absence or inaccessibility of such employment explains why, in most cases, it has taken so long for former mill workers to find a new occupation. The period of idleness was necessary to allow them to adjust their aspirations to a much lower level. As mentioned earlier, this adjustment was more difficult for some than for others, while a significant group refused to take a step back at all.

The former mill workers would prefer to find work under a permanent contract, but the security and protection provided by such a status ended when they were made redundant. The closest they have come to that now is an unwritten, and even unspoken, contract through which employer and employee agree by implication to continue the relationship until the contract is terminated. This is the basis upon which workers are taken on by factories or workshops as wage labourers for an indefinite period, or as guards by companies that specialize in security for industrial premises, offices, or residential quarters. As long as the work they do fulfils the requirements of the employer, they can be sure of a job. But they can derive no rights from this employment. Casual labourers, who are hired on a daily basis or until a job is done, are in an even more vulnerable position. This arrangement is standing practice in the building industry. These people assemble early in the morning at one of the many labour markets, which may be a road junction, a square, or a bus station, where they wait for the jobbers and sub-contractors to come and recruit the labour they need. Sometimes, a relative, neighbour, or friend may have asked them to tag along as an extra hand or told them to report directly to the building site. This meeting of supply and demand is not based on legally valid terms of employment and the covert agreement is very vague and fluid.

More numerous than these regular and casual wage labourers are those who are self-employed, working on their own account. Three of the most common occupations in this respect are *rickshaw* drivers, street vendors (of cloth and garments, food and drinks, crockery, vegetables), and repairing or recycling waste materials. Others work at home, making garments, paper, toys, or plastic articles on a sub-contracting basis. Although they are without doubt economically active, they find it difficult to specify their main occupation. This is also because many of them have to be engaged in several trades to earn enough to keep their heads above water. Then there are those who are active only occasionally. They work some days and not others, depending on the demand for their services. They are not overly active in seeking work, but do not refuse it if it is offered to them.

The ex-mill workers are now employed in jobs that typically require a far lower level of capital investment than the work they performed in the mills. If mechanized power is involved at all, it is in the form of simple machines (a rickshaw motor; a sewing machine; or other simple equipment, for example, for repairing clocks and watches, radios, bicycles, or household articles; or craft tools for producing handmade commodities, such as leather goods, furniture, *ambar charkha*, or paintbrushes). Only the weavers in the powerloom sheds work on the same machines that they used in the mills, which were sold as scrap. The skill level outside the industrial sector of the economy is much lower, and it is especially in these branches (small-scale trade, transport, and services) that a large proportion of the former mill workers have ended up. Many of them have lost the skills that they learned in the mills. On the other hand, their work now demands much greater physical effort. Complaints from construction labourers, pedal rickshaw drivers, cart pullers, head porters, and ambulant street vendors about being exhausted at the end of the day must partly be seen in the light of the fact that they now work far less with machines.

The work in the mills had a daily rhythm of eight hours, leaving enough time to spend with the family, do household chores, and engage in activities outside the home. This is now completely impossible. On paper, the powerloom workshops are supposed to operate according to a three-shift roster. As everyone knows, however, the working hours are split up into a day shift and a night shift, each lasting ten to twelve hours. The employers will not take anyone on for less. More is, of course, always possible. If someone does not turn up for work, a member of the previous shift can simply work another ten or more hours. Home workers can decide for themselves how many hours they work, but the pressure to earn more by starting early in the morning and working until late in the evening is great. Often, all the members of the household play some part in the production, leaving very little leisure time for them to spend together.

Others who work in the open air at their own expense can determine the length of their own working day. Street vendors offer their wares long after night has fallen and have to be up and ready to replenish their stocks at the break of day. Lastly, there are the not inconsiderable numbers who have to spend part of the day or night doing a second job to supplement their low income. The former mill workers have to cope not only with much longer but also much more irregular working hours. Although they used to work three eight-hour shifts, the shift schedule was drawn up in advance and they were paid extra for overtime. Such bonuses are a thing of the past and the regular cycle of their working lives has been replaced by erratic and unpredictable interruptions and long periods of idleness during which they are not paid. The fact that they show up for work is no guarantee that they will actually be employed on any particular day. It is often uncertain whether the working day will begin at all and how it will develop, and the workers are expected to adapt to these major and often unpredictable fluctuations. Free days and leave have become a luxury and are never paid.

More than any other criterion, the enormous drop in income illustrates the degree to which the quality of life of the former mill workers has deteriorated. The weavers, who now earn their living in small enterprises, do the same work, but for much lower pay. Nor can they always be sure that there will be work for them. Most ex-mill workers who earned a daily wage of between Rs 90 and Rs 100 before the mills closed, for an eight-hour day, six days a week, amounting to between Rs 2,000 and Rs 3,000 a month, now earn less than half of that, while a sizeable minority have to make do with less than one-third of what they earned previously. The fall in income is so dramatic that other members of the household are forced to work. The wage brought home by the man of the house was sufficient to allow customs to be observed or imposed, but following the closure of the mills, there has no longer been the financial freedom for such sensitivities. Home working allowed Muslim and some Hindu women to take an active part in earning income for the household without them having to break the social code of public behaviour. Sewing and embroidering clothing, making incense sticks, and rolling cigarettes are prime examples of activities in which all household members, particularly women and children, can take part. But, in many cases, women and children also are forced to engage in work outside the house. They are employed in garment workshops, but may also have to seek work as domestic servants. Collecting paper and other waste (such as scrap metal or empty plastic bottles), which has a low status and earns very little, is the business of dalit women and girls.

In some of the households of former mill workers, the shortage of income has sometimes become so acute that impoverishment has given way to outright pauperization. The household members can no longer afford to buy the basic necessities to survive. But, even in the much larger numbers of households where the fall in earnings has been less severe, it is still hard to make ends meet. As a result of the gap between income and expenditure, the proportion of the household's budget that has to be spent on food is much larger than before and many have been forced to cut back on both the quantity and quality of their daily food consumption. The tradition of celebrating family events with lavish meals and new clothes has been abandoned and little or no money is left for the purchase of consumer durables. Although the lifestyle of the industrial workers allowed for few comforts, the large majority of ex-mill workers are connected to electricity and water supply, and two-thirds have a toilet in or close to the house. A bicycle and a table or ceiling fan are relatively normal and the majority have a radio and a sewing machine. A little under half still enjoy the luxury of a television set or a pressure cooker, purchased in better times. Many have had to sell such valuable possessions, and even more are no longer able to repair them if they breakdown. About half own the house they live in. The remaining rent their homes for around Rs 100–Rs 150 a month. Although many of these tenements are located in what have now become slum districts, this does nothing to impair their value for those who live in them. The quality of the dwellings has, however, suffered across the board, as the residents find themselves unable to afford even the most basic repairs, for example, to roofs or walls. And rent that was formerly well within their means has now become an almost unbearable burden.

A greater threat to the well-being of the former mill workers and their families than the deterioration in their food intake is the loss of their right to free or cheap medical care. In the past, they were members of the Employees State Insurance Scheme (ESIS), set up by the government in 1948 for employees of public and private sector enterprises. Employees and employers fund ESIS from contributions, while the government also provides a sizeable subsidy. Under the statutes of the scheme, the workers' families are eligible for medical services, which are provided free of cost. The ESIS has its own hospitals and neighbourhood clinics, with its own doctors who see patients and prescribe medicines. When workers retired or were unable to go on working due to disability, insurance coverage continued for them and their wives, but those who lost their jobs for other reasons were automatically excluded from the scheme. To their great anguish and resentment, this is what happened to the mill workers when they were dismissed. The benefit that the workers derived from their membership of ESIS was much greater than the contribution they paid into the fund and represented not less than 10–15 per cent of their salary. Now that they are no longer insured, they try to rely on self-help and only call in low-grade doctors and quacks if they have no choice. These practitioners, who are often not properly trained, charge much more for a consultation or an injection than the insurance scheme. And there is neither the money nor the professional expertise for the treatment of the stress and other mental problems that arose during and after the redundancy period.

The future of the new generation of children is in jeopardy because their schooling is cut short. Parents can no longer afford to invest in improving the life chances of their offspring. Primary school attendance is not affected much, but the impact on more advanced education has been much greater. Apart from the fact that the cost of intermediate and vocational schooling far exceeds the household budget, the labour power of youngsters is a much needed source of income that has to be tapped at an early age. As a consequence, the level of knowledge of the new generation when they enter the labour market at a very young age is often lower than that of the mill workers when they started their working lives many years ago.

Former mill workers also worry a great deal about their children's life partners and the cost of marriages. Looking for suitable candidates is time consuming and assumes that the parents have the opportunity to deliberate carefully on their choice. Financial considerations play a decisive role in the negotiations, which aim to secure the best candidate at the lowest price. In the absence of a reasonable dowry, gifts of money, and commodities with which the arrangement is sealed, girls, in particular, are forced to accept partners who would never have been eligible before. A lower status, not only for the individual but also for the whole family, is the price that has to be paid.

Building up the reserves needed in times of crisis is now completely out of the question. And setbacks occur more often and with greater intensity than before the mill closures. Initially, the workers could use their redundancy benefits, but these varied greatly in size and many received nothing at all. How was this money used? A small minority managed to deposit at least part in a savings account and were resolved not to eat into it until the time came for which it was intended, usually for the purchase of a house, future repairs, or the marriage of sons or daughters. A much larger number indicated that they had to use the money to pay for medical care, urgent home repairs, or the repayment of debts. By far, the largest share was spent on day-to-day expenses since, with the difficult adjustment to a lower level of income, this was the only way that the households could meet their recurrent needs. Clearly this situation, in which expense exceeded income, came to an end when the reserves were exhausted. Redundancy payments were far less than most of the workers were entitled to and, moreover, were paid in instalments over an extended period. This explains why workers could not resist the temptation to spend the money as it came in. Most of them therefore clung to their previous way of life and consumption pattern for much longer than they were able to afford.

The dramatic fall in the standard of living of the former mill workers undermined their self-confidence. After the shock of being expelled from the mill, came the discouraging experience of looking for a new job, accompanied as it was by the loss of skill and a much lower wage. We heard how the men were completely at a loss in the early days following their dismissal. They would not talk for days on end and refused to take food. Their loss of vitality was so great that even the lightest of physical activity was seen as too exhausting. Some stayed at home, others left the house early in the morning and came back late at night, refusing to disclose where they had been or what they had been doing. This state of shock easily led to health problems, which had previously received little attention. Such ailments were used as an excuse to avoid helping with the daily household chores. The ESIS medical records show an increasing number of patients in the industrial neighbourhoods with heart problems and high blood pressure. The greatest demand was for social care and psychological counselling, but this was not covered by the insurance. Social relationships within the family suffered. Husbands and wives quarrelled, often leading to violence by the man, and sometimes even vice versa. Tensions also increased between parents and children. According to primary and secondary school teachers in the industrial neighbourhoods, children became unruly and 'difficult', had problems concentrating, and complained about troubles at home.

No visitor to Ahmedabad can fail to observe the sprawling slums on the east bank of the river, which have spread rapidly over the past few decades. A large segment of the city's population is cramped together in these deprived quarters, exposed to environmental degradation and excluded from the most elementary civic amenities. There is a close link between living in a slum and working in the informal sector of the economy. The tall chimneys marking the industrial landscape have disappeared and the factory compounds, which for a century or more were congested worksites with people constantly milling around, are vacated and deprived of their economic significance. Working-class neighbourhoods no longer surround the new wastelands, which are filled with the rubble of demolished buildings and now dominate this part of the city. The lack of steady employment and a sharp fall in incomes have transformed these habitats of the former mill workforce into slum localities.

The alienation of the ex-mill workers from mainstream society finds expression in their reduced access to public services and institutions, including those that are intended for each and every citizen of Ahmedabad. This state of exclusion is accompanied by a loss of control over the conditions that determine the quality of their lives now and in the future. Market discrimination in how they live and work reinforces their acute sense of deprivation and ensures that they do not enjoy equal opportunities to improve their situation. Members of stigmatized groups naturally seek contact with their own kind—Muslims, dalits, and other social minorities exposed to discriminatory practices, individually and collectively—for mutual support and protection. A life of dependency, however, goes hand in hand with restricted choice and downward mobility. Indebtedness forces the former mill workers to sell their own labour power and that of other household members and to settle for a lower wage in exchange for advance payment. Such dependency restricts other options and investment in forms of horizontal solidarity that cut across primordial loyalties. There is an impelling need to retreat into their own communal niche and to stay aloof from other social segments.

The retrenched textile workers are not the only inhabitants of the industrial districts to have suffered from the collapse of the large-scale textile mills. The impact on petty trade, services, and transport in the mill areas has been enormous, because demand for the services of a wide variety of shopkeepers, street operators, and craftsmen came predominantly from this leading segment of the working population employed in the formal sector of the economy. Many of their customers have become their competitors. The influx of households expelled from the formal sector has put even greater pressure on the already fragile existence of workers in the informal economy. Competition for work has led to much tension and conflict, both in residential areas and at the workplace. The process of levelling down to the bottom has become manifest in the spread of squalour and has helped to create an atmosphere of undiluted depression.

## Grades of Vulnerability

From early morning until late in the evening, the *chali*s and side roads are crowded with people. The large majority are males of all ages, lying, sitting, or standing in front of their houses or hanging around in small clusters. They take to the streets to kill time because there is not much else for them to do. Women who are not engaged in outside work tend to stay at home, not only because of a code of conduct which does not allow them to move about freely, but also because they are busier than their male partners with all kinds of household chores and in making use of their labour through gainful employment.

Few labourers in the informal sector of the economy succeed in working more than twenty days a month. Street vendors seem to be the most susceptible to seasonal fluctuations, which prevent them from achieving a fixed rhythm of work. On days when it is raining, cold, or very hot, there is less demand for their services and they have to face a considerable drop in income. Daily wage labourers are similarly affected. On such days, they go to the various labour markets in the city where workers are hired early in the morning, only to be turned away. It is the same story at the building sites, where they seek work as unskilled hands. It would, however, be incorrect to attribute the unpredictable nature of work in the open air purely to inclement weather. It may also by interrupted by public holidays, or by disturbances of the public order, such as riots or political tensions. Seasonal swings in the city's economy, caused by not so transparent flows of industrial and mercantile capital in the informal sector, have a greater impact on the mass of workers in this sector than on their counterparts in the better-regulated formal sector. Not much is known about the nature and effects of these cyclical and erratic trends. They also affect home workers, whose means of earning a living are wholly concealed from public view. The fact that they are apparently available for work at all times does not mean that they have work all the time. The delivery of raw materials is irregular, the power supply is unreliable, and contractors pass on fluctuations in demand for the end product without the slightest scruple.

The large amount of time not spent in gainful work does not mean that this vast reserve army enjoys the many and erratic hours of non-activity at their disposal. Leisure used to be a familiar notion that grew out of the pattern of regular employment in the mill. When they were not on night shift, the men would congregate in small groups after the evening meal and sing devotional songs or just engage in small talk together on street corners. Going alone or with the whole family to the Sunday market on the riverbank or to visit relatives living in other neighbourhoods were favourite outings during the weekend. These days are gone. Although there is more 'idle time' available now, there is neither the money nor the energy to enjoy it as leisure.

Not all workers who have lost their mill jobs have fallen below the poverty line. There are those who do not have to rely solely or predominantly on the sale of their unskilled labour power. These include the owners of petty means of production, such as motorized rickshaws, handcarts, or street cabins, or of parcels of land or small buildings in the slum areas, who not only use this property themselves but rent or lease it out. Although the percentage of workers having access to various forms of petty capital should not be exaggerated, their households are certainly better off than those who have no means of production themselves. At the opposite end of the spectrum, there is an extremely vulnerable segment of ex-mill workers who, because of ill fortune or disability, are alienated both from means of production and consumption. The households to which they used to belong have broken up. There are instances of men deserting their wives and children, unwilling to provide for them any longer, but there are also cases of men being thrown out of their houses soon after losing their jobs at the mill. Such people, the ultra-excluded, roam the streets as lost souls, begging and afflicted by acute pauperization. They depend for their irregular and inadequate meals on *ramroti*, free food distribution centres run by religious charities.

Slum life is not only characterized by signs of want, deprivation, and neglect. The closure of the mills has also led to a shrinking of public space in the settlements surrounding them. Places where people used to meet their workmates and others with different social identities are nowadays difficult to find. Certainly, in the past too, the mill hands used to spend most of their time off in or around the home, mainly within the confines of the particular communal circle to which they happened to belong. Life-cycle events or religious festivals were public functions, which were largely celebrated in the open. The neighbourhood schools run by the municipality were a point of contact where children not only demonstrated the skills picked up within the intimacy of family life in dealing with 'others', but where they also made friends from the other side of the fence. People living nearby were invited to share in the food and fun, even if they observed other customs themselves. There were clubs, which gave training in wrestling, boxing, and other sports to all-comers, irrespective of their caste or communal background. And the spectators at the matches were also mixed. The reading rooms set up by the Textile Labour Association (TLA) throughout the industrial districts were also important meeting places. Classes were held in the mornings and evenings to teach adults and those who had dropped out of school at an early age how to read and write. Later on, many of these centres were taken over by the Labour Welfare Board, an official agency set up under the auspices of the municipal government. In recent years, several of these places have closed down for lack of funds. The municipal corporation decided to cut down on social expenditure and the clientele has dwindled. Apart from the inability of the clients, men as well as women, to pay the very modest fee charged for the various courses or for the crèches where toddlers can be left a few hours each day, they have also lost their appetite for spending 'free' hours in constructive activities. Their time is eaten up in the search for work, or just in remaining 'idle'. Venturing out into mainstream society has become an option that many households in the milieu of ex-mill workers can no longer afford.

## THE FALLACY OF PARALLEL DEVELOPMENT

A paradigm, which has dominated post-colonial development literature in the second half of the twentieth century, suggests that inclusion is a historical trend encompassing more and more people in different parts of the world. This particular brand of wishful thinking suggests that the process of transformation, as it has taken place in western economies, will be repeated at the global level and will, in the end, give rise to the kind of industrial–urban society that initially emerged on both sides of the Atlantic Ocean in the northern hemisphere. No doubt, that historical trajectory was also difficult to predict when it first commenced. Towards the end of the nineteenth century, there were strong doubts that the underclasses in western societies would be able to find their place in the new industrial society that was being constructed. The doctrine of social Darwinism was based on the assumption that not all poor people could or, for that matter, should be raised to a life of human dignity. In the struggle for survival, only the fittest in the process of natural selection would be able to qualify for a better future. When compared with the deserving poor, kept in waiting as a reserve army of labour, the non-deserving poor were labelled as a burden to themselves and to society at large. This sizeable segment of the poor was blamed for its own poverty. Having nothing useful to add, the very presence of these people was considered to be a risk to social stability and cohesion.

The subsequent inclusion of these marginalized groups into mainstream society was the outcome of a highly labour-intensive process of industrialization. The low level of technology, although rapidly increasing, allowed for the insertion into the workforce of households pushed out of the rural–agrarian economy. What came to be redefined as *the social question*, conditioned, on the one hand, by growing assertiveness from below and, on the other, by acceptance among the higher classes that the cost of exclusion might be higher than inclusion, had its origin in an expanding economy which required the labour power of the masses living in poverty. There is no clear indication that this development scenario, which took place within the framework of the nation-state, has been replicated at the transnational level a century later. On the contrary, the enormous gap between non-poor and poor people is still widening.

The assumption of parallel development explains why, in the postcolonial era, politicians and policymakers have gone on record as saying that 'soon' or in 'the foreseeable future' people would no longer have to live in poverty. While they might have conceded that the fight against deprivation would take time and was dependent on all kinds of preconditions, they did not state that bringing increasing numbers and, ultimately, all people above 'the poverty line' was something that could not, or even should not, be contemplated. A well-known example of that mode of thinking was the idea of 'trickle down', which promised that people with few or no assets were eventually going to benefit from the process of economic growth.

In line with the notion of inclusion as a historical trend, the British sociologist, T.H. Marshall, specified various dimensions of the process of inclusion and ranked them in sequential order: first, the granting of legal rights which extend the rule of law to all citizens; next, the granting of political rights which proclaim universal suffrage and promote the participation of all in a democratic framework; and finally, the granting of socio-economic rights which find their apex in the welfare state.[27]

There have been episodes in the recent history of developed societies which have seemed to signal that the trend towards inclusion could be abruptly halted or even reversed, resulting in a slide back into exclusion. The world economic recession in the 1930s once again exposed many people in the industrialized countries to a situation of vulnerability, which they found difficult to accept, precisely because of their improved well-being in the preceding decades. In 1933, a book was published, entitled *Die Arbeitslosen von Marienthal*, consisting of an empirical study of the effects of long-term unemployment.[28] The book became one of the classic works of social scientific literature on the significance of the loss of paid employment for working-class households in an industrial society.

The setting of the study was a small community on the outskirts of Vienna, which had one large textile mill and not much else by way of economic activity. After cutbacks in production and working hours in the late 1920s, against the background of the economic crisis which affected the whole of industrial Europe, the mill closed in 1930. This signified the disappearance of what was essentially the only source of employment in this rural township. With the complete workforce made redundant, no less than three-quarters of the local population, 367 of the 478 households, found themselves in a situation of acute and stark poverty. In summing up their findings, the authors spoke of *die müde Gesellschaft* (the tired community). This subtitle of their study expressed the feelings of powerlessness and hopelessness that overwhelmed these

---

[27] T.H. Marshall, *Social Policy in the Twentieth Century*, 4th edition, London: Hutchinson, 1975.

[28] M. Jahoda, P. Lazarsfeld, and H. Zeisel, *Die Arbeitslosen von Marienthal* (The Unemployed of Marienthal), Leipzig: Hirzel, 1933.

people. Only a small proportion of the population managed to stay in paid work, in the service sector outside the village, and a number of older people received a pension.

The study describes the response of the affected households in subsequent phases: how they proceeded from initial resolve to resignation, going on to despair, and finally, apathy. The social–psychological approach illustrates how these people lost their sense of time and how their daily routine, which is so important for a meaningful life, was eroded. Outside the household, there was a noticeable increase in isolation, a declining involvement in the world outside, institutionally and organizationally, together with symptoms of envy and suspicion instead of mutual help. The tenor is clear: a process of marginalization and a shrinking of the psychological space, leading to alienation. The portrait demonstrates how tempting it is to hold the poor themselves accountable and responsible for the state of exclusion in which they are made to live.

How did the dismissed Austrian workers survive in those years of crisis? Certainly not through being able to find paid employment, but by partially retreating into self-sufficiency. They grew vegetables or bred rabbits on a small piece of land rented to them by the mill or the local council. Much more important than these modest contributions towards imposed autarky, however, was the unemployment benefit that they received from the state every fortnight. The economic cycle of the households affected by the mill closure revolved around this paltry payout. The benefits were funded from contributions by employers, workers, and the local authority, and the total accumulated in the years prior to the closure of the mill meant that there were enough funds to last for twenty or thirty weeks. After that, the former mill workers were eligible for the lower benefits provided by a government 'dole' system. Sporadically, such as on religious holidays, the municipality or charity organizations would provide them with food packages. In the early 1930s, the welfare state in Europe was still under construction. It would not be expanded and completed until well after the end of Second World War, but the foundations had already been laid in the early years of the twentieth century. When the economic crisis struck in the early 1930s, governments in the industrialized part of the world responded to the sudden onset of unemployment and impoverishment with relief programmes. These took the form of both financial support and job creation through the commissioning of public works. It is precisely this type of public scheme which, in the free market-driven policies towards the end of the twentieth century, has been lacking or soft-pedalled in the global fight against poverty.

The essence of my argument in the previous pages has been that past experiences are relevant to defining, analysing, and resolving the dynamics of inclusion–exclusion in what is called the developing world. In order to promote incorporation into mainstream society, and to forestall a return with a vengeance of the doctrine of social Darwinism in the globalized economy, the deeply skewed balance between capital and labour will have to be redressed. Such a corrective policy needs to be carried out at the transnational, national, and local levels and requires: (i) capital redistribution (land reforms in the first place); (ii) employment creation and job security; and (iii) the provision of social welfare, concretized in terms of health, housing, and education.

The huge disparities that have been created in today's world cannot be undone without connecting the mechanisms of inclusion to those of exclusion. As Seabrook, for example, has argued, it seems to be the object of official political discourse to suppress any such connections:

The easiest alibi, as always, is to blame 'nature', drought, over-population, the spread of the desert; when it is our own nature that is deeply implicated, above all the nature of our society and its development, which has succeeded in re-creating a lasting sense of impoverishment out of the very riches it has accumulated, and has made us believe that the simple goal of sufficiency for all represents for us, the rich, not emancipation, but a terrifying loss not to be contemplated.[29]

[29] J. Seabrook, *Landscapes of Poverty*, London: Blackwell, 1985, p. 175.

# 11

# The Political Economy of Unfree Labour in South Asia

## Determining the Nature and Magnitude of Debt Bondage*

In a recent report entitled, *The Curse of Coercion*,[1] the International Labour Organization (ILO) draws attention to a form of coercion that occurs on a wide scale, especially on the subcontinent of South Asia: the fact that millions of men, women, and children are not free to dispose of their labour power as they wish, but are bonded by debt to their employer. Debt bondage is described as:

The status or condition arising from a pledge by a debtor of his personal services or of those of a person under his control as security for a debt, if the value of these services as reasonably assessed is not applied to the liquidation of the debt or the length and nature of those service are not respectively limited and defined.[2]

A loan extended to an employee by an employer cannot always be seen as a form of bondage. The relationship can only be referred to as one of

* Originally published as 'The Political Economy of Unfree Labour in South Asia: Determining the Nature and Scale of Debt Bondage', *Indian Journal of Labour Economics*, vol. 52, no. 1, January–March 2010.

[1] Global report on the follow-up to the International Labour Organization (ILO) Declaration on Fundamental Principles and Rights at Work, International Labour Office, Geneva, 2009, Report I (B). The ILO addresses unfree labour practices in its annual reports and publishes regular reports on the theme. The most recent ILO report on forced labour was published in 2005.

[2] Ibid., p. 8.

bondage if the loan is provided with the aim of disposing over the labour power of the borrower, and if the amount of the loan is disproportionate to the terms imposed, in scale and duration. Many of those who belong to the huge army of land-poor and landless labourers, who make up a large segment of the working population, are drawn into a state of servitude by accepting a small or larger advance on the rendition of their labour power, either from an employer or his agent, and undertaking to work off the subsequent debt. Debt bondage is part of a wide range of unfree labour practices, of which forced labour is the generic format. While the latter has to be performed under threat of punishment and is based on duress, bondage is a form of servitude which does not have to be enforced with non-economic sanctions. Of their own 'free will', that is, because they have no choice, bonded labourers enter into a relationship of subordination which denies them any real power to dispose of their own labour power. It is worth pointing out that while it may be possible to distinguish between voluntary and involuntary in theory, it often turns out to be quite difficult to do so in practice. To demonstrate this lack of clarity: when a labourer enters into an employment agreement based on an advance payment, his wife and children have no other choice than to join him in bondage. There is no question at all of free will in their cases.

How many people live and work in a state of unfreedom? The 2009 ILO report states that 12.3 million people worldwide are entrapped in regimes of coercion—varying from slavery, forced, or bonded labour to human trafficking—adding that this figure, given the lack of reliable or even basic records, is without doubt a very substantial underestimation of the problem's true size. This uncertainty about the scale of unfree labour has its roots not only in the unwillingness of official agencies to gather statistical information on the phenomenon but also on the difficulty of establishing a clear dividing line between free and unfree labour. The lives of the working masses at the bottom of the labour system in South Asia display a wide range of aspects that testify to far-reaching deprivation and discrimination, making the designation of free and unfree labour a very elastic concept. In other words, practices of free and unfree labour cannot be described as an absolute dichotomy, but have to be seen in terms of a sliding scale, a continuum on which only the extremes are in clear and sharp contrast to each other. Having said that, some sources claim that, for South Asia alone, the magnitude of unfree labour is almost double that estimated for the world as a whole in the 2009 ILO report, namely, around 25 million people. Furthermore, that estimate covers only the category of debt-bonded labourers. I would suggest that the reservations that can be made about the reliability and, more especially, the verifiability of the statistical data do not alter the fact that debt bondage on the South Asian subcontinent is a significant feature of the misery in which the lower echelons of the working population find themselves. The argument that follows is based on the precept that excessive poverty must be seen as the main cause of this mode of unfree labour.

## THE FADING AWAY OF AGRARIAN BONDAGE

Bondage is a form of submission that, in various part of South Asia, dates back to the pre-colonial past. It was a relationship of servitude in which the landless were bonded to large landowners in a pre-capitalist agrarian system. Servants were distinguished from masters, who were usually members of a higher caste, by their subservient position at the foot of the social hierarchy. Originating from a low caste or tribal community, they had to acknowledge the economic as well as social superiority of their masters. The landowner did not only exploit the labour power of his employee and other household members but also made use of his farm servant, together with servant's wife and children, to gain in power and status. As well as being an employee, the farm servant was also the client of a patron and as such, obliged to display servility and obedience. Conversely, the patronage relationship meant that, as a client, the farm servant could claim the support and protection of his landowning master. What it came down to was that, in exchange for performing the tasks assigned to him and his family on the land, in and around the employer's house, caring for the cattle, or other activities—work that varied from season to season as well as with the changing demands of the master—the farm servant received a wage that was considered sufficient to support himself, his wife, and children. Ideally, becoming a bonded servant meant being guaranteed that their basic needs would be met.

The account on my first fieldwork in south Gujarat, conducted in 1962 and 1963, addresses the existence and disappearance of the *hali* system, as this traditional form of servitude was known in the region where I conducted my research.[3] My conclusion was that the progressive commercialization of agriculture and the transition to capitalist

---

[3] J. Breman, *Patronage and Exploitation: Changing Agrarian Relations in South Gujarat, India*, Berkeley: University of California Press, 1974.

production in this primary sector of the economy radically changed the nature of the relationship between landlords and the landless. The disappearance of the patronage aspect in the interaction between farmers/ landowners and the landless, together with the formers' decision to switch to crops that required less labour and, above all, less permanently employed labour, meant they were no longer interested in having attached servants. With the growing monetization of consumption, the landowning upper class of rural society realized that it was cheaper to replace a permanent workforce with casualized labour. The change took place over a long period, from the end of the nineteenth to the middle of the twentieth century, and was reflected in the gradual replacement of farm servants by daily wage workers. For their part, there was increasing resistance among the halis against the state of bondage in which they were forced to live. As I have argued elsewhere, it is a misconception to believe that they submissively accepted the yoke they were forced to bear.[4] The diversification of the rural economy in the post-colonial era led to expansion of the labour market. The younger generation of landless responded to this development by refusing to attach themselves in bondage. As direct stakeholders, both landowners and landless labourers can, in the first instance, be held responsible for the disintegration of the hali system. Much less important, in my assessment, is the role of the colonial and post-colonial authorities in the eclipse of the former agrarian relationship in south Gujarat, while I consider the half-hearted attempts from civil society to bring about the emancipation of the working underclass as marginal. Without wishing to cast doubt on their good intentions, I had to conclude in my retrospective analysis that, by emphasising mutual harmony instead of a conflict of interests, the social movement set up along Gandhian lines to achieve this emancipation resulted in a fiasco.

Has the traditional form of bondage disappeared elsewhere in South Asia as well? In India as a whole, this is undoubtedly what has happened, as many regional studies detail. As far as Pakistan is concerned, I hesitate to conclude that this is the case everywhere. Local elites continue to have far-reaching authority over the extensive underclass of labourers. In other words, the civil or military government—the army has taken over the reins of government for long periods of time since independence—has systematically failed to honour or defend the fundamental rights of the

---

[4] J. Breman, *Labour Bondage in West India: From Past to Present*, New Delhi: Oxford University Press, 2007.

working population to live in freedom. This applies, for example, to the
landless peasants in Sindh, who till the land appropriated by a class of
large landowners on a sharecropping basis and are compelled to do so
in a way in which naked force is inherent. Their employment relationship is founded on debt, and the repressive regime to which they are
exposed renders them the physical captives of the local political elite.
Conducting research into these practices was a shocking endeavour,
an experience exacerbated by the patent unwillingness of the international organization to which I was to report my findings to put a stop
to the unfreedom of the sharecroppers by calling for a programme of
necessary reforms.[5]

The fact that the situation I encountered shortly after the turn of the
century in Sindh was by no means exceptional is shown by the employment contracts that tie farm labourers to their employers in central and
southern Punjab. They work as servants for landlords and are attached
to their masters in a way that no longer occurs in India. The difference
is undoubtedly related to the authoritarian nature of the political order
in Pakistan. Unlike in India, where the state system was set up along
democratic lines immediately after independence, the subjugation of
the lower classes has remained intact in rural Pakistan. The enormous
mass of land-poor and landless peasants remains at the mercy of local
landlords, who may constitute a small minority of the population but
possess the lion's share of total farmland in the country. Agricultural
activity largely continues to be founded on landlordism. The complete
absence of any land reform, under civil or military governments, has
not only preserved the sharp dividing lines between social classes, but
strengthened them with the growth of population.

In India, too, the landless have been excluded from the redistribution
of land ownership, but in the democratic set-up introduced in
1947, political parties and the government have to take account of
the demands of the most deprived groups for improvement of their
situation. Although these demands have not led to deliverance from the
severe poverty in the bottom ranks, at the village level, there are clear
limitations on the dominance of substantial landowners, the caste–class
on which agricultural labourers depend for making a living. The
dismantling of the hali system in south Gujarat must be seen partly

---

[5] J. Breman and K. Lieten, 'A Pro-Poor Development Project in Rural Pakistan:
An Academic Analysis and a Non-Intervention', *Journal of Agrarian Change*, vol. 2,
no. 2, 2002, pp. 331–55.

in the light of this radical change in the social climate. In Punjab, in Pakistan, the tillers of the land, deprived from their own means of production, remain trapped in a relationship that denies them any freedom of action. In fact, their situation has deteriorated as a result of landowners switching, in the 1970s, to the cultivation of crops that are not only less labour intensive but also offer employment in an irregular cycle of peaks and slacks. By replacing what was a sharecropping arrangement by wage labour, this change has resulted in progressive proletarianization of the landless peasantry. The landowners recruit servants from among their numbers, though they only make limited use of their labour for agricultural purposes. As servants, the landless are at the disposal of their masters for agricultural work, but they are also clients with whom landowners surround themselves as evidence of their power and status. The local elite's preference for a semi-feudal lifestyle calls for them to maintain a cluster of underlings. The patron surrounds himself with servants not only to make use of their labour power but also to acquire greater prominence, recognition as someone who can claim notability, and, more importantly, can use his attached entourage to demonstrate his authority in the village and beyond, with a show of manpower and, if necessary, backed up with the exercise of violence.

In a study based on extensive fieldwork, anthropologist Nicolas Martin has described the economic, political, social, and cultural dimensions that determine the relationship of servitude in which the landlords in a district in central Punjab maintain the landless segment of the population in a far-reaching state of subordination.[6] During my recent sojourn in Pakistan (2009), I was able to confirm his description and analysis. The lack of adequate work offering prospects of a better life in the urban economy contributes to the confinement of this rural proletariat. Although many industrial workshops may have opened in the main towns of the region such as Faisalabad, Sialkot, and Multan, they have little to attract the rural landless as they offer jobs only on the basis of informal terms of employment (that is, temporary rather than permanent work and on the basis of a low piece rate). The underclasses in the countryside stagnate in unemployment and, in that situation, servitude to a landlord is grasped as an option that at least guarantees a landless worker can meet his basic needs. However, despite the behaviour of a

---

[6] N.E. Martin, 'Politics, Patronage and Debt Bondage in the Pakistani Punjab', PhD thesis, London School of Economics and Political Science, 2009.

patron that the landlords project and which obliges them to see to it that their clients enjoy a basic living standard, in practice, they do not practice the generosity expected of them. The servants are bonded in debt to their masters but do not get the credit as an advance on their services that they require to survive. Forced to live and work in a state of subjugation, they are expected to fulfil their client's duty of unconditional obedience, but do not receive the reward they need to lead a somewhat secure and dignified existence. It means that this rural proletariat must be available as a labour reserve and lacks the room to escape practices that cannot bear the light of day. The fact that *lumpen* can be hired from this landless underclass, excluded from sufficient work and income, to perform activities that fall beyond the limits of the law, shows that poverty has reached a level that borders on pauperization. Identifying all kinds of activities that far exceed the boundaries of legality, such as widespread dealing in drugs and weapons, and the use of excessive violence as a way to warn or punish opponents and competitors, should not conceal the fact that behind the perpetrators who do the dirty work are the landlords, with their contacts in politics and government. The situation that has developed in Pakistan also explains why the land-poor and landless masses, persistently excluded from economic and social progress, have little reason to be loyal to a state that is responsible for their marginaliza-tion from mainstream society. Nor should it be surprising that, in the absence of any improvement in their living standards, these impover-ished classes are receptive to the tenets of a religious movement that aims to dismantle the state and restructure society radically along funda-mentalist lines.

In Nepal, agrarian bondage used to occur in the form of sharecropping in agriculture. Under the *kamaiya* system, farm labourers undertook to work for the owner of the land they cultivated. The debt which ensured that the sharecropper remained dependent on the landlord was known as *saunki*. A servant from a low caste who, as a result of his servitude, earned less than a free labourer was known as a *haliya*. As mentioned earlier, the kind of agrarian bondage as is still practised in Pakistan, can no longer or hardly be found in India. Although the class of substantial landowners continued to hold the dominant position they had already acquired, the land reform introduced in the wake of independence has resulted in the demise of landlordism. Consequently, the agricultural economy has undergone a different development than in Pakistan. A second, perhaps more important, difference between the two countries is the ongoing process in India of replacing attached farm servants with casual daily wage labourers. In addition, agrarian servitude has been reduced to a pure employment modality, as a result of the removal of the patronage and the political dimension in the contract with the landowners. It has, in fact, evolved into an unsatisfactory arrangement for both parties, as the employer still expects his servant to act with loyalty and deference, while the latter tries to demand a manner and level of cash payment that enables him to meet the basic daily needs of his family and protect them against deficiency and setbacks. What could have resulted in progressive vulnerability was mitigated by a diversification of the rural labour market, which expanded more forcefully than in Pakistan. This has meant that the landless underclass has more opportunity to find employment outside agriculture and the village. Furthermore, the establishment of a democratic political system has made an important contribution to the erosion of the traditional state of agrarian bondage. Despite the outright and sustained reluctance from political quarters to support the emancipation of landless labour, it has proved impossible to ignore this substantial segment of the rural electorate completely. The Congress party, in particular, presented itself in the national arena as the benefactor of the interests of the economically and socially most deprived segment of the population.

Time and again, however, deeds have failed to live up to promises, even to the extent that, in some states, a once loyal and reliable support base has transferred its allegiances, voting in elections for parties that have pledged, or at least pretended, to make every effort to reduce the ingrained inequalities in social hierarchy. Having said that, it is important to note that the comparison with Pakistan shows the importance of a state apparatus that has committed itself to upholding the rights—to freedom and representation—of all its citizens. Undoubtedly, social practice in India can be criticized for not devoting sufficient attention to the recognition and, especially, the affirmation of basic rights for the mass of poor people. Yet, it is not difficult to identify a multitude of programmes and facilities intended to relieve their deprivation and the discrimination under which they are forced to live. Already at an early stage, attempts were made to increase the active participation of the most deprived and denigrated communities in political decision making by reserving seats for candidates from these underprivileged segments in representative institutions right down to village level. The policy of positive discrimination in obtaining access to education and jobs in the public sector also demonstrates the effort made to give priority to reducing the gap between the haves and have-nots.

During the course of my fieldwork-based research for close to half a century, I have not been able to observe a reduction in inequality—in fact, the trend seems to be moving in the opposite direction—but there have certainly been changes in social balance. There is no doubt that the non-poor have benefited much more from economic expansion, but the poor have not become poorer, and their social deprivation and degradation has not become deeper or more harrowing. In my opinion, those living at the foot of society have become more assertive and show themselves increasingly dissatisfied with the lack of progress in improving their condition. That change indicates the development of an awareness that precludes a return to subjugation and servitude. I do not conclude from the difference in emancipatory consciousness between the landless classes in Pakistan and India that farm labourers in Pakistan lack any desire for freedom and equality. They are forced, however, to operate in a political economy that allows them no space to express this desire. In rural India, the former system of servitude has certainly left its traces in the lives of the working classes. The problem of the rural proletariat in India is, however, no longer enforced subjugation from above or, conversely, being powerless to resist that subjugation from their inferior station at the foot of society, but how to survive when they are unable to satisfy their basic needs due to a combination of too little work and a too meagre wage.

## THE PREVALENCE AND SPREAD OF NEO-BONDAGE OUTSIDE AGRICULTURE

Does the disappearance of agrarian servitude in large parts of South Asia, at least in the form in which it formerly occurred, mean that the working population is now in a position to determine for themselves where, when, and for whom they work? That conclusion would be compatible with the classical assumption that the transition to a capitalist mode of production is characterized by a labour system based on freedom to move around. It is, however, an assumption that needs to be reconsidered, certainly in the case of South Asia. Debt bondage proves not to have disappeared, but still exists on a large scale. Perhaps, even to a greater extent than traditional forms of bondage in agriculture. It is a form of unfree labour that has received a strong boost as the capitalist economy has risen to dominance.

I first encountered this form of bondage during my first visit to south Gujarat in 1962–3. In one of the villages where I conducted my fieldwork, land-poor and landless labourers would leave their homes at the end of the harvest, as the rain season was coming to an end, to work in brick kilns or salt pans near Mumbai. They would return shortly before the start of the first rain. My informants told me that their parents and grandparents were already accustomed to spending part of the year away from the village to perform this seasonal work. The stories I listened to were indeed confirmed by an early village monograph.[7] The labourers were recruited by an agent working for the employer, who sealed the agreement made with the owner of a brick kiln or salt pan by paying them earnest money. This committed the migrants to go with the job-ber when he gave them orders to leave a few months later, after the monsoon was over. By giving the members of the gang he contracted an advance, he enabled them to survive through the period of heavy rainfall, when work in the fields was almost at a standstill. This allowed them to fulfil their basic needs, despite not earning enough from farm work. For his part, by paying the advance through his agent, the em-ployer secured the quantity of labour he required so that, when the dry season arrived, production could get under way again at his brick kiln or salt pan. The advance was larger if the man's wife and children were also contracted. The seasonal migrants repaid the debt as they worked. The jobber now became a foreman charged with supervising the gang he had recruited. The piece rate that the migrants earned was not paid out. Instead, they received a two-weekly grain allowance for food and a small sum of money to pay for other necessities. This did not change once they had paid off the debt. From then on, they built up savings, which were not paid out until the end of the season when they returned home. In other words, the bondage entailed not only repayment of the advance but continued in the form of withholding payment of wages and settling the balance only at the end of the season. The labour process itself, extremely heavy with a working day-and-night of fourteen hours or longer, and the miserable life the migrants were forced to lead, will not be discussed in this essay.

What I wish to focus on is that the state of debt bondage in which the migrants find themselves denies them any say in the terms of their employment or the fruits of their labour. The brick makers, for example, do not even know what the rate is per 1,000 bricks, on the basis of which they are finally paid off. This rate is only determined at the end of the season when the employer has marketed his bricks and knows

---

[7] G.C. Mukhtyar, *Life and Labour in a South Gujarat Village*, Bombay: Longmans, Green and Co., 1930.

what price his production has fetched. It means, in fact, that a large part of the employer's risk is transferred to his workers. In the many rounds of fieldwork that followed, my attention has remained focused on the employment of rural migrants in brick kilns. It is an industry that I have persistently continued to study, not only in Gujarat but also in Pakistan and Nepal. In Pakistan, the debt with which the owners of brick kilns contract their workforce in bondage is known as *peshgi*. My interest in this traditional branch of industry with such a large army of labour lies in its significance for the process of urbanization. The location of brick kilns in the vicinity of cities is related to the enormous expansion of construction work, and therefore, of the market of their products. Brick making is very similar throughout the whole of South Asia: it is a seasonal activity, largely performed by migrant labour recruited in debt. It is important to note here that, in the half a century that I have been visiting brick kilns, the organization of the labour process has hardly changed. It remains largely small scale and with minimum use of technology, with a flexibility that enables it to be tailored to demand. Despite the high labour intensity, the wages of the temporary bonded labourers account for only a small proportion of the total production costs. This is undoubtedly one of the main reasons that labour has not been replaced by capital.

A second case of neo-bondage is to be found in the agro-industry in the region of my research. The construction of a network of irrigation canals, completed around the middle of the previous century after the building of a dam in the Tapti river, led to a radical change in the cropping pattern on the fertile plain of south Gujarat. The cultivation of rice, millet, cotton, and pulses which provided employment throughout the year for the local landless, by far the largest class in the agricultural economy, was replaced especially by sugarcane, which accounted for an increasing share of the cultivated acreage. This brought about a radical change in the labour system. Sugarcane is a labour-intensive crop that requires a large army of cutters in the harvest period. The cooperative sugar mills set up to process the cane delivered by the farmers followed the example of the existing agro-industry in Maharashtra and hired labour from outside for the cutting season, rather than make use of the reserve pool of farm labourers locally available. Agents for the mills contract gangs of cane cutters from far-off regions for the campaign, which begins at the end of October and lasts, depending on the size of the harvest, until well into May. They are recruited in the monsoon, because the land-poor and landless peasants in the hinterland then have no income to meet their basic needs. The mill agent pays jobbers an advance, which they use to recruit a gang they will lead for the duration of the harvest campaign. In their contracts, the jobbers also undertake to accompany the cutting teams—usually consisting of a man, his wife, and at least one child—that make up their gang on the journey from their homes and to return again with them at the end of the season.

I have reported in a number of publications on the way in which this itinerant army of labourers is set to toil day and night; the way the work is divided among the gangs and the cutting teams; the camps which they erect in the open air and have to move from place to place; and how these activities are organized by the mill management.[8] Here, I concentrate on the debt bondage which is the organizing feature of their seasonal employment. The mode of payment for work performed on a piece-rate basis is identical to that customary in the brick kilns. The acceptance of an advance implies acquiescence with a debt relationship that leaves the labourer no other choice than to depart from home when the mill gives the jobbers the sign. Failing to honour the agreement at this crucial moment is tolerated only if the labourer who has received the advance can find someone else to go in his place. Cane cutters, too, repay their debt with their labour power. What stops them from repossessing their freedom after reaching this turning point and leaving is that the balance of their wages is not paid until the end of the season. Until then, they receive an allowance in kind that is just about sufficient for their daily food requirements. If one of the teams of cutters decides to leave early, they forfeit the balance of their wages that the mill is 'safeguarding' for them. The combination of paying for labour power in advance *and* after the season has finished means that the bondage starts when the labourers are recruited and lasts until the migrant army is demobilized at the end of the season.

The two forms of debt bondage just described, which are prevalent in south Gujarat, the region where I have conducted repeated fieldwork over the past half a century, are both related to the seasonal migration that has expanded to such a grand scale in the modern economy. The opening up of the countryside, given a considerable boost by the greater ease with which distances can be covered, has allowed the widespread

---

[8] Compiled in J. Breman, *Wage Hunters and Gatherers: Search for Work in the Urban and Rural Economy of South Gujarat*, New Delhi: Oxford University Press, 1994, chapters 2, 3, and 5.

mobility of labour. This happens in a way, however, that does not improve the bargaining power of the seasonal migrants. As we have seen, they are mobilized in a state of immobility. In the first case, the land-poor and landless migrate out of their villages to work in far-away brick kilns, while in the second case, a similar army of migrant labour is brought in to cut the sugarcane. It is important to emphasize that the influx of bonded labour from elsewhere is not evidence of a local shortage. As mentioned already, the cooperative sugar mills in south Gujarat refuse to employ farm labourers from their own region, who are available in abundance, to cut the cane. The same applies to the employment of labour in the brick kilns. When, during a new round of fieldwork, I came across a kiln on the outskirts of one of the localities of my earlier research, I discovered that the workers did not come from the village. The latter went to work in brick kilns near Mumbai, as they had done for many years, while seasonal migrants were recruited from far away to work in the kiln that had been opened in the village. Why?

Migrants are cheaper but can also be called on to work at all times, day and night. Employers can exercise much more control over these outsiders and know how to extract the maximum amount of labour power from them. I was able to supplement these case studies with many others in the region of my research and reported in various publications on what has become a widespread practice. For example, in the countryside of south Gujarat, I found bonded labourers working in stone quarries and on the construction of roads and canals. In the towns, too, I encountered such workers in diamond-cutting ateliers and other industrial workshops held captive in unfree employment conditions by their employers.[9] By way of these examples, I wish to make it clear that debt bondage is: (i) not a remnant of an earlier form of servitude; (ii) has expanded to such a scale in both the rural and urban economies that it is as widespread, or even more prevalent, than the state of unfreedom in which farm labourers used to live; and (iii) frequently, though not always, entails a modality of employment that requires labourers to migrate away from their homes. Lastly, I have no reason at all to believe that the sites of my research are exceptional in this respect. There is no lack of evidence to show that the employment regimes I have described are typical of labour systems in the lower circuits of the economy throughout South Asia.

---

[9] J. Breman, *Footloose Labour: Working in India's Informal Economy*, Cambridge: Cambridge University Press, 1996.

Is this system, in fact, fundamentally different to the form of agrarian servitude that characterized the relationship between landlords and the landless in the pre-capitalist era, both in south Gujarat and elsewhere on the subcontinent? After all, the subordination of the farm servant to his master was also based on the debt into which he entered at the start of his employ. Just as the hali was not forced to work but entered into the arrangement voluntarily, the land-poor and landless, driven by their need to survive, have no option but to sell their unused or underutilized labour power in advance. By entering into a debt that can run up to 10,000 rupees or more, they have no other choice than to surrender their freedom. Furthermore, they do so in the knowledge that they are consenting to terms of employment that allow them no say at all in the volume, nature, or manner of the work they will be expected to perform or what they will earn from their efforts. In an interesting argument, Mohapatra interpreted cause and effect in the opposite direction.[10] In his view, the driving factor in the pre-capitalist agrarian system was a shortage of labour. An underclass excluded from access to land was prepared to work for the landowners in exchange for a guarantee of survival. Subsequent forms of bondage, in Mohapatra's interpretation, arose when labour became less scarce as a result of population growth and its strong bargaining power initially turned into vulnerability. What had previously been acknowledged as a right to a basic living standard, increasingly, took on the character of a debt relationship, a decisive shift that the colonial authorities backed up by imposing sanctions when indebted workers refused to do what they had committed themselves to on receipt of the earnest money.

Present-day employers are prepared to enter into an agreement with a 'loan' in the certain knowledge that that they can set the price of labour unilaterally, usually at the lowest possible level and without having to account for it in advance, and can subject their catch of men, women, and children to a rhythm of production that yields the highest profits. Like the former masters of the halis, today's employers also have far-reaching powers over their workforce by binding them through debt. Those powers remain intact even when the debt is paid off and is converted into credit by the employers' refusal to pay the accumulating

[10] Prabhu P. Mohapatra, 'From Contract to Status? Or How Law Shaped Labour Relations in Colonial India, 1780–1880', in J. Breman, Isabelle Guérin, and Aseem Prakash (eds), *India's Unfree Workforce: Of Bondage Old and New*, New Delhi: Oxford University Press, 2009, pp. 96–125.

balance of wages while they continue to require the labour power they have laid claim to. The similarity I identify between the situation then and now is strengthened by the fact that servitude is deeply embedded in a milieu that is exposed to economic vulnerability and social deprivation. There is a demonstrable link between debt bondage and origins in the lowest castes, tribal communities, and religious minorities.

In my view, all reservations about the distinction between practices of servitude in the past and present do not change the fact that there has been a fundamental change. The debt bondage typical of the current capitalist mode of production strongly displays the characteristics of an employment relationship in which other than economic dimensions are largely or completely absent. The employer is not interested in gaining in power or raising his status, nor is he obliged to guarantee that his employees can meet their basic needs, irrespective of how long the employment contract lasts. He lays claim to their labour power and that, not a need to act as a patron, is why he is willing to pay an advance. Between the employer and the debt-bonded labourers, there is often an intermediary who has an identity similar to the labourers he recruits and who is expected to act as a gang boss in the production process, but who will—like his employer—do no more than lay claim to the labour output of his gang. The employment contract contains none of the social and cultural aspects that gave the relationship between bonded farm servants and their masters a much more encompassing quality. This reduction to a labour commodity, pure and simple, is also apparent from the exact specification of who falls under the contract. In addition to those to whom the agreement first applies, usually a man, the amount of earnest money increases if his wife and children are also ready and willing to work. This means, in effect, that the man can demand a higher advance by expanding his own bondage to include the members of his household. A second significant difference is that employment contracts are now valid for a limited time. Especially in the case of seasonal migration, the lifelong attachment that was characteristic of traditional agrarian bondage, often passing on from generation to generation, is lacking. I am inclined to attribute the shorter duration of employment contracts in the practices of neo-bondage to the unwillingness of employers to hire labour any longer than is strictly necessary. The regular replenishment of the workforce is in any case not motivated by any voluntary limitation of the employers' span of control. Workers are always hired and fired where, when, and to the extent that the material benefits exceed the costs.

By limiting the advance paid to prospective employees, employers try to protect themselves against the risk of default on the part of the former. For their part, the labourers attempt to restrict the size of the debt they enter into. They know full well that bondage reduces the value of their labour power and means that they have no say in the terms of their employment. They are also aware that the lack of freedom inherent in debt bondage reduces their self-respect and imposes on them a behaviour of subordination that is incompatible with their desire to live and work in freedom. The acceptance of earnest money can be caused by a permanent inability to meet the household's basic needs, earn sufficient income, or find enough work. The need to capitalize on their labour power in advance, however, may also stem from the lack of alternatives to raise money for covering the costs of life-cycle events like births, deaths, and marriages; to build a house; or to pay for medical treatment. In such cases, bondage offers a solution in exchange for a temporary deprivation of freedom. This variability is one reason why it is difficult to quantify the volume of the workforce exposed to debt bondage every now and then.

## THE MAGNITUDE OF UNFREE LABOUR AND THE HALF-HEARTED ATTEMPTS TO END DEBT BONDAGE

Various methods have been applied to specify criteria helpful in the definition of unfree labour practices. A ruling by the Supreme Court in India some years ago stated that not paying the statutory minimum wage could be seen as evidence of bondage. That is, however, possibly an overly rigorous yardstick and produces unreliable results. Deviating from the statutory minimum wage does not necessarily mean that workers are entrapped in a state of bondage. Providing estimates of debt bondage on the basis of case studies in various branches of economic activity and their regional spread may be a very laborious method of gathering factual evidence but is undoubtedly more accurate. A superficial inventory of workers involved in a debt-based employment relationship shows that it is indeed a standing practice in many sectors of the economy. First and foremost, of course, in agriculture. The number of farm labourers who are employed throughout the year by substantial landowners has rapidly declined in the past decades, but agro-industrial enterprises make widespread use of indebted labour for a wide range of operations, especially during the harvest. In south Gujarat, this is largely to cut sugarcane, but bonded labour is used all over rural South Asia to pick cotton, harvest and process tobacco, in rice milling plants, on tea estates, and other plantations.[11] Debt bondage in the forestry and fishing sectors is also widespread but difficult to identify. Since the end of the 1970s, the rural economy has undergone a process of diversification accompanied by new employment opportunities, often on the basis of debt bondage. That applies in the case of manufacturing industries, which are almost without exception organized on informal lines, such as brick kilns and stone quarries, mining, road construction and repair, digging irrigation canals, laying pipelines, and other infrastructural projects.

Forms of neo-bondage also occur in the urban informal sector on a large scale, in diamond cutting and polishing, processing gems, making bangles, glass blowing, fabrication of cloth, garment manufacture, embroidery, carpet weaving, the manufacture of incense sticks and matches, producing packaging materials and toys, etc. A host of service providers fall into the category of bonded labour, such as street vendors who are indebted to their suppliers, and a wide-ranging category of cleaners and domestic servants, who are, for the same reason, not free to change their employ. Often, but by no means always, bonded labourers are seasonal migrants who are engaged for a season or an unspecified period. Their workplace is sometimes a commercial premise, perhaps in the open air, but in other cases, they work at home. A wide variety of documents illustrate the existence of practices of bondage in all these branches of economic activity. The distribution of gender and age groups varies from sector to sector. Sometimes an employment contract will apply to all the members of a household who are able to work, but at others, it applies specifically to a man, woman, or child. Taking all variations in degree and duration into account, I estimate that not less than 10 per cent of the working population in the informal sector of the urban and rural economy in India, which totalled 395 million people in 2005,[12] is employed on terms that amount to debt bondage. Of course, the number of people in the whole of South Asia working in a state of temporary or permanent debt bondage is far higher than the figure I have taken as an estimate for India—about 40 million men, women, and children. In the absence of reasonably reliable statistics on the volume, sector-wise distribution, and, especially, the occupations and

[11] Breman *et al.*, *India's Unfree Workforce*.
[12] Government of India (GoI), National Commission for Enterprises in the Unorganized Sector (NCEUS), *Report on Conditions of Work and Promotion of Livelihoods in the Unorganised Sector*, New Delhi: Academic Foundation, 2008, pp. 3–4.

mode of employment of the economically active population in Pakistan, Nepal, and Bangladesh, my estimate for the subcontinent as a whole must remain incomplete.

The employment of unfree labour is not permitted and, as signatories to the ILO conventions, the governments of South Asia have committed themselves to take action to prevent or end it. The freedom to choose where, when, and for whom to work was, in fact, already included in the Indian constitution, but the article was never effectively implemented. Partly as the result of international pressure, India introduced the Bonded Labour System (Abolition) Act in 1976. In 1992, Pakistan announced introduction of the same law, and Nepal followed suit in 2000 with a ban on the kamaiya system. Despite the sanctions linked to these statutory provisions—including redemption of the debt—there is no official monitoring to ensure compliance. Registration by the authorities is not systematic, resulting in records that seriously underestimate the extent of unfree labour practices. A Director-General of the Indian Ministry of Labour has stated that the number of bonded labourers in the years before the turn of the century was restricted to a few thousand and that, in the years since, that number has fallen to not more than a few hundred. A different department of the same ministry, however, claimed that, between 1996 and 2006, 286,000 bonded labourers had been identified in the various states of the union, of whom 266,000 were duly rehabilitated. Again, a study commissioned by the Supreme Court in 1995 reported that, in the state of Tamil Nadu alone, there were a million bonded labourers. These figures are all exemplary in the extent of their randomness. The only conclusion that can be drawn from them is that official bodies are extremely reluctant or even simply not prepared to investigate the true scale of bonded labour, even approximately. The National Commission for Enterprises in the Unorganized Sector (NCEUS), to which I have referred earlier, summarizes the lack of reliable information in the following terms:

No credible estimate of the magnitude of bonded labour is yet available. In any case, the Commission views the problem as a huge one in view of the overwhelming empirical evidence arising from a number of studies and surveys. Officials have tended to underplay the incidence of bonded labour. In fact, it is almost an non-existent problem if one takes the reported figures of bonded labour seriously.[13]

---

[13] Ibid., p. 108.

Before considering the question of which stakeholders other than government agencies exercise influence on the prevalence and abolition of unfree labour practices or, alternately, benefit from their preservation, I would first like to devote attention to the striking ineffectiveness of repeated bans on debt-based bondage. In the first place, there is the point-blank denial that the problem even exists. A good example of this evasive attitude was the refusal of the Bombay provincial government in 1948 to implement the recommendation of an official committee of investigation to abolish the hali system in Gujarat. The ministers responsible at the time, Morarji Desai—who would later become Prime Minister of India—and Gulzarilal Nanda—who later in his career officiated as President of India—promulgated that since the system of bonded labour had never been legally recognized, it could not be declared illegal.[14] Another reason for not taking any official action is the lack of insight in government circles into the structure and dynamics of the informal sector. The 1976 law banning unfree labour incorrectly assumed that debt bondage was restricted to the agricultural economy. The ban was based on the assumption that the form of servitude that formerly tied landless and their landlords was still in existence. This was a misperception that completely ignored the practices that I have referred to as neo-bondage, within and beyond the agricultural sector and in both town and countryside.

The last reason for the far-reaching official indifference, expressed in benign disregard, is the retreat of the government from meddling in the economy and from abandoning its role as arbiter in ensuring fair and just consideration of the interests of both employers and employees. At the end of the twentieth century, neo-liberal ideology seized the upper hand, leaving no space for any other doctrine than that which preached non-intervention and the undiluted sway of the free market. The tripartite structure which had been the backbone of labour legislation disappeared, to be replaced by negotiations between direct stakeholders, with the mode of employment left to the working of supply and demand. The informalization of the economy, which developed at ever-increasing speed, was accompanied by the repealing or sidelining of laws designed to protect labour against exploitation. These included doing away with the Minimum Wage Act, which prescribed the mandatory payment of a piece rate or time-based wage; the Contract of Labour (Abolition) Act,

<hr />

[14] Breman, *Labour Bondage in West India*, pp. 174–5.

which called for casual labourers to be given permanent employment contracts; and the Interstate Migration Act, under which jobbers had to register themselves to prevent abuses in the recruitment of migrants and their transport to far-off sites of work. Compliance with these laws had been reasonably lax from the beginning, but towards the end of the twentieth century, the machinery was also lacking for effective monitoring. The labour inspectorates in both India and Pakistan received instructions to stop inspecting and bothering employers by checking on their labour practices. In fact, the labour inspectors did not use the legislation to prosecute negligent employers, but only to threaten them. For example, instead of imposing a fine on the owners of brick kilns and sue them for back pay, they would take a lower amount in hush money, which they considered a bonus on top of their salaries. The workers were aware of this widespread corruption among government officials, but assumed—correctly—that with the abolition of laws intended to offer them protection, they were now entirely at the mercy of their employers. That explains why, when brick makers at the outskirts of Lahore went on strike in January 2008, their demands for higher wages were accompanied by a call for the minister responsible to instruct the labour inspectors to resume their duties. At the end of the march during which the strikers chanted these demands, the police broke up the demonstration with batons under the pretext of restoring peace and order.

The assumption that the government has stopped interfering in the economy must be qualified in the sense that the support and protection of the state for capital has increased rather than decreased. One aspect of the state bias in interest mediation that has come about is that the authorities neglect to track down and identify employers in the lowest circuits of the informal sector economy who use bondage to minimize the costs of labour, and in such a way that their workers are left with no space to resist their captivity. In recent years, there has been a growing awareness in political and policy circles that debt bondage is a mode of employment that occurs on a large scale and in many branches of industry. The longstanding tendency to see it as a remnant of the traditional relationship between landowners and the landless in the agricultural sector is no longer tenable. The recent ILO report on unfree labour observes that it has at least become possible to discuss the problem, and that the taboo that prevented it from receiving attention from official agencies has been removed. Indicative of this reappraisal is a recent memorandum in which a head of department within the

Indian Ministry of Labour sets out the essence of bonded labour in the following points:

1. The character of bonded labour in India was evolving and changing over time and was no longer characterized as a practice affecting the agriculture sector alone.
2. Monetary advances to employees by employers, earlier the principal root of debt bondage, now existed in various alternative monetary arrangements. However, the major characteristic of debt bondage remained the absence of regular payment by an employer to an employee at market value for provided labour and services. In some instances, workers received no remuneration at all.
3. Victims of debt bondage often belonged to vulnerable and marginalized groups (scheduled caste/scheduled tribe [SC/ST]), who were not able to ascertain their rights, whether knowingly or unknowingly, and the lack of available alternative formal credit facilities.
4. The role of intermediaries (middlemen) hiring labour for the principal employer was complicating matters and always violating the principles of international labour standards that such services should be provided free of cost to workers.
5. Definitional problems compounded by a number of judgments by the Supreme Court of India in an attempt to make the act more effective.
6. Weak implementation in states in relation to the complicated enforcement system of the act and its rules, often exacting action by an already overburdened district administration.

In summary, the memorandum (undated and not signed)[15] closes by commenting that, while the socio-cultural connotation attached to unfree labour has changed radically, poverty and the conditions that lead to impoverishment must be identified as the main causes of bondage. I heartily endorse this promising conclusion. It is, however, not followed up with a concrete programme of action. The memorandum refers to the need to strengthen the economic status and social power of the household, without stating how this is to be achieved. Labourers who are freed from bondage are, however, pledged a higher amount for their rehabilitation (5,000 rupees rather than the 1,000 rupees they now receive) and a temporary unemployment benefit until they have found other waged

---

[15] GoI, *Bonded Labour: Report of the Sub-Group on Child Labour and Bonded Labour*, New Delhi: Ministry of Labour, 2009.

work or turn to self-employment in line with the latest policy fashion. A national fund is also to be set up to enable these measures to be better implemented. I have two critical comments on these recommendations. First, public funds should not be used to buy the freedom of labourers from employers who use debt bondage to maximize their profits. Second, the obligation to find other, better-paid work cannot simply be imposed on people who are forced by excessive poverty to work and live in a state of persistent and recurring unfreedom.

## INTERVENTION NECESSARY TO END BONDED LABOUR

In answer to the question how to phase out bonded labour, I distinguish two complementary forms of intervention, one based on direct action and the other more indirect. First, government intervention in the labour system by introducing a ban on the kind of neo-bondage described earlier, making employers who violate the ban punishable by law, and ensuring strict enforcement, would undoubtedly achieve the intended goal in a reasonably short time span. At the same time, it should be clear that this direct approach has little or no chance of success. Across the board, the government continually fails to impose any restraints on the exploitation and subjugation in which the most vulnerable segment of the working population, the underpaid and uneducated mass at the broad base of the informal sector, is forced to live. This refusal is founded on the assumption that economic growth stands or falls with keeping faith or not in the cheap labour policy. This is also why a series of labour laws dating back to the 1960s and 1970s were only enforced half-heartedly, if at all, and, during a later phase of even greater reticence, were repealed or suspended until further notice. In the light of this dismal record, it is very unlikely that the government would enforce a ban on debt bondage.

The regional office of the ILO has argued for an approach based on tripartite consultations between employees, employers, and official agencies. Reports on pilot projects at the district level in South India describe them as reasonably successful, but my hunch is that more objective evaluation by non-stakeholders might not confirm the claim that, if the current course is pursued, the end of debt bondage is in sight. My reservations are based, in the first place, on the lack of sufficient representation from the bonded labourers' own milieu—a segment that is exposed to discrimination and is hardly, if at all, capable of defend-ing its interests through collective action. The district administration is involved in the Joint Action Forum or Vigilance Committees that have been set up in a way that is reminiscent of the arbitration role that the government used to play in the past. But these committees prove only to exist on paper and their members hardly or never meet to discuss what should be or has been done.[16] The argument that the local government apparatus is too overburdened to be able to fulfil this extra task adequately conceals the real reason for refusing to intervene: official indifference or downright sabotage of efforts to put a stop to the social deprivation and subordination generated by this labour modality. But, in my view, the failure of what is presented as a concerted effort by all stakeholders is largely the result of the unwillingness of employers to cooperate voluntarily with regulations that would deny them the right to employ labour in a state of servitude. Their determination to maintain this system is based on the way they use it not only to save on labour costs, but also to have at their disposal a workforce that they can deploy and exploit as they see fit. They succeed in their endeavour to recruit a cheap and pliable workforce by relying on the mediation of agents who operate as jobbers and gang bosses. Agreeing to an employment relationship in which the freedom of the worker takes priority would inevitably lead to a rise in the price of labour. Achieving a shift in the balance between the greatest possible profit for the employer and the costs of a decent standard of living for his workforce will not come easily. Any strategy aimed at liberating labour that relies on the approval of those who minimize their costs of production by tying down the workers they contract is doomed to end up in a fiasco.

The reluctance of the South Asian policymakers to take resolute action against practices of unfree labour, in combination with the arbitrary nature and negligible impact of official interventions which, given the government's international commitments, could not be ignored altogether, means that those wishing to see an end to debt bondage should place their hopes in building up pressure from civic society. In this perspective, social movements fight to emancipate labour, by doing what politicians and bureaucrats fail to do. Civic action, however, does not always take the form of unconditional support for the oppressed. Gandhian social workers, for example, campaigning both before and after independence to put a stop to the hali system in Gujarat, called on the landless proletariat to improve their lifestyles by giving up all kinds of 'bad habits' which made them appear uncivilized. From

---

[16] Breman *et al.*, *India's Unfree Workforce.*

the Gandhian viewpoint, self-improvement and reconciliation of the conflict of interests between farm servants and landowners were the only way to achieve progress. The organization, set up to improve the lives of the poor, was doomed to certain failure from the very beginning because of this patronizing attitude.[17]

At the other end of the spectrum, we find activists who are not afraid to confront employers, but who do this in such a way that their success is short-lived and may even turn out to defeat the very objective of their intervention. By this, I mean the 'rescue and release' operations which focus on liberating unfree labourers from their sites of work. Raids are carried out on a rural brick kiln or an urban workshop to free men, women, and children from the confinement in which they are held. The raids and their outcomes are filmed in a dramatic attempt to mobilize public empathy with the victims. My criticism of this method is, first, that it suggests that the victims are forced to work under the threat of physical violence. With a few exceptions, this assumption is false and rests on the misconception that debt bondage is imposed by the employer, without the worker consenting to it. My second reservation is more essential: the impact the raids intend to achieve is only short term. The social activists who carry them out do not have the capability to extend their support to genuine rehabilitation, that is, to offer the people they have released prospects of a better life. Without that, the liberation will be only temporary and a fall back into servitude with the same or another employer inevitable. The concrete involvement of non-governmental organizations is exceptionally useful and desirable as long as their willingness to take action is accompanied by recognition of the limits to what they can achieve, both in terms of impact and consequences. In my view, direct action aimed at putting a stop to debt bondage comes up against a reluctant and resistant government, downright opposition from employers, the inadequate reach of civil society organizations, and a lack of collective assertion among the segment of the working population exposed to debt bondage. This conclusion does not mean that all civic efforts to solve the problem are doomed to failure. However, when severe poverty is the main cause of people's need to sell their labour power in advance and, therefore, enter into an employment contract that curtails their freedom of movement for a longer or shorter period, action aimed at alleviating poverty is a necessary detour that leads to the ultimate goal.

[17] Breman, *Labour Bondage in West India*.

The choice for indirect action brings me to examine a number of options which, to remain realistic, link up with existing practices of policy implementation. Straightaway, I want to reject one approach that enjoys considerable support: preventing or solving debt bondage by providing microcredit. The current popularity of this form of intervention in policy circles seems to be founded on the idea that the poor can overcome their indigence themselves by using the high-interest loans extended to them to raise the yield from their labour. However, workers who accept an advance which they pay off with their labour do so because they lack wherewithal. They cannot increase their deficient income with the aid of a loan, nor can they provide any collateral for repayment, one of the conditions for receiving microcredit, as they simply have nothing to offer. Investing in improving their lives brings with it an unacceptably high risk, and it is even impossible to blame them if do not meet their side of the bargain. The dire need in which they live leaves them no other choice than to use the money they eventually have been granted as a loan for instant consumption rather than production-related expenditure. To back up my viewpoint that microcredit does not offer a solution to debt bondage, I quote from the following report which refer to the situation in South India: 'The bonded and extreme poor cannot benefit only from loan based schemes ... improving livelihoods in less favoured areas, and among extreme poor households is the only long term way out of bondage';[18] and in the same vein, Rajasekhar and Suchitra express themselves with equal clarity:

Income-Generating Activities (i.e. sponsored by micro-credit programmes) should not be promoted where they are unlikely to be viable, that is, until a household can meet most of its basic household consumption needs without dependence on borrowing of any sort, it should not be forced to take up any Income-Generating Activities.[19]

Greater success can be expected from a programme aimed at improving the lives of the rural land-poor and landless by generating employment through public works. The programme that set out to do so got off to

[18] S. Premchander, V. Prameela, and M. Chidambaranathan, 'Prevention and Elimination of Bonded Labour: The Potential and Limits of Microfinance-Led Approaches', Delhi, July 2008, p. 5.

[19] D. Rajasekhar and J.Y. Suchitra, 'Micro-Finance Programmes and Vulnerability to Debt Bondage', in Gopal K. Kadekodi and Brinda Vishwanathan (eds), *Agricultural Development, Rural Institutions, and Economic Policy: Essays for A. Vaidyanathan*, New Delhi: Oxford University Press, 2009, p. 53.

a slow and rather haphazard launch, but has been expanded recently, with the growing realization that it would create a vote bank for the Congress party, which then gave its blessing for a nation-wide scheme. Each state is obliged to provide employment to at least one member of the eligible households for at least two months a year and at the statutory minimum wage. The National Rural Employment Guarantee Act (NREGA), which was introduced in 2006, followed the *modus operandi* of the Government of Maharashtra, which already decided as early as 1976 to implement public works to compensate for the widespread lack of employment during the lean months in the agrarian cycle. Men and women were given the opportunity to work in small-scale earthmoving projects, such as road repairs, widening irrigation canals, and building check dams, enabling them to earn an income and upgrade to physical infrastructure. On the basis of this precedent, the central government has adopted the same method of handing over total responsibility—from the choice of projects to their execution and completion—to authorities operating below district level. The strategy aims to increase transparency from below and involve the targeted workforce in the decision-making process and daily progress of the project. It also intended to make it more difficult for low-ranking civil servants, sub-contractors, politicians, and other local VIPs to engage in the wide variety of malpractices that seem inherent in pro-poor interventions. That objective has only been marginally successful and there is no dearth of reports pointing to widespread fraud and corruption in the implementation of this national programme.

One special point for attention is the hope that the seasonal migration that often accompanies debt bondage will decline as a consequence of the public works now being undertaken in the rural hinterlands of India. There are indeed indications that fewer people are migrating from Bihar to Punjab. However, the expectation that the same would happen in Maharashtra has not yet materialized. The exodus of an army of cane cutters at the start of the dry season from the villages in the western districts of the state to the plain of south Gujarat seems not to have tapered off so far. The source on which I base this tentative conclusion reports that one important reason is the disinterest of the authorities at the local level, with the consequence that the target group turns its back on joining the land army.

We notice that political as well as bureaucratic will is absent in the new scheme under the guidelines of the NREGA. The poor had become weary of the scheme because of lack of regularity and assurance of wages and where erring officials were not punished and nor was unemployment allowance granted to any labourer who was not provided with work. Seasonal migration has been on the rise as a result of this situation.[20]

That this is not an exceptional case can be seen from the recent complaint of the Governor of the newly formed state of Jharkhand, where the representative of the central government had to take charge after a fall-out between the ruling political parties. During my recent visit to the area to collect more information on practices of bonded labour, the governor stated in a press release that he was being forced to send half of the budget received for the NREGA back to Delhi because there was insufficient administrative and political willingness to implement a large-scale programme of public works. To this I would add that indifference, sometimes bordering on hostility, is prevalent throughout the whole of South Asia when it comes to fighting poverty, and not only at the top of the political and civil service apparatus. In other publications, I have drawn attention to the leaking away of funds and benefits aimed at curbing discrimination and indigence. In addition to the illegal skimming off of funds, there is also—and perhaps even especially—at local level, systematic obstruction and sabotage of schemes aimed at promoting a measure of economic, social, and political equality. This resistance from a close-knit coalition of established interests wishing to preserve the hierarchical social structure must be taken into account in efforts to put a stop to debt bondage. In the case of the NREGA, it is still too early to draw up the balance of its impact. Recognizing the need to bring about improvement in the extremely unstable existence of those living at the foot of the economy by creating employment means that high priority must be given to further close monitoring of the successes and failures of this important initiative.

The same applies to another intervention, the introduction of a package of elementary social care arrangements. This concerns the Social Security Bill, enacted at the end of 2008, which aims to alleviate the vulnerability inherent in the lives of a large segment of the working population in India that is faced with too little work for an inadequate wage. As I explained earlier, setbacks of all kinds—fragile health, acute illness, pregnancy and, more generally, temporary or permanent loss of labour power—are one of the main causes of debt bondage. Under

---

[20] C. Datar, 'Failure of National Rural Employment Guarantee Scheme in Maharashtra', *Economic and Political Weekly*, vol. 42, no. 34, 25 August 2007, p. 3547.

the new law, although the loss of income remains uncompensated, the costs of illness, an accident, or pregnancy are insured. The right to an old age pension if children are unable to provide support means that concerns for the future—the fear of a fall in income once one's labour power has been exhausted—are rendered less acute. To be sure, political opposition at the highest level led to the original proposals being diluted and being incorporated in a bill. The refusal to set up a central fund and locate responsibility for implementing the act at national level means that the individual states have the freedom to implement the plan on the basis of existing schemes for providing social care. The wide variety between different parts of the country in this respect will not make it easy to monitor the working and impact of what is intended as a basic packet of social security. But again, close monitoring is necessary to determine the effectiveness of this intervention for preventing and phasing out debt bondage.

The current campaign for the introduction of a Food Security Act can also be seen as an example of a strategy aimed at safeguarding basic needs. The argument behind this initiative is founded on the notion that food security is a basic right for all. On the world rankings for hunger, India is in a low ninety-fourth place. South Asia accounts for around a third of all the people in the world living in hunger. A persistent shortage of food of sufficient quantity and quality is one of the outstanding indications of poverty. That applies even more to the state of extreme poverty that accompanies debt bondage. Social recognition of the right to a dignified existence, and its expression in political and administrative terms, incorporates not only the right to a sufficient daily intake of food but also to decent shelter. In comparison with the basic needs described earlier, this fundamental right has received preciously little attention. Going around the slums of the large cities, and a tour of the colonies in which the poor find their habitat in the countryside, testifies to the urgent need to ensure that people have adequate and proper space to live. Building such accommodation would be a perfect opportunity for a large-scale programme of public works. The right to a homestead, a plot of land with a house, reduces the risk of falling into and becoming stuck in a state of debt bondage.

Calls for the recognition of basic rights should further include release from the stigma of illiteracy. That would end the debt bondage in which an enormous mass of children are put to waged work, individually or as 'helpers' for their parents, in rural or urban worksites, in the open air or under cover, essentially confined for a season or for an unlimited period. Child labour is widespread throughout the whole of South Asia, although school attendance has risen strongly in the past quarter of a century. That progress deserves attention and has meant, for example, that the number of children not attending school in India fell from 13.3 million in 1993–4 to 8.6 million in 2004–5.[21] The improvement has been made possible by both growing public care provision and increased awareness among parents that education offers their children a real chance of leading better lives. This does not, however, change the fact that children who fall prey to debt bondage not only have no opportunity to attend school but are predestined to spend their adult lives in the extreme poverty of the milieu from which they hail.

The common denominator in all the interventions discussed is that they are based on an indirect approach to the problem of debt bondage. The policy recommendations made here are founded on the assumption that direct action to liberate unfree labour will meet with such resistance and unwillingness to act that, without actually abandoning this strategy entirely, it is not advisable to rely on it alone or even primarily. My argument to follow, in general terms, a course of indirect action is based on the principle that the main reason why the land-poor and landless have no other choice than to sell their labour in advance is excessive poverty. Their acute and severe lack of basic security compels them to enter into an agreement that robs them of their freedom of action temporarily or permanently, and of a say in the terms of their employment and the income they receive from it. As a consequence, they find themselves caught up in a spiral of poverty with little chance of escaping. Does this mean that my notion of combating debt bondage essentially boils down to efforts to improve the lives of the poor in general? Only to a certain extent, as the approach I propose assumes a genuine difference in the nature, duration, and especially, the intensity of deprivation. The interventions I advocate do not, therefore, cover the whole spectrum of poverty alleviation but focus on the numerous people who are exposed to it in its most extreme form. What I have in mind is establishing a floor of basic social rights to ensure that indigence does not reach a level below which it is no longer possible to lead a dignified human existence. Related to this is the acknowledgment that everyone should enjoy these entitlements and that civic society has a duty to ensure that economic growth is inclusive.

---

[21] GoI, *Report on Conditions of Work and Promotion of Livelihoods in the Unorganised Sector*, p. 130.

Two more rights have to be added to the rights already mentioned (to gainful work, social security, food security, shelter, and schooling): the much earlier recognized right to a minimum wage and to terms of employment that guarantee a decent use of labour. Establishing such a floor of rights should offer protection against sliding down into a state of exclusion and should correspond to what the NCEUS refers to in its report as a minimum package.

Such a conclusion points to the need for laying down, at the least, a minimum standard for conditions of work, a national floor below which no trade or occupation based minimum wage should be set and a minimum package of social security. Given the federal character of the polity, these minimum standards should be applicable to the whole country backed by national legislation.[22]

If I do not doubt the ultimate emancipation of labour, it is because I discern a growing assertion at the foot of the economy. When I take as my point of departure the land-poor and landless milieu in south Gujarat that has been my field of study close to half a century, I see no attitudes of lethargy and even less so, any internalization of subordination with respect to employers or the better-off social classes in general. Nor do those who spend their working lives in debt bondage give the impression of quietly accepting their fate. Docility is certainly not a marked feature of their behaviour. The state of dependency in which they live is the reason why they are unable to escape their servitude. But they will respond alertly and effectively to any initiative from outside to expand their narrow room for manoeuvre. Living in servitude erodes their self-respect and the desire to dignify their lives does not need to be imbued from outside.

As opposed to the establishment and recognition of a floor of rights that guarantee inclusion in the social order, it is also possible to identify the contours of a lower limit. Exclusion results in such an advanced degree of deprivation that it not only renders granting the right to a dignified human existence impossible but also completely precludes recognition of any claim to such a right. If that is the case, a point has been reached at which a state of advanced inequality, as is inherent to practices of debt bondage, results in systematic abuse of human rights. That occurs when the means of subsistence in a country are distributed extremely unevenly between its citizens. The slightest attempt to

---

[22] NCEUS, *Report on Conditions of Work and Promotion of Livelihoods in the Unorganised Sector*, p. 48.

change that situation is met with determined resistance by those who have established themselves as masters of those resources. They use their monopoly of power and authority to prevent redistribution and regard any demand to that effect as illegal and subversive. In this description, it is possible to recognize the regime that has led to the unbridled dominance of the landlords in rural Pakistan, sometimes in collaboration with the warlords, sometimes sharing power in turn. This is an alliance that upholds the exclusion of the land-poor and landless underclasses in defence of its own interests. The servitude in which sharecroppers and farm labourers are forced to work is accompanied by a lack of political space that leaves little opportunity to mobilize the property-less mass in the struggle for social justice and equality. That this is not a completely hopeless exercise can be seen from the abolition of the kamaiya system in Nepal by recognizing sharecroppers as owners of the land they farmed. In Sindh, the landlords are making no moves at all to transfer ownership of their farmland to their *haris*. Yet it is here, in this transfer of ownership, that the solution lies to the agrarian bondage that emerged only recently, with the transition to a capitalist mode of production. Going by a news item that I read while completing this essay, published in the Karachi edition of *Dawn* on 21 January 2010, not much seems to have changed in Sindh.

Umerkot, 20 January: As many as 66 bonded labourers, including children and women, were recovered in police raids on two agricultural farms near here on Wednesday. The Umerkot police raided the farm of landlord Allah Rakhio Rajar near Berchhan and recovered 32 bonded labourers, including eight women and 17 children. Jumo Bheel had submitted an application in the district and sessions court, stating that Rajar had made his relatives and other peasants bonded labourers. The district and sessions judge ordered the police to recover the bonded labourers. The police raided the farm and recovered the bonded labourers. They were produced in the court, where they were set at liberty after recording their statements. The freed bonded labourers told *Dawn* that their accounts were manipulated, their movement was restricted and they were not allowed to visit their relatives even for attending a marriage or condoling a death. Meanwhile, the Chhor police in a raid on the farm of landlord Lal Mohammad Soomro recovered 34 bonded labourers.

*Dawn*, Karachi edition, 21 January 2010

Certainly, these agricultural workers were set free by the police but rather than being inspired by a concern for the plight of haris—no mention is made if and how this lot is going to be rehabilitated—it is more likely that the raid was carried out because of political strife between local landlords. The route to emancipation seems longer and more difficult in Pakistan than elsewhere in South Asia, but this must not be an excuse for not striving to achieve it.

# 12
# Myths of the Global Safety Net*

Media reports on the economic meltdown have mainly concentrated on the impact of the crisis on the rich nations, with little concern for the mass of the population living in what used to be called the Third World. The current view seems to be that the setbacks in these 'emerging economies' may be less severe than expected. China's and India's high growth rates have slackened, but the predicted slump has not materialized. This line of thought, however, analyses only the effects of the crisis on countries as a whole, masking its differential impact across social classes. If one considers income distribution, and not just macro-calculations of gross domestic product (GDP), the global downturn has taken a disproportionately higher toll on the most vulnerable sectors: the huge armies of the poorly paid, undereducated, resourceless workers that constitute the overcrowded lower depths of the world economy.

To the extent that a major segment of the globalized workforce is incorporated into the production process, it is as informal labour, characterized by casualized and fluctuating employment and piece rates, whether working at home, in sweatshops, or on their own account in the open air; and in the absence of any contractual or labour rights, or collective organization. In a haphazard fashion, still little understood, work of this nature has come to predominate within the global labour force at large. The International Labour Organization (ILO) estimates that informal workers comprise over half the workforce in Latin

* Originally published as 'Myths of the Global Safety Net', *New Left Review*, no. 59, September–October 2009, pp. 1–8.

America, over 70 per cent in sub-Saharan Africa, and over 80 per cent in India; an Indian government report suggests a figure of more than 90 per cent.[1] Cut loose from their original social moorings, the majority remain stuck in the vast shanty towns ringing city outskirts across the global South.

Recently, however, the life of street hawkers in Cairo, tortilla vendors of Mexico City, *rickshaw* drivers in Kolkata, or scrap mongers of Jakarta has been cast in a much rosier light. The informal sector, according to the *Wall Street Journal (WSJ)*, is 'one of the last safe havens in a darkening financial climate' and 'a critical safety net as the economic crisis spreads'.[2] Thanks to these jobs, former International Monetary Fund (IMF) Chief Economist, Simon Johnson, is quoted as saying, 'the situation in desperately poor countries isn't as bad as you'd think'.[3] On this view, an admirable spirit of self-reliance enables people to survive in the underground circuits of the economy, unencumbered by the tax and benefit systems of the 'formal sector'. These streetwise operators are able to get by without expensive social provisions or unemployment benefit. World Bank economist, W.F. Maloney, assures the *WSJ* that the informal sector 'will absorb a lot of people and offer them a source of income' over the next year.[4]

The *WSJ* draws its examples from Ahmedabad, the former mill city in Gujarat where I conducted fieldwork in the 1990s. Here, in the Manek Chowk market—'a row of derelict stalls', where 'vendors peddle everything from beans to brass pots as monkeys scramble overhead'—Surajben Babubhai Patni sells tomatoes, corn, and nuts from a makeshift shelter: 'She makes as much as 250 rupees a day, or about $5, but it's enough to feed her household of nine, including her son, who recently lost his job as a diamond polisher.'[5] Enough: really? Five dollars for nine people is less than half the amount the World Bank sets as the benchmark above extreme poverty: one dollar per capita per day. Landless

---

[1] International Labour Organization (ILO), *Decent Work and the Informal Economy*, Report submitted to the 90th Session of International Labour Conference, Geneva, June 2002; National Commission for Enterprises in the Unorganized Sector (NCEUS), *Report on the Conditions of Work and Promotion of Livelihoods in the Unorganised Sector,* New Delhi: Academic Foundation, 2008.

[2] Patrick Barta, 'Global Economics: The Rise of the Underground', *Wall Street Journal,* 14 March 2009.

[3] Ibid.

[4] Ibid.

[5] Ibid.

households in villages to the south of Ahmedabad have to make do with even less than that—on the days they manage to find work.[6]

Earlier in 2009, I returned to the former mill districts of the city to see how the economic crisis was affecting people there. By 2000, these former working-class neighbourhoods had already degenerated into pauperized quarters. But the situation has deteriorated markedly even since then. Take the condition of the garbage pickers—all of them women, since this is not considered to be man's work. They are now paid half of what they used to get for harvesting waste paper, rags, and plastic gleaned from the waste dumps in their daily rounds. To make up the loss, they now begin their work at 3 a.m. instead of 5 a.m., bringing along their children to provide more hands. The Self-Employed Women's Association (SEWA)—which started to organize informal sector workers in the city and has now expanded its activities across India and even beyond—reports that 'incomes have declined, days of work decreased, prices have fallen and livelihoods disappeared'.[7] Their recent newsletter presents statistics testifying to the crash in prices for the 'goods' collected on the dumps (see Table 12.1).

TABLE 12.1   Prices Paid to Ahmedabad Waste Collectors

| Items | Price in Rs/kilo April 2008 | Price in Rs/kilo Jan 2009 | Percentage decrease |
|---|---|---|---|
| Waste steel | 6 | 3 | 50 |
| Steel sheets | 10 | 5 | 50 |
| Plastic bags | 8 | 5 | 37.5 |
| Newspaper | 8 | 4 | 50 |
| Hard plastic | 15 | 7 | 53 |
| Soft plastic | 10 | 4 | 60 |
| Dry bones | 4 | 2 | 50 |
| Waste hair | 1,000 | 300 | 67 |

*Source:* Self-Employed Women's Association (SEWA), 'We the Self-Employed', SEWA electronic newsletter, No. 18, 15 May 2009.

A SEWA activist based in Ahmedabad reports on the anguish she met when visiting local members. One of these, Ranjanben Ashokbhai

[6] J. Breman, *The Poverty Regime in Village India: Half a Century of Work and Life at the Bottom of the Rural Economy in South Gujarat,* New Delhi: Oxford University Press, 2007.

[7] Self-Employed Women's Association (SEWA), 'We the Self-Employed', SEWA electronic newsletter, No. 18, 15 May 2009.

Parmar, started to cry: 'Who sent this recession! Why did they send it?' I was speechless. Her situation is very bad, her husband is sick, she has 5 children, she stays in a rented house, she has to spend on the treatment of her husband and she is the sole earner in the family, how can she meet her ends? When she goes to collect scrap she takes along her little daughter, while her husband sits at home and makes wooden ice-cream spoons, from which he can earn not more than Rs 10/- a day. In the industrial city of Surat, 120 miles south of Ahmedabad, half the informal labour force of the diamond workshops was laid off overnight at the end of 2008, with the collapse of worldwide demand for jewels. Some 200,000 diamond cutters and polishers found themselves jobless, while the rest had to contend with drastic reductions in hours and piece rates. A wave of suicides swept the dismissed workers, who—with a monthly income of little more than $140—were reputed to belong to the most skilled and highest paid ranks of the informal economy. These bitter experiences of the recession-struck informal economy in Gujarat can be repeated for region after region across India, Africa, and much of Latin America. Confronted with such misery, it is impossible to concur with the World Bank and WSJ's optimism about the sector's absorptive powers. As for their praise for the 'self-reliance' of those struggling to get by in these conditions, living in a state of constant emergency saps the energy to cope and erodes the strength to endure. To suggest that these workers constitute a 'vibrant' new class of self-employed entrepreneurs, ready to fight their way upward, is as misleading as portraying children from the *chawls* of Mumbai as slumdog millionaires.

## RURAL ROPE'S END

The second option currently being touted by the western media as a 'cushion for hard times' is a return to the countryside. As an Asian Development Bank official in Thailand recently informed the *International Herald Tribune (IHT)*, 'returning to one's traditional village in the countryside is a sort of "social safety net"'. The complacent assumption is that large numbers of rural migrants made redundant in the cities can retreat to their families' farms and be absorbed in agricultural work, until they are recalled to their urban jobs by the next pick up of the economy. The *IHT* evokes a paradisial rural hinterland in northeast Thailand.

Even in the dry season, there are still plenty of year-round crops—gourds, beans, coconuts and bananas among them—that thrive with little rainwater. Farmers raise chickens and cows, and dig fish ponds behind their homes ... Thailand's king, Bhumibol Adulyadej, has long encouraged such self-sufficiency.[8]

Similar views were published at the time of the Asian financial crisis in 1997. Then, World Bank consultants assumed that agriculture could act as a catchment reservoir for labour made redundant in other sectors, based on the notion that the army of migrants moving back and forth between the country and urban growth poles had never ceased their primary occupation. The myth persisted that Southeast Asian countries were still essentially peasant societies. These tillers of the land might go to the city to earn extra wages for cash expenditure, but if they lost their jobs, they were expected to reintegrate into the peasant economy with no difficulty. This was far from the case, as I wrote then.[9]

Returning to west Java this summer, I listened to the latest stories of men and women who had come back to the village, having lost their informal sector jobs elsewhere, and find no work here, either. Of course not: they were driven out of the village economy in the first place because of lack of land or other forms of capital. There is no family farm to fall back on. The departure of the landless and the land-poor was a flight, part of a coping strategy. Now that the members of this rural proletariat have become redundant in Jakarta or Bangkok, or as contract workers in Taiwan or Korea for that matter, they are back to square one, due to an acute and sustained lack of demand for their labour power in their place of origin. A comparable drama is taking place in China. Out of the 120–150 million migrants who made the trek from the rural interior to the rapidly growing coastal cities during the last twenty-five years, official sources report that about 10–15 million are now unemployed. For these victims of the new economy, there is no alternative but to go back 'home' to a deeply impoverished countryside.

The Asian village economy is not capable of accommodating all those who possess no means of production; nor has the urban informal sector the elasticity to absorb all those eager to drift into it. According to policymakers' notions of cross-sectoral mobility, the informal economy should swallow up the labour surplus pushed out of higher-paid jobs, enabling the displaced workforce to stick it out through income-sharing

[8] Thomas Fuller, 'In Southeast Asia, Unemployed Abandon Cities for Their Villages', *International Herald Tribune,* 28 February 2009.

[9] See J. Breman and Gunawan Wiradi, *Good Times and Bad Times in Rural Java: Socio-economic Dynamics in Two Villages Towards the End of the Twentieth Century,* Leiden: KITLV Press, 2002.

arrangements until the economic tide turned again. I have never found any evidence that such a horizontal drift has taken place. Street vendors do not turn into *becak* riders, domestic servants, or construction workers overnight. The labour market of the informal sector economy is highly fragmented; those who are laid off in their branch of activity have no alternative but to go back 'home', because staying on in the city without earnings is next to impossible. But returning to their place of origin is not a straightforward option, given the lack of space in the rural economy. Nevertheless, my informants do not simply lay the blame for their predicament on the economic meltdown. From the perspective of the world's underclasses, what looks like a conjunctural crisis is actually a structural one, the absence of regular and decent employment. The massive army of reserve labour at the bottom of the informal economy is entrapped in a permanent state of crisis which will not be lifted when the Dow Jones Index goes up again.

## NEW ECONOMIC ORDER

The transformation that took place in nineteenth century Western Europe, as land-poor and landless peasants migrated to the towns, is now being repeated on a truly global scale. But the restructuring that would create an urban–industrial order, of the sort which vastly improved the lot of the former peasants of the Northern hemisphere, has not materialized. The ex-peasants of the southern zones of our planet have failed to find secure jobs and housing on their arrival in the cities. Struggling to gain a foothold there, they have become mired for successive generations in the deprivation of the shanties, a vast reserve army of informal labour.

In the 1960s and 1970s, western policymakers viewed the informal sector as a waiting room, or temporary transit zone: newcomers could find their feet there and learn the ways of the urban labour market. Once savvy to these, they would increasingly be able to qualify for higher wages and more respectable working conditions. In fact, the trend went in the opposite direction due, in large part, to the onslaught of market-driven policies, the retreat of the state in the domain of employment, and the decisive weakening of organized labour. The small fraction that made their way to the formal sector was now accused of being a labour aristocracy, selfishly laying claim to privileges of protection and security. At the same time, the informal sector began to be heralded by the World Bank and other transnational agencies as a motor of economic growth. Flexibilization became the order of the day—in other words, dismantling of job security and a crackdown on collective bargaining. The process of informalization that has taken shape over the last twenty years saw, among other things, the end of the large-scale textile industry in South Asia. In Ahmedabad itself, more than 150,000 mill workers were laid off at a stroke. This did not mean the end of textile production in the city. Cloth is now produced in powerloom workshops by operators who work twelve-hour days, instead of eight, and at less than half the wages they received in the mill; garment manufacture has become home-based work, in which the whole family is engaged day and night. The textile workers' union has all but disappeared. Sliding down the labour hierarchy has plunged these households into a permanent state of crisis, both economic and social.

It is not only that the cost of labour at the bottom of the world economy has been scaled down to the lowest possible level, fragmentation also keeps the underemployed masses internally compartmentalized. These people are competitors in a labour market in which the supply side is now structurally larger than the—constantly fluctuating—demand for labour power. They react to this disequilibrium by trying to strengthen their ties along lines of family, region, tribe, caste, religion, or other primordial identities which preclude collective bargaining on the basis of work status and occupation. Their vulnerability is exacerbated by their enforced rootlessness: they are pushed off the land, but then pushed back onto it again, roaming around in an endless search for work and shelter.

The emergence of the early welfare state in the western hemisphere at the end of the nineteenth century has been attributed to the bourgeoisie's fear that the policy of excluding the lower ranks of society could end in the collapse of the established order.[10] The propertied part of mankind today does not seem to be frightened by the presence of a much more voluminous *classe dangereuse*. Their appropriation of ever-more wealth is the other side of the trend towards informalization, which has resulted in the growing imbalance between capital and labour. There are no signs of change of direction in this economic course. Promises of poverty reduction by global leaders are mere lip service, or photo opportunities. During his campaign, Obama would, once in a while, air his appreciation for Roosevelt's New Deal. Since

[10] Abram de Swaan, *In Care of the State: Health Care, Education and Welfare in Europe and the USA in the Modern Era*, Cambridge: Polity and New York: Oxford University Press, 1988.

his election, the idea of a broad-based social welfare scheme has been shelved without further ado. The global crisis is being tackled by a massive transfer of wealth from poor to rich. The logic suggests a return to nineteenth-century beliefs in the principle and practice of natural inequality. According to this view, it is not poverty that needs to be eradicated. The problem is the poor people themselves, who lack the ability to pull themselves up out of their misery. Handicapped by all kinds of defects, they constitute a useless residue and an unnecessary burden. How to get rid of this ballast?

# 13

# The Eventual Return of Social Darwinism*

The universal disregard of the poverty condition in which a sizable part of mankind continues to live, and the inadequacy of strategies selected to tackle this prime social question, is connected to the return of inequality as a fashionable doctrine both at the national and global level. Elaborating on the ideological push in favour of more and not less inequality, my point of departure is a recent study outlining the main tenets of social Darwinism.[1] The central proposition of Darwin's *The Origin of Species* was that the development of organisms must be seen as a struggle to survive over a period of millions of years.[2] The principle of natural selection implied continual adaptation to the surrounding environment in a way that ensured that superior species would emerge, succeeding where those which lacked the necessary qualities to survive had not. The ultimate appearance of man was proof of this progressive biological selection process. Darwin's theory represented a break in the

* Originally published as 'The Eventual Return of Social Darwinism', *Economic and Political Weekly*, vol. 39, no. 35, 2004, pp. 3869–72.

[1] Cor Hermans, *De dwaaltocht van het sociaal-darwinisme: Vroege interpretaties van Charles Darwins theorie van natuurlijke selectie, 1859–1918* (The Quest of Social-darwinism: Early Interpretations of Charles Darwin's Theory of Natural Selection, 1859–1918), Amsterdam: Uitgeverij Nieuwezijds, 2003. The study originated as a PhD thesis at the University of Amsterdam. The author discusses in rich detail the history and variety of social Darwinist thinking from the middle of the nineteenth century until the end of the second decade of the twentieth century. In my essay, I have summarized the main features of his work and line of argumentation.

[2] Charles Darwin, *The Origin of Species by Means of Natural Selection, or the Preservation of Favoured Races in the Struggle for Life*. Republished by J.W. Burrow (ed.), London: Harmondsworth, 1983 [1859].

static interpretation of nature according to which all forms of life were ranked in a hierarchy in which man had occupied the highest position since 'the beginning'. The application of Darwin's ideas to social and political theory became known as social Darwinism.

One of the leading pioneers of this school of thought was Herbert Spencer who had already vented ideas similar to those of the British biologist. Darwin adopted his expression of 'the survival of the fittest' as a more expressive formulation of the mechanism of natural selection for social development. Initially, this process was closely linked to the *laissez-faire* doctrine, which suggested that the struggle to survive would produce the best results if left to its own devices. Such a formula precluded any form of interference with what was considered to be a natural process. Very quickly, however, this hands-off approach became replaced by more pessimistic views which no longer automatically associated evolution with progress. The last phase of development of the theory towards the end of the nineteenth century was marked by the socio-biological programmes of Ernst Haeckel and others, who were preoccupied by the dangers of degeneration. Despite their many differences, the ideas on human and social development that laid the foundations for the emergence of social Darwinism were logically connected and came about over a period of a few decades only. They spread surprisingly fast in the international arena, Europe and North America in particular. The first to actually use the term 'social Darwinism' was the French anarchist, Emile Gautier, in 1879.

The initial conceptualization subsequently acquired strongly negative connotations. It was seen as extremely individualistic, denying any form of state intervention and overemphasizing the importance of competition as opposed to solidarity as the driving force of social interaction. This viewpoint does not do justice to a completely different interpretation of Darwinism which, rather than sing the praises of unbridled individualism, actually criticizes it fundamentally. From the latter perspective, it formed the basis of calls for public intervention to harness the free play of social forces. Here, the emphasis lay on the possibility for people, in the struggle for survival, not to fight against each other, but to work together and towards the well-being of all. The aim to put an end to unfettered self-interest through cooperation and solidarity also denied the evangelism of inequality, which would countenance no concession to the principle of 'every man for himself'. What attracted radical reformers to Darwinism was the way it broke through the hierarchic order which still prevailed. The egalitarian traits these critical minds identified in the theory did not glorify atomistic individualism, but promoted collectivism. This was at the root of the emancipatory interpretation that both Marxists and Fabians gave social Darwinism. But collectivism also had a conservative if not reactionary variant. In the theory of eugenics, which was rapidly gaining ground, the survival of the fittest was presented as the right of the strongest, and led to calls to liberate society and mankind as a whole from undesirable elements, who were a burden to themselves as well as to the world at large.

The conservative–progressive dichotomy is not useful as a means of clarifying social Darwinist thought. The proponents of industrial capitalism, founded on harshness and inequality, were reformist in the sense that they rejected the religious–aristocratic social order and sought refuge and support in modern science. The original laissez-faire approach was definitely anti-authoritarian and anti-traditionalist, radical in its individualism and its resistance to the supremacy of the pre-industrial alliance of church and state. This does not change the fact that the reversal in the social interpretation of Darwinism—from a predominantly optimistic liberal individualism to a pessimistic and socially conservative collectivism—had a strong influence on the triumph of the latter in the later discussion on human and social development. Darwin was convinced that his theory of evolution had brought about a sea change in thinking on society and civilization. Yet, the mechanism of natural selection he described cannot be seen in isolation from ideas on political economy which had been around for much longer. The biologist was strongly influenced by Thomas Malthus, who had warned half a century earlier of the disruption of the natural order resulting from the unbalanced growth of food supply and population. According to Malthus, it was necessary to allow all forms of social misery—pestilence, hunger, and war—to continue unhampered, regrettable as this may be, to avoid an unsustainable demographic explosion.

The conclusion quickly followed that the mechanism of natural selection was not active—or at least, not active enough—in civilized society. While Darwin was still working on his sensational publication, a fierce debate raged in British parliament inspired by the long drawn-out struggle to introduce the first piece of industrial labour legislation. In the well-to-do circles to which Darwin belonged, there was widespread and sharp criticism of the intolerable generosity of the Poor Laws. Government support must not and could not be used to halt the ongoing process of pauperization. One solution to the problem of what to do with the inferior and redundant elements in the population

if they came into contact with western civilization. Their limitations were genetic. Black people were seen as children for whom growth to adulthood was excluded.

Herbert Spencer was a social Darwinist *avant la lettre*. The affinity between the ideas of the two men did not mean that they agreed with each other in all respects. One difference of opinion that remained irreconcilable was Spencer's belief in the self-regulating capacity of industrial society. Spencer took the stance of a prophet of liberalism that was, in fact, ultra-conservative, and his hyper-individualism, together with a virulent anti-statism, made him a favourite of Andrew Carnegie and other American captains of industry. By contrast, Darwin did not go beyond expressing his concern that the development of civilized society would cancel out the effect of natural selection. He feared that the spread of pauperism would have a detrimental effect on the biological strength of the British people. Without losing his faith—he retained the belief that humanity would continue to benefit, also in modern society, from the unhindered working of the process of natural selection—Darwin proved sensitive to the argument that some degree of government intervention was required to see to it that the 'favoured races' keep their privileged position. The ultimate consequence of this standpoint was the necessity of social engineering to ensure that the struggle to survive in a global society was decided in favour of those who had shown themselves to be the fittest and the strongest.

The ongoing confrontation with the weaker elements somehow surviving at the bottom of industrial society was, however, interrupted when increasing tensions abroad required closing the ranks at home. The creation of a strong state was increasingly seen as a necessity for national survival. The support of the lower classes was indispensable in the imperialist fight against other nations and races. This geopolitical realization was expressed in the award of basic rights to the working masses and was accompanied by an improvement in living standards at the base of industrial society. The principle of competition still prevailed but in the social Darwinist variant of imperialist ideology, the focus of the struggle to survive no longer lay in efforts to weed out the unworthy in our own midst. It was directed outwards, in the engagement resulting from the inequality between people and races. Their subjection was a matter of denigration and discrimination. In the racist practice of colonial statecraft, more than in western societies themselves, social Darwinism came into its own. Such racist overtones can, again, be discerned in current debates on the ongoing process of globalization;

more specifically, in the variant suggesting and promoting a clash between civilizations.

I would like to conclude with some additional comments which relate the past, dealt with by Hermans in fascinating detail, to the present. In the first place, how to explain the disappearance—or at least the declining prominence—of social Darwinism from the early twentieth century onwards? The question is relevant because of a possible re-emergence of ideas on society and culture inspired by social Darwinism. The neo-liberalism in vogue at the end of the twentieth century heralds, in some ways, a return to social Darwinism of the more extreme kind *à la* Spencer. The reason to go back to an earlier round is not because it provides a retrospective interpretation of a historical school of thought, but because it comes at a time when debates in the social sciences are contextualized in the setting of the turbulent and ever-advancing process of globalization.[4]

A number of the factors which contributed to the erosion of this heavily charged ideology at the beginning of the twentieth century were highlighted in the literature belonging to the first round of the debate on the merits and demerits of social Darwinism. First, there was the widely shared belief that sending the poor to the colonies, whether or not of their own volition, would solve the problem of pauperization at home. In this way, internal tension could be discharged by external expansion. Mass migration to what were seen as empty regions—which often resulted in the enforced evacuation or elimination of the 'natives' and alienation from their right to dispose of the means of production they owned—is no longer an option in the current structure of the global economy for societies wishing to rid themselves of those they consider counterproductive because of their apparent incapacity to help increase the national surplus. Whereas Darwin explained the flow of emigrants to America as the process of natural selection at work, people who nowadays seek to escape poverty at home and find a better exist-ence in the more highly developed parts of the world are stigmatized as economic refugees. In the past, however, migration to the city or overseas was the traditional escape valve in Europe for the people from the rural hinterlands who suffered worst in the fight to survive.

[4] I pointed out the parallels between past and present in a collection of essays. See 'The Renaissance of Social-Darwinism', in J. Breman, *The Labouring Poor in India: Patterns of Exploitation, Subordination and Exclusion*, New Delhi: Oxford University Press, 2003, 'Introduction' and chapter 1.

The eclipse of social Darwinism at the end of the nineteenth and the beginning of the twentieth centuries must, however, be seen primarily in the light of the burgeoning resistance to the cruelties of the industrial society. The working masses proved to be militant and forced improvements in their situation. What were initially little more than the weapons of the weak and desperate—recalcitrance, sabotage, and other forms of subversive behaviour—were gradually replaced by emancipatory activities organized collectively and on the basis of solidarity which resulted in the alleviation of poverty. This change for the better was partly prompted by an increasing fear among the bourgeoisie that continued exclusion would result in the propertyless hordes rising in revolt. The problems associated with including what was seen as *les classes dangereuses* were considered to weigh less heavily than the unrest that would eventually erupt into open hostility if this expanding segment at the base of society continued to be refused access to civil life and respectability.[5]

But whether the declining popularity of social Darwinism at that moment in time can be explained by the increasing pressure from below or the enlightened self-interest of the better-off, the fact that the social and economic value attached to labour—and consequently, the price that had to be paid for it—increased was a significant factor in the change that occurred. This slow but steady trend towards embetterment, empowerment, and growing respectability can be traced back to an early pattern of industrialization and a production system which was still heavily labour intensive. For the masses in western societies, who had been expelled from their rural–agrarian existence during the nineteenth century, the cities and other sectors of the economy appeared, at first, to offer insufficient employment opportunities. The inevitable consequence of this was impoverishment and eventual pauperization. However, the relatively low level of technology that characterized this phase of industrialization ultimately enabled a mass of people, until then written off as superfluous and of no use, to be employed gainfully in moving the process forward. The industrial reserve army turned out to be much more than useless ballast. Skilling and schooling put an end to the combination of underemployment and too low wages. Around the turn of the century and in the early years of the twentieth century, the poor succeeded in becoming fully fledged participants in the labour

---

[5] For arguing along these lines, see A. de Swaan, *In Care of the State: Health Care, Education and Welfare in Europe and the USA in the Modern Era*, Cambridge: Polity and New York: Oxford University Press, 1988.

process of western societies and contributed to the growth in prosperity. The increasing dignity of the working classes led to greater political representation and was a logical outcome of this trend towards equality.

I have sketched this process briefly to suggest that the rebirth of social Darwinism is caused by the absence of the factors which, in the first round, helped temper or even dissipate an ideology which held a substantial part of the world's population themselves responsible for the defects of their existence. Social theories prevailing in an earlier round of globalization considered improvement impossible for these people because they lacked the required qualities for improvement; at the same time, any claim by or on behalf of the underprivileged masses to a real-location of the resources needed to survive was considered illegitimate.

In the beginning of the twenty-first century, awareness seems to grow that continuation of the current economic and social policies at global level will make it impossible to solve the problem of mass poverty. This agonizing reappraisal also applies to the post-industrial societies where despite—or perhaps because of—rapidly expanding wealth, resistance to a more even spread of property, power, and status has grown in recent decades. The recent trend towards greater inequality affects all of those who live down below, at the bottom of society, but in particular the segment of the unskilled and unqualified whose origins lie 'elsewhere'—those with different skin colour, ethnicity, or religion. After their arrival, supposedly 'temporarily', in the prosperous zones of the world, they are not given permission to settle permanently, or have great difficulty in receiving that permission. In an incomparably harsher way, a much higher percentage of people are exposed to destitution in countries where the triumph of capitalism is a more recent phenomenon. The circumstances which eventually allowed their predecessors in the early industrialized countries access to the mainstream society do not apply to these latecomers. The once 'empty' regions of the world are considered 'full' and their resources have been appropriated by earlier waves of settlers. Moreover, technological advances have made production much less labour intensive.

Finally, the informalization of gainful employment which has be-come a major trend, especially in developing countries, in this late phase of capitalism hampers steady increase in the wretchedly low wages and replaces regular employment with casual, irregular, and spasmodic work arrangements, paid not in time-based wages but on piece rates. An economic regime of this kind discourages militancy and obstructs the mobilization of the labouring poor into unions and other mass-based organizations.[6] The countervailing power of the working masses to resist is extremely weak. The agendas of the transnational institutions with a mandate to steer the global economy pay lip service to combating poverty, but in the neo-classical policies that lie behind them, the increasingly vocal message is that the poor masses mainly have themselves to blame for their plight. What other explanation is there for the fact that they do not possess a greater proportion of the world's wealth? Deprivation and subordination has not yet been transformed into a policy-systematic exclusion. But the idea seems to have been revived that it is not poverty itself, but the degenerated human material suffering from it, that represents an unacceptable burden for the better-off of the world. In that reactionary perspective, rather than poverty the poor themselves constitute an intolerable nuisance.

---

[6] I have devoted a number of publications to this development, including 'A Question of Poverty', my valedictory address at the Institute of Social Studies, reprinted in *The Labouring Poor in India*, chapter 6, pp. 194–220.

# Index